LEARNING TEXT

CONSTITUTIONAL AND ADMINISTRATIVE LAW

LEARNING TEXT

CONSTITUTIONAL AND ADMINISTRATIVE LAW

Peter Cumper LLB, LLM

Lecturer in Law, Leicester University

with

Terry Walters LLB, M.Phil, MIMgt

Visiting Professor, Nottingham Law School

and

Judith Ward BA (Hons), Solicitor

Senior Lecturer in Law, Nottingham Law School

 BLACKSTONE
PRESS LIMITED

First published in Great Britain 1996 by Blackstone Press Limited,
Aldine Place, London W12 8AA.   Telephone 0181–740 2277

© Nottingham Law School, Nottingham Trent University, 1996

First edition 1996
Second edition 1999

ISBN: 1 85431 813 6

British Library Cataloguing in Publication Data
A CIP catalogue record for this book is available from the British Library.

Typeset by Style Photosetting Limited, Mayfield, East Sussex
Printed by Livesey Limited, Shrewsbury, Shropshire

FOREWORD

The books in the LLB series have been written for students studying law at undergraduate level. There are two books for each subject. The first is the *Learning Text* which is designed to teach you about the particular subject in question. However, it does much more than that. By means of Activities, Self Assessment, and End of Chapter Questions, the *Learning Text* allows you to test your knowledge and understanding as you work. Each chapter starts with 'Objectives' which indicate what you should be able to do by the end of it. You should use these Objectives in your learning — check them frequently and ask yourself whether you have attained them.

The second book is a volume of *Cases and Materials*. This is cross-referenced from the *Learning Text*. It contains the primary sources of law such as statutes and cases plus subsidiary sources such as extracts from journals, law reform papers and textbooks. This is your portable library. Although each volume can stand alone, they are designed to be complementary.

The two-volume combination aims to support your learning by challenging you to demonstrate your mastery of the principles and application of the law. They are appropriate whatever your mode of study — full-time or part-time.

CONTENTS

PREFACE

Constitutional and administrative law is a challenging subject to study. Taught usually in the first year of most law degrees, it is rather unlike the other legal subjects which most law students will (at that point) be studying. In particular, students from overseas or those lacking a detailed knowledge of British political life, may be overwhelmed by a subject in which non-legal principles, rooted in British history, are of considerable contemporary importance.

The aim of this book is to de-mystify constitutional and administrative law, and it is hoped that it will stimulate an interest in a subject which is of day-to-day relevance. The book is split into three parts. Chapters 1–8 deal with the sources of the British Constitution; Chapters 9–11 concentrate on civil liberties; and Chapters 13–16 focus on administrative law. Chapter 12, on the rule of law, is relevant to each of these three areas and I have used it to tie together some of the central themes in constitutional and administrative law.

Chapters 9 and 10 were written by Terry Walters; Judith Ward wrote Chapter 15.

Thanks are extended to Heather, Mandy and Paula and all at Blackstone Press who made publication of the book possible.

The law is correct as of 1 July 1998, although a few minor additions were made later at the proof stage.

Peter Cumper

TABLE OF CASES

TABLE OF STATUTES

INTRODUCTION

Definitions

Constitutional and administrative law is essentially about power and accountability. The power to make law and the accountability of those charged not only with enacting the law, but also with applying and enforcing it. This area of law can be distinguished from private law subjects such as contract or property law, which regulate legal relationships between private individuals. Instead constitutional and administrative law is concerned with the distribution and exercise of power within the State and the relationship between the individual and the State.

Distinguishing between constitutional law and administrative law is not easy. The two cannot always be clearly separated from one another. However, one possible distinction is to see constitutional law as the law relating to the constitution of a State. All States have a constitution of some form and it will incorporate the body of rules by which the State is governed. Administrative law, on the other hand, is concerned with rules which control the exercise of governmental power, particularly controls exercised by the courts.

In the United Kingdom, Parliament is the supreme law-making authority. Parliament exercises this power through the enactment of legislation (i.e., statutes). Such Acts of Parliament are therefore a primary source of *constitutional law*. But where a minister, as the representative of the government of the day, appears to act unreasonably or illegally, the legality of such action may be tested in the courts. This is the *administrative law* procedure of judicial review.

This subject is also concerned with an individual's rights. Take a minute to think about this. What rights do you as a citizen enjoy? What powers are vested in the State? What rights do you have if approached or arrested by the police? And how can you challenge an unfair decision taken by a government body or agency? At the end of this course you will be able to answer these questions. In effect this course is divided into three sections. The first section covers the main principles of constitutional law. We shall then look at the powers of the police. The final section will deal with some of the general principles of administrative law.

Studying Constitutional and Administrative Law

Constitutional and administrative law is unlike other subjects you may have studied such as crime, contract, tort or land law where the law is fairly clearly expressed in statutes and case law. The sources of constitutional law are more diverse than this and are not always formally written down. In addition, much of this subject is based on constitutional principles, embedded in history, which sometimes seem to be political rather than legal in origin. When studying constitutional law you will have to discuss and analyse such principles. In so doing, you will often be expected to answer essays although parts of the syllabus (such as the chapters on police powers and public order) are more associated with problem questions.

By now you may be feeling a little concerned about the breadth of this subject – by its very nature constitutional law encompasses not just the law, but also historical and political issues. A basic understanding of how Parliament and government work is beneficial but do not be put off if your knowledge in this field is limited. You can quickly pick up the key elements of the British Constitution, by reading quality newspapers and watching the news on television.

To get the most out of constitutional law you will need to study it in the context of what is happening around you. Constitutional issues are continually discussed and analysed in the media reflecting changes in the law and society's values. For example, Tony Blair's Labour Government, which took office in May 1997, was elected on a manifesto pledge to reform the House of Lords and it has also introduced a Bill to incorporate the European Convention on Human Rights into British law which, at the time of writing, is going through Parliament. The Human Rights Act 1998 will have a significant impact when it comes into force as, for the first time, people living in the UK will be able to invoke a document in the British courts which guarantees their fundamental rights and freedoms. The creation recently of regional assemblies for Scotland, Wales and Northern Ireland is relevant to this subject, as is that perennial constitutional issue, the UK's membership of the European Union. Therefore it will enhance your studies considerably, and make the subject even more interesting, if you are able to follow contemporary issues of constitutional importance. After all, as citizens in a democracy, we are all affected by issues relevant to constitutional and administrative law in our daily lives.

CHAPTER ONE

WHAT IS A CONSTITUTION?

1.1 Objectives

At the end of this Chapter you should be able to:

■ explain what is meant by the term 'constitution';

■ understand the difference between 'rigid' and 'flexible' Constitutions;

■ describe the constituent elements of the British Constitution;

■ be familiar with the changes to the Constitution initiated by the Labour Government.

1.2 Definition of Constitutions

What is a constitution? This is not an easy question to answer. Usually it is defined as a document which sets out the distribution of powers between, and the principal functions of, a State's organs of government. In addition, most constitutions include a list of the rights which people living in the State enjoy. An example of a written constitution which is well respected and has been the basis for other constitutional documents is that of the United States of America. It was framed in 1787 and remains in force today although over the years there have been several amendments.

Where a constitution is codified in documentary form, the powers of the State are clearly discernible. For example, art. 1 of the US Constitution vests legislative power in Congress; art. 2 reveals that executive power is conferred on the US President and art. 3 provides information about the terms of office and the powers of the judiciary.

The rights of a nation's citizens can also be ascertained from a written constitution. Many written constitutions are supplemented by a Bill of Rights, which is a written list of rights and freedoms to which the people living in that society are entitled. For example, in the USA, the principles of freedom of speech and religion ('. . . Congress shall make no law respecting an establishment of religion or prohibiting the free exercise thereof; or abridging the freedom of speech, or of the press . . .') are enshrined in the 1st Amendment to the US Constitution; similarly, other amendments such as the right to 'bear arms' (art. 2), trial by jury (art. 6) and vote without any distinction 'on account of race, colour, or previous condition of servitude' (art. 15) are examples of constitutionally protected rights in the United States.

Although we have only referred to the US Constitution so far, it is important to remember that every constitution is different. For example, the constitutions in Western nations tend to stress 'civil and political' rights, such as the right to a fair trial, freedom of expression, religion or assembly. On the other hand, third world and socialist States emphasise 'social, economic and cultural' rights, such as the right to food, work, shelter, a fair wage and a clean environment. The nature of the society concerned will dictate the form of its constitution.

ACTIVITY1

Read the extract 'The Constitution: Morals and Rights' in *Cases and Materials* (1.1). According to Sir John Laws, what is a 'constitution'?

Due to the unwritten nature of the UK Constitution, it is arguably more difficult to determine whether something is or is not 'unconstitutional' in the United Kingdom than in the United States of America. In the USA, reference can always be made to the written document and any breach of the principles contained therein will clearly be 'unconstitutional'. The US Federal Supreme Court has responsibility for determining such issues and has the power to rule on the constitutionality of actions taken by the President, the government and even the legislature (Congress): *Marbury* v *Madison* (1803) 1 Cranch 137.

Although it is fairly easy in most countries to propose new legislation, where changes to its constitution are required, a more elaborate procedure has to be followed. The special legal sanctity accorded to written constitutions means that constitutional amendments must usually comply with a specified procedure. This differentiates *ordinary law* from *constitutional law* and ensures that there will be no variation of the fundamental principles of the constitution without adequate consultation.

Again if we use the United States as an example, before an amendment can be made to the US Constitution, the amendment must have been: (a) proposed by a two-thirds majority vote in both Houses of Congress and (b) ratified by a three-quarters majority of all the State legislatures.

Obviously the procedures for amendment vary in different constitutions. However, in most countries it is generally true to say that where a law is passed purporting to alter the written constitution, this proposed law will be declared invalid or unconstitutional if the correct procedure has not been followed. In cases of doubt the power to arbitrate on such matters is vested in that particular nation's courts.

SAQ 1

What is the difference between *ordinary* law and *constitutional* law? Do constitutions matter? For some thoughts on this please turn to the views of Finer, Bogdanor and Rudden in *Cases and Materials* (1.1).

Explain what is meant by the term 'constitution'. (See the views of Wheare in *Cases and Materials* (1.1).)

The United Kingdom does not have a written constitution in the sense which has been discussed (i.e., there is no single document or group of documents which can be called the constitution). Indeed de Tocqueville remarked, rather dismissively, that in England 'there is no constitution'. This statement is a gross oversimplification, but it is perhaps understandable. As Sir John Marriot (*English Political Institutions* (1910), p. 26) points out: 'On the lips of a Frenchman familiar with a long succession of written constitutions . . . the remark is not merely intelligible but obvious'. So, you may be asking, particularly after **SAQ 2**, what exactly is a 'constitution?' An authoritative definition has been provided by Bolingbroke. He defined it as: 'that assemblage of laws, institutions, and customs . . . that compose the general system, according to which the community has agreed to be governed'. This is a theoretical definition. So how does it relate to the United Kingdom's Constitution? Examples of this assemblage of laws in the UK include:

(a) the method of choosing the head of state,

(b) his or her powers and royal prerogatives,

(c) the composition, powers and privileges of the legislature and the relationship betwen the two chambers (the Lords and Commons),

(d) the status of Government Ministers and the position of their civil servants,

(e) the control of the armed forces,

(f) treaty-making powers,

(g) the power to raise and spend public money,

(h) the tenure of judges,

(i) the liberties of the individual, and

(j) the right to vote in elections (the franchise).

Although the UK's Constitution cannot be found in any single written document, this list clearly proves that Britain has a constitution.

Read the article by Lord Scarman in *Cases and Materials* (1.1). What are the four safeguards which Lord Scarman claims that the UK Constitution should embody?

1.3   Classification

The fact that not all constitutions are codified in a document has led to two separate categorisations: 'written' and 'unwritten' constitutions. All such classifications are, of course, far from perfect. However, we will consider some of the classifications that exist:

1.3.1   WRITTEN AND UNWRITTEN

The United Kingdom, New Zealand and Israel are the only countries in the world which lack a written constitution (although New Zealand has a number of rules codified in its 1990 Bill of Rights). The UK Constitution is unwritten mainly as a result of history. It has not been thought necessary to frame a single document which would deal with matters relating to the constitution. This has been due to the gradual development of the UK Constitution and the absence of any event which might have precipitated an abrupt change in the constitution, such as a revolution, a defeat in war, or a major change in political ideology.

Although the UK Constitution is classified as 'unwritten', it has 'written' elements in the sense that rules of constitutional importance are contained in statutes and law reports. However, there is no single document entitled 'the British Constitution'.

One consequence of this unwritten constitution is that it is relatively easy to change the constitution. Legislation of constitutional significance can be introduced through the ordinary law-making process. Unlike most States, which have a written constitution, there are no technical or special procedures in the UK relating to constitutional amendments. Such flexibility is advantageous as well as potentially dangerous. (See **Chapter 12** on the rule of law.)

Why has the UK never had a written constitution? If you still are unsure, consult the extracts from Munro in *Cases and Materials* (1.2.1).

1.3.2 RIGID AND FLEXIBLE

The terms 'rigid' and 'flexible' were used by Dicey (*The Law of the Constitution*, ed. Wade, 10th edn, 1959). They have formed the basis of this classification. Dicey described a 'flexible' constitution as:

> one under which every law of every description can legally be changed with the same ease and in the same manner by one and the same body.

He defined a 'rigid' constitution as:

> one under which certain laws generally known as constitutional or fundamental laws cannot be changed in the same manner as ordinary laws.

Following these definitions the United Kingdom Constitution is *flexible* because the Queen in Parliament can easily change any law of any description.

The United States Constitution, on this basis, would be classified as *rigid* because special procedures are required to change the fundamental rules of the constitution which do not apply to ordinary laws. As Marshall and Moodie (extracts in *Cases and Materials* (**1.2.2**)) point out:

> A constitution which is inflexible and difficult to amend in the formal sense may have been amended without difficulty in fact. Conversely a constitutional system which is flexible in the sense of having a formally uncomplicated procedure for legal change may be one in which for political or social reasons fundamental changes are extemely difficult to bring about.

Thus, whilst the UK Constitution may **legally** be flexible, **political** factors may impede radical constitutional reform. To illustrate this point de Smith notes that there would have to be extraordinary circumstances for legislation to be enacted which would abolish the Monarchy or extend the life of a Parliament in the UK.

SAQ 4

Explain in your own words, the difference between a 'flexible' constitution and a 'rigid' constitution. What are the advantages and disadvantages of each? You may find it useful in this matter to consider the comments of Finer, Bogdanor and Rudden in *Cases and Materials* (1.2.2).

There are two main types of States: Federal and Unitary.

1.3.3 FEDERAL

You are probably familiar with the word 'federal', or at least its derivative, the term 'federalism', which is often used in a contemporary European context. Dicey defined federalism as 'the distribution of the force of the State among a number of co-ordinate bodies each originating in and controlled by the constitution'. But what does this mean in practice?

In a federal constitution several 'units' (e.g. provinces) are joined together under one constitution — however each of those 'units' has the responsibility for dealing with certain matters within its own jurisdiction. The powers and functions of government are divided between the national government and the 'units', (e.g. States, provinces etc.) Examples of federal constitutions are the United States of America, Canada and Australia. A common characteristic of federations is that they presuppose a desire for some form of union among independent provinces which, nevertheless, still wish to preserve their identity and some measure of independence. Consequently, certain areas are within the competence of the Federal government (e.g. foreign affairs) while others are retained by the State or provincial government (e.g. local taxation). Thus, for people living in countries which are based on a federal system, there are two types of law — Federal law and State law.

1.3.4 UNITARY

A unitary State is where power is concentrated in one body or in a single source. Dicey noted that it means 'the concentration of the strength of the State in the hands of one visible sovereign power be that Parliament or Czar'. Thus, a unitary system has no separate provincial government. Were the United Kingdom to become a federation, it seems that much of the constitution would have to be reduced to writing in order to determine the relationship between the federal government and the provincial governments, something which is now even more arguably necessary following the referendums which recently paved the way for the establishment of regional Assemblies in Scotland, Wales and Northern Ireland.

Read the extract from McAuslan and McEldowney on the fundamental principles of the British Constitution in *Cases and Materials* (1.2.3). You might compare their opinions with the views of Sir Ivor Jennings (in *Cases and Materials* (1.2.3)).

1.4   Sources of the UK Constitution

These sources may be summarised as:

(a) **Rules of law:**

    (i)   Legislation: Acts of Parliament and enactments of other bodies upon which Parliament has conferred power to legislate, particularly delegated legislation (i.e., statutory instruments).

    (ii)   Judicial precedent: decisions of the courts interpreting the common law and interpreting statutes.

(iii) European Community law: a fairly recent source following Parliament's enactment of the European Communities Act 1972.

(b) **Advisory sources**:

Constitutional law theorists and writers of authority (e.g., Dicey, Jennings, Wade etc.).

(c) **Conventions**:

Influential political rules and ethics, which are not enforced by the courts.

These sources will now be considered in more detail.

1.4.1   RULES OF LAW

1.4.1.1   Primary legislation

Acts of Parliament are an important source of the British Constitution. Examples of statutes which are particularly significant from a constitutional point of view include:

- **Magna Carta, 1215**: The aim of Magna Carta was to afford protection against arbitrary punishment and to assert the right to a fair trial and justice so may be seen as an early attempt to codify some of the main principles of constitutional government.

- **The Petition of Right, 1628**: it forbade taxation without the consent of Parliament.

- **The Bill of Rights 1689**: Following the Revolution of 1688 it made illegal:
  — the execution of laws by Royal authority without the consent of Parliament;
  — the dispensing with of laws, or the execution of laws, by Royal authority;
  — the levying of money by the Crown, without the permission of Parliament;
  — and the raising or the keeping of a standing army in time of peace, without the consent of Parliament.

- **The Act of Settlement 1701**: the Monarch must be a communicant of the Church of England. Thus Roman Catholics and persons marrying Roman Catholics are excluded from the throne. It also provided that judges hold office during good behaviour and can be dismissed 'upon the address of both Houses of Parliament'.

- **The Union with Scotland Act 1707**: the Scottish and English Parliaments were merged.

- **The Parliament Acts 1911 and 1949**: they assert the primacy of the House of Commons over the House of Lords in the event of a conflict.

- **The European Communities Act 1972**: it incorporates European Community law into the UK.

- **The Human Rights Act 1998**: it incorporates the European Convention on Human Rights into UK law.

Finally, almost all areas of constitutional law have, at some stage, been affected by Acts of Parliament. For example, the law relating to civil liberties has been altered radically by the Police and Criminal Evidence Act 1984, the Public Order Act 1986, and the Criminal Justice and Public Order Act 1994. Similarly the Crown Proceedings Act 1947, the Parliamentary Commissioner Act 1967 and the Supreme Court Act 1981 have directly influenced administrative law, while statutes such as the European Communities Act

1972, the European Communities (Amendment) Act 1986 the European Union (Accessions Act) 1994 and the European Communities (Amendment) Act 1998 have affected the most basic principle of British Constitutional law, the supremacy of Parliament (see **Chapters 7 and 8**).

1.4.1.2 Delegated legislation

As well as primary legislation in the form of Acts of Parliament, subordinate or delegated legislation is also a source of constitutional law. This takes the form mainly of statutory instruments of which there may be two types:

(a) An Act of Parliament which confers upon a Minister the power to make regulations. This generally means he/she will fill in the details of an Act, the framework of the legislation having been agreed upon in principle by Parliament. (For example, s. 99 of the Police and Criminal Evidence Act 1984 empowers the Home Secretary to make regulations concerning procedures for dealing with complaints against the police.)

(b) Parliament also confers on the Queen in Council power to legislate by Order in Council. Orders in Council serve the same purpose as the regulations described above, but are also very useful in times of emergency, when Parliament is not in session. For example, when direct rule from Westminster was imposed on Northern Ireland in 1972, the Northern Ireland (Temporary Provisions) Act 1972 provided that Orders in Council could be made on any matter within the competence of the Northern Ireland Parliament.

Local authorities may also be given the power to make by-laws which are also a form of delegated legislation (e.g., by-laws forbidding cycling on footpaths). On delegated legislation generally see **Chapter 13**.

1.4.1.3 Judicial precedent

Case law comes from the decisions of judges in the superior courts, i.e., the Queen's Bench Division of the High Court, the Court of Appeal, the House of Lords and the Judicial Committee of the Privy Council. Often seemingly trivial fact situations raise serious constitutional issues. The decision in *Congreve v Home Office* [1976] QB 629 is a good case in point. Until 31 March 1975, a colour television licence cost £12 for 12 months. From 1 April 1975 it was increased to £18. Thousands of people renewed their licences before 1 April, in order to save £6. Eager to recover this lost revenue, the Home Office warned those who had obtained their licences at the £12 rate that they should pay an extra £6, or their new licences would be revoked after only eight months. The Court of Appeal held that this threat was an improper exercise of the Home Secretary's discretionary power of revocation, under the Wireless Telegraphy Act 1949. It relied on the long-established principle that taxation may not be raised without the consent of Parliament. Thus, the Home Secretary could not use his power 'as means of extracting money which Parliament had given the executive no mandate to demand' (per Lane LJ).

There are many examples of judicial decisions which have affected the development of the British Constitution. Such cases include:

(a) *Case of Proclamations* (1611) 12 Co Rep 74: on the question of whether the King could create new law without Parliament, Coke CJ held: 'the King by his proclamation or other ways, cannot change any part of the common law or statute law . . . also the King cannot create any offence by his prohibition or proclamation which was not an offence before'.

(b) *Stockdale v Hansard* (1839) 9 Ad & E 1: which decided that the Commons cannot change the law by passing a resolution claiming a new privilege.

(c) *Attorney-General* v *Wiltshire United Dairies* (1921) 37 TLR 884: which established that no prerogative power existed to levy a tax without the consent of Parliament.

(d) *Christie* v *Leachinsky* [1947] AC 573: the House of Lords held that an 'arrested man is entitled to be told what is the act for which he is arrested'. This rule was codified in s. 28(3) of the Police and Criminal Evidence Act 1984.

(e) *Ridge* v *Baldwin* [1964] AC 40: it established the principle that the rules of natural justice could apply irrespective of whether a decision-making body was judicial or merely administrative.

(f) *Council of Civil Service Unions* v *Minister for the Civil Service* [1985] AC 374 (the GCHQ case): which redefined the grounds on which an application for judicial review may be made. Lord Diplock classified these as 'illegality', 'irrationality', and 'procedural impropriety'.

(g) *M* v *Home Office* [1992] QB 270: Ministers of the Crown can be held in contempt of court.

Judges interpret statutes passed by Parliament. As most powers of government departments and local authorities are now derived from statute, this is a very important source of the Constitution. As we shall discover later, this interpretative role of the judiciary carries with it some law-making potential.

1.4.1.4 European Community law

European law became a source of British Constitutional law following the encactment by Parliament of the European Communities Act 1972. This Act provides that some European legislation is to be given the same effect as Acts of Parliament passed by the United Kingdom Parliament.

There are three types of European 'legislation': Regulations, Directives and Decisions.

(a) **Regulations**. A Regulation is of 'general application . . . binding in its entirety and directly applicable in all member States' (EC Treaty, art. 189).

(b) **Directives**. A Directive is 'binding as to the result to be achieved, upon each member State to whom it is addressed' (EC Treaty, art. 189). This leaves to each member State a choice of method to achieve the required result. However, a Directive may be 'directly effective' where it creates rights for individuals which are enforceable in national courts (see *Van Duyn* v *Home Office* [1975] Ch 358).

(c) **Decisions**. A Decision is 'binding in its entirety on those to whom it is addressed' (EC Treaty, art. 189).

We shall examine the influence of European law and its erosion of the principle of Parliamentary supremacy in **Chapter 8**.

1.4.2 ADVISORY – WRITERS OF AUTHORITY

In the absence of a written British Constitution, the writings of prominent Constitutional lawyers have acquired a greater significance than in most other areas of the law. Experts such as the Victorian jurist A.V. Dicey (*The Law of the Constitution*, ed Wade, 10th edn, 1959), Jennings, (*The Law and Constitution*, 5th edn, 1959), W. Bagehot (*The English Constitution*, 1963) and de Smith (*Judicial Review of Administrative Action*, ed Brazier, 7th edn, 1994), have directly influenced British constitutional law. Whilst their theories are not binding legally, they remain extremely persuasive.

1.5 Devolution

1.5.1 INTRODUCTION

The United Kingdom is one the most centralised States in Europe. Perhaps mindful of this, the Labour Government fought and won the General Election in 1997 on a manifesto which included a promise to devolve powers to elected regional assemblies. Thus, in accordance with the Referendums (Scotland and Wales) Act 1997, the Scots and the Welsh (in September 1997) voted in favour of having their own regional assemblies while, in June 1998, a Northern Ireland Assembly was established to end the 'direct rule' of that province from Westminster.

There are a number of reasons why the Government supports the principle of devolution. First, devolution is advantageous because it brings the machinery of government closer to the people. An elected regional assembly should (at least in theory) be more in tune with the feelings of local residents and better equipped to respond to the needs of a particular area than, say, a distant and remote centralised legislature. Secondly, as a corollary of this, locally elected assemblies tend to increase people's confidence in the nation's political system — local communities feel that the are listened to, that they have a 'voice' locally, and that their local representatives can even influence government policy centrally. Thirdly, an elected local assembly can foster a sense of a regional identity so that local traditions are protected. As William Rees-Mogg claimed, after the result in the referendum which narrowly approved the establishment of a Welsh Assembly, '[f]or Wales it is the [Welsh] culture that matters most, and the Welsh Assembly can contribute to its preservation' (*The Times*, 22 September 1997).

1.5.2 THE WELSH ASSEMBLY

In the referendum for Wales, the people of that region voted for a Welsh Assembly. It is questionable just how much influence this Assembly will possess in the future. It is expected that it will have 60 seats (40 directly elected and 20 elected by proportional representation), but it will lack any tax raising powers and will also be unable to introduce legislation which conflicts with laws that have been passed at Westminster. Indeed, the fact that the present Labour Government has ruled out giving the Welsh Assembly powers that would replace the many quangos (non-elected public bodies) which were appointed for Wales by John Major's previous Government, even led to three Labour MPs to break ranks and criticise, publicly, the Government's plans for limited devolution in Wales during the actual referendum campaign.

The Welsh Secretary encouraged a 'yes' vote at the referendum by posing the question, 'whether that power which everybody agrees should be devolved, should be exercised by democratically elected representatives of the people, or whether it should be exercised by a Secretary of State for Wales' (*The Guardian*, 9 September 1997). However, while the people of Wales eventually supported the proposal for a Welsh Assembly, just 50 per cent of the total electorate actually voted and of these voters only 50.3 per cent of them supported the Assembly.

Supporters of the Welsh Assembly point out that it will have the power to distribute the £7 million budget of the Welsh Office and that the Assembly is expected to take over the decision-making functions of the Welsh Office in areas such as food and agriculture, economic development, education, health care, local government, roads and transport, and finally, the arts, culture and recreation. It is expected that the first elections to the Welsh Assembly will take place in May 1999, and it remains to be seen whether the Welsh Assembly will continue to live in the shadow of its much stronger neighbour North of the border in Scotland, which we will now consider.

1.5.3 THE SCOTTISH PARLIAMENT

The referendum for Scotland was held on 11 September 1997, and Scottish voters were asked to consider two proposals: (a) should a Scottish Parliament be created and, if so, (b) should it have tax-varying powers? Just over 74 per cent of Scots supported the first proposal and 63.5 per cent supported the second, giving this new Parliament tax varying powers. On the day of the referendum, the Secretary of State for Scotland, Donald Dewer, announced that '[w]hat is on offer is direct democratic control over a large area of Scotland's domestic affairs' (*The Independent*, 11 September 1997), a claim we will now proceed to examine.

The Scottish Parliament will be located in Edinburgh and will be composed of 129 Members of the Scottish Parliament (MSPs). It is anticipated that 73 MSPs will be directly elected from existing constituencies in Scotland while the remaining 56 MSPs will be elected by proportional representation from the eight European Parliament constituencies (i.e., seven from each constituency). Members of the Scottish Parliament will be elected for four years and must be aged over 21, although all British citizens, as well as EU or Commonwealth citizens resident in the UK, will be eligible to stand for election. Just as any MP can, at present, simultaneously retain a seat in both the British and European Parliaments, future MSPs may choose also to be members of the Westminster or European Parliaments.

Elections to the Scottish Parliament will take place in 1999, and the party with the highest number of seats in the new Parliament will control the Scottish Executive (Cabinet) which will be composed of a First Minister, who will work with a team of Ministers and law officers. Just as the executive is accountable to Parliament at Westminster, so too will the Scottish Executive be accountable to the new Scottish Parliament and select committees of MSPs will be created to scrutinise the actions of Ministers.

The Scottish Parliament and Executive will have power over a wide range of issues such as: economic development, education, the environment, food standards, health, housing, law and order, transport, agriculture and fisheries, sport and the arts. However, matters which will fall outside its remit and remain under Westminster's control will include: the British Constitution, social security, economic policy, employment legislation, transport policy, the nuclear industry and the control of the border. Thus, just as the power which is to be devolved to Scotland is essentially of a 'local' or 'regional' nature, so 'international' matters such as foreign policy, national security and relations with the rest of Europe, will also continue to be dealt with by Westminster.

Perhaps the most significant facet of the recent plans to devolve powers to Scotland is the fact that the new Scottish Parliament will have the power to raise income tax above Westminster levels by up to 3 pence in the pound. Scotland will continue, however, to receive its share of UK public expenditure (its 'block grant', which is at present approximately £14 billion), although public spending levels will, in the future, be determined by the Scottish Parliament. Both the Scottish Parliament and Executive will be held accountable for the way in which the block grant is spent and levels of expenditure will be audited by the UK's financial watchdog, the Comptroller and Auditor General.

ACTIVITY 4

Please turn to *Cases and Materials* (1.3) and read what Brazier has to say about the Scottish Executive's future relations with the Scottish Parliament and the Crown.

The Prime Minister, Tony Blair, has said that the new Scottish Parliament 'allows the Scottish people to take decisions closer to them, closer to their own priorities' (*The*

Independent, 11 September 1997). However, critics of Scottish devolution oppose these reforms on a number of grounds. First, they point to the expense not merely of setting up a new Parliament for Scotland (this may be as much as £40 million) but also of administering it (approximately £20–£30 million), although supporters of the Government's proposals may respond with the argument that an important principle such as improving local democracy should never be subject to financial considerations.

Secondly, fears have been expressed that Westminster's future relationship with the new Scottish Parliament may be less than harmonious. It is expected that MSPs may take their seats in the new Scottish Parliament in January 2000 and that the 72 Scottish MPs, presently at Westminster, would be permitted (at least initially) to continue to represent these constituencies and participate fully in proceedings at Westminster. This has been called 'the West Lothian Question' and has generated controversy because of the anomaly that, after devolution, English MPs (at Westminster) will not be able to vote on 'Scottish' matters (i.e., those dealt with by the Scottish Parliament), but that Scottish MPs at Westminster will retain jurisdiction over 'English' affairs. The former Prime Minister, John Major, has called this 'a nonsense' and has warned that 'English MPs, and their constituents, would not — and should not — tolerate this situation for long' (*The Times*, 30 August 1997). It remains to be seen whether an agreement can be reached, presumably under the auspices of the Parliamentary Boundary Commission Review which is expected to recommend that in the next but one General Election (probably in 2007) there will be fewer Scottish MPs at Westminster.

Thirdly, the most serious criticism of the Government's plans for Scotland from a constitutional point of view is the claim that these reforms will, in the words of John Major, 'be the first step in breaking up our country' (*The Times*, 30 August 1997). Advocates of this view attach great significance to the fact that many leading Scottish and Welsh nationalists see devolution as the first step towards full independence for their regions and that this would precipitate the break up of the United Kingdom. On the other hand, it can be argued that devolution gives recognition to the fact that the United Kingdom is composed of regions which have different priorities, cultures and traditions. Therefore, by at last taking cognisance of this, devolution, in the words of Professor Vernon Bogdanor, 'will strengthen national unity not weaken it' (*The Times*, 22 December 1997). There is no doubt that the Government's plans to devolve more power to the regions have profound constitutional implications for everyone living in the United Kingdom. The full extent of this however is, as yet, unclear. It remains to be seen whether devolution will fan the flames of nationalism and threaten the unity of the country or defuse the latent tension which has simmered between the regions over the past two decades.

1.5.4   THE NORTHERN IRELAND ASSEMBLY

Unlike the Welsh Assembly, the Northern Ireland Assembly has recently had its first election. It consists of 108 members, elected by proportional representation, and it will have power to take decisions in the areas of agriculture, education, the environment, finance, health and the economic development of Northern Ireland. David Trimble, the leader of the largest single party in Northern Ireland (the Official Unionists) has been elected, by the Assembly's members, as its First Minister and Seamus Mallen (of the SDLP) has become his deputy. The Northern Ireland Assembly is significant from a constitutional perspective in that it returns power to the province for the first time since 1972 when the Government, concerned that the local Stormont Assembly (controlled by the majority Unionist population) was discriminating against the minority Nationalist population, dissolved the Stormont Assembly and imposed direct rule from Westminster. The success of the Northern Ireland Assembly will ultimately be determined by political factors and only time will tell whether it will not merely introduce local government to Northern Ireland, but can also provide a forum in which a way can be found for ending a conflict which has lasted for generations.

1.6   The Human Rights Act 1998

A Bill of Rights is a written catalogue of rights and freedoms which are extended to everyone living in a particular State. Such rights are often included in the written constitution of each nation but, perhaps not surprisingly in view of the fact that the British Constitution is not codified, there has never been such a Bill of Rights in the United Kingdom. Thus, in an effort to rectify this anomaly, the Labour Government in its White Paper, *Rights Brought Home: The Human Rights Bill* (published in October 1997) introduced plans to incorporate the European Convention on Human Rights (ECHR) into British law (see *Cases and Materials* (1.4.1)). At the time of writing, the Human Rights Bill is still going through Parliament but it is most likely to come into force without any significant changes, so we can safely assume that what is written here, and in *Cases and Materials* on the Bill, will also apply to the final Human Rights Act 1998.

1.6.1   THE MODEL FOR THE HUMAN RIGHTS ACT

The European Convention on Human Rights (ECHR) 1950 is an international human rights treaty which was drafted under the auspices of the Council of Europe at the end of the Second World War. The aims of the ECHR's drafters were clear. Europe had been devastated by Nazi aggression and the statesmen of Western Europe were determined that this should never happen again. Thus, the factors which led a number of Western European countries to sign and ratify the ECHR included: a desire to prevent another European 'holocaust'; the promotion and establishment of common democratic values in Western Europe which would help to prevent the spread of Communism from the Soviet Empire in the East; and a desire to foster co-operation for the future between the peoples and countries of Western Europe. British statesmen and diplomats were involved in the drafting of the ECHR and, since 1966, the United Kingdom has allowed people living in this country to refer complaints against the UK to the European Commission and Court of Human Rights, the ECHR's organs of implementation. Ironically, however, the UK was one of the few States in Europe never to incorporate the ECHR into its domestic law and, obviously mindful of this, the Home Secretary, Jack Straw, on the publication of the White Paper said: 'The UK had a major role in drafting the Convention and was the first to ratify it . . . Now, nearly 50 years later, the British people's rights are coming home'. Thus, the Human Rights Act will not merely provide a mechanism by which a citizen's grievances against the State may be remedied but, for the first time, individuals resident in the UK will have a document which formally sets out their rights.

ACTIVITY 5

Please turn to the copy of the ECHR in *Cases and Materials* (1.4.1). What rights are protected by the ECHR? How would you categorise these rights? Is it a radical document? What does Sir Stephen Sedley (*Cases and Materials* (1.4.1)) say about it? Do you agree with the view expressed by Lord Bingham (*Cases and Materials* (1.4.1)) that 'incorporation of the Convention would . . . restore this country to its former place as an international standard bearer of liberty and justice'?

As you will have seen, the rights guaranteed in the ECHR seem rather basic. For example, every society in the world today, at least in theory, claims to respect the right to life (art. 2), the prohibition of torture, inhuman and degrading treatment (art. 3), the prohibition of slavery (art. 4), the right to liberty (art. 5) and a fair trial (art. 6). However, approximately half a century ago, human rights were largely unknown to international law so that when the ECHR was first drafted and it was not merely a vague piece of paper with noble platitudes, but a workable document with its own organs of implementation (Commission and Court), it was seen as a radical and standard setting treaty. As the ECHR approaches its fiftieth birthday, it is perhaps showing its age, for it only protects what one might normally term 'civil and political' rights (e.g., the rights to privacy (art. 8), religion (art. 9), expression (art. 10) and assembly (art. 11)), as opposed to 'economic, social and cultural' rights, so that there is, for example, no right to food, water, shelter, health care, employment or social security. The advantage of adopting this approach (at least from a State's perspective) is that with the former, a government is, generally, only under an obligation to refrain from interfering with human rights (i.e., not to take life, torture, enslave etc.) rather than under a 'positive' duty to enforce rights (i.e., such as providing everyone with a job, a house, etc.). Despite the rather limited range of human rights which are guaranteed under the ECHR, and the fact that compared to many other contemporary human rights documents its provisions are rather modest, it is important to recognise the effect which the ECHR has had on human rights jurisprudence. It is unquestionably the world's most successful human rights document and was the natural choice for any government seeking a model on which to base a British Human Rights Act. However, in order to examine Lord Bingham's bold claim about it in **Activity 5**, we must first proceed to consider how the Human Rights Act 1998 will work in practice. Before we do this, please consider the following question.

In the past, when a person living in the UK was a victim of a human rights violation under the ECHR, he or she had to exhaust domestic remedies before submitting a complaint to the European Commission which, acting as a filter system, would refer meritorious cases to the European Court of Human Rights at Strasbourg. It would then consider the respective arguments and would rule on the merits of the alleged violation. What do you think was the most obvious effect of the UK not incorporating the ECHR into its domestic law, but still allowing individuals to submit complaints to the Court of Human Rights?

1.6.2   THE AMBIT OF THE HUMAN RIGHTS ACT 1998

As we have seen, the Human Rights Act will incorporate the substantive rights which are guaranteed by the ECHR. Thus, the Human Rights Act 1998 provides that it will be 'unlawful for a public authority to act in a way which is incompatible with one or more of the Convention rights' (s. 6(1)). Also, who will it cover? The Human Rights Act will only cover the actions of 'public authorities', a term which has been defined to include courts, tribunals and 'any person . . . whose functions are functions of a public nature', although the definition of public authority specifically excludes both Houses of

Parliament (s. 6(3)). This means that the Human Rights Act will cover not merely the actions of central and local government, but also institutions ranging from the BBC and the Advertising Standards Authority to the companies which are responsible for managing the privatised utilities. Therefore, where a 'public authority' has acted contrary to the rights in the ECHR, an individual will be able to institute proceedings against that authority on the basis of s. 7 of the Human Rights Act 1998 (see *Cases and Materials* (**1.4.1**)). In principle the ambit of the Human Rights Act will be quite wide. However, in practice, as a result of the rather vague definition of 'public authority' (see s. 6 generally in *Cases and Materials* (**1.4.1**)), the fact that this definition may not cover the 'private' acts of a 'public authority' and, in view of the problems generally which judges in the past, have experienced when distinguishing a 'public' authority from a 'private' one, it seems likely that a great deal of litigation will be needed before one can identify with confidence what is a 'public' authority.

When we look at judicial review (**Chapter 15**), you will discover that if an individual wants to challenge the decision of a public body (i.e., the ruling of a Minister, a court or a local authority), he or she must have a personal interest in the case ('*locus standi*') before being allowed to be heard by the court. The Human Rights Act 1998 imposes a similar requirement. It stipulates that 'the applicant is to be taken to have a sufficient interest in relation to the unlawful act only if he is, or would be, a victim' of the alleged breach of the ECHR by the public authority (s. 7(3)). In interpreting the comparable 'victim' require- ment under Article 25 of the ECHR, the European Commission and Court of Human Rights have given quite a wide interpretation to the word 'victim'. For example, parents have been permitted to bring cases on behalf of their children (e.g., in *Campbell and Cosans v UK* (1980) 4 EHRR 293, where two mothers objected to the use of corporal punishment in State schools) while a gay male was held be a victim of a law criminalising homosexuality even though he had never been formally arrested or prosecuted under it (*Dudgeon v UK* (1981) 4 EHRR 149). Moreover, it is not merely the European institutions which have been prepared to extend the boundaries of the citizen's right to bring a legal challenge. As we will see at **15.3.4.2**, recent years have witnessed a greater judicial willingness to interpret the locus standi requirements in British cases increasingly flexibly, so perhaps one may be cautiously optimistic that, in the future, the UK courts will avoid an excessively narrow interpretation of the 'victim' requirement under the Human Rights Act.

Finally, what are the remedies offered, and the sanctions provided, by the Human Rights Act? Where a court or tribunal has considered that there has been a violation of the ECHR, it 'may grant such relief or remedy, or make such order, within its jurisdiction as it considers just and appropriate' (s. 8(1)). Thus, in determining whether to award damages, and the amount of any such award, judges 'must take into account' the principles which are applied by the European Court of Human Rights in relation to the awarding of compensation (s. 8(4)). It is perhaps significant that when such awards have been made at Strasbourg, they have tended to be lower than might have been the case in the British courts.

ACTIVITY 6

Read the article by Lord Browne-Wilkinson in *Cases and Materials* (**1.4.2**). Why does he claim that 'some form of protection of fundamental human rights seems to me to . . . be necessary'?

1.6.3   THE INTERPRETATION OF THE HUMAN RIGHTS ACT 1998

Prior to the publication of the White Paper, but following the Government's pledge to incorporate the ECHR into UK law, the director of the pressure group Liberty, John Wadham, suggested that 'the real test of the commitment of the new Parliament will be whether it is prepared to allow the courts to give a higher status to the Convention than other legislation' (*The Times*, 14 May 1997). Thus, it followed that the most radical proposal for incorporating the ECHR involved giving British judges the power to strike down Acts of Parliament which were incompatible with the Human Rights Act. This could have been based on the model of the European Community Act 1972 (see **Chapter 8**), whereby the courts have the power to set aside a statute where it is incompatible with European Community law (*R v Secretary of State for Transport, ex parte Factortame (No. 1)* [1990] 2 AC 85, *R v Secretary of State for Transport, ex parte Factortame (No. 2)* [1991] AC 603). However, the Government rejected this proposal and chose not to give the judiciary the power to strike down legislation, presumably on the basis that it would have been incongruous with the principle of parliamentary sovereignty, would have politicised the judiciary, and would have probably been resisted by many judges themselves.

Therefore, although judges lack the power to strike down legislation which is inconsistent with the ECHR, the Human Rights Act 1998 provides that '[s]o far as it is possible to do so, primary legislation and subordinate legislation must be read and given effect in a way which is compatible with the Convention rights' (s. 3(1)) and this requirement also extends to all such legislation 'whenever enacted' (s. 3(2)(a)). Lord Steyn calls s. 3(1) 'the pivotal provision' (see *Cases and Materials* (**1.4.3**)) and it is clear that it puts the protection of human rights very much in the hands of the judiciary. The exact limits of this power are hard to predict. As Geoffrey Marshall comments, '[w]hat interpretation the courts will place on Section 3 is impossible to know' (see *Cases and Materials* (**1.4.3**)) and this uncertainty has led to two different fears. First, some claim that the Human Rights Act will give judges too much power which they may misuse. Francis Bennion claims that it will give 'a blank cheque to our judges to develop the Convention's open textured articles as seems good to them' and as a consequence of this the 'State is likely to suffer' (*New Law Journal*, 3 April 1998). Thus, judges may be too interventionist and this may lead to uncertainty and vexatious litigation.

On the other hand, it must be remembered that most of the provisions of the ECHR are drafted with clauses which 'claw back' rights for the State. For example, if you turn to *Cases and Materials* (**1.4.1**) and read arts 8 to 11, you will observe the wide limitations placed on these rights. Thus, it is possible that, say, if parts of the Public Order Act 1986 or the Criminal Justice and Public Order Act 1994 (see **Chapter 11**) are challenged as being incompatible with art. 11 of the ECHR, a British court might interpret art. 11(2) of the ECHR very widely and reject the individual's complaint. Of course, this is mere conjecture but, as Lord Steyn concedes, s. 3 of the Human Rights Act 'will present judges with the challenge of a radical departure from traditional techniques of statutory interpretation'. It remains to be seen whether judges, generally, will be bold or timid when they come to interpret legislation in accordance with s. 3.

ACTIVITY 7

Please turn to *Cases and Materials* (**1.4.1**) and read s. 3 of the Human Rights Act 1998. What could it mean? Compare your ideas to the views of Lord Steyn and Geoffrey Marshall in *Cases and Materials* (**1.4.3**).

SAQ 6

Does the United Kingdom actually need a Human Rights Act? How were the rights of people living in the United Kingdom protected in the past? Are these mechanisms still appropriate for the protection of individuals' rights today? Is there even any need for the European Convention on Human Rights to be incorporated into British law? Compare and contrast the views of the former Attorney-General, Sir Nicholas Lyell, and the Lord Chancellor, Lord Irvine, in *Cases and Materials* (1.4.3).

1.6.4 DECLARATIONS OF INCOMPATIBILITY

When judges in the High Court, or above, are unable to interpret legislation in conformity with the Convention, they are required to make a *declaration of incompatibility*, that the relevant 'provision is incompatible with one or more of the Convention rights' (s. 4(2)). Such a declaration will not 'affect the validity, continuing operation or enforcement of the provision in respect of which it is given' (s. 4(6)(a)) and will not be 'binding on the parties to the proceedings in which it is made' (s. 4(6)(b)). Thus, a declaration of incompatibility is intended to bring public attention to a conflict between primary or secondary legislation and the UK's obligations under the Convention, leaving it up to the Government to amend the offending legislation in accordance with the court's interpretation of the Human Rights Act 1998.

The Human Rights Act 1998 provides for a 'fast track' route, whereby a Minister may, by statutory instrument, amend legislation in response to a declaration of incompatibility. Thus, '[i]f a Minister of the Crown considers that, in order to remove the incompatibility, it is appropriate to amend the legislation . . . he may by order make such amendments to it as he considers appropriate' (s. 10(2)). Such an order requires the approval of both Houses of Parliament and the actual procedure is described in s. 12 of the Human Rights Act 1998 (see *Cases and Materials* (1.4.1)).

It is assumed that the political pressures of being seen to take human rights obligations seriously will force most governments to comply with declarations of incompatibility. Also, even if a government refuses to change the law following a declaration from a court, the complainant, having exhausted all available domestic remedies, will still be able to refer his or her case to the European Court of Human Rights in Strasbourg. Nevertheless, these are early days, and perhaps the success of the new system will depend on two factors: the willingness of the courts to issue declarations of incompatibility; and the extent to which Parliament chooses to respond, vigorously or not, to any such declarations.

So far we have concentrated on how the Human Rights Act will regulate *existing* legislation. However, it is important to point out that the Act will also introduce safeguards for the human rights of individuals with regard to *subsequent* legislation. In the future, a Minister who is sponsoring a Bill through Parliament must pledge publicly either that the Bill's provisions are compatible with the ECHR (s. 19(1)(a)), or else the

Minister must make a written statement 'that although he is unable to make a statement of compatibility the government nevertheless wishes the House to proceed with the Bill' (s. 19(1)(b)). This requirement closely resembles what is often called a 'notwithstanding clause', i.e., a provision in a Bill of Rights (of which perhaps the best contemporary example is the Canadian Charter) which provides that later legislation will only be exempted from the Bill of Rights if this is expressly provided for in the legislation itself. The main difference between the British Human Rights Act and the Canadian Charter is that British judges (unlike their Canadian counterparts) are unable to set aside statutes which are incompatible with the ECHR and have been passed without such a 'notwith-standing clause'. Perhaps, however, much of this is mere conjecture for, at least in the short term, British governments may be reluctant to attract domestic criticism as well as incurring the wrath of the international community, by affirming publicly that they are planning to legislate contrary to the ECHR. Since one of the main reasons why the UK chose to incorporate the ECHR was to avoid the embarrassment of being taken before the European Court quite so often, it would hardly be logical for Britain to incorporate the ECHR, only for the Government to tarnish its international image by routinely passing legislation which was contrary to its Convention obligations.

Please turn to *Cases and Materials* (1.4.4). What does the Lord Chancellor, Lord Irvine, mean when he says that the Human Rights Act will lead to 'a rights based system within the field of civil liberties'?

1.6.5   THE HUMAN RIGHTS ACT 1998: FUTURE PROSPECTS

Notwithstanding the apparent enthusiasm for the Human Rights Act, as you will have seen in *Cases and Materials*, some reservations have been expressed. These are some of the arguments which have been made against the Act.

First, it is said that it will, in the words of the former Lord Chancellor, Lord Mackay, 'draw judges into making decisions of a far more political nature'. Certainly few would want British judges to be tarred by the brush of party politics, as has so often been the case with the judiciary in the USA, but such claims have been rejected by the present Lord Chancellor, Lord Irvine (see *Cases and Materials* (1.4.3)).

Secondly, it is claimed by some (e.g., the former Conservative Party Chairman, Sir Brian Mawhinney) that the Human Rights Act 1998 is incongruous with the principle of the sovereignty of Parliament (see **Chapter 7**). This is the argument that since Ministers may amend statutes using the 'fast track' procedure without having to first obtain Parliamentary approval it will 'erode the sovereignty of Parliament' (Editorial, *The Daily Telegraph*, 25 October 1997). To counter this, however, one might point out that in adopting a model to incorporate the ECHR, the Government chose to protect the sovereignty of Parliament by basing the Human Rights Act on the New Zealand Bill of Rights 1990, thereby denying judges the right to strike down Acts of Parliament.

Thirdly, some argue that the Human Rights Act is unnecessary for human rights are already adequately guaranteed in the United Kingdom, so that it will create unrealistic expectations and lead to frivolous litigation. However, as you may have already realised when considering **SAQ 5**, a consequence of the fact that British courts were, in the past, unable to enforce the ECHR in the domestic courts, was that a disproportionately high number of cases were brought to the European Court of Human Rights by British applicants. As Lord Browne-Wilkinson once commented, 'that this country should be found so repeatedly in breach of its international obligations is very shocking' (*The Independent*, 28 September 1995). Despite the arguments advanced by Sir Nicholas Lyell (see *Cases and Materials* (**1.4.3**)), it is undeniable that successive British governments were in the past embarrassed not merely by the number of these cases, but also by the negative publicity it generated for the UK. Prior to incorporation, Lord Lester QC lamented the fact that 'Britain's dirty washing has been washed slowly, expensively and inefficiently in Strasbourg' (*The Independent*, 28 September 1995), but now, as a result of the Human Rights Act 1998, many of these cases can be dealt with much more 'quietly' and less embarrassingly, in the UK's domestic courts.

Fourthly, it has been argued that the Human Rights Act is 'un-British'; i.e., it departs from the traditional British model of not codifying fundamental rights and is 'a giant step towards the continental [European] model' (Editorial, *The Daily Telegraph*, 25 October 1997). There are at least three responses to the claim that a constitutional document guaranteeing rights is somehow not 'British'. First, a number of Commonwealth countries, whose legal systems are largely based on the 'British' model, such as New Zealand (1990) and Canada (1960 and 1982), have chosen to enact Bills of Rights. Secondly, Britain has helped to draft Bills of Rights for a number of its former colonies (e.g., Hong Kong, Nigeria, Jamaica, Kenya etc.) in recent years, thereby quashing the notion that there is any thing quintessentially 'un-British' about a Bill of Rights. Thirdly, the idea that the principles upon which the UK's Constitution are based upon today are only 'British' is fallacious in view of the increasing influence of European Community law.

Finally, the Human Rights Act is opposed by some on the ground that it will give judges more influence than they should enjoy in a parliamentary democracy. There is no doubt that the Act will give judges extra power and it is suggested that this is the strongest objection to the Human Rights Act. Even the Lord Chancellor, Lord Irvine, has conceded that 'incorporation will involve a very significant transfer of power to the judges' (*The Daily Telegraph*, 25 October 1997). As we noted earlier, parts of the Human Rights Act are rather vague (e.g., s. 3), so many challenges lie ahead for Britain's judges in interpreting this legislation in a way which protects the rights of the individual yet does not erode the sovereignty of Parliament.

The Government has said that it has not 'closed its mind' on the idea of setting up a Human Rights Commission (*The Guardian*, 25 October 1997), which would help implement the Human Rights Act 1998. What is a Human Rights Commission? How would it work and what are the arguments for establishing it? You will find the answers to these questions in the extract from Sarah Spencer and Ian Bynoe in *Cases and Materials* (1.4.5).

1.7   Conclusion

In this chapter we have established that the British Constitution is rather unusual in that it is not contained in a single document. However, these are changing times for the UK's Constitution. Ironically the political ideology of 'Thatcherism' which had such a significant influence on the administration of the country in the last decade, never quite extended to constitutional reform. Thus, the present Prime Minister, Tony Blair, has claimed that his Government's policy of reforming the Constitution 'is something which has not been seen in this country for nearly a century' (*Evening Standard*, 22 April 1998). He has pledged to take Britain's 'working constitution, respect its strengths, and adapt it to modern demands for clean and effective government while at the same time providing a greater democratic role for the people at large' (*The Economist*, 14 September 1996). It is up to you whether you agree or disagree with his proposals but at this stage you should at least be able to appreciate a number of the arguments for and against further constitutional reform.

Tony Blair's previous statement refers to the 'strengths' of the present system. Perhaps the most obvious of these is the British Constitution's flexibility and, in the next chapter, we will examine the constitutional conventions which have enabled the Constitution in the past to respond smoothly and successfully to changing social and political developments.

1.8 End of Chapter Assessment Question

'. . . if we are moving inevitably . . . towards some sort of constitutional crisis too deep-seated in its causation to be capable of achieving piecemeal adjustment, it is at least worthwhile examining the means of achieving fundamental reform without recourse to the disastrous expedient of revolution.' (Lord Hailsham, *The Times*, 1975.)

Discuss with reference to the case for the codification of the British Constitution.

(See *Cases and Materials* (1.6) for a specimen answer.)

CHAPTER TWO

CONVENTIONS – THE RULES OF THE GAME

2.1 Objectives

At the end of this Chapter you should be able to:

- define the nature and characteristics of conventions;

- distinguish between conventions and rules of law;

- evaluate the significance of conventions and their role in the UK Constitution;

- assess the convention of individual Ministerial responsibility in terms of its effectiveness in holding ministers to account, particularly in the light of recent political events;

- consider the arguments for and against the codification of conventions.

2.2 Introduction

In **Chapter 1** we looked at the term 'constitution' and sought to define both what a constitution is, and what is meant by constitutional law. In doing so we observed that Britain has no written constitution in the formal sense of possessing a written document. Instead, it was noted that a constitution can be found to exist amongst a variety of sources ranging from legal rules (e.g., statutes and case law) to non-legal rules (e.g., customs and conventions). Conventions play an important role in the British Constitution. For example, even the office of Prime Minister owes its existence to a constitutional convention. Therefore, in order to understand how the UK's Constitution operates, it is crucial that we appreciate both the influence of conventions and the extent to which they, as 'rules of the game', are observed.

2.3 Definitions of Conventions

We have already encountered difficulties in trying to ascertain what is meant by 'a constitution' – conventions themselves are no easier to define.

Think of an organisation or body of which you are a member – it might be related to work or leisure. Now list, on a separate sheet of paper, as many rules and regulations as you can concerning the organisation of that body and the conduct of its members.

(a) Does the group meet on a regular basis? How are its meetings conducted? Who takes control? How are decisions made? What happens if an individual objects?

(b) Is any standard of moral behaviour required? What would happen if one of the members was found to be having an extramarital affair with another member? Would it be any different if a member was alleged to be involved in unlawful activities?

(c) What would happen if any of these 'rules' were broken?

(d) Of all the rules and regulations you have listed, how many, as far as you know, are actually written down?

Conventions are non-legal rules, which may include constitutional practices, customs, habits, agreements and understandings. They underpin the framework of the operation of government. Conventions may demand particular forms of political and professional behaviour. Whilst conventions cannot be enforced in the courts because they are non-legal rules, in practice they are of considerable constitutional significance. No doubt some of the characteristics of conventions are similar to the rules you identified as operating within your chosen organisation. It may be an unwritten rule that you finish early on Friday, or meet for a drink at lunchtime. It may be expected that people attend and a practice may have developed, but there is probably no formal sanction that can ensure attendance. Private peccadillos may be tolerated as long as they do not interfere with the effective operation of the group. If an individual's behaviour becomes troublesome, this could lead to pressure being exerted to curb that behaviour. Ultimately there may remain the threat of expulsion.

These are all examples of conventions or practices which may be found in any organisation. Such 'conventions' are usually necessary to enable the group to function effectively and their role is not significantly different in constitutional terms. (A list of some important constitutional conventions is provided in *Cases and Materials* (2.1).)

2.3.1 THE VIEWS OF DICEY AND JENNINGS

It is very difficult to define constitutional conventions because of their nature and the fact they are not formally codified. A.V. Dicey, is credited with formulating the term 'convention'. Dicey distinguished conventions from law. He defined conventions as 'rules which make up constitutional law', and 'rules for determining the mode in which the discretionary powers of the Crown (or of the Ministers as servants of the Crown) ought to be exercised'. Dicey equated the term 'law' with statute and judge-made law. On the other hand conventions are 'understandings, habits and practices which are not enforced by the courts but which regulate the conduct of members of the sovereign power'.

Sir Ivor Jennings in his book, *The Law and the Constitution* (see *Cases and Materials* (2.1.1)) commented that whilst Dicey's definition is 'plain and unambiguous', it is too simplistic. Jennings doubted whether such a distinction between law and convention could be drawn. His justification for this was that 'conventions are like most fundamental rules of any constitution in that they rest essentially upon general acquiescence'. Jennings stressed that it is this which sets conventions apart from the law – they are obeyed and followed rather than *enforced* by the courts. Thus, just as conventions will not exist if they are not respected or obeyed, so neither will a written constitution have any legal force unless its provisions are accepted and obeyed by the community. Although Jennings accepted that courts will *recognise* their existence, but take no action in the event of a breach of a convention, Jennings claimed that '[t]he real question which is presented to the Government is not whether a rule is law or convention, but what the House of Commons will think about if a certain action is proposed'. Thus, for Jennings there were real similarities between law and conventions, but he conceded that there were three important differences.

Read the extract from Jennings, *The Law and the Constitution*, in *Cases and Materials* (2.1.1). What are the three important differences he identifies between legal rules and conventions?

Jennings's interpretation has since been refined by many other constitutional writers. For example, Marshall and Moodie (*Some Problems of the Constitution*, 5th edn, 1971) define conventions as:

> . . . certain rules of constitutional behaviour which are considered to be binding by and upon those who operate the Constitution, but which are not enforced by the law courts (although the courts may recognise their existence), nor by the presiding officers in the Houses of Parliament.

Similarly, Hood Phillips (*Constitutional and Administrative Law*, 7th edn, 1988) suggests that conventions are:

> . . . rules of political practice which are regarded as binding by those to whom they apply, but which are not laws as they are not enforced by the courts or by the Houses of Parliament.

What conclusion can you draw from the fact that respected constitutional writers have failed to achieve a common definition of conventions?

2.4 Determining the Existence of Conventions

Because conventions are unwritten and are somewhat elusive concepts, it is often extremely difficult to be sure whether a particular rule or practice has in fact been crystallised into a convention. First, it would seem relatively straightforward to distinguish beween conventions and legal rules, so perhaps this is a good starting point.

2.4.1 DISTINGUISHING BETWEEN CONVENTIONS AND LEGAL RULES

What factors or characteristics distinguish conventions from legal rules?

Conventions   *Legal rules*

■ Laws are usually to be found in written form (in statutes, delegated legislation or case law); conventions are not codified.

■ Laws develop systematically and formally; conventions evolve.

- Laws can be enforced through the courts; conventions are only recognised by the courts.

- The breach of a law or legal rule normally results in formal legal punishment; there is no clear legal sanction for disobeying a convention.

Dicey said that conventions are 'a body not of laws but of constitutional or political ethics'. On the other hand, laws are 'rules enforced or recognised by the courts'. There are however exceptions to this general rule. As we will see in **Chapter 6**, not all breaches of law are enforced by the courts (e.g., Parliament has the authority and jurisdiction to deal with matters of Parliamentary privilege and to commit individuals for being in contempt of the House).

Dicey drew a clear distinction between conventions and laws. He concluded that conventions are not enforceable by the courts, unlike formal legal rules. However, Dicey considered that a breach of a convention could lead to a violation of the law. As an example he cites the convention that Parliament must assemble at least once a year. Suppose Parliament was prorogued, and did not sit for two years, this would be a breach of convention, although not a breach of the law. However, the result would be that statutes which must be passed annually to govern the country, would not be re-enacted (e.g., Acts relating to the keeping of an army or taxation). Thus, the keeping of an army and the collection of taxes would become illegal. Although this is a clear example of such a consequence, it fails to explain why conventions are generally observed. One possible explanation is that of political expedience (e.g. government Ministers and those subject to conventions like to occupy the 'moral high ground' in being seen to respect constitutional conventions).

2.4.2   DISTINGUISHING CONVENTIONS FROM USAGES

It is important to compare conventions to usages. A 'usage' would include a custom, practice, habit or rule, but unlike a convention, it is not obligatory. As examples of usages Hood Phillips (*Constitutional and Administrative Law*, 7th edn, 1988) cites the existence of political parties (which is a fact), and the Chancellor taking the dispatch box containing the Budget speech to the House of Commons before delivering the Budget (a custom).

According to K C Wheare (*Modern Constitutions*, 2nd edn, 1966), a convention is 'an obligatory rule' while a usage is a 'rule which is no more than the description of a practice and which has not yet obtained obligatory force'.

The obligatory nature of a convention makes it prescriptive. However, a usage is descriptive. In other words conventions require that people behave in a certain way, because they feel obliged to, whereas usages are actions taken subconsciously.

Sir Ivor Jennings advises that the existence of a convention can be determined by asking three questions:

(a)   What are the precedents?

(b)   Did the actors in the precedents believe that they were bound by a rule?

(c)   Is there a reason for the rule?

Jennings goes on to say that 'a single precedent with a good reason may be enough to establish the rule. A whole string of precedents without such a reason will be of no avail, unless it is perfectly certain that the persons concerned regarded themselves as bound by it'.

Why do you think conventions are generally observed?

What happens if conventions are not obeyed? Look again at the list of examples in *Cases and Materials* **(2.1) and assess the consequences.**

2.4.3 WHY ARE CONVENTIONS OBSERVED?

What is it that makes the actors within the constitution usually respect conventions? We have established that there is no legal sanction for breaking a convention. So why are conventions of constitutional significance? Sir Ivor Jennings suggests that 'conventions are observed because of the political difficulties which arise if they are not'.

What might these political difficulties be?

2.4.3.1 Practical difficulties

Clearly, if certain conventions were not followed this would lead to major difficulties in the functioning of government and Parliament. Dicey's earlier example of Parliament not meeting annually would have severe practical consequences.

2.4.3.2 Changes in law

As already mentioned, a breach of convention can lead to a change in the law, e.g., the Parliament Act 1911. Similarly, in 1947, the House of Lords failed to observe the convention of yielding to the House of Commons. The Lords also rejected a second Bill to reduce its powers further but this was eventually enacted as the Parliament Act 1949.

2.4.3.3 Political consequences

If a government is defeated in a vote of no confidence in the Commons, it is expected to resign and call a general election. Notwithstanding political considerations, perhaps this is a subtle way of ensuring that a government acts responsibly! (See the extract from R. Brazier in *Cases and Materials* (**2.2.2**), on conventions and the resignation of Ministers.)

Hood Phillips (*Constitutional and Administrative Law*, 7th edn, 1988) concludes that obedience to conventions is therefore both political and psychological. This is a view echoed by de Smith (*Constitutional and Administrative Law*, 7th edn, 1994), who refers to the '. . . force of habit, inertia, desire to conform, [and] belief that it is right to obey them and wrong to disobey them because they are reasonable rules'.

So, in conclusion, it would appear that what induces obedience to conventions is a fear of the practical consequences which may follow if they are ignored. Conventions are politically 'binding' but there is no mechanism for identifying, applying or interpreting them.

2.5   The Characteristics of Conventions

All constitutions, whether written or unwritten, embody certain fundamental rules. However, the application of these rules is governed usually by an additional set of non-legal rules: conventions. For example, even in the United States (a country with a written constitution) conventions have an important constitutional role. There, the office of Secretary of State, a position held by important international statesmen in recent years such as Warren Christopher or Henry Kissinger, is a creature of convention.

The main advantage of conventions is flexibility. However, because conventions are not formally written down, they are often very difficult to identify. This explains why it is virtually impossible to provide a definitive list of them, as you may have concluded from **SAQ 8**. So how do we know if the origin of a particular practice is a constitutional convention or a formal legal rule? A useful starting point would be to look for the common characteristics of conventions. Some of these are identified in the following paragraphs.

2.5.1   CONVENTIONS ARE NOT FORMULATED IN WRITING

Conventions are not enacted. There is no 'official list' which denotes all of the existing conventions. (See, however, *Cases and Materials* (**2.1**) for a summary of the most common ones.) Conventions are the unwritten rules of political practice. Thus, even a convention of major constitutional significance, such as the rule that the Monarch does not refuse the Royal Assent to Bills passed by both Houses of Parliament, is not formally codified.

Why do you think conventions are not recorded or written down?

2.5.2 THE DEVELOPMENT OF CONVENTIONS IS AN EVOLUTIONARY PROCESS

Since conventions are continually changing and developing to reflect new situations, there is sometimes uncertainty as to whether a certain practice actually has been recognised as a constitutional convention. Nevertheless, an example of a fairly recent convention is the requirement that a Prime Minister must be a member of the House of Commons. This convention did not become firmly established until 1963 when the former Earl of Home was invited to become Prime Minister. Having disclaimed his peerage under the Life Peerages Act 1963 (see **Chapter 6**) he was elected to the House of Commons in a by-election and, as Sir Alec Douglas Home, became Prime Minister. Thus, had Tony Blair, the leader of the Labour Party, failed to win his own seat in the 1997 General Election, he could not have become Britain's Prime Minister.

What are the advantages of a system in which a convention naturally evolves? For some ideas turn to the extract from Dorey on the 'Origins and Widening of Collective Responsibility' in *Cases and Materials* **(2.2.1).**

2.5.3 CONVENTIONS REGULATE THE CONDUCT OF THOSE HOLDING PUBLIC OFFICE

Ministers of the Crown, as holders of public office, are subject to constitutional restraints through convention. Ministers are, at least in theory, individually responsible to Parliament for the running of their departments. In practice, however, the 'whipping' system, whereby MPs are pressurised into supporting their party's line by 'whips' or party managers, reduces the likelihood of government ministers receiving criticism from their own backbenchers. We will return to this in more detail shortly but, as an introduction to this topic, it is useful to consider what Lord Nolan, in *The Making and Remaking of the British Constitution* (1997) has described as the three aspects of ministerial accountability:

First, ministerial accountability is a convention without statutory force. Second, there has never been universal agreement about the terms of that accountability. Third, there is no independent source of authority which can determine whether the convention has been observed in a given circumstance.

2.5.4 SANCTIONS FOR A BREACH OF CONVENTION ARE POLITICAL

The violation of a convention would appear to be 'unconstitutional' – yet since the courts cannot enforce conventions, there is no legal sanction. The only sanction is therefore political. For example, when a Minister flouts a convention, he or she is expected to resign – and if the Minister is unwilling to leave office, pressure may be exerted by the Prime Minister, Cabinet or press. If you think carefully, you will probably remember some former Cabinet resignations.

For example, in 1992, David Mellor, the former Heritage Secretary, was forced to resign following press reports of his affair with a Spanish actress and his acceptance of a holiday paid for by Mona Bauwens, the daughter of a senior Palestine Liberation Organisation official while, in 1994, Tim Yeo was forced to resign as Environmental Minister, after admitting that he had fathered a child out of wedlock at a time when the Government had pledged itself to supporting traditional family values. Most recently, in October 1998, Ron Davies resigned as the Welsh Secretary following an incident, which he described as a 'serious lapse of judgment', when he was robbed while walking alone at night in a central London park. Thus, the sanction for conduct unbecoming that of a Minister (be it professional or even moral) is the loss of political office. However, resignation on purely *moral* grounds is thought of as being increasingly unlikely, following the lack of political reaction to the decision of Robin Cook, the Foreign Secretary, to leave his wife in 1997 for a ministerial aide (whom he later married) and Sir Richard Scott's view that what Ministers do in their private lives is 'nothing whatever to do with the constitutional principle of ministerial responsibility' (see *Cases and Materials* (2.3.1).

According to Richard Rose (see *Cases and Materials* (2.2.2)) what is the purpose of the Cabinet? Who sits in the Cabinet? A list of Cabinet positions in Tony Blair's government (1998) is also provided in *Cases and Materials* (2.2.2).

One of the most famous resignations in the late twentieth century was the decision of Lord Carrington (then Foreign Secretary) and two other Ministers to resign, in 1982, as a result of the Argentinian invasion of the Falkland Islands. They took the blame for the UK Government's failure to predict the Argentinian military junta's hostile intentions. However, examples of such ministerial resignations are rare. In recent years it would seem that a loss of confidence in a Minister or pressure to go from party members is often the real reason why Ministers have resigned although, as the Public Service Committee conceded in its second report (1995–96), '[t]here have always been elements of ambiguity and confusion in the convention of individual ministerial responsibility' so that 'the way in which it is used in practice tends to be variable and inconsistent.'.

(a) Lord Nolan (*The Making and Remaking of the British Constitution*, 1997, p. 38) has suggested that 'forcing a Minister to resign has little or nothing to do with rectifying mistakes . . . and much or all to do with political warfare' and that 'inviting or compelling a Minister to put things right . . . is almost certainly more valuable' than forcing him or her to resign. Do you agree?

(b) The following Ministers were forced to resign. What were the reasons for their departure? Check your answer in *Cases and Materials* (2.2.2).

Minister	Reason for resignation
Cecil Parkinson (1983) (Trade and Industry Secretary)	
Leon Brittan (1986) (Trade and Industry Secretary)	
Edwina Currie (1988) (Parliamentary Secretary, Department of Health)	
Nicholas Ridley (1990) (Trade and Industry Secretary)	
David Mellor (1992) (Heritage Secretary)	
Michael Mates (1993) (Northern Ireland Minister)	
Tim Yeo (1994) (Environment Minister)	
Neil Hamilton (1994) (Junior Trade Minister)	
Allan Stewart (1995) (Scottish Office Minister)	
John Redwood (1995) (Secretary of State for Wales)	
Rod Richards (1996) (Junior Welsh Office Minister	
David Willetts (1996) (The Paymaster General)	
Ron Davies (Welsh Secretary)	

Can you think of any occasions in recent years where ministers, under pressure to resign, have refused to do so?

Despite these examples, there have been a number of occasions, in recent years, where Ministers, under pressure to resign, have refused to do so. The defiant response of a former Home Secretary in refusing to resign, following the Court of Appeal's ruling that he had acted in contempt of court in deporting a Zairian asylum seeker despite a court order (*M v Home Office* [1992] QB 270), is considered by Marshall in *Cases and Materials* (2.2.2). Similar refusals by Ministers, such as that of Douglas Hurd (the former Foreign Secretary) to resign over the Pergau Dam affair (see *R v Secretary of State for Foreign Affairs, ex parte WDM* [1995] 1 All ER 611, in *Cases and Materials* (15.1.3.1)) and the decision of Michael Howard (the former Home Secretary) to sack the former Director General of the Prison Service, Derek Lewis, rather than to take the blame himself for a number of prison breakouts, even led the House of Commons to debate the motion (in

February 1996) '[t]hat this House deplores the erosion by Her Majesty's Government of the principle of ministerial responsibility'. However, it was the failure of any Ministers of the Crown to resign following the publication of the Scott Report (1996), set up to investigate the 'arms to Iraq' affair, which was particularly controversial. Professor Vernon Bogdanor claims that the Scott Inquiry shows 'how inadequate our conventional notions of ministerial accountability are in actually pinning down responsibility' (*Parliamentary Affairs*, 1997, No. 1, vol. 50, p. 71) and we will return to the Scott Report in more detail later in this chapter.

Read the extract from Colin Turpin, 'Ministerial Responsibility' in *Cases and Materials* (2.2.2).

How does he describe the convention of ministerial responsibility and what is its purpose?

The convention of ministerial reponsibility is not just one 'convention' but, as Turpin puts it, is 'an assemblage of conventions which control and govern ministerial conduct'. Two main conventions have developed - the doctrines of (a) collective responsibility and (b) individual ministerial responsibility. Having already looked at individual ministerial responsibility, we must now turn to collective responsibility.

The principle of collective responsibility may have a number of different connotations. At its most fundamental level it means that the government is collectively responsible and should **collectively resign** if it loses a vote of confidence in the House of Commons. This tends to be rare and only two governments have lost the confidence of the House since 1924 — Ramsay MacDonald's (1924) and James Callaghan's (1976) minority Labour governments.

Collective reponsibility is also taken to refer to the convention that the Cabinet 'speaks as one'. When Ministers speak in their official capacity, they are speaking on behalf of the government. All Cabinet Ministers therefore assume responsibility for Cabinet discussions and all Ministers are expected to present a united front. The convention is that it is constitutionally improper for a Minister to remain in office if that Minister has dissassociated himself or herself from Cabinet policy. A Minister should therefore resign if in dissent as Michael Heseltine did over the Westland affair (1986). He favoured a European-based financial reconstruction of the ailing British Westland helicopter company, whereas others in the Cabinet were in favour of a United States rescue package. Similarly, when Margaret Thatcher was Prime Minister, both Geoffrey Howe and Nigel Lawson resigned from the Cabinet because they failed to agree with her policies, particularly those on Europe. When a senior government Minister resigns on the ground that he or she opposes government policy, the Prime Minister may be seriously weakened and many commentators believe that Geoffrey Howe's decision to leave the Government, particularly his resignation speech in the House of Commons, inflicted serious political damage on Margaret Thatcher.

The convention of collective responsibility also means that once a Cabinet decision has been taken, Ministers must not publicly express any contrary opinions in public. This is justified on the ground that full and frank discussions will have been expressed earlier in the Cabinet. The disclosure of Cabinet discussions might curb full debate. (For a discussion of collective responsibility, see the extract from Brazier in *Cases and Materials* (2.2.2).)

The confidentiality of Cabinet discussions was considered in *Attorney-General* v *Cape Ltd* [1976] QB 752, where the court recognised, but refused to enforce, the convention of the collective responsibility of Cabinet Ministers. Jonathan Cape wished to publish the diaries of Richard Crossman, a former Minister. After his death the diaries were edited because they contained extracts of Cabinet meetings but the publishers did not agree to all of the cuts and revisions suggested by the Cabinet Secretary. The government sought an injunction to restrain publication as the Attorney-General (on behalf of the government) argued that the material was confidential and would be prejudicial to the public interest if printed. The court held that the convention of collective responsibility placed Ministers under a duty of confidentiality. However, as the meetings in question had occurred 10 years earlier it was held that there was no reason to grant an injunction restraining publication, as there was now no risk to the collective responsibility of the Cabinet. Since this argument of Cabinet confidentiality failed the Attorney-General could not block publication and Lord Widgery CJ accepted that 'a true convention [is] . . . an obligation founded in conscience only'.

Read the extract from the *Jonathan Cape* case in *Cases and Materials* (2.2.2).

What arguments were presented to the court on behalf of the defendant to support the proposition that the court had no jurisdiction to enforce the convention of collective responsibility?

You should also look at the brief case summaries of *Carltona Ltd* v *Commission of Works* (1943) and *Liversidge* v *Anderson* (1942) in *Cases and Materials* (2.2.2).

2.5.5 IN THE EVENT OF A CONFLICT BETWEEN LAW AND CONVENTION THE COURTS MUST ENFORCE THE LAW

The principle that a rule of law overrules any convention where there is a conflict is shown in the following two cases, concerning the procedures by which independence was granted by Westminster to former Commonwealth colonies. In *Madzimbamuto* v *Lardner-Burke* [1961] 1 AC 645, the Judicial Committee of the Privy Council had to decide whether a statute passed by Parliament (the Southern Rhodesia Act 1965) should take priority over a convention. The Judicial Committee is where the Law Lords sit as the final appeal court for those countries of the Commonwealth that still recognise its jurisdiction. The convention required that Parliament should legislate for a Commonwealth country only with the consent of that country's government. The Southern Rhodesian government (today this State is known as Zimbabwe) unilaterally declared independence, and in response Parliament passed the statute reasserting the right of Westminster to legislate for Southern Rhodesia. The Privy Council held that the UK statute, although passed in breach of the convention (as the Southern Rhodesian government had not consented to its enactment), took priority and was valid.

Similarly, in *Reference re Amendment to the Constitution of Canada* (1982) 125 DLR (3d) 1, a valuable discussion of constitutional conventions took place in the Canadian Supreme Court. The Canadian government, which was in the process of asking the Westminster Parliament to pass a new statute to amend the British North America Act 1867 (which had created the Dominion of Canada), requested an advisory opinion. The issue facing the court was whether or not the consent of the provinces was required before the Canadian Parliament made that official request. Some of the Canadian provinces had argued that there was a constitutional convention, which required their agreement to any proposed changes to the Canadian Constitution. The Canadian Supreme Court agreed that this convention did exist, but that it did not have the status of a rule of law and so could not be enforced. The court held that to enforce the convention 'would mean to administer some formal sanction . . . But the legal system from which they [the conventions] are distinct does not contemplate formal sanctions for their breach'. As a result the Federal Government negotiated a new agreement with all of the disaffected provinces (except Quebec), and the Canada Act 1982, passed by Westminster, granted Canada its independence.

What is the main purpose of constitutional conventions? For an answer to this question turn to the extract from *Reference Re Amendment of the Constitution of Canada* (1982) in *Cases and Materials* (2.2.3).

2.5.6 CONVENTIONS ARE CAPABLE OF BEING ENACTED INTO STATUTE

A failure to observe an important constitutional convention may precipitate a change in the law, with Parliament legislating to prevent any such recurrence. One example of a convention being codified in the form of a statute is the convention that the House of Lords should yield to the elected body, the House of Commons. In 1909 the House of Lords disobeyed this convention (see **Chapter 6**). As a result, the Liberal government presented a Parliament Bill (under the threat of creating more Liberal peers in the Lords to ensure its successful passage), which limited the powers of the Lords, and in effect ensured that they must yield to the Commons. This was enacted as the Parliament Act 1911. A convention still exists (the 'Salisbury convention') that the Lords should not offer outright opposition to the Commons.

Another example is s. 4 of the Statute of Westminster 1931 (see *Cases and Materials* (2.2.4)), which enacts the established convention that Parliament will not legislate for dominion territories unless so requested.

If conventions are so important why are they not codified as legal rules?

2.5.7 THE CLOSE RELATIONSHIP BETWEEN CONVENTIONS AND LAW

The line between strict law and convention is blurred. Often the two are closely linked or related. (For example, see the extract from Munro in *Cases and Materials* (2.2.5)).

Conventions may dictate how individuals, within the constitutional framework, should exercise their legal powers. Equally a statute may presuppose the existence of a convention. The office of Prime Minister, that of Leader of the Opposition and even the very existence of the Cabinet, are assumed to exist by the legislation which provides for their salaries.

Fill in the table below by looking at the list of conventions in *Cases and Materials* (2.2.5).

Legal rule	*Convention*
The Monarch must give the Royal Assent to a Bill.	
The Monarch appoints the Prime Minister.	
The Monarch appoints and dismisses Ministers.	
The Monarch summons and dissolves Parliament.	
The Monarch may pardon convicted prisoners or remit or reduce a sentence.	

2.6 The Purpose of Conventions

Read the second extract from Jennings, *The Law and the Constitution* in *Cases and Materials* (2.1.1). What does he say is the purpose of conventions and what metaphor does he use to describe their function?

We have already seen that conventions supplement strict rules of law. From your answers to the SAQs in the preceding section, you should by now have concluded that they are flexible — conventions are not written down anywhere, so this allows them to evolve and develop as necessary. Their main advantage is flexibility — no complicated procedures are required to introduce a fresh convention. As a new rule or political practice is formulated, it may become a convention. In addition to Jennings's metaphor that conventions 'provide the flesh which clothe the dry bones of the law', he has also described them as 'oiling the wheels of government'. Think of a skeleton — the dry bones of the law are contained in Acts of Parliament, the common law and prerogative powers. What does a skeleton need to function as a living organism? It needs flesh and clothes to protect those bones, muscle to provide motion, oxygen and blood to allow the system to breathe and make the individual organs work as one effective, functioning body. This is the purpose of conventions. Conventions enable the law and the constitution to operate, by providing those components which allow the constitution to live and breathe.

The three main purposes of conventions are:

(a)   to change and develop the constitution,

(b)   to regulate both internal and external relations, and

(c)   to provide a control mechanism.

Select an example of a convention from *Cases and Materials* (2.1) to illustrate each of these purposes.

2.6.1   A MEANS OF CHANGING AND DEVELOPING THE CONSTITUTION

Conventions are a means of bringing about constitutional change and reform without the need for complicated and formal changes to the law. Conventions can be found to a greater or lesser extent in all constitutions whether written or unwritten. In the United States it was a convention that a person could only serve as President for two successive terms. The Second World War led to Franklin Roosevelt being elected President for a third term in 1940 and then again for a fourth term in 1945. This prompted the 22nd amendment to the US Constitution limiting the life of a presidency to two terms (another example of a convention becoming a legal rule).

2.6.2 CONVENTIONS REGULATE BOTH INTERNAL AND EXTERNAL RELATIONS

Conventions provide the means of co-operation and practice with regard to both:

(a) Internal relationships, e.g., relations between government departments and Parliament or between departments and the Sovereign, and

(b) External relationships, e.g., allowing members of the Commonwealth to co-operate in matters of foreign affairs and defence.

2.6.3 CONTROL AND ACCOUNTABILITY

Dicey highlighted the regulation of any discretionary use of power as a primary function of conventions. Conventions are therefore an important mechanism in holding to account those in public office, by providing a check on their actions. Perhaps the convention which is most synonymous with holding a government to account is that of ministerial responsibility and, in the light of the findings of the Scott Inquiry, there has been much recent discussion about how this convention should operate in practice. Thus, it is necessary to consider why the Report was commissioned, what it found, and the lessons which can be learnt following its publication.

Why do conventions play such an important role in our constitution?

2.7 The Scott Report

2.7.1 THE BACKGROUND TO SCOTT

The Scott Report was commissioned following the unsuccessful prosecution of three directors of Matrix Churchill, a British machine tool company. They had been accused of unlawfully exporting, to Iraq, machinery which was capable of being used in the production of weapons of destruction, contrary to government export regulations. The defendants argued that the British Government not merely knew of their exports to Iraq but that one of the defendants (Paul Henderson) had even been using his influence and contacts in this area to pass on useful information to the British intelligence services. In an effort to corroborate these claims, the defendants tried to obtain documents from the relevant Government Departments. However, acting on the advice of the Attorney-General, Government Ministers (although one Minister, the former President of the Board of Trade, Michael Heseltine, still had some reservations about doing this) signed

Public Interest Immunity (PII) certificates thereby denying the defendants access to this information, on the ground that the disclosure of these documents would be injurious to the public interest.

It was not until the former junior Defence and Trade Minister, Alan Clark, gave evidence at their trial that the full version of events became public. Under cross-examination from counsel for the defendants, Clark provided answers in court which conflicted with a written statement he had made earlier and this was the catalyst for the revelation that the Government (without telling Parliament) had altered its guidelines (the Howe Guidelines) on arms sales, thereby sanctioning a less stringent policy on the export of defence equipment to Iraq. The revelation that Ministers were prepared to sign PII certificates which concealed information that, without which, might have led to innocent men being sent to prison, caused a public outcry. Thus, on 23 November 1992, the day after the collapse of the trial, the Prime Minister (John Major) announced that an inquiry into the trial and 'any other similar cases', would be set up under the Chairmanship of the then member of the Court of Appeal, Lord Justice Scott (his title changed to Sir Richard Scott when he subsequently was appointed to the position of Vice-Chancellor and head of the Chancery Division of the High Court).

When should a Minister resign from office? Ought he or she be held responsible for the acts and omissions of others? Make a brief note of when a Minister should resign from office and compare what you have written with the views of Sir Richard Scott, which we will look at later in this chapter.

2.7.2 SCOTT'S CONCLUSIONS

Perhaps the most obvious thing initially to notice about the Scott Report was its sheer size — it comprised of four volumes of text, with more than 1,800 pages, and a fifth volume of appendices.

The main findings of the Report are as follows:

■ There had been a change in the 'Howe Guidelines' and Parliament should have been informed of this shift in policy. The less restrictive policy towards Iraq had been concealed from Parliament in order to prevent a public debate on the matter; similarly, information given by the Government in 1989 and 1990 about the export of arms had 'consistently failed to discharge the obligations imposed by the constitutional principle of ministerial responsibility' (Report, para. D4.63). Thus, the Government had failed, deliberately, to 'inform Parliament of the current state of Government policy on non-lethal arms sales to Iraq' (Report, para. D4.25).

■ William Waldergrave, a Foreign Minister at the time, was criticised for misleading Parliament, for he had sent 38 letters to MPs between March and July 1989, in which he denied that there had been any policy change. However, Scott accepted that Waldergrave honestly believed that the policy had not changed and that he had not intended 'to be misleading' (Report, para. D4.12).

■ The Matrix Churchill directors should never have been prosecuted and, instead, HM Customs and Excise should have investigated the claims and allegations of the defendants. Moreover, at the trial itself, the Attorney-General should have informed the court that one Minister (Michael Heseltine) had been reluctant to sign the PII certificate.

■ Finally, the Attorney-General (Sir Nicholas Lyell) was also criticised for interpreting the law on PII certificates incorrectly, by suggesting that Ministers had a duty to sign such certificates when requested to do so. Thus, the Attorney-General should have provided his ministerial colleagues with accurate information about the consequences of using PII certificates.

2.7.3   REACTIONS TO SCOTT

For those who hoped that the Scott Report would not merely provide an independent, impartial and critical evaluation of the events surrounding the Matrix Churchill trial, but that it would also unambiguously apportion blame and attribute fault, there was disappointment. The Report satisfies the first, but not the second criteria. Despite Sir Richard Scott's criticisms, not a single Minister was forced to resign and, having survived a critical Commons motion by a single vote, the controversy generated by the Report soon abated, endorsing William Waldergrave's opinion that for the Government 'it would be hairy for ten days but that will be all' (*The Guardian*, 14 August 1996).

There are a number of reasons why the Scott Report failed, certainly in the short term, to have the effect which many had hoped that it would. First, in the month prior to the Report's publication, senior figures, such as the former Foreign Secretary, Lord Howe, attacked its credibility by suggesting that, in gathering evidence for the Report, there had been a denial of the rules of natural justice. Secondly, the Government was given access to the Report eight days in advance of its publication, but it prevented the Opposition from seeing the Report until the morning of 15 February 1996 (the day of the initial debate on the Report), leaving Opposition leaders with just under four hours to read the Report's five volumes. This is a clear illustration of the old maxim 'information is power', so the opposition parties were clearly at a disadvantage in rebutting the arguments of well-briefed Ministers in the early days of the Report's publication, a fact made even worse by the Report's omission of a summary of its conclusions and recommendations. Finally, and perhaps most significantly, Sir Richard Scott tended to apply a *subjective* test to the actions of Ministers. Thus, even if they had failed to act in accordance with what was actually in the public interest, the Ministers had, at least, taken decisions in good faith, although a more rigorous *objective* standard (e.g., would a reasonable Minister have signed the PII certificates etc.) might have led to a more critical report and increased the pressure for ministerial resignations.

2.7.4   LESSONS FROM SCOTT

Sir Richard Scott made a number of recommendations and these include:

■ the creation of a Parliamentary Officer to examine the claims of Ministers that it may be 'in the public interest' to conceal certain information;

■ a 'comprehensive review' of the subjects and topics on which Government Ministers can choose not to answer questions, a task later undertaken by the Public Select Committee in July 1996; and,

■ in the light of the fact that civil servants had been permitted to give evidence directly
to the Scott Inquiry, more opportunities for civil servants to 'give information about
what they have done in the discharge of their duties, not in the formation of policy,
but in the application of policy'.

Despite these recommendations, perhaps the most enduring legacy of the Scott Report
will be the guidance it offers on ministerial accountability and responsibility. In this
regard it is particularly ironic that Scott's original remit made no explicit reference to
ministerial accountability, but it is submitted that the credibility of his report demanded
that he consider these issues. In doing so Scott accepted the distinction, which is drawn
by the Cabinet Secretary (Sir Robin Butler) between ministerial accountability (which
cannot be delegated) and ministerial responsibility (which can be transferred to officials).
This distinction is not always easy to draw in practice and you will find an extract from
an article by Sir Richard Scott in [1996] *Public Law* 410, in which he expounds his views
on ministerial accountability.

Please turn to *Cases and Materials* (2.3.1) and read the extract from Sir Richard Scott's
article. What does he mean by 'constitutional accountability'?

In the light of what you have read so far, what is the distinction between ministerial
'responsibility' and ministerial 'accountability'? You will find some useful guidance
in the extract from Diana Woodhouse in *Cases and Materials* (2.3.1).

In conclusion, perhaps the final lesson from the Scott Inquiry and the subsequent Report
is the fact that, in the words of Sir Richard himself, '[t]he key to ministerial accountability
must surely be the obligation to give information'. As pointed out earlier, 'information
is power' and at present both members of the public, and even Parliament itself, have
little power when it comes to gaining full access to information. Thus, perhaps only a
Freedom of Information Act will cut through the veil of secrecy which seems to have
shrouded the activities of successive governments and, in so doing, will ensure that
Ministers are properly held to account.

2.7.5 FREEDOM OF INFORMATION

What are the arguments for freedom of information legislation? Some of the arguments can be found in the extract from Patrick Birkinshaw in *Cases and Materials* (2.3.2).

On 11 December 1997, the Labour Government published a White Paper (*Your Right to Know*, Cm 3818), which is expected to form the basis of a future Freedom of Information Act. This Act is expected to cover a wide range of people and bodies, including all government departments, local authorities, quangos, nationalised industries, privatised utilities, public corporations, the NHS, the armed forces and the police. However, this proposed Freedom of Information Act excludes both the activities of Parliament (on the basis that these are already public) and the security services (as such legislation would make it impossible for them properly to carry out their duties).

The White Paper anticipates the appointment of an independent Information Commissioner who will have the power to intervene in cases where disclosure is refused. This Commissioner will be empowered to order the disclosure of information and will be able to obtain search warrants to further an investigation. In cases where an individual wants to challenge the refusal of the Commissioner to grant a disclosure order, there will be no right of appeal to the courts, although the Commissioner's decisions will be subject to judicial review. (The differences between appeal and judicial review, and the area of judicial review generally, are considered in **Chapter 15**.)

The Government's proposals provide that there will be a 'presumption of openness', but there are a number of categories which are exempt from disclosure. These will include information relating to: national security; defence and international relations; the safety of the individual; personal privacy; law enforcement; commercial confidentiality; and information which has been received in confidence from foreign governments. The test for disclosure will be whether it is necessary in the public interest, and the ways in which the Government, the Information Commissioner and the courts interpret these exceptions will be crucial to the overall success of the legislation.

The Scott Report may have increased the pressure for a Freedom of Information Act but, if the White Paper's proposals had been law at the time of the Matrix Churchill affair, would it have made any difference? There would seem to be no easy answer to this question. One the one hand, the Government might have been tempted to hide behind the national security exception to disclosure; yet, on the other, perhaps the enactment of a Freedom of Information Act would have, at least to some extent, fostered a culture of greater openness in Whitehall, making it harder for Ministers to withhold the documents which would have vindicated the Matrix Churchill directors. Of course, all of this is mere speculation but what does seem certain is that, in the future, much will depend on the way in which the Government intends to enact and administers the Freedom of Information Act.

Tony Blair while in opposition promised, in a speech given at an event organised by the Campaign for Freedom of Information in March 1996, that a Freedom of Information Act would 'signal a new relationship between government and people: a relationship which sees the public as stakeholders in the running of the country'. It remains to be seen whether this legislation can purge government of the endemic secrecy which was graphically illustrated by the Matrix Churchill affair.

Do you think that this reliance on 'inherent' obedience, as opposed to a formal legal sanction, provides adequate safeguards for the individual?

2.8   Codification

In **Chapter 1** we established the fact that the UK's Constitution is rather unusual in that, unlike most other nations, it is not codified in a single document. Clearly conventions play a crucial role in the effective working of the British Constitution, but just as there is a strong case for codifying the Constitution, so too are there a number of arguments for codifying the very conventions which traditionally have provided the flexibility which has allowed this country's unwritten constitution to adapt and respond to changing societal developments. In a decade which has witnessed Government Ministers consolidating their power, while at the same time many commentators accept that there has been a diminution of Parliament's role (e.g., Ministers often leak information to the press before it is released formally to Parliament) and its prestige (e.g., recent allegations of Parliamentary 'sleaze'), some argue that the unwritten codes of behaviour which regulated government in the past are no longer appropriate for Britain as it approaches the millennium and that an effort should be made to codify some of the most important conventions, in order to ensure that they are respected.

What are the main advantages and disadvantages in codifying conventions?

2.8.1 THE CASE FOR CODIFICATION

The obvious advantage of codifying conventions is certainty. Codification may reveal the scope of individual conventions. However, it is unlikely that codification could provide answers to deal with every possible constitutional problem (e.g., the conventions relating to the powers of the Monarch to dissolve Parliament are far from clear). Could the Monarch refuse a request to dissolve Parliament? And even if such a scenario was to be covered by codifying that particular convention, drafting it would be politically controversial. The experience of Commonwealth countries seems to suggest that while the codification of conventions has led to greater certainty, the courts have been called upon to consider politically sensitive issues. As de Smith comments: 'Whatever the outcome, the prestige of the judiciary will probably suffer'.

2.8.2 THE CASE AGAINST CODIFICATION

As conventions evolve, so the constitution can change and develop, without the need for formal and often time-consuming legislation. The flexibility of conventions is therefore a compelling argument against codification. Such flexibility facilitates constitutional change. It allows the constitution to move with the times and reflect contemporary social and political attitudes. In addition, the difficulty of *defining* conventions could mean that the actual drafting of conventions into a written code would be practically impossible. And remember, there are conventions in almost every constitution, both written and unwritten. Therefore, it is likely that new unwritten conventions would soon start to emerge, even if the traditionally recognised conventions were codified.

2.9 Conclusion

We have seen that conventions play a significant and unique role in the UK's Constitution. Despite the events which precipitated the setting up of the Scott Inquiry and the frequent press allegations of governmental maladministration, it seems fair to say that, on a day-to-day basis, the vast majority of conventions are respected by those in positions of power. A cynic might claim that the system only works because Britain, at present, benefits from a reasonably stable economy and political system, and that if there was a major constitutional or economic crisis, conventions could be easily ignored or overridden by Ministers in an arbitrary government. Of course, who is to say that this might or might not happen some day but, rather than speculating on possible future political developments, we should concentrate on the position at present. In contemporary Britain conventions are generally observed because of the political difficulties which would result if they were not. Ministerial responsibility, as Turpin points out, 'provides the grounds and focus for Parliamentary scrutiny and criticism of the executive, and we should be unwise to depreciate a principle that legitimates efforts to restrain executive dominance in our constitution'.

Therefore, in the UK, conventions provide flexibility and allow the constitution to change and adapt to new situations. Over the past 400 years the balance of power has shifted within the British Constitution, from the Sovereign to the House of Commons. This change has in large part been facilitated by constitutional conventions, and it is a graphic illustration of their constitutional significance.

2.10   End of Chapter Assessment Question

'What are constitutional conventions is often a matter of both legal and political dispute, although it is hardly contestable that our system in Britain depends on conventions, which, if broken, would lead to its very breakdown.'

Explain this statement and consider whether a breakdown of the 'system' could be avoided if conventions were codified.

(See *Cases and Materials* (2.5) for a specimen answer.)

CHAPTER THREE

THE CONTROL OF POWER

3.1 Objectives

At the end of this Chapter you should be able to:

■ recognise where power is vested in the British Constitution;

■ identify the political control mechanisms in operation to prevent an abuse of power;

■ explain what is meant by the principle of the 'separation of powers' and its relevance to the UK Constitution;

■ compare and contrast the operation of this 'separation of powers' principle in the USA and the UK.

3.2 Introduction

At the end of **Chapter 2** we considered two issues: the Scott Report and the question of whether constitutional conventions should be codified. What each of these topics have in common is that they, albeit separately, illustrate how important it is that there are checks and balances in operation which can prevent, or at least curb, the abuse of power by the State. As the British historian, Lord Acton, observed in 1887: 'power tends to corrupt and absolute power corrupts absolutely'.

By this stage of the book you should have realised that constitutional law is concerned primarily with power and the accountability of those who exercise it. Lord Acton clearly believed that, unless controls are placed on those who exercise power, those with power in government will abuse it (a view which we will return to later in **Chapter 12** when we consider the 'rule of law'). However, in the meantime, we will concentrate on two areas. First, the bulk of this chapter will be devoted to checks and balances on State power and, in this context, we will consider the principle of the separation of powers. But before turning to the ways of controlling power, we need to identify where power is actually concentrated in the State.

There are three obvious sources of power in the United Kingdom:

(a) the Prime Minister;

(b) the Cabinet;

(c) Parliament.

We will now proceed to consider each of these in turn, before examining the extent to which they are subject to any 'checks and balances'.

3.2.1 THE PRIME MINISTER

There is no doubt that the powers of the Prime Minister are considerable. He or she must be the leader of the majority party in Parliament and is head of the government. The Prime Minister controls the Cabinet (e.g. determines the Cabinet agenda, may sack, reshuffle or appoint Ministers) and is the Chairperson of the most important Cabinet Committees. Other members of the Government (i.e. non-Cabinet Ministers) are appointed by the Prime Minister.

In international affairs the Prime Minister is the United Kingdom's chief spokesperson, and may sign treaties on behalf of the nation without any formal ratification by Parliament. Moreover, the decisions to send British troops to the Falkland Islands in 1981 and to participate in Operation Desert Storm to liberate Kuwait in 1990 were taken by the Prime Minister, not Parliament.

The Prime Minister is also the political Head of the Civil Service and has enormous powers of patronage (e.g. dispensing titles, creating peers and awarding honours). In view of this David Dilks claims that:

> . . . There are other heads of government whose powers are much greater . . . [but] there is no headship in government in any country of comparable importance . . . which bears the same combination of duties.

Tony Benn also believes that the wide range of powers possessed by the Prime Minister 'has gone too far and amounts to a system of personal rule in the very heart of our Parliamentary democracy'. On the other hand, suggestions that British Prime Ministers have almost 'presidential' like powers can be countered by the fact that Margaret Thatcher was forced to resign in 1990, while still in good health, as a result of pressure from within her own party while John Major, in 1995, was forced to resign and seek re-election as the leader of the Conservative Party following a challenge from a Cabinet colleague, John Redwood. Thus, while it is undeniable that the Prime Minister has considerable influence, political factors (i.e., his or her level of support in the Cabinet, Commons, media etc.) may determine the extent to which the holder of this office is in a position to exercise real power.

ACTIVITY 20

Do you agree with the claim made earlier by the MP and former Minister Tony Benn? You will find an extract from Benn's 'The Case for a Constitutional Premiership' in *Cases and Materials* **(3.1.1).**

And what of a previous Prime Minister's view? Read the observations of James Callaghan on the role of a Prime Minister in his autobiography *Time and Chance* **(see** *Cases and Materials* **(3.1.1)). You will also find a list of former British Prime Ministers since the Second World War in** *Cases and Materials* **(3.1.1).**

What are the powers of the Prime Minister? Note that Peter Hennessy provides a detailed list of Prime Ministerial powers in *Cases and Materials* (3.1.1). Why, according to Philip Norton, have the post-war years 'seen a significant increase in the size and responsibility of government'? You will find Norton's explanation for this in *Cases and Materials* (3.1.1).

3.2.2 THE CABINET

The term 'Cabinet government' is often used to describe the system of British government. In theory the Cabinet is only a committee of the government but in practice it is the most important element in the formulation of government policy. According to Professor Kavanagh 'for the last century and a half the sovereignty of the Crown in Parliament has been vested in the Cabinet'. So what are the characteristics of the Cabinet?

Unlike the USA, where the President may appoint people from other parties or from outside politics to his Cabinet, in the United Kingdom Cabinet members are usually chosen from the party with the majority in the House of Commons.

However, in July 1997, the Prime Minister (Tony Blair) created a new Cabinet Committee with membership split between the Prime Minister, four Cabinet Ministers and five senior Liberal Democrats, including their leader Paddy Ashdown. A Government spokesman claimed that the move was 'part of our fulfilment of a new politics' (*The Times*, 23 July 1997) and most commentators agree that this move was significant as, apart from two joint Cabinet Committees in 1931 (disarmament) and 1935 (defence research), such an invitation is unprecedented in British politics. Thus, since a British Cabinet consists of members with similar political views, it is expected to formulate and carry out an agreed policy. Cabinet members are bound to support this agreed policy in public (the convention of 'collective responsibility') and where a Minister disagrees with a Cabinet decision, the Minister should resign (e.g. the resignation of Michael Heseltine as Secretary of State for Defence in January 1986 over the Westland affair).

The function of the Cabinet is threefold. First, it is the body where government policies are formulated (e.g. Government Ministers are expected to thrash out an agreed party line on issues such as defence, education, Europe etc.). Secondly, the Cabinet plans the business of the House (e.g. it approves the timing and details of Bills which are to travel through Parliament). Thirdly, the Cabinet will co-ordinate policy between different government departments. This may range from standardisation of departmental policies to arbitrating between 'warring' departments (e.g. a clash between the Treasury, which controls the purse strings, and the Department of Education, which wants money to improve standards in schools and colleges).

The Cabinet exercises considerable power, though a former Cabinet Minister, Richard Crossman, once claimed that over the last 40 years there has been a transformation 'of Cabinet government into Prime Ministerial government'. Similarly, John MacKintosh (*The British Cabinet*) has claimed that with the Prime Minister's powers increasing in relative terms to those of the Cabinet, one should now refer to Prime Ministerial, rather than Cabinet government. An obvious explanation for this has been an increase in the role of committees of the Cabinet, often under the chairmanship of the Prime Minister. Such Cabinet Committees have existed since the beginning of the 19th century, but in recent years they have become increasingly important. For example, many key decisions taken during Margaret Thatcher's premiership (e.g. the GCHQ trade union ban in 1984, the granting of permission to US planes which bombed Tripoli in 1986 to take off from British air bases, and decisions during the Miners Strike 1984 and Gulf Conflict 1990) appear to have been originally taken by Cabinet Committees. John Major continued this policy of relying on Cabinet Committees as has Tony Blair. Information released in April 1998 revealed that there are 27 Cabinet Committees, and that the Deputy Prime Minister (John Prescott) sits on 14 of them, the Chancellor of the Exchequer (Gordon Brown) on 13, the Home Secretary (Jack Straw) on 12, the Lord Chancellor (Lord Irvine) on 11, the Foreign Secretary (Robin Cook) on 10 and finally and perhaps rather surprisingly, the Prime Minister (Tony Blair) only sits on four Cabinet Committees. However, the fact that Peter Mandelson, who at that time, was not a formal member of the Cabinet, but sat on the highest number of Cabinet Committees (15), attracted considerable press comment and, in an editorial, *The Independent* suggested (18 April 1998) that 'decision making' may have not just have moved out of the Cabinet, but even 'beyond Cabinet Committees' and that today policy is formulated in 'the informal group around the Prime Minister', although this is a charge which the Government would reject.

(a)   Read the articles by Brazier and James *Cases and Materials* (3.1.2)) Why, according to Brazier and James, are Cabinet Committees established?

(b)   What are the two changes which Martin Burch (see *Cases and Materials* (3.1.2)) identifies 'in the central executive in the period since 1974'?

3.2.3   PARLIAMENT

We will look at the powers of Parliament in **Chapter 5** (the Commons and Royal Assent) and **Chapter 6** (the House of Lords).

3.3   The Separation of Powers

In this chapter we will be referring to the three main organs of government and their functions. They are the legislature, the executive and the judiciary.

3.3.1   THE LEGISLATURE

The legislature consists of the House of Commons, the House of Lords and the 'Queen in Parliament'. As we shall see later in **Chapter 7**, Acts of the legislature may not be challenged in the courts (the principle of Parliamentary supremacy).

3.3.2   THE EXECUTIVE

In theory the Queen is the head of the Executive, but in practice the real power is exercised by the Prime Minister. Thus, the UK is a 'constitutional monarchy' in that virtually all of the Monarch's powers are exercised by her Ministers. The Executive therefore consists of the Queen, the Prime Minister, the Cabinet, other Government Ministers and, in so far as it carries out the day-to-day running of the country, the Civil Service. There are now approximately 500,000 civil servants and, of these, about 3,000 are senior policy advisors (i.e., Permanent Secretaries, Under Secretaries etc.), who offer confidential advice to Ministers. Civil servants are expected to be politically neutral and anonymous but it has been claimed that, between 1979–1985, the appointment of senior civil servants by Margaret Thatcher endangered the traditional political neutrality of the Civil Service. The attitude of senior figures in the Labour Government to the Civil Service is considered in the extract from the article by Theakson in *Cases and Materials* (**3.2.1**).

3.3.3   THE JUDICIARY

As we saw in **Chapter 2**, judges, by convention, are expected to retain their political independence and their constitutional role is to interpret the law.

ACTIVITY 22

(a)   Complete the following table by writing in the appropriate words from the list provided.

Institution	Composition	Function
■ The Executive	(QUEEN) PM CAB, CIVIL SERVICE	DAY-DAY RUNNING OF COUNTRY
■ The Legislature	HC. HL. QUEEN.	PARLI
■ The Judiciary		

(b)   To test whether you filled in the table correctly think of the collection and expenditure of our taxes.

Who has the legal authority to raise taxes?   LEGISL .

What body is responsible for collecting taxes?   EXEC

Who resolves any dispute between a tax collector and a taxpayer?   JUDIC

(See *Cases and Materials* (**3.2.2**) for the answer.)

3.3.4   MONTESQUIEU

The principle of the separation of powers is regarded as having its modern origins in the writings of Montesquieu, a French political philosopher, who visited England in 1732 and later wrote *De l'esprit des lois* in 1748. This idea of a separation of powers, the notion that the three functions of government (legislative, executive and judicial) should be discharged by separate bodies to avoid misgovernment, was not completely novel. A similar theory previously had been put forward by Aristotle, while in the 17th century John Locke (*Second Treatise on Civil Government*) and in the 18th century, Blackstone (*Commentaries on the Laws of England*) had both referred to the importance of an independent judiciary operating as a check on a government's power. However, the theory of the separation of powers is particularly synonymous with Montesquieu. Montesquieu wrote:

> When the legislative and executive powers are united in the same person, or in the same body . . . there can be no liberty, because apprehensions may arise, lest the same Monarch or Senate should enact tyrannical laws, to execute them in a tyrannical manner.

> Again there is no liberty if the judicial power be not separated from the legislative and executive. Were it joined with the legislative, the life and liberty of the subject would be exposed to arbitrary control; for the judge would then be the legislator. Were it joined to the executive power, the judge might behave with violence or oppression.

(a)   What is the purpose of the separation of powers?

(b)   What is meant by a 'pure doctrine' of the separation of powers?

You will find the answers to these questions in *Cases and Materials* (3.2.3).

Read the extract on the separation of powers from C. Munro in *Cases and Materials* (3.2.3). How does he characterise the 'academic orthodoxy' in this area and what lessons, if any, are to be learnt from it.

Hopefully, by now, you will have an understanding of what is meant by the separation of powers. In answer to item (a) of **SAQ 22** you should have written something like this:

The separation of powers concerns the division of State power between the legislature, the executive and the judiciary. Individual liberty and democracy are best protected if one class of function is concentrated in no more than one organ of government.

The ultimate objective is therefore the ideal of law, liberty and democracy. Tyranny and dictatorship cannot thrive where power is divided amongst the three organs and there are effective checks and balances. Alternatively, you may have suggested that the aim of the separation of powers is to achieve a balance of power, where each institution acknowledges all others as equal in terms of status and respect. This interpretation of the doctrine suggests that the three institutions need not be totally independent of one another, but that absolute power should not be vested in only one person or body. Thus, the exercise of power by one institution should be checked by the other two. Whilst the UK Constitution does not conform to the 'pure' doctrine of the separation of powers, to some extent it may reflect this latter interpretation.

Sir Ivor Jennings is sceptical about the separation of powers securing liberty in our constitution. What does he think is responsible for maintaining our freedom? (See *The Law and the Constitution* by Sir Ivor Jennings in *Cases and Materials* (3.2.3).) For an analysis of Jenning's view see the extract from Barendt in *Cases and Materials* (3.2.3).

3.4 The US Constitution

The US Constitution (1787) actually creates a system in which each of the three branches of government is independent of the others. The purpose of this was to prevent any single branch from becoming too powerful, providing a series of checks and balances. The American Constitution is therefore based firmly on Montesquieu's doctrine of the separation of powers.

Look at the extract from Yardley in *Cases and Materials* (3.3) and complete the following:

		Composition	*Function*
Legislature	=		
Executive	=		
Judiciary	=		

In fact the most significant 'check' in the United States is not even found in its written constitutional document. Instead the Supreme Court of the United States, under the inspiration of Chief Justice Marshall, assumed for itself the power of declaring invalid Acts of Congress and of the President, when such legislation is contrary to the US Constitution (*Marbury* v *Madison* (1803) 1 Cranch 137).

No equivalent rule exists in the UK whereby judges can strike down an Act of Parliament on the ground that it is 'unconstitutional'. Why not? If you are unsure, the answer will appear later in this chapter.

Even in the United States there is not a totally complete and distinct separation of powers. After all, not every power can be executed independently of the others. The doctrine in the United States may be represented diagrammatically as follows:

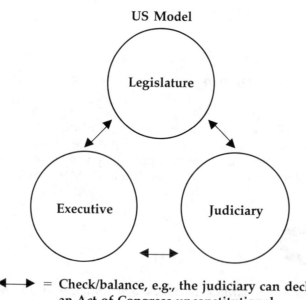

US Model

←——→ = Check/balance, e.g., the judiciary can declare an Act of Congress unconstitutional

Complete the diagram by labelling the circles (i.e., which body is the legislature etc.), and then, with reference to the US Constitution itself, see if you can add the 'checks and balances' built into the Constitution as represented by the arrows.

See *Cases and Materials* (3.3) for a suggested completed diagram.

In the United States, power is divided as follows:

(a) **Legislative power** – vested in *Congress*

Congress is composed of two Houses – an Upper House, the Senate, which has 100 members (two from each State, elected for a two-year term); and a Lower House, the House of Representatives, which has 435 members elected for six-year terms.

(b) **Executive power** – vested in *the President*, Bill Clinton.

(c) **Judicial power** – vested in *the US Supreme Court*, the nine most important judges in the United States.

The founding fathers of the US Constitution were profoundly influenced by the doctrine of the 'Separation of Powers'. Practical examples of these 'checks and balances' are as follows:

(a) No member of one branch of government may also be a member of another, e.g. the President cannot sit or vote in Congress.

(b) The President holds office for a term of four years. The President can be elected to no more than two four-year terms.

(c) The President is elected separately from Congress. Therefore, the President may be of a different party from that which has a majority in Congress. In the 1980s Republican Presidents, Reagan and Bush, experienced difficulties in persuading a Democrat-controlled Congress to pass the laws they wanted. More recently, Democrat President Bill Clinton has faced similar problems as Congress has, at various times, been controlled by the Republican Party.

(d) Any member of Congress who hopes to become President must resign from Congress to assume the Presidency of the United States.

(e) The President can veto legislation of Congress. However, this may be overridden by a two-thirds vote in the Senate.

(f) The President appoints judges to the US Supreme Court. Such appointments are often controversial and arguably politicise the judiciary in the United States. One example of a particularly controversial appointment was President Bush's successful nomination of Clarence Thomas as a member of the US Supreme Court. Claims were made that Clarence Thomas was only nominated because of his race (he is an African American) and for his conservative views, and that there were other candidates who were much better qualified to hold this judicial office.

(g) Finally, the US Supreme Court may declare Acts of Congress, the President, or of any of the 50 State Legislatures, unconstitutional (illegal): *Marbury v Madison* (1803) 1 Cranch 137.

As you may have realised in answer to **SAQ 23** there is no US equivalent to the UK principle of Parliamentary Supremacy (see **Chapter 7**) which prevents judicial review of acts of the legislature.

SAQ 24

Madison wrote that the government should be arranged so 'that its several constituent parts may, by their mutual relations, be the means of keeping each other in their proper places'. Explain this statement with reference to the US Constitution.

3.5 The UK Model

There is no formal separation of powers in the UK. (See the extract from Munro in *Cases and Materials* (**3.2.3**).) The functions of the legislature and the executive are closely interrelated. An illustration of this is the fact that Ministers in the Cabinet are members of both the legislature (by Convention, a Minister must be a member of either the House of Lords or of the Commons), and the executive. We will return to consider this point in more detail shortly.

Draw a diagram representing the UK Constitution, using circles for each of the three institutions.

Professor Wade concludes that a complete separation of powers is possible neither in theory nor in practice. However, he defines the notion of separation as meaning at least three different things:

(a) that no person or body of persons should form part of more than one of the three organs of government;

(b) that one organ of government should not exercise the functions of either of the other two organs;

(c) that one organ of government should not interfere with or seek to exercise control over the functions of the other two organs.

To test the existence of a separation of powers in the UK Constitution, it is useful to consider these three meanings with reference to the shared functions or 'pairings' of the organs of government.

Try to think of as many examples as you can from the British Constitution which offend Wade's three principles. Give examples of where there is a *duality of function or joint membership* of the main institutions. To get you started here are two examples:

(a) **The Queen is head of both the executive (Her Majesty's government), the judiciary, and is an integral part of the legislature (the Queen in Parliament).**

(b) **Administrative tribunals exercise a judicial function but are part of the executive.**

Add as many other examples as you can.

Legislature/Executive

Personnel

Functions

Checks

Executive/Judiciary

Personnel

Functions

Checks

Legislature/Judiciary

Personnel

Functions

Checks

Now look at the diagram you drew to illustrate the UK Constitution. It should look something like this:

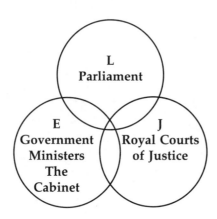

Draw a larger version of this diagram and where the circles overlap write in examples which can be found in more than one category. For example, where would you put the following:

Law Lords   Queen
Lord Chancellor   Cabinet
Home Secretary   Delegated legislation

(See *Cases and Materials* (3.4) for the answer.)

It would appear therefore that, in the British Constitution, a formal separation of powers is absent. There are many overlaps. In answer to **Activity 27** you should have noted that the following anomalies exist in the United Kingdom.

3.5.1 LEGISLATURE AND EXECUTIVE

3.5.1.1 Personnel

Sovereign – she or he is Head of both.
Cabinet Ministers – they are members of both.
Lord Chancellor – she or he is usually a Cabinet member who also sits in the House of Lords.

3.5.1.2 Functions

In view of the problems associated with administering a modern State it has become necessary for Parliament to delegate power to Ministers (e.g. delegated legislation). The main principles are set out in Acts of Parliament and Ministers are given powers to implement those principles by detailed regulations. Delegated legislation is necessary because of increasing pressure on Parliament's time. It is also a way of dealing with local variations and is more flexible than Acts of Parliament. However, to ensure that the executive is not usurping the powers of the legislature, there is scrutiny by the courts and Parliament. We will consider delegated legislation and these safeguards in more detail in **Chapter 13**.

3.5.1.3 Checks

The question remains, does the legislature control the executive or does the executive control the legislature? In one sense Parliament (through the House of Commons) controls the executive, as a government can be ousted by a Commons vote of no confidence. However, as long as the Cabinet retains a Commons majority, it can influence the passage of legislation and, in practice, most legislation is initiated by Government Ministers with the support and approval of the Cabinet.

Party loyalties are also a relevant consideration and Lord Nolan (see *Cases and Materials* (**3.4.1**)) has conceded that 'the dominance of the executive has undoubtedly rested on the party system'. The Cabinet is mainly composed of members of the majority party in the House of Commons. Backbench MPs usually are reluctant to vote against their party leaders; after all, a defeat in the Commons could lead to the dissolution of Parliament, a new general election, and the possibility of a loss of political office. Therefore, although Parliament is in *theory* supreme (see **Chapter 7**), in *practice* the government enjoys considerable influence over Parliament.

Why did Walter Bagehot remark that '[t]he efficient secret of the English [sic] Constitution may be described as the close union, the nearly complete fusion of the executive and legislative powers'?

3.5.2 EXECUTIVE AND JUDICIARY

3.5.2.1 Personnel

Sovereign – she or he is Head of both.

Judicial Committee of the Privy Council – it is part of the judiciary and is a committee of the Privy Council, which is an executive organ.

Lord Chancellor – she or he is a Cabinet Minister and is also a senior member of the judiciary.

3.5.2.2 Function

There has been a tendency in recent years to entrust some justiciable matters to administrative bodies (i.e., tribunals). Various reasons are put forward to justify this:

■ it saves time and money;

■ the belief that judges, with only 'legal' training, are not the best people to decide issues involving 'administrative' policy;

■ and finally, the argument that certain complicated technical issues are best dealt with by specialist tribunals.

Thus, where a dispute concerns issues such as pensions, social security or income tax, it may be handled best by highly qualified specialist bodies (i.e., tribunals). These tribunals perform the tasks of a court and have the characteristics of a court (e.g., publicity, precedent where possible, and the publication of decisions with reasons).

Read the extract from Barendt in *Cases and Materials* (3.4.2) on the separation of powers and administrative authorities.

The executive plays a role in the appointment of the judiciary. Judges (up to and including the High Court) are appointed by the Lord Chancellor, while the Law Lords and Appeal Court judges are appointed by the Prime Minister who acts on the advice of the Lord Chancellor. Indeed, the person holding the office of Lord Chancellor is selected by the Prime Minister. Despite this, the executive normally exerts little control over the judiciary and tends to leave the judges to apply and interpret the law.

An independent judiciary is a safeguard against the abuse of power. The judiciary tends to check rather than control the actions of the executive. For example, Michael Howard, the former Home Secretary, was admonished by the judiciary in *R* v *Secretary of State for the Home Department, ex parte Fire Brigades Union* [1995] 2 AC 513, when he was held to have acted unlawfully in ignoring the will of Parliament by introducing a criminal injuries compensation scheme which was radically different from that authorised by Parliament. Also, in *R* v *Secretary of State for Foreign and Commonwealth Affairs, ex parte World Development Movement Ltd* [1995] 1 WLR 386, the former Foreign Secretary, Douglas Hurd, was censured for authorising £234 million in aid for the Pergau Dam project in Malaysia. These cases are examined in more detail later in this book and extracts from them can be found in *Cases and Materials*.

3.5.3   LEGISLATURE AND JUDICIARY

3.5.3.1   Personnel

Sovereign – she or he is Head of both.

House of Lords – the Law Lords sit in the highest Appeal Court in the land and are also part of the legislature (although by convention they remain apolitical).

Lord Chancellor – he or she is the Speaker of the House of Lords in its legislative capacity and is the head of the judiciary under the Crown.

3.5.3.2   Functions

Both Houses of Parliament may exercise a judicial function to punish members and others who are in breach of House privilege or in contempt of Parliament (see **Chapter 5**).

Moreover, Parliament has delegated powers to Ministers, on occasion, to exercise a quasi-judicial function. For example, during the Second World War, the powers of a Minister to detain on suspicion anyone he or she believed to be a threat to national security could not be questioned in the courts: (*Liversidge* v *Anderson* [1942] AC 206). Although such disputes may on occasion be dealt with by special committees or tribunals, some argue (e.g., civil liberties pressure groups) that matters involving personal liberty should only be resolved by an independent judiciary.

Finally, it is also clear that sometimes judges, in fact, make law — the common law itself is evidence of this — however, the extent to which this creative role of the judiciary usurps Parliament's legislative function is a matter for debate, which will be considered later in this book.

3.5.3.3 Checks

Senior judges (e.g. members of the High Court and above) can only be removed from office by the Queen after a Resolution has been passed by both Houses of Parliament. This has only ever happened once when an Irish judge, Jonah Barrington, was found guilty in 1830 of financial impropriety. It is much more usual for a senior judge who has acted inappropriately to be censured by the Lord Chancellor, or to resign voluntarily as Mr Justice Harman did in February 1998, when he was criticised in the Court of Appeal for taking 20 months to reach a decision in a case without the assistance of his trial notes which he had earlier misplaced. Nevertheless, Parliament does exercise a power over the judiciary in so far as the Judicial Pensions and Review Act 1993 imposes the requirement that judges appointed after 1993 must normally retire when they reach 70, while those who accepted judicial office before that date may not sit over the age of 75. All judges are affected by this except the Lord Chancellor, whose unique constitutional position has exempted the holder of this office from the compulsory retirement legislation.

Conversely, it must also be remembered that judges have power. While the judiciary cannot declare Acts of Parliament invalid, even under the Human Rights Act 1998, judges may exert some control over the legislature, in practice, through the way in which they interpret legislation. This will be considered in more detail in **Chapter 4** while other examples of the powers of judges will be provided when we look at European Community law (**Chapter 8**), in particular the courts' ability to suspend UK legislation where it conflicts with European Community law (*R* v *Secretary of State for Transport, ex parte Factortame Ltd (No. 2)* [1991] AC 603, as well as judicial review (**Chapter 15**).

How can Parliament control the judiciary?

Since the UK does not have a written constitution, there are few visible legal rules to provide the checks and balances which are necessary to prevent an abuse of power. So it is now to conventions (non-legal rules) that we must briefly return.

In **Chapter 2** we discovered how conventions have enabled the UK Constitution to move with the times. However, constitutional conventions are also relevant in considering the checks and balances imposed upon those on whom power is vested. For example particularly important conventions in this context include:

(a) The convention that the Law Lords should not participate in overtly party political debates in the House of Lords. This is consistent with the convention that judges should be politically neutral.

(b)   The convention of Ministerial Responsibility and the accountability of ministers to Parliament.

(c)   The convention that a government must resign if it is defeated in a vote of confidence in the House of Commons.

(d)   The convention that a Minister must divest himself or herself of any position which appears to be incompatible with the holding of ministerial office (e.g. the Secretary of State for Defence should not be the majority shareholder in a private company which manufactures tanks since there would appear to be a conflict of interest on the occasion of defence procurement contracts).

Turn back to **Chapter 2** and think of any other constitutional conventions which seek to prevent misgovernment and the abuse of power.

Read the article by Lord Steyn in *Cases and Materials* (3.4.3). Do you agree with Lord Steyn's claim that 'the proposition that a Cabinet member must be the head of our judiciary in England is no longer sustainable on either constitutional or pragmatic grounds'?

In response to **SAQ 27** you may have concluded that Parliament has the power to make and change the law. Thus, if Parliament is unhappy with a decision of a court, it can pass legislation (retrospectively) to repeal it. For example the Northern Ireland Act 1972 was passed to overturn the decision in *R (Hume)* v *L'Derry Justices* [1972] NILR 91. We will consider the validity of such retrospective legislation in **Chapter 7** when we look at Parliamentary supremacy.

3.6   Constitutional Significance of the Separation of Powers

The constitutional significance of the separation of powers is perhaps best illustrated by case law. Look at the extracts from *Duport Steels Ltd* v *Sirs* [1980] 1 WLR 142, *British Airways Board* v *Laker Airways Ltd* [1984] QB 142 and *R* v *Her Majesty's Treasury, ex parte Smedley* [1985] QB 657 in **Cases and Materials** (3.5). In the last two cases, Lord Donaldson made a number of pertinent observations relating to the separation of powers. Lord Donaldson also addressed these issues in *M* v *Home Office* [1992] QB 270.

In *M* v *Home Office*, a 28 year-old Zairean teacher had arrived in the UK in September 1990 seeking political asylum, claiming to have been tortured in Zaire. The Home Office rejected this claim. Twenty-four hours before he was due to be deported, his lawyers passed a medical report to the Foreign Office supporting his claims of torture. M's legal advisers managed to secure an order from Garland J that the asylum seeker should be kept in the UK while his case was being considered. However, the Home Secretary and various Home Office officials failed to prevent M's departure and neglected to intercept his flight at Paris to prevent his outward journey to Zaire, from where he disappeared.

The main question to be answered by the court was whether a Minister could be guilty of contempt of court.

In the Court of Appeal Lord Donaldson, in delivering the main judgment, held that Ministers are not immune from legal ruling which ordinary citizens have to obey and that 'It would be a black day for the rule of law and the liberty of the subject' if Ministers could not be held to account. Lord Donaldson added that individual citizens should be able to look to the courts for protection under the law, and that the judiciary could not simply trust the government. Judges had to ensure that civil servants and Ministers are accountable to the law (i.e., courts) for their personal actions. Similarly, Nolan LJ, on the relationship between the executive and the judiciary, commented:

> . . . the proper constitutional relationship of the executive with the courts is that the courts will respect all acts of the executive within its lawful province, and that the executive will respect all decisions of the court as to what its lawful province is.

Thus, the Court of Appeal, by a majority of 2 to 1, found Kenneth Baker to be the first Minister in UK legal history, to be guilty of contempt of court. The House of Lords [1994] 1 AC 377 rejected Baker's appeal and held that the contempt jurisdiction of the courts extended to Ministers of the Crown. This is an important case and Professor Jeffrey Jowell has described the ruling as an 'assertion of judicial authority'.

ACTIVITY 31

What does Professor Jowell mean by an 'assertion of judicial authority?' Read the extract from M v Home Office in Cases and Materials (3.5). Is it possible that judges may 'over assert their authority?'

A case which is often cited as illustrating the dangers of judges 'over asserting their authority' is Shaw v DPP [1962] AC 220. Shaw planned to publish a 'ladies' directory', giving details of prostitutes and their services. After consulting his lawyers and the police, he was advised that in the event of publication, he would not be committing an offence. Nevertheless, a conviction of 'conspiracy to corrupt public morals' was upheld by the House of Lords (even though such a conviction was unprecedented and there was no such statutory offence). Viscount Simonds spoke for the majority of the Lords when he stated:

> In the sphere of criminal law I entertain no doubt that there remains in the courts of law a residual power to enforce the supreme and fundamental purpose of the law, to conserve not only the safety and order but also the moral welfare of the State, and that it is their duty to guard it against attacks which may be the more insidious because they are novel and unprepared for.

This is a striking example of judicial creativity by the House of Lords but it should be added that such cases are rare. Most judges are loath to acknowledge any ostensibly creative role for the judiciary.

Read the extract in *Cases and Materials* (3.5) from *R* v *Secretary of State for the Environment, ex parte Hammersmith and Fulham London Borough Council* [1990] 1 AC 521 at 560 and 561. There the House of Lords rejected an application for judicial review of the Secretary of State's decision to 'charge cap' a number of local authorities which had imposed excessively high community charges. It was held that the Secretary of State had acted neither illegally nor had there been any procedural impropriety.

According to Lord Donaldson MR, what should be the role of a judge?

(a)   Explain how the rulings in *M* v *Home Office*, *Shaw* v *DPP* and *R* v *Secretary of State for the Environment, ex parte Hammersmith and Fulham London Borough Council* illustrate the principle of the separation of powers.

(b)   Of the three organs – legislature, executive and judiciary – which is potentially the most powerful? Which is actually the most powerful? For some ideas turn to the views of Sir John Laws in *Cases and Materials* (3.5).

3.7   Conclusion

The accountability of those holding power is a theme which runs through this book. As Lord Scarman wrote in *Why Britain Needs a Written Constitution* (1992), 'a government above the law is a menace to be defeated'. Therefore, in response to **SAQ 28**, you will no doubt have explained that it is imperative for there to be checks and controls on the three institutions of State. *Shaw* v *DPP* is an example of how the judges can exercise their law-making potential and, in effect, usurp Parliament's power to legislate. However, Parliament can always pass legislation to reverse any such decision of the courts.

M v *Home Office* is a good example of the courts checking the actions of the executive by holding Kenneth Baker, the then Home Secretary, to account. Lord Donaldson MR described the role of the judiciary in *R* v *Secretary of State for the Environment, ex parte Hammersmith and Fulham London Borough Council* as one of a referee. Parliament makes the rules, supplemented by the common law. It is up to the courts to determine whether or not those rules have been broken and not to comment or express an opinion about the way in which 'the game' has been played.

The legislature is theoretically the most powerful of the three organs of government. The principle of Parliamentary supremacy means that Parliament is able to pass any law it chooses. However, where a government can rely on the support of a majority of MPs in the Commons, and most members of the House of Lords, it can easily push legislative proposals through Parliament.

Therefore, in the British Constitution there is no separation of powers in the strict (or US) sense between the executive and the legislature. The extent to which this is a weakness of the UK Constitution is something for you to consider. As Professor Robert Stevens in *The Independence of the Judiciary: The View from the Lord Chancellor's Office* (1993) points out: 'Nothing underlines the atheoretical nature of the British Constitution more than the casualness with which it approaches the separation of powers.'

CHAPTER FOUR

THE INDEPENDENCE OF THE JUDICIARY

4.1 Objectives

At the end of this Chapter you should be able to:

■ understand the role of the judiciary within the British Constitution;

■ distinguish between the interpretative and the active 'law-making' powers of British judges;

■ appreciate the influence of judicial creativity in the law-making process;

■ evaluate the independence of the British judiciary.

4.2 Introduction

Many of the chapters in this book overlap. As we saw in **Chapter 3**, judges play a crucial role within the British Constitution. They are an essential prerequisite of any system which seeks to prevent the abuse of power and, by means of judicial review (**Chapter 15**), actions of individual Ministers may be scrutinised to ascertain whether or not a power has been lawfully exercised. For example, think back to *M v Home Office* [1992] QB 270, CA and [1994] 1 AC 377, HL, where the Home Secretary was personally liable and in contempt of court, for disregarding a High Court judge's order. But what are the limits of a judge's power? The Lord Chancellor once commented: 'I am a complete supporter of judicial review . . . [b]ut the courts must keep in their place' (*The Times*, 16 October 1995). Later in the book we will return to judicial review, but first in this Chapter we must examine the nature, role and 'place' of the judiciary in the United Kingdom.

4.3 Why is an Independent Judiciary Desirable?

SAQ 29

Why is an independent judiciary desirable?

Turn to *Cases and Materials* (4.1) and the extracts from the judgments of Lords Scarman and Diplock in *Duport Steels Ltd* v *Sirs* [1980] 1 WLR 142 for some reasons.

In many written constitutions there is a clause which 'guarantees' the independence of the judiciary. Whilst the UK lacks any such written constitution, the Act of Settlement 1700 secures judicial independence in this country. Other than the rather unique role of the Lord Chancellor, who serves both as head of the judiciary and as a Cabinet Minister, judges (as we observed in **Chapter 3**) are expected to remain apolitical.

So, what are the consequences of judicial independence? One such consequence is that judges are often called upon to chair public inquiries on controversial issues. The last decade has witnessed a number of these, and they include: the reports of Mr Justice Popplewell and Lord Taylor into the football ground disasters at Bradford and Hillsborough; Lord Butler-Sloss's inquiry into child abuse in Cleveland; Lord Bingham's inquiry into the collapse of the financial institution BCCI; Lord Justice Woolf's investigation into the Strangeways prison riots in Manchester; Lord Scott's Inquiry into the Matrix Churchill affair; and most recently, the appointment of a former High Court judge, Sir William Macpherson, as the chairman of the inquiry into the racially-motivated murder of black teenager, Stephen Lawrence.

In answer to **SAQ 29** you may have mentioned some of the following reasons for an independent judiciary:

(a) Judges are the 'guardians of the constitution'. Because the UK has no written constitution, and there is no separate Supreme Constitutional Court, constitutional issues are resolved in the ordinary courts of law.

(b) The judiciary must be free, from outside interference, to ensure that cases against the executive (i.e., government) are dealt with impartially. Thus, in December 1996, the former Lord Chancellor, Lord Mackay, said that 'the independence of the judiciary must connote not only independence from the executive but also that of one judge from another'.

(c) The public must have faith in the judicial system. This requires confidence in the integrity and impartiality of the judiciary.

(d) Finally, no one should be above the law (see **Chapter 12** on the rule of law). As Lord Denning once wrote (*The Family Tree*, 1981), 'The keystone of the rule of law in England is the independence of judges.' Thus, everyone (including judges) should be answerable and accountable to the law.

4.4 The Basis of Judicial Independence

The Act of Settlement 1700 secures the independence of the judiciary by establishing the principle that superior judges, (i.e., High Court judges and above) cannot be dismissed by the executive except by an address to the Crown from both Houses of Parliament.

The independence of the judiciary is secured by a number of other factors:

4.4.1 APPOINTMENTS

All judges, up to and including those in the High Court, recorders, stipendiary and lay magistrates, are appointed by or on the advice of the Lord Chancellor. Recently, the Lord Chancellor proposed that High Court judges should only be chosen following their application for office, rather than merely by invitation and, on 24 February 1998, the first ever advertisement for the position of a High Court judge appeared in the *The Times*. Superior court judges (members of the House of Lords and the Court of Appeal) are appointed by the Prime Minister on the advice of the Lord Chancellor. Therefore, the role of the Lord Chancellor is highly significant in terms of the appointment, promotion and removal of judges. Ironically, whilst Britain's judiciary is by convention independent, the position of the Lord Chancellor is itself a political appointment—Tony Blair appointed the current Lord Chancellor, Lord Irvine, who (as noted in **Chapter 3**), is not merely the head of the judiciary, but is also the peer who acts as the Speaker in the House of Lords and is the Cabinet member ultimately responsible for law reform, at the heart of the executive.

What is the constitutional basis of judicial independence? For some ideas on this you should refer to the views of Kate Malleson in *Cases and Materials* (4.2.1).

4.4.2   JUDICIAL IMMUNITY

Judicial proceedings are privileged in the same way as debates and proceedings in Parliament. Absolute privilege attaches to all parties, counsel and witnesses, covering words uttered in the course of judicial proceedings. Judges also enjoy absolute privilege, even for possibly defamatory remarks. The justification for such privilege is the public interest in the proper administration of justice.

As a general rule, provided that judges act in the honest belief that their conduct is within their jurisdiction, they will be protected from liability for anything said or done in court proceedings. In *Sirros* v *Moore* [1975] QB 118, the majority of the Court of Appeal (Lord Denning MR and Ormerod LJ) stated that every judge was entitled to protection from liability in respect of what she or he has done, provided she or he has been acting judicially and honestly. Lord Denning observed that 'each [judge] should be able to do his work in complete independence and free from fear. He should not have to turn the pages of his books with trembling fingers, asking himself: "If I do this, shall I be liable in damages?"'

4.4.3   POLITICAL INDEPENDENCE

In return for this immunity, judges are expected to remain politically impartial. By convention, a judge must sever all political ties on appointment to the bench. However, this 'myth of judicial neutrality' has been challenged by Professor J.A.G. Griffith. Griffith notes that 'what is or is not in the public interest is a political question which admits of a great variety of answers'. According to Griffith, the judicial concept of the public interest includes the preservation of law and order, the protection of property rights and the promotion of political views commonly associated with the Conservative party. Griffith's conclusion is that, 'on every major social issue which has come before the courts during the last 30 years the judges have supported the conventional, established and settled interests'. Griffith's views tend to be favoured by those on the political left, and his claims of judicial bias have been vigorously denied by the judiciary.

ACTIVITY 33

Read the extract from Griffiths in *Cases and Materials* (4.2.2). Do you agree with his claim that in 'both democratic and totalitarian societies, the judiciary has naturally served the prevailing political and economic forces'?

4.4.4 REPRESENTATIVE OF SOCIETY?

British judges have long been regarded as a socially elite group, unrepresentative of the wider community. Of the 3,151 judges in England and Wales, 306 are women and all but 15 are white. If we break these figures down we discover that of the nation's 97 High Court judges, there are just seven females and no one of ethnic minority origin; in the Court of Appeal, there is only one female and not a single appeal court judge from an ethnic minority; and finally, of the 12 Lords of Appeal in ordinary in the House of Lords, there are no women and no one of ethnic minority origin. Thus, there is statistical evidence to support Professor Griffith's claims, with which you should be familiar from the last Activity, that judges in the United Kingdom are overwhelmingly white, male, middle aged, middle class and, in the main, the products of private fee-paying schools and the universities of Oxford and Cambridge.

Of course, the old adage that there are 'lies, damned lies, and statistics' may also, to some extent, apply. It is difficult to refute the statistics in the last paragraph, but judges may raise a number of arguments in their own defence. First, the anomaly that there are so few women and ethnic minorities on the bench is a problem, not so much with the judiciary, but with the legal profession generally. For example, as only 14 per cent of barristers with more than 15 years' experience are female, the pool from which women may be appointed as judges is very shallow. Successive Lord Chancellors have pledged to remedy this situation and since 43 per cent of new recruits to the bar in 1997 were women, it can be argued that it is only a matter of time before the 'trickle down' (or perhaps in this case, 'trickle up') effect means that more women and other minorities will be appointed as judges.

The main problem with this argument is that whilst it recognises that change may come in the long term, many are impatient for much more rapid reform. In a recent Editorial, *The Independent* (10 October 1997) appeared to speak for many when it claimed that the 'white, male, privately-educated bias of the judiciary is a blot on British justice'. Aware of such sentiments, the Lord Chancellor, in November 1997, announced a number of proposals for reforming the judiciary, ranging from making it possible for prospective applicants for judicial office to 'shadow' a judge, so giving them an insight into what it is like to sit judicially, to a scheme whereby District and Circuit judges would 'mentor' their junior colleagues. These proposals are considered in more detail in *Cases and Materials* (4.2.3) (see the extract from Drewry), but they stop short of introducing the 'affirmative action' or 'positive discrimination' policies which have been used previously in the United States to redress racial and gender inequality on the Bench. Instead, Lord Irvine has said that, '[Judicial] appointments must be made on merit — irrespective of ethnic origin; sex; marital status; political affiliation; sexual orientation; religion; or disability'.

This approach avoids the political controversies which would be synonymous with selecting people as judges merely because of factors such as their gender, skin colour, and sexual orientation, but it means that reform is likely to be a slow process. In the meantime, judges in the United Kingdom face a more immediate problem — a recent British crime survey found that 80 per cent of British people think that judges are out of touch and that their interests and values are different from those of 'ordinary people'.

In their defence to this, judges can argue that they are frequently misrepresented by the media. The fact that a particular judge has not heard of a celebrity, or makes a remark which titillates the tabloid press, does not mean that *all* judge are out of touch with contemporary values. As one of the newly appointed Law Lords, Lord Saville, has suggested of the public's attitude to the judiciary: 'They think that we start work at eleven, finish at three, spend two hours sipping sherry and that we are totally removed from anything to do with real life. It is certainly not true' (*The Times*, 6 January 1998).

The fact that many judges will have been criminal barristers before sitting on the bench, and will have had a chance to see the 'real world' through the problems of their clients, also helps rebut the presumption that judges are somehow remote from the rest of the community. Also, the fact that they are mainly white, male, middle class, and middle aged, should not mean that they are any less qualified to hold judicial office — after all, most members of the Cabinet, both Chambers of Parliament and the upper echelons of the Civil Service, the Army, and the Church of England (to name but a few examples) are white, middle aged and middle class. Thus, judges will argue that, unless there is evidence to suggest that they tend to deliver judgments which are flawed because of their social class and backgrounds (and they will of course deny this), there is no reason for the public to doubt their entitlement to hold judicial office.

ACTIVITY34

Do you think that Grifflith's criticism of the judiciary is unfounded? Turn to *The Judiciary in the 90s*, by the former Lord Chief Justice, Lord Taylor, in *Cases and Materials* (4.2.3). How did he respond to criticism of the judiciary? Then read the extract from Gavin Drewry's comment on the Labour Government's proposals for reforming the judiciary.

4.5   Usurping the Legislative Function?

The doctrine of Parliamentary supremacy (see **Chapter 7**) ensures that Parliament is invested with the sole power to make law in the form of statutes. The role of the judges was traditionally one of interpretation and dispute resolution but increasingly members of the judiciary have shown a willingness to act as 'law-makers'. Beverley McLachlin, a Canadian judge, has written that 'in the latter part of the 20th century, the law-making role of the judges has dramatically expanded . . . Increasingly, it is invading the domain of social policy, formerly the exclusive right of Parliament and the legislatures' (*Law Quarterly Review*, 1994, p. 260).

Some examples of this 'social policy', which often has a moral or ethical dimension, include:

(a)   *Gillick v West Norfolk Area Health Authority* [1984] 1 All ER 365.

The House of Lords ruled that children under 16 years of age could consent to medical treatment (contraception) without the approval of their parents, provided that they were sufficiently mature.

(b)   *R v R* [1992] 1 AC 599.

The House of Lords decided that a husband could be guilty of raping his wife if there was intercourse without her consent. The Lords rejected the proposition that by marriage a wife must submit to sexual intercourse in all circumstances. This decision overturned a 256-year rule and Lord Keith commented: 'The common law is . . . capable of evolving in the light of changing social, economic and cultural developments'.

(c)   *Airedale NHS Trust v Bland* [1993] AC 789.

The House of Lords ruled that it was perfectly reasonable for responsible doctors to discontinue the supply of treatment to keep Tony Bland (a victim of the Hillsborough soccer disaster) alive because they had reached the conclusion that it was not providing any positive benefits. Thus, the doctors would not be acting unlawfully even through the termination of medical treatment would almost inevitably lead to Bland's death.

(d)   *R v Human Fertilisation Embryology Authority, ex parte Blood, The Times*, 7 February 1997.

The Court of Appeal held that sperm which had been taken from an unconscious man prior to his death, which his wife wanted to use to have a child, should not have been preserved and stored; and that the Human Fertilisation and Embryology Authority had acted lawfully in preventing Mrs Blood (the wife) from either using the sperm in the UK or from travelling abroad to another EU country where such a practice was lawful.

(e)   *St George's Healthcare National Health Service Trust v S, R v Collins, ex parte S, The Times*, 8 May 1998.

The Court of Appeal decided that in the case of a pregnant woman of sound mind who, against her will, had been forced to have a Caesarean section because of her medical condition, should have had a right to refuse this treatment even though this could have resulted in the death of an unborn child.

It is important to remember that while decisons such as these illustrate the potential of the creative 'law making' role of the judiciary, they also tend to be rather unusual.

Moreover, of the five cases mentioned earlier, it is submitted that, with the exception of *R v R* which all right thinking people will surely welcome, these decisions raise complex philosophical questions to which there are no easy answers. All of these cases generated considerable interest in the press and media, and it is suggested that they are controversial because, at their heart, there is a conflict of rights or interests. For example, in *Gillick*, the court had to strike a balance between the interests of the parent and the rights of the child; in *ex parte S*, it was the rights of the mother and those of the unborn child; in *ex parte Blood*, the interests of Mrs Blood had to be weighed against the expertise and policy considerations of the Human Fertilisation and Embryology Authority; and in *Bland*, the court had to balance the rights of Tony Bland, his family, the opinions of doctors, and the danger that this case would be seen as opening the door to euthanasia.

Finding the correct answer to these cases may require the contemporary equivalent of the wisdom of Solomon. Yet are judges, particularly in view of their privileged social backgrounds, the best people to be making such decisions on behalf of society generally? Some might argue that they are not: the press and public's critical reaction to the Court of Appeal's ruling in *Blood*, which led to the Authority later permitting Mrs Blood to attend a fertility clinic in Belgium with her husband's sperm (*The Times*, 28 February 1997), illustrates how judges can sometimes be out of touch with ordinary public attitudes and opinions. Despite the superficial attraction of this argument, such criticism can be easily rebutted by pointing out that judges are answerable to the law and not to fickle whims of public opinion. Also, for those who are suspicious of judges dealing with such controversial issues generally, it is difficult to think of any other people, bodies or institutions, who could handle this task any better.

SAQ 31

Normally one might have expected Parliament to have legislated on issues in these cases. Why has Parliament failed to pass legislation on these matters?

To what extent has the judiciary *created law* in these cases? What *reasons* can you put forward in favour of such a role?

ACTIVITY 35

Look at Anthony Lester's article in *Cases and Materials* (4.3).

(a) What does Lester mean when he says that judges have 'shackled themselves in chains of their own making'?

(b) Why were Lord Denning and Lord Simonds in dispute and why was Lord Denning's approach condemned as a 'constitutional heresy'?

In the past there was a rule that the courts were prohibited from referring to *Hansard* (the record of debates in Parliament) to ascertain the intention of Parliament. However, in a bold decision which abandoned a practice which had existed for over two hundred years, the House of Lords accepted in *Pepper* v *Hart* [1993] AC 593 that where an act is ambiguous or unclear, a court may use *Hansard* as an aid to statutory interpretation. *Hansard* may enable judges to discover the meaning of legislation, but there would appear to be some areas where the courts concede that they dare not tread. It seems that only Parliament has the right to make law on certain issues. For example:

(a) *R* v *Chief Metropolitan Stipendiary Magistrate, ex parte Choudhury* [1992] 1 QB 429.

   Here the Divisional Court refused to extend the offence of blasphemy to religions other than Christianity, pointing out that Parliament was the appropriate forum for such reform.

(b) *R* v *Brown* [1994] 1 AC 212.

   The House of Lords rejected an argument that consent to sadomasochistic practices, although freely given, could be recognised as a defence to a charge of aggravated assault.

(c) *R* v *Clegg* [1995] 1 All ER 334.

   Following the conviction of Private Clegg, a soldier serving with the British army in Northern Ireland, for the murder of a young woman who had been shot dead while travelling in a stolen car, the Northern Ireland Court of Appeal suggested that Parliament should consider a change in the law — that it should allow a conviction for manslaughter where a soldier or police officer, acting in the course of their duty, causes another person's death wrongly, without malice or an improper motive. The House of Lords affirmed that any such change should only be made by Parliament. Lord Lloyd of Berwick noted: 'I can hardly conceive of circumstances less suitable than the instant . . . to arrogate to ourselves so momentous a law-making initiative.'

(d) *R* v *Secretary of State for Defence, ex parte Smith and Others* [1996] 1 All ER 257.

   An attempt to seek judicial review of a policy maintaining a ban on homosexuals in the armed forces was unsuccessful. The Court of Appeal rejected the argument that this policy was irrational as it had been supported by both Houses of Parliament and by those in the armed forces (i.e., senior officers) to whom the Ministry of Defence looked for professional advice.

(e)   *C (a Minor)* v *DPP* [1996] 1 AC 1.

In the case of a 12 year old boy, who was convicted of attempted theft, the Divisional Court rejected the traditional rule that children who are aged between 10 and 14 must be shown to know that their actions are unlawful before they can be found guilty. The House of Lords refrained from following this approach and choose not to change the law. Instead, Lord Lowry noted that:

The distinction between the treatment and punishment of child 'offenders' has popular and political overtones, a fact which shows that we have been discussing not so much a legal as a social problem [which] . . . should be within the exclusive remit of Parliament.

What areas of law should be left solely to Parliament to legislate on?

One obvious reason for judicial creativity is the fact that Parliament sometimes appears to be slow to react to gaps or anomalies in the criminal law; thus, the courts intervene to plug these gaps and to rectify these anomalies. A good example of this fairly recently was the response of judges to the problems of harassment and stalking. In the absence of legislation which specifically covered such anti-social behaviour, the House of Lords interpreted the Offences Against the Person Act 1861 flexibly. Therefore, in *R* v *Ireland* [1997] QB 114, persistent silent telephone calls could constitute assault occasioning actual bodily harm (s. 47 of the 1861 Act), while in *R* v *Burstow* [1997] 3 WLR 534, harassment involving telephoning and photographing the victim, was deemed by the House of Lords to be grievous bodily harm (s. 20 of the 1861 Act).

The initiative of the judges in these cases was generally welcomed and Parliament has now responded to the problem by passing the Protection from Harassment Act 1997. However, such judicial creativity in the area of criminal law has not always been so warmly welcomed. For example, in **Chapter 3** we touched on the case of *Shaw* v *DPP* [1962] AC 220. Shaw had published a 'ladies directory', an illustrated guide to prostitutes and their services. The House of Lords upheld Shaw's conviction for conspiracy to corrupt public morals, although this was not a statutory offence and there had never previously been a conviction for this offence.

Viscount Simonds explained that 'there remains in the courts of law a residual power . . . to conserve not only the safety and order but also the moral welfare of the State'. Also, in *Knuller (Publishing, Printing and Promotions) Ltd* v *DPP* [1973] AC 435, the House of Lords upheld another conviction of conspiracy to corrupt public morals. This was after the appellants had published a magazine which contained advertisements by male homosexuals seeking to meet other homosexuals. These cases may be seen as examples of judicial creativity, but not all judges welcomed these decisions and, in a powerful dissenting judgment in *Shaw* v *DPP*, Lord Reid rejected the notion that the courts should be the guardians of public morals.

SAQ 33

Critics of the decision in *Shaw* v *DPP* argued that only Parliament should make changes to the criminal law.

What arguments support this view? On some of the dangers of judicial creativity, refer to the extract from Hillyard and Percy-Smith in *Cases and Materials* (4.3).

It is important to remember that the charge of 'judicial creativity' has not only been levelled at British judges. The Court of the European Community (see **Chapter 8** for more details), the European Court of Justice (ECJ), has been accused by Professor T.C. Hartley of interpreting EC legislation 'contrary to the natural meaning of the words used, an activity to which the phrase "judicial legislation" may be justifiably applied'. Indeed, Professor Hartley even claims that the ECJ's rejection of 'the natural meaning' of the Community's Treaties 'has taken place in persuance of a settled and consistent policy of promoting European federalism' ((1996) 112 LQR 95). Hartley's claims are rejected by Professor Anthony Arnull, who doubts whether they 'command widespread acceptance among objective students of the Court', and defends the 'value of the part played by the Court in promoting the proper functioning of the Community' ((1996) 112 LQR 411).

Just as the judges of the European Community may be said to have had a creative role in developing EC law, the members of Europe's other major court, the European Court of Human Rights, have interpreted the European Convention on Human Rights (ECHR) in a way which most of those who drafted the ECHR in the late 1940s would have never imagined. With more than 500 judgments, there are plenty of examples of creative decision-making, but for our purposes we will concentrate briefly on one aspect of art. 3, which prohibits torture, inhuman and degrading treatment.

The ECHR does not expressly guarantee a human right not to be deported or extradited, but the European Court of Human Rights has interpreted art. 3 of the ECHR to cover situations where an individual's deportation or extradition might be contrary to the prohibition of inhuman or degrading treatment under art. 3. For example, in *Soering* v *UK* (1989) 11 EHRR 439, the European Court held that if Britain granted an extradition request from the State of Virginia that Soering, a German national, be returned to the US to stand trial for the murder of his girl friend's parents, there would be a violation of art. 3 as, with a 'real risk' of the death penalty being imposed, it would mean that Soering would then be kept on 'death row' for a number of years, pending execution. In this case the European Court avoided considering the death penalty *per se* (probably because it is permitted under certain circumstances in art. 2, and not all States have ratified the optional Protocol 6 which abolishes it), but it considered that, on the facts (i.e., the number of years which Soering was likely to spend on 'death row', the extreme conditions there, his youth, his confused mental state, and lack of any previous criminal record), for Britain to return Soering to face capital murder charges would be inhuman treatment, contrary to art. 3. Thus, in complying with this decision, the UK only extradited Soering on the condition that he would not be subject to the death penalty if found guilty at his trial; and on his return to the US he was subsequently found guilty and sentenced to life imprisonment.

An equally wide view was taken of art. 3 in *R v UK, The Times*, 12 May 1997, when the European Court held that the UK's decision to deport a drug dealer with AIDS, to his home in St Kitts on his release from prison in Britain, was a violation of his human rights. The Court accepted that since the applicant would not have access to medical facilities on St Kitts, to send him there would amount to inhuman and degrading treatment. This decision, like that in Soering, was criticised by some as being too 'soft on crime', but irrespective of whether one agrees with the actual decisions which were reached, they certainly illustrate the European Court's willingness to give a bold interpretation to the ECHR.

How did you answer **SAQ 31**? You probably observed that cases which involve questions of ethics and morality (such as *Gillick* and *Airedale NHS Trust* v *Bland*) tend to be controversial. Parliament is often reluctant or slow to respond to these issues. Usually they are addressed in Parliament in the form of a Private Member's Bill (see **Chapter 5**). Without government support most Private Member's Bills fail. An unusual exception is the Human Fertilisation and Embryology Act 1990, which was passed after much controversial debate, following Baroness Warnock's Committee of Inquiry into Human Fertilisation and Embryology. In view of Parliament's traditional reluctance to address such moral and ethical issues, Britain's judges often find themselves on 'the front line', hearing cases which almost inevitably have a law-making dimension.

4.6   Conflict between the Judiciary and the Executive

It would appear that the past decade has witnessed, particularly in the final years of John Major's previous administration, increasing tension between the executive and members of the judiciary. This reached its climax when a call was made by the former Conservative Party Chairman, Brian Mawhinney, at the 1995 Conservative Party Conference, for members of the public to write to judges and magistrates if they wanted to complain about lenient sentences in particular cases. His comments, and their endorsement by a number of senior Conservative politicians, were seen by many as undermining the principle of the separation of powers, and possibly were the catalyst for the publication of an article in *The Guardian* by Lord Donaldson, the retired Master of the Rolls. Lord Donaldson considered that the 'attack by politicians on the judiciary as a whole' was 'without precedent' and raised 'very serious constitutional issues', for 'to mount a campaign of abuse and criticism of the judiciary as a whole' was 'unpardonable'. The reaction to the expression in public of the trenchant views of a recently retired senior judge who had, ironically, never been thought of as a 'liberal', even led to some suggestions in press reports that the Lord Chancellor had planned, in the draft of a speech which he was shortly expected thereafter to give, to warn judges to 'keep in line'. This was later denied by the Lord Chancellor but, amidst allegation and counter allegation few facts appeared to be certain, what seemed clear was that relations between the executive and the members of the judiciary were, in a number of areas, rather strained.

ACTIVITY 36

Read Lord Donaldson's article in *Cases and Materials* (4.4). Do you agree with the views which are expressed?

So, why has the past decade witnessed a deterioration in the relationship between certain members of the executive and the judiciary? There are a number of reasons, the most obvious of which is perhaps the growth and increasing availability of judicial review. As you will later see, in **Chapter 15**, judicial review is a discretionary public law remedy and applications for leave to apply for judicial review must be made to a judge who has the power to refuse to grant it. The rapid increase in the number of applications for leave to apply for judicial review (applications have risen from 160 in 1974 to approximately 3,800 in 1996), and the increasing willingness of judges to grant these applications (in 1995, out of 3,604 applications for leave received, 41% were granted) have, perhaps in recent years, certainly increased the likelihood of conflict between members of the judiciary and the executive.

Secondly, the willingness of British judges to give a bold interpretation to the European Communities Act 1972, as vividly illustrated by the decision of the House of Lords to recognise the supremacy of EC law in R v *Secretary of State for Transport, ex parte Factortame* [1990] 2 AC 85, has increased tensions between judges and those members of the executive who might be described as having 'Eurosceptic' tendencies.

Thirdly, recent Government proposals to curb civil legal aid for personal injury claims and to expand 'no win, no fee' arrangements for a number of civil disputes, have also aroused criticism from members of the judiciary. No less a figure than the Lord Chief Justice, Lord Bingham, has warned 'of the difficulties and the potentially fateful consequences of any radical change to the current arrangements' (*The Times*, 12 June 1998).

Finally, the issue of sentencing has been perhaps the most controversial and emotive of the areas of disagreement between judges and ministers in recent years. For example, judges have long been opposed to mandatory life sentences where the length of the sentence is determined ultimately by the Home Secretary. The argument in favour of this power is that the Home Secretary, as an elected MP and Minister, should have a say, in order to represent the views of the public. Against this view, however, it could be argued that the Home Secretary's involvement means that a sentence could be imposed for party political reasons (e.g., to demonstrate a government's commitment to tackling the perpetrators of crime), rather than on the particular facts of the case and in the interests of 'justice'. This conundrum has been at the heart of two recent decisions which arouse powerful emotions, as they both involve the murder of young children. In R v *Secretary of State for the Home Department, ex parte Venables and Thompson* [1997] 2 WLR 67, Venables and Thompson, who were both aged 10, were convicted of the murder of Liverpool toddler, James Bulger. At their trial, the judge recommended that the two boys serve ('a tariff') eight years, but the Lord Chief Justice then recommended a term of 10 years. However, following a number of complaints from members of the public about the leniency of the sentence, the Home Secretary raised their tariff to 15 years, a decision which the boys then challenged by way of judicial review. In hearing this action, the Court of Appeal agreed that the Home Secretary had acted unfairly when, in fixing the tariff, he had taken account of irrelevant considerations, such as the views and opinions of the public. This decision was greeted, predictably, by howls of protest which will no doubt be even louder if the European Court of Human Rights upholds the complaints of Venables and Thompson in an action brought by them, which is currently pending at the time of writing.

As with the murder of James Bulger, the killing of a number of young children by Myra Hindley, in what are commonly known as the 'Moors murders', touched the nation's nerve and any question of her release, even after 31 years in prison, generates considerable controversy. In R v *Secretary of State for the Home Department, ex parte Hindley, The Times*, 19 December 1997, Hindley sought judicial review of the decision of the Home Secretary, that the principles of retribution and deterrence demanded that her tariff (on which there had been no guidance from the trial judge) should be fixed for her 'whole life'. Her challenge failed as Lord Bingham ruled that the Home Secretary has the power to decide that a life sentence 'will mean life'. However, Lord Bingham appeared to express some unease about the Home Secretary's sentencing powers when he commented: [t]here is room for serious debate whether the task of determining how long convicted murderers should serve . . . should be undertaken by the judiciary . . . or, as now, by the executive'. Myra Hindley may now bring her case before the Court of Appeal and the House of Lords and, if she takes this course of action, it will be interesting to see how British judges respond once the ECHR is incorporated into British law and Hindley is able to invoke art. 5(4) of the ECHR (see *Cases and Materials* (1.4)). In view of the emotion generated by this case, what seems clear is that any decision which might lead to the release of Hindley would be extremely controversial.

SAQ 34

In what ways, if any, does judicial review contribute to or exacerbate antagonism between judges and government Ministers? On this, see the views of Lord Nolan in *Cases and Materials* (4.4). Do you find his arguments convincing?

SAQ 35

How would you describe the judiciary's relationship with both the legislature and the executive? For some ideas turn to the extract from Lord Steyn's article, in *Cases and Materials* (4.4).

4.7 Conclusion

There have been many changes to the judiciary over the last three decades. First, the judiciary has increased in size from approximately 200 judges in 1970, to just under 2,000 judges today. However, notwithstanding this increase, most judges are still overwhelmingly white, male, middle class and middle aged. Secondly, judges have increasingly been willing to comment on legal issues. In the 1960s the Lord Chancellor, Lord Kilmuir, discouraged judges from expressing their opinions in public but recently, to some extent, this veil of secrecy has been lifted. A combination of an information hungry press and the more tolerant and open approach of recent Lord Chancellors, has led to some judges expressing opinions on some matters (e.g., ranging from mandatory life sentences to the legalisation of soft drugs) which, 30 years ago, would have been unimaginable. Thirdly, and perhaps most importantly, judges appear to have more power today than ever before. The Human Rights Act 1998 seems likely to increase the powers of Britain's judges even further, and perhaps this document will give them the courage to defend human rights in the way in which the mere existence of the US Constitution has often been thought of as being the catalyst for some of the US Supreme Court's most bold decisions (e.g., its rulings challenging racist transport and educational policies in certain Southern States in the 1960s).

The success of the Human Rights Act 1998 will certainly depend on how it is interpreted by the nation's judiciary. In retaining public confidence, it will be crucial for judges to act, and to be seen to act, independently. Unlike those countries with written constitutions, which have provisions expressly guaranteeing the independence of the judiciary, judicial independence in Britain is maintained through a combination of laws, practices and conventions. Of course you must decide whether these 'traditional' ways of guaranteeing judicial independence are still appropriate, or are in need of modification and reform, as we move towards the new millennium. Certainly it should be noted that whatever criticisms may be made of the British judiciary, they have avoided the allegations of political bias which have been levelled at many holders of judicial office in the United States. Thus, as Wade once noted: 'In many constitutions the separation of powers has meant an unhampered executive. In England, it means little more than an independent judiciary.'

4.8   End of Chapter Assessment Question

'It behoves the courts to be ever sensitive to the paramount need to refrain from trespassing upon the province of Parliament and I hope and would expect that Parliament would be similarly sensitive to the need to refrain from trespassing upon the province of the courts' (per Sir John Donaldson MR in R v *Her Majesty's Treasury, ex parte Smedley* [1985] QB 857).

To what extent is this an accurate reflection of the relationship between Parliament and the courts?

(See *Cases and Materials* (4.6) for a specimen answer.)

CHAPTER FIVE

PARLIAMENT AND THE LAW-MAKING PROCESS – I FUNCTION, PRIVILEGES AND PARLIAMENTARY CONTROLS

5.1 Objectives

At the end of this Chapter you should be able to:

■ explain the role and function of Parliament;

■ critically analyse the rules of Parliamentary privilege;

■ assess the effectiveness of Parliamentary checks on the government's power;

■ argue the case for the reform of Parliament.

5.2 Introduction

How would you define the word 'Parliament'? In the United Kingdom it would appear to have at least three different meanings. It is commonly used to describe:

(a) **The Legislature in the UK**

Parliament is composed of three elements: the House of Commons, the House of Lords and the Monarch (sometimes referred to as the 'Queen in Parliament'). The legislature is *bicameral* – that is, it consists of two chambers, the Lords and the Commons.

(b) **The period of time between general elections**

After a general election a new Parliament is formally opened and declared. Since no Parliament may last for more than five years (Parliament Act 1911, s. 7), Parliament must be dissolved and its life end within this period.

(c) **The Palace of Westminster**

In this sense 'Parliament' is used simply to describe the physical structure and buildings of Westminster, where the House of Commons and House of Lords are located. The two Houses are merely tenants in a Royal palace which dates back to 1099. The palace is owned by the Crown and is managed by the government on its behalf.

In addition to these three meanings, it is worth pointing out that the word Parliament is sometimes erroneously used to refer to the House of Commons. The fact that those who sit in the Commons are called Members of Parliament and that the House of Commons is where most power is vested within Parliament are probable reasons for this confusion. However, it is important to note that the House of Commons is only *one* of the *three* constitutent elements of Parliament, the other two being the House of Lords and the Queen in Parliament.

Philip Norton suggests that Parliament has three functions. What might they be? You can discover what they are by referring to the extract from his book *Parliament in the 1980s* in *Cases and Materials* (5.1).

5.2.1 MEETINGS OF PARLIAMENT

Parliament should 'meet frequently' (Bill of Rights 1689, Art. 13), and at least every three years (Meeting of Parliament Act 1694). Although there is no formal legal rule which expressly requires that Parliament should assemble annually, a convention has developed that this does in fact happen. This is primarily because a Finance Act must be passed each year, which renews the authority for taxes to be collected and enables any changes in taxation proposed during the Chancellor's Budget speech to be made. Therefore, if this convention was broken and Parliament did not meet annually, no money could be raised or spent, and there would be a breakdown of government.

5.2.2 LENGTH OF PARLIAMENTS

No one Parliament can last for more than five years (Parliament Act 1911, s. 7). However, in exceptional circumstances, Parliament can pass legislation to extend its own life. For example, during both the First and Second World Wars, the danger of general elections disrupting the war effort led to an extension of the Parliamentary term.

Parliament is nearly always dissolved by the Monarch exercising the Royal prerogative before the five years are up (see **Chapter 14**), acting on the advice of the Prime Minister who, by convention, can request dissolution. This allows the Prime Minister some flexibility in choosing the most appropriate time for a general election.

Parliament is formally opened by the Sovereign in person, or by Royal Commissioners in the House of Lords with much pomp and pageantry. A Speaker is elected to the House of Commons and all MPs subsequently swear an oath of allegiance. Members of the Lords also swear an oath and shortly afterwards the Queen's speech is read in the House of Lords. This is, in fact, written by the Prime Minister and Cabinet, and it outlines the government's policies for the coming legislative session. A general debate on this speech starts off the proceedings for each Parliament in both the Lords and Commons.

The dates on which Parliament is opened (summoned) and closed (prorogued), e.g. the beginning and end of a Parliamentary session, are fixed by Parliament itself. Each Parliament is subdivided into a number of sessions normally of about one year in length. Sessions tend to run from early November to late October and each session is terminated (prorogued) by a short speech from the Monarch or a Royal Commission summarising the achievements of that session. Thus, apart from the continuing judicial duties of the House of Lords, prorogation brings all business in a Parliamentary session to an end.

5.3 The Function of Parliament

Parliament's main role is the formal enactment of legislative proposals. Each government's policy is put into effect through legislation. In particular, proposals for taxation and expenditure must receive Parliamentary approval. The powers of Ministers need formal approval through Bills assented to by Parliament. Parliament is also responsible for providing and maintaining an effective government, providing a forum for debate on matters of general public concern, and supervising the executive through the doctrine of Ministerial Responsibility.

Legislation is not required where *prerogative* powers are exercised (primarily by Ministers) to pursue government policy (e.g. the signing of foreign treaties, decisions on defence matters, granting pardons, etc.). We shall return to prerogative powers (ancient powers of the Crown now exercised by Ministers) later in **Chapter 14**.

5.3.1 LEGISLATION

Parliament's main role is to pass legislation. In recent years there has been a huge increase in the amount of legislation enacted by Parliament. In 1951, 675 pages of legislation were published, while in 1994 the figure had risen to 3,012 pages (41 Acts) and more than 10,000 pages of delegated legislation (more than 3,300 statutory instruments). There are perhaps two reasons for this dramatic increase in the volume of Parliamentary legislation. First, Parliament has had, over the last decade, to implement an increasing number of directives from the European Community. Secondly, governments in recent years have been increasingly eager to show they have not run out of ideas, so they have pressed ahead with wide-ranging proposals for legislative change. This dramatic increase in primary and secondary legislation has led to fears that some legislation, passed recently, may be ill conceived in principle and poorly drafted in practice. Thus, it is particularly important that such legislation is carefully scrutinised.

SAQ 37

An obvious consequence of this growth in legislation is that government Bills proceeding through Parliament may not be as carefully scrutinised as they should be. Bear this in mind when you cover the ways in which Bills become law. Griffith and Ryle also note that the increasing volume of legislation passed by Parliament has had three important effects on the conduct of proceedings of the House of Commons. What are these effects? (You will find the answer in *Cases and Materials* (5.2.1).)

5.3.2 TYPES OF BILL

Laws begin life as legislative drafts or Bills which are presented to Parliament for amendment and approval. There are four main types of Parliamentary Bills: (a) Public Bills, (b) Private Members' Bills, (c) Private Bills, (d) Hybrid Bills.

(a) Public Bills

Public Bills relate to matters of general importance and usually originate from within government departments. The annual Finance Bill and Appropriation Bills for authorising government expenditure and the raising of taxes must be introduced in the Commons, whereas any other public Bill can originate either in the Commons or in the Lords. In the 1995–96 session, 43 government Bills were introduced into the Commons and all of them ended up on the statute book.

(b) Private Members' Bills

An MP (who is not a member of the Cabinet) or a peer can seek to introduce a private members' Bill. Perhaps the best known recent example of this is Mike Foster's Bill to ban fox hunting in 1997 which, despite gaining the support of more than 400 MPs in a Commons vote, failed after MPs tabled more than 150 amendments in order to 'talk it out' of Parliament. On the other hand, in January 1995, MPs gave their backing to a Private Members' Bill requiring compulsory registration of outdoor activity centres, prompted by a canoeing tragedy at Lyme Regis in 1993. Twelve Fridays each session are set aside for Private Members' Bills. These can be introduced if the member is one of 10 MPs placed highest in a ballot. It is rare for a Private Members' Bill to pass into law, since most fall prey to strict Parliamentary time limits (e.g., in the Commons session of 1995–96, only 60 hours were allocated to Private Members' Bills), so that those which survive almost inevitably have the support of the government.

(c) Private Bills

These deal specifically with issues that affect a particular group, individual or company and are introduced by that person or body. Bills of a personal character are less common but were used in the past for divorces and private railways. Private Bills are generally promoted by local authorities wishing to acquire further powers and have been used by other public corporations such as the Coal Board and British Railways (prior to privatisation).

(d) Hybrid Bills

In addition you might also come across hybrid Bills. Erskin May defined a hybrid Bill as 'a public Bill which affects a particular private interest in a manner different from the private interests of other persons or bodies of the same category or class'. In other words they alter the law, but have a specific effect upon a certain section of the population. An example of a Hybrid Bill is what later became the Channel Tunnel Act 1987.

SAQ 38

Explain the difference between Public Bills and Private Members' Bills.

And why does Brazier suggest that the fact that 'a dozen or so Private Members' Bills become law in each session is attributable to luck and the acquiescence of the government?' You will find the reasons for this statement in *Cases and Materials* (5.2.2).

5.3.3 STAGES OF A BILL

A Bill will often start life in the form of a 'Green Paper', which will set out the government's provisional proposals. Having consulted interested parties and taken into account the public's reaction to its plans, the government may then issue a 'White Paper' which states the government's position on that particular issue. Since coming to power, Tony Blair's Government has presented White Papers on a number of areas including those dealing with the incorporation of the ECHR, a Freedom of Information Act and a proposed Greater London Authority.

For a Public Bill to be introduced into the House of Commons it must comply with the following procedure:

(a) First Reading

(b) Second Reading

(c) Committee Stage

(d) Report Stage

(e) Third Reading

Bills can be introduced in either the Lords or (as is usually the case) the Commons. Money Bills, however, must start in the Commons.

(a) **First Reading**

The title of the proposed Bill is read out in the Commons (or the Lords), and the Bill is ordered to be printed and published. The first reading is essentially a formality, indicating that the government intends to introduce a Bill.

(b) **Second reading**

The Minister or proposer of the Bill explains its aims and moves that the Bill be read a second time. This is the first opportunity for the Bill to be debated on the floor of the House. No amendments to individual clauses are allowed. The principles and merits of the Bill are considered and a vote taken on whether it will be given a second reading. It is rare for a government Bill to be defeated at this stage although, in 1986, a government Bill to reform the law on Sunday shopping was defeated on its second reading in the Commons.

(c) **Committee stage**

The Bill is normally then referred to a standing committee consisting of between 16 and 50 members, including representatives of all the main parties. The committee considers the Bill in detail, clause by clause, and makes amendments.

(d) **Report stage**

Having passed the Committee Stage, the amended Bill is then presented to the whole House for debate. Further amendments may be made to the Bill.

(e) **Third reading**

This is the stage where the Bill, in its final form, is debated once more by the whole House. A vote is then taken and only verbal amendments are permitted.

It is worth noting that the vast majority of amendments to government Bills are usually as a result of changes requested and proposed by Ministers themselves.

The Bill is then sent to the Lords where virtually the same procedure is followed. As the House of Lords has no standing committee, the committee stage is usually undertaken by a committee of the whole House. Any amendments are referred back to the Commons for consideration. The Commons can either reject or uphold such amendments. If upheld, the Bill can proceed to receive the Royal Assent. If rejected, the two Houses must reach a solution or compromise. If the Lords refuse to give their assent to a public Bill, it can be presented for Royal Assent without their approval (see **Chapter 6**).

The assent of the Sovereign is required by law, after a Bill has passed through both Houses. By convention such assent has not been withheld since Queen Anne refused her assent in 1707. (Royal Assent has not been given by the Monarch in person since 1854 and today Commissioners notify each House of the assent on behalf of the Monarch: Royal Assent Act 1967.)

Which is the most important stage of a Bill? Explain why. Also, do you agree with the view expressed by the Select Committee on the Modernisation of the House of Commons in 1997 that 'more thorough scrutiny of legislation is necessary and long overdue'? You will find some of the recommendations of this Committee in *Cases and Materials* (5.2.3).

ACTIVITY 37

Read the extract from R. Rose in *Cases and Materials* (5.2.3). In what ways are laws, according to Rose, important?

5.4 The Speaker

The Speaker is the senior officer of, and chairs proceedings in, the House of Commons. The Speaker does not participate in debates and has no vote. Responsible for deciding which of the amendments proposed at the report stages are to be debated, the Speaker will also call upon members to speak, rule on points of order and endeavour to maintain good order! Generally the Speaker is elected at the beginning of every new Parliament. It is a convention that, on taking office, all party connections and allegiances are severed, although the Speaker remains an MP. Unable to represent the interests of his or her constituency in the House, the Speaker can take up individual grievances with government departments. Historically the Speaker had the unenviable task of telling the Monarch that the Commons had refused to grant the money that he or she had requested so the job was not a popular one. Thus, by custom, a newly elected Speaker is 'forced' into the Speaker's chair whilst 'protesting'. Recent Speakers have included George Thomas (the late Viscount Tonypandy) and Bernard Weatherill (now Lord Weatherill), while today the office is held by Betty Boothroyd, the first woman Speaker and a former Labour MP.

The Speaker has no control over when Parliament shall sit or the duration of business and debate. These are matters within the sole jurisdiction of the House. The Speaker has the power to:

- maintain discipline in the House by demanding silence or calm, by normally repeating the words, 'Order! Order!'.

- name a member who has disobeyed a ruling (such a member must then leave or be forcibly ejected);

- choose who shall speak next in a debate;

- decide how many supplementary questions may be asked at question time;

- ensure that the Commons rules of procedure are correctly applied; and

- rule on points of order.

A number of deputies assist the Speaker, acting as substitutes where necessary. The Deputy Speaker has the title of Chairman of Ways and Means and there are two additional deputies to that title – the First and Second Deputy Chairmen of Ways and

Means. The office of Speaker carries much authority and it is a key element in the successful operation of the House of Commons.

Read the brief extract in *Cases and Materials* (5.3) from Griffith and Ryle, *Parliament: Functions, Practice and Procedures*. **What qualities do the authors ascribe to the office of a successful Speaker?**

'The Speaker is both master and servant of the House.' **Explain the meaning of this description of the Speaker's role?**

At the beginning of every Parliament, the Speaker claims certain privileges for Parliament from the Sovereign. These include: freedom of speech and debate; freedom from imprisonment and arrest for civil wrongs (traditionally it covered debt, but today this is largely unheard of) and freedom of access to the Queen 'whenever occasion shall require'. Therefore, it is to the privileges of Parliament that we now turn.

5.5   Parliamentary Privilege

Members of both Houses of Parliament enjoy certain privileges and immunities not enjoyed by the ordinary citizen. This enables each House to maintain its independence with its members able to discharge their duties without undue interference. Both the Lords and Commons have exclusive jurisdiction over all questions which arise within their own walls and they may punish anyone for the breach of a specific privilege. As Erskine May notes, 'Parliamentary privilege is the sum of peculiar rights, enjoyed by each house individually, without which they could not discharge their functions'.

The privileges of the Commons fall into two groups:

(a) Those claimed by the Speaker from the Sovereign at the beginning of each new session as 'their ancient and undoubted rights and privileges':

(i)   Freedom of speech and debate (guaranteed by art. 9 of the Bill of Rights 1688).

(ii) Freedom from civil arrest – (*Stourton* v *Stourton* [1963] P 303).

(iii) Freedom of access to the Crown through the Speaker.

(b) Those not so claimed:

(i)   The right of Parliament to regulate its own composition. In *Bradlaugh* v *Gossett* (1884) 12 QBD 271, Lord Coleridge CJ said 'What is said or done within the walls of Parliament cannot be inquired into in a court of law . . . The jurisdiction of the Houses over their own Members, their right to impose discipline within their walls, is absolute and exclusive.' Therefore, the court in this case (see *Cases and Materials* (**5.4**)) lacked the power to strike down a resolution of the Commons that Bradlaugh, an atheist, should be prevented from taking the oath to be sworn by all MPs, and excluded from the House. Parliament may expel any member which it feels is unfit to serve.

(ii) The exclusive right to regulate matters arising within the House. For example, in 1994 the *Sunday Times* published claims that MPs had been offered and accepted payments for the tabling of Parliamentary questions. In reponse to these allegations, the 17-member cross-party Commons Privileges Committee recommended that two Conservative MPs should be temporarily suspended from the Commons without pay. This subsequently became known as the 'Cash for Questions' affair and is discussed later in this chapter. Thus, as Lord Simon in *Pickin* v *B.R.B.* [1974] AC 765 noted: 'Among the privileges of the Houses of Parliament is the exclusive right to determine the regularity of their own internal proceedings'.

(iii) The right to punish members and others for breach of privilege and contempt of Parliament. In 1947 Garry Allighan MP was held in contempt for making unsubstantiated allegations against other members. The House voted to expel Mr Allighan even though he was a member of the Labour Party which was in Government with a large Commons majority. As Erskine May points out: 'any act or omission which obstructs or impedes either House of Parliament in the performance of its functions . . . or which has a tendency, directly or indirectly, to produce such results, may be treated as a contempt.' Nine examples of House contempts are provided by Griffiths and Ryle in *Cases and Materials* (**5.4**).

'Proceedings' in Parliament attract *absolute privilege*. Thus, no Member may be legally liable for words spoken in the course of Parliamentary proceedings. Matters relating to Parliament, but which are not actually 'proceedings in Parliament', may attract the common law defence of *qualified privilege* if it can be shown that the person making the statement was motivated by a legal, social or moral duty. But what of speech which is not protected? If a member feels that a breach of privilege has occurred, the normal procedure is that the Speaker should be privately informed. The Speaker will then decide whether it should take precedence over other Commons business and be officially announced in the Commons. The House may either drop the matter or refer it to the Select Committee on Privileges (a committee of 17 of the most senior members of the House) to investigate and report back with their findings and recommendations.

The Speaker is responsible for determining which punishment should be meted out if someone is found to be in contempt of the House. Punishments include:

■ Expulsion – but this cannot prevent re-election. In 1948, Garry Allighan was expelled for having made false allegations against other MPs. In 1954, Peter Baker was expelled, having been convicted of forgery and sentenced to seven years in prison.

■ Suspension. In April 1988, Ron Brown was suspended for 20 days from the House of Commons for damaging the Mace. However, a member has not actually been suspended for a breach of privilege since 1911.

■ Imprisonment – members are sent to the Clocktower in the Tower of London, while 'strangers' are consigned to an ordinary prison. In the past more than one member was imprisoned and Sir John Eliot died there: *Eliot's Case* (1629) 3 St Tr 294. However, the House has not used this power to commit for contempt since 1880. Imprisonment is during the 'pleasure of the House' but cannot last beyond a session, i.e. approximately one year. The Committee on Privileges has recommended its abolition.

■ Reprimand or admonishment by the Speaker. This penalty can be imposed on any offender, such as on an MP (Tam Dalyell in 1968) or on a journalist (Mr Heighway in 1947).

Hatsell (1818) claimed that 'the privileges of Parliament are rights which are absolutely necessary for the due execution of its powers'.

Why should Parliament be permitted to enjoy certain privileges?

Although the House of Commons is entitled to regulate its own composition, certain categories of people are disqualified from sitting and voting in the Commons. What should prevent a person from becoming an MP? A list of the major disqualifications can be found in *Cases and Materials* (5.4).

5.5.1 FREEDOM OF SPEECH AND DEBATE

Freedom of speech is an essential prerequisite of every free legislature. It is a right which was claimed by the House of Commons as long ago as the fourteenth century in *Haxey's Case* (1397). It is also guaranteed by art. 9 of the Bill of Rights. Each member is under a duty to refrain from any action which might jeopardise his or her freedom of speech, (e.g., through association with groups which could limit a member's independence).

In *Church of Scientology of California* v *Johnson-Smith* [1972] 1 QB 522, Browne J held that a 'member must have a complete right of free speech in the House without any fear that his motives or intentions or reasoning will be questioned or held against him thereafter'. Therefore, the Church of Scientology's attempt to sue an MP who it claimed had slandered the Church and its members failed, since the church was unable to rely on a speech made by the MP in Parliament. The MP's words were held to be absolutely privileged.

Similarly, in *Prebble* v *Television New Zealand Ltd* [1955] 1 AC 321, Lord Browne-Wilkinson (in the Privy Council) said that art. 9 of the Bill of Rights prevented a court from entertaining any action against members of the legislature, who therefore enjoy complete immunity in respect of their words in Parliament.

SAQ 42

Why is freedom of speech and debate so important in Parliament?

5.5.2 PROCEEDINGS IN PARLIAMENT

As we have just seen, everything that a member says or does during the course of a debate in the chamber is absolutely privileged. No legal proceedings can be brought for slander (words spoken) or libel (the written word). However, comments made by a member outside Parliament do not attract *absolute privilege*. In such a case the member could claim the common law defence of *qualified privilege* only if it could be shown that the comments had been made in good faith. Thus, qualified privilege gives the maker of an untrue or defamatory statement a defence to an action, unless the plaintiff can prove that the defendant was motivated by malice.

However, what of things said or done outside the chamber? For example, a situation where discussions take place outside the Commons chamber, but which are still associated with Parliamentary business. Are they still 'proceedings in Parliament'? There is no complete definition of the phrase 'proceedings in Parliament', but in identifying such 'proceedings', two factors which may be taken into account are: the place where the statement was made; and the form in which it was made (e.g. in a letter).

5.5.2.1 The place where the statement is made

It would seem that any statement made within the confines of the House, which has no connection with Parliamentary proceedings, will not be protected by absolute privilege: (*Rivlin* v *Bilainkin* [1953] 1 QB 485). A defamatory statement in a letter from Bilainkin to a Member of Parliament concerning the conduct of Bilainkin's former wife, was not protected by Parliamentary privilege, because it was in no way connected to any proceedings in Parliament.

However, a statement made by one Member to another outside the Commons Chamber, but within the precincts of the House may, on occasion, be a proceeding in Parliament. In *Duncan Sandys's Case* (1939) it was held that a private conversation between two members outside the chamber, but within the precincts of the House, would only be a proceeding in Parliament if the conversation related to matters pending or likely to be considered in the House. The Select Committee on the Official Secrets Acts said that on matters such as 'communications between one Member and another, or between a Member and a Minister, so closely related to some matter pending in, or expected to be brought before the House, that, although they do not take place in the Chamber or a committee room, they form part of the business of the House'. The House itself later in this case agreed with the Committee's recommendation.

In 1987, however, when some MPs proposed to show a film about a secret defence project code-named 'Zircon' (the publication of which had been banned by an injunction earlier that day) the Committee of Privileges held that the showing of the controversial film in a committee room would not constitute a proceeding in Parliament. Therefore, it was not protected by Parliamentary privilege.

In the absence of a statutory definition of the words 'proceedings in Parliament' the exact limits of this term remain unclear, although this uncertainty gives the House flexibility in interpreting its privileges.

5.5.2.2   Letters

The issue of whether a letter from a member to a Minister is to be regarded as a proceeding in Parliament was considered in the case of *Strauss* [1958] AC 331. Here Strauss (the member) wrote a letter to a Minister on a matter unrelated to that Minister's responsibility and therefore outside the scope of a Parliamentary question. The letter contained allegations of improper conduct on the part of the Electricity Board (a nationalised industry). The Minister sent a copy of the letter to the Board for its observations and the Board replied demanding an apology from the member, failing which damages for libel would be sought. The member raised the question of privilege in the House. The matter was referred to the Committee of Privileges which reported that the letter was a proceeding in Parliament and the Board was in breach of privilege. However, the House (on a free vote) decided by a majority of five, that the letter was not a proceeding in Parliament, so was not privileged. Thus, the effect of the decision in *Strauss* (which was later criticised by the Committee of Privileges) is that a letter from an MP is only privileged to the extent that it relates to an official parliamentary question or to an issue being considered in the House.

In *R v Rule* [1937] 2 KB 375 a constituent wrote a defamatory letter to his MP, complaining about the conduct of a magistrate and certain police officers. He requested that his complaint be referred to a Minister. It was held that although the letter was not a proceeding in Parliament, it could attract qualified privilege.

Turn to *Cases and Materials* (5.4.1) and consult Griffith and Ryle's table of privilege cases in the House of Commons. Compare the recommendations of the Committee of Privileges to the action taken by the House.

5.5.3 PARLIAMENTARY PAPERS

In the 19th century a major conflict between Parliament and the Courts developed over the question of whether or not the House had sole authority to publish Parliamentary debates and reports. In the leading case of *Stockdale* v *Hansard* [1839] 9 Ad & E 1, Stockdale contended that he had been libelled in a report on prison conditions, which had been prepared and published by order of the Commons. He claimed damages from Hansard, then the official printer to the House. On the instructions of the House of Commons, Hansard pleaded that the report was covered by Parliamentary privilege, the Commons having passed a resolution declaring the report to be a proceeding in Parliament. It was held that the report was not a proceeding in Parliament and that a resolution of the Commons alone could not change the law and make it so. As a result damages were awarded to Stockdale.

The House of Commons then ordered Hansard not to pay any damages and the Sheriff of Middlesex sought to seize Hansard's property to satisfy the judgment. The Sheriff and his officers were accordingly arrested and imprisoned on the order of the House of Commons for contempt of the House. This led to the *Case of the Sheriff of Middlesex* [1840] 11 Ad & E 273. Habeas corpus proceedings were brought to secure the release of the Sheriff and his officials. They were unsuccessful as the court held that the Commons was entitled to imprison for contempt of the House. Thus the House of Commons has the power to commit individuals for contempt for whatever conduct it considers amounts to contempt. This is a wide power which was last exercised in 1880.

As a result of these cases, it would seem that the following principles apply:

■ As long as the Commons can show a privilege exists in law, the Commons has sole jurisdiction over it.

■ The Houses of Parliament have never expressly renounced their claim to be the judges of their own privileges.

■ The authority of the House is no defence to a claim that defamatory material was published outside the House.

■ The courts are bound to give way when the House chooses to enforce its power to commit for contempt.

■ No new privileges can be created except by statute.

In recent years Parliament's reputation has suffered, particularly following revelations that some MPs had accepted money for tabling questions in Parliament. We will proceed to the 'cash for questions' controversy shortly, but some have argued that in view of these allegations it appears wrong that Parliament should, without legislation, claim the exclusive right to decide the scope of its privileges when this may lead to adverse consequences for citizens. Do you agree? With judges probably unwilling to become involved because of the danger that they will be tainted by party politics, the question remains as to who should be the final arbiter in cases of conflict concerning Parliamentary privilege.

ACTIVITY 41

Consider whether the rules of Parliamentary privilege apply in the following cases.

(a) During an impromptu press conference in her Westminster office Mrs Yoke MP, a Government Health minister, repeats a defamatory remark about the dangers of eating eggs sold by Mr Shell, a well known chicken breeder that she had made earlier in a Commons debate about public health and food poisoning. Mr Shell claims that this has adversely affected his business and now threatens his livelihood. He plans to bring an action for defamation against Mrs Yoke. Advise her.

(b) During Parliamentary question time Mr Ladd, the member for Kidsville, reads out a letter received from one of his constituents, which makes a scurrilous attack on the management of the recently formed Family Support Department. Advise Mr Ladd.

(c) A Commons resolution has just given the House power to fire those who breach rules of Parliamentary privilege.

Now check your answers in *Cases and Materials* (5.4.1).

5.5.4 ALLEGATIONS OF 'SLEAZE'

It has been difficult for anyone living in Britain, in the last few years, not to have noticed the attention which has been paid by the press to allegations of what has come to be known as 'sleaze' in Parliament. The catalyst for this was a report in 1994 that a *Sunday Times* journalist, posing as a businessman, had offered 20 MPs £1,000 to ask a question in Parliament and that two Conservative MPs had not immediately rejected this proposal. This led to considerable public unease and was followed by allegations, in *The Guardian*, that two Ministers (Tim Smith, the junior Minister for Northern Ireland and Neil Hamilton, the Trade and Industry Minister), having accepted money from a wealthy businessman to ask questions in Parliament, had failed to reveal this in the Register of MPs' interests. Tim Smith admitted having taken such money from Mohammed Al Fayed (the owner of Harrod's) and he quickly resigned, but it was Neil Hamilton's stubborn rejection of these and subsequent claims, as well as his decision to bring, and then drop, a libel action against *The Guardian*, which seemed to exacerbate latent doubts in the public's mind that the behaviour of parliamentarians was beyond reproach. The then Prime Minister, John Major, acknowledged that 'this matter is poisoning British politics' and, in an effort to restore public confidence, announced that a wide ranging inquiry would be set up under the chairmanship of the Law Lord, Lord Nolan, to examine the conduct of those holding public office.

The Nolan Committee (which was composed of experienced MPs from different parties, a former Clerk to the House of Commons, a Professor of politics, and those who had experience of public life) was instructed to consider:

(a) the rules that should govern the links between MPs and commercial interests;

(b) whether former Ministers should be allowed to work for companies they had helped privatise; and

(c)   how appointments were made to quangos (quasi-autonomous non-governmental organisations) after allegations had been made that many quango members had only been nominated for political reasons.

The Nolan Committee published its report in May 1995. It identified 'seven principles of public life', which should apply to all areas of public life, and these are: selflessness, integrity, objectivity, accountability, openness, honesty and leadership. Further details of these can be found in the extract from Dawn Oliver's article in *Cases and Materials* (5.4.2).

Whilst the Nolan Committee refused to say that standards in public life had 'declined', it noted that 'conduct in public life is more rigorously scrutinised than it was in the past'. It concluded that 'the principle reason for public disquiet' was the fact that 'people in public life are not always as clear as they should be about where the boundaries of acceptable conduct lie'. Thus, the Committee made a number of recommendations which include:

■   the requirement that ex-Ministers seek clearance for jobs taken in private industry within two years of leaving office;

■   the establishment of a new Public Appointments Commissioner to ensure high standards and fair play in all appointments to quangos;

■   a rule that members must declare all of their earnings derived from services offered as MPs, for 'the financial question which gives rise to most public concern is the paid outside employment of Ministers';

■   more effective investigation of allegations against serving Ministers and greater protection for Whitehall whistle blowers;

■   and finally, the creation of an independent Parliamentary Commissioner for Standards to investigate complaints against MPs.

Perhaps the appointment of a Parliamentary Commissioner for Standards will be seen as being, in time, the most significant of these recommendations. Following the publication of the Nolan Report, a Parliamentary Commissioner for Standards was appointed in 1995 by the House of Commons, with a duty to report to the Select Committee on Standards and Privileges. It is the dependence of the Parliamentary Commissioner for Standards on the Committee on Standards and Privileges which perhaps distinguishes this office from that of the Parliamentary Commissioner for Administration (PCA), which we will consider later in **Chapter 16**.

There are a number of differences between the PCA and the Parliamentary Commissioner for Standards. First, unlike the PCA, who is susceptible to judicial review (*R v PCA, ex parte Dyer* [1994] 1 All ER 375), the Parliamentary Commissioner for Standards is not subject to judicial review. In *R v Parliamentary Commissioner for Standards, ex parte Al Fayed* [1998] 1 All ER 93, Lord Woolf explained that: 'Activities of Government are the basic fare of judicial review . . . [while] . . . [a]ctivities of Parliament . . . are accepted in general . . . to be not subject to judicial review'. Secondly, unlike the PCA who has the power independently to publish his or her reports, the Parliamentary Commissioner for Standards is dependant on the approval of the Select Committee on Standards and Privileges for the publication of his or her reports. This latter difference (as noted earlier) illustrates the fact that the Parliamentary Commissioner for Standards does not have an independent, 'regulatory' function but is, rather, constrained by the 'self-regulatory' factors which govern the management of Parliament.

SAQ 43

Why does Nicholas Bamforth suggest that, in the light of the 'history of Parliamentary privilege,' the Court of Appeal's decision in *R v Parliamentary Commissioner for Standards, ex parte Al Fayed* [1998] 1 All ER 93 is 'unsurprising'? You will find the answer in the extract from Bamforth in *Cases and Materials* (5.4.2).

The duties of the Parliamentary Commissioner for Standards are:

(a)   to maintain the Register of Members' Interests and to advise MPs on matters relating to the registration of their interests;

(b)   to give advice to MPs, and to members of the Select Committee on Standards and Privileges, on the interpretation of the Code of Conduct that was adopted by the House of Commons in July 1996 and which incorporates Nolan's seven principles of public life;

(c)   to monitor the way in which this Code is operated in practice; and

(d)   to investigate complaints which have been received about the conduct of individual Members of Parliament.

The first holder of the office of Parliamentary Commissioner for Standards was Sir Gordon Downey, the former Comptroller and Auditor General, and it was not long before he had an opportunity to investigate the complaint which is usually known as the 'Neil Hamilton affair'.

As noted earlier, Neil Hamilton, a former Minister at the Department of Trade and Industry, had been accused of having accepting cash for asking questions in Parliament on behalf of Mohammed Al Fayed, the owner of Harrod's. Hamilton, who then resigned as a Minister but not as an MP, vehemently denied the allegation that he had failed to comply with the Commons' rules on the registration of financial interests. The House of Commons proceeded to refer this matter to the Select Committee on Members' Interests but, because Hamilton had earlier issued a writ for libel against *The Guardian*, the Members' Interests Committee (which has now been replaced by the Select Committee on Standards and Privileges), chose to postpone their investigation of the complaint against Hamilton until after the completion of his libel action. In September 1996 Neil Hamilton abandoned his libel action, agreeing to pay a contribution to *The Guardian's* costs and, five days later, John Major announced that he would send all of the evidence, in what the press had termed the 'cash for questions' affair, to Sir Gordon Downey (the Parliamentary Commissioner for Standards) who had subsequently re-started his investigation into the allegations against Hamilton.

In July 1997, Sir Gordon's Report was published. It ran to three volumes, contained just under 900 pages, and dealt with complaints which had been made against 25 MPs.

Particularly significant was Sir Gordon's conclusion that there was 'compelling' evidence that Neil Hamilton had accepted money from Mohammed Al Fayed in return for asking questions in the Commons. Geoffrey Robertson QC suggests that the 'real lesson of the Downey Report is that never again should MPs be regarded . . . as above the law' and that as self-regulation of Parliament 'is not enough', the Government should now establish an independent commission (headed by a judge) to investigate complaints of corruption against Ministers, MPs and public servants (*The Guardian*, 4 July 1997).

Please read the extracts from Dawn Oliver's articles, 'Standards of conduct in public life — what standards?' and 'Regulating the conduct of MPs', both in *Cases and Materials* (5.4.2).

What does she mean when she claims (in the latter article) that 'there has been a problem of political corruption in the British Parliament for a number of years'?

Professor Vernon Bogdanor (see *Cases and Materials* (5.4.2)) claims that the Downey Report is 'a constitutional innovation of the first magnitude' and that Parliamentary privilege 'can no longer be trundled out in defence of traditional procedures' (*The Guardian*, 4 July 1997), but the *long*-term effect of the Downey Report remains unclear. Certainly, in the *short* term, the political reaction to the Report of the Parliamentary Commissioner for Standards has been rather mixed. As noted earlier, the Parliamentary Commissioner for Standards works through the Standards and Privileges Committee and, when it considered Sir Gordon Downey's Report in November 1997, it failed to unequivocally endorse it. The Committee failed to reach a verdict on whether Hamilton had ever taken cash for questions and ruled that there was 'no absolute proof that such payments were or were not made', but this conclusion seems to have pleased no one. First, Neil Hamilton was left dissatisfied and he criticised the Committee's decision as a 'complete abdication of responsibility' (*The Daily Telegraph*, 7 November 1997), for it had failed to absolve him of the charges against him. Secondly, many Conservative MPs, such as Ann Widdecombe, who resigned from the Standards and Privileges Committee in protest at its procedures, complained that the Committee had acted contrary to the rules of natural justice (see **Chapter 15**), by deciding not to question all of those who had made allegations against Hamilton, particularly Al Fayed. Thirdly, those who had thought that, in the words of Committee member Dale Campbell-Savours, the 'post-Nolan reforms would herald in a period of unblinkered objectivity' (see *Cases and Materials* (5.4.2)), were disappointed by the fact that the Standards and Privileges Committee, in this case, was split across traditional party lines, with the dissenting voices coming mainly from its Conservative members. Certainly the difficult issues raised by the 'Neil Hamilton affair' were always likely to create serious problems for Parliament's system of self-regulation, but a *Daily Telegraph* editorial (7 November 1997) summed up the views of many when it suggested that 'everyone . . . emerges the loser from this unhappy episode'.

SAQ 44

Is self-regulation of Parliament either possible or even desirable? For some ideas on this you should refer to the views of Professor Vernon Bogdanor, Dale Campbell-Savours MP and Lord Nolan in *Cases and Materials* (5.4.2).

Perhaps the main lesson which has been learnt, 'post-Nolan', is the realisation that even at Westminster, the 'mother of Parliaments', power can also be abused. As the political columnist Peter Riddel remarked: the '"cash for questions" affair knocked away the final argument for the old approach of "MPs are good chaps who can be trusted"' (*The Times*, 4 July 1997). Allegations of 'sleaze' had an inexorably damaging effect on John Major's chances of re-election at the last General Election, and even Tony Blair's new Labour administration, which in opposition had waged war on public 'sleaze,' has found itself tainted by this very charge. In the Autumn of 1997, the Government had to return a £1 million donation to Bernie Ecclestone, the head of Formula One racing, because of public concern that there was a link between the donation and the Government's decision to abandon its opposition to a ban on some tobacco sponsorship and in July 1998 there were claims that former Labour ministerial aides had passed on, improperly, confidential information to lobbying companies.

Press reports suggest that Tony Blair is already committed to setting up what has been called a 'new "sleazebuster" to police the activities of Ministers' (*The Times*, 23 March 1998), and the person who has been thought likely to be given this post is Lord Neill, the successor to Lord Nolan as the Chairman of the Committee on Standards in Public Life. Paradoxically, however, some might think that the comment in the Nolan Report, that 'people in public life are not always as clear as they should be about where the boundaries of acceptable conduct lie', might perhaps even have been applied to Lord Neil for, in June 1998, he aroused controversy by agreeing to act as a legal adviser for the former Conservative Westminster Council leader, Dame Shirley Porter, who had earlier been found guilty by a district auditor of 'disgraceful gerrymandering'. This dual role led to allegations that there was a clear conflict of interest, and Lord Neill subsequently declared that he would no longer represent Dame Shirley Porter. However, this event perhaps illustrates how even an experienced and distinguished public servant can, on occasion, struggle to gauge the public mood as to what is appropriate for a person holding public office.

5.5.5   REFORM

As we have seen, although each House is the sole judge of its privileges, there is a form of dual jurisdiction whereby the courts determine the existence of a privilege. If one exists then the House has sole jurisdiction over it. If not then the Commons and Lords can always create new privileges by enacting a statute (e.g., the Parliamentary Papers Act 1840). However, in recent years, the privileges of Parliament have been subject to criticism. An initial complaint relates to the unsuitability of a 'political' assembly

(Parliament) dealing with 'judicial' matters. For example, in proceedings such as contempt of the House, the Commons will be both prosecutor and judge. As noted earlier, this seems incongruous with the principles of natural justice (see **Chapter 15**).

A second criticism is that the rules of Parliamentary privilege are not codified. The conduct of MPs is governed by a hotchpotch of resolutions, rulings by the Speaker and recommendations from the Committee of Privileges. There is no single document which lists the required standards. As Lord Lester told *The Times* (20 October 1994): 'Parliament assumes that all MPs can be counted upon to apply unwritten principles of honour and good judgment and so it grants them great discretion in resolving ethical dilemmas: without strong monitoring and enforcement procedures, the entire edifice is susceptible to corrosion from within'.

Despite these criticisms, the majority of commentators still believe that Parliament is justified in seeking to protect itself against external interference through the rules of Parliamentary privilege. Provided such privileges are not abused, there is general agreement that these rules are both acceptable and necessary for Parliament to function effectively.

5.6 Parliamentary Controls

Patrick Gordon Walker, a former MP, has written that the 'Cabinet dominates Parliament,' but 'The Cabinet is always conscious of the House of Commons and wary of it.' (For a detailed explanation of this you should refer to *Cases and Materials* (**5.5**).) In holding the Cabinet and the Government to account, Parliament can utilise (a) backbench MPs in the House of Commons, (b) the opposition, (c) Parliamentary Committees, (d) and the House of Lords (see **Chapter 6**).

5.6.1 BACKBENCH MPs IN THE HOUSE OF COMMONS

The role of the government is to govern (not rule)! On the other hand, Parliament is responsible for keeping a check on the executive. In theory backbench MPs should seek to hold the government accountable. In practice it tends to be rather different. Party political loyalties often mean that the most detailed scrutiny of Ministerial actions is undertaken by opposition members of Parliament.

More than two hundred year ago, the English political theorist Thomas Paine, in his seminal work, *The Rights of Man* (1791), complained of Parliament's failure to control government Ministers. Paine observed that: 'The Minister, whoever he at any time be, touches it [Parliament] as with an opium wand, and it sleeps obedience.' Today, notwithstanding the many criticisms which can be levelled at Parliament and, in particular, the House of Commons, it would seem rather harsh to claim that it 'sleeps obedience'. For example, Professor Philip Norton (see *Cases and Materials* (**5.5.1**)) has suggested that, in recent years, MPs have been increasingly willing to challenge the government in power.

Nevertheless, despite these remarks, the present Government would not appear to have much to fear from backbench MPs for at least three reasons. First, as a result of its victory at the General Election in 1997, Tony Blair's Government is in control of 64.4 per cent of the seats in the House of Commons (Labour has 418 seats, the Conservatives 165, Liberal Democrats 46, and the remaining parties 30 seats) so, unless there is a massive 'backbench' rebellion, the Government is unlikely to lose any votes in the Commons. Secondly, the Parliamentary 'whipping' system, whereby party managers 'whip' MPs into supporting the party line on particular issues, tends to obviate the danger of disunity. Thirdly, if the 'stick' metaphorically waved by the whips is not enough to compel obedience, the 'carrot' of promises of promotion or patronage, which is often waved by party managers, often manages to secure the acquiescence of wavering MPs. Thus, as the former Minister, William Waldergrave, wrote of the House of Commons in his book *The Binding of Leviathan* (1978): 'the majority, once obtained, can be whipped into line on virtually any measure . . . by its Prime Ministerial ring-master who holds the whip of a dissolution over it, and dangles fat bunches of patronage carrots under its nose.'

Of course, it must be remembered that there are always independently minded MPs who steadfastly refuse to adopt the party line on certain matters. Every party has, what government Ministers might term as, 'the awkward squad', who are not afraid to criticise the government in public or defy the party whips. However, with 'New Labour' proud of its party discipline and the Government enjoying a comfortable Commons majority, it is almost inconceivable that Tony Blair will have to do deals with any parties to stay in power, in the way that John Major, aware of his fragile Commons majority, was forced to negotiate with the Ulster Unionists in the last days of his Government.

The Home Secretary, Jack Straw, has said that the Government is unlikely to change the present 'first past the post' electoral system before the next General Election (*The Guardian*, 10 March 1998). If MPs were elected on the basis of proportional representation, rather than the present 'first past the post' method, might the House of Commons become more effective in holding the Government to account? For an analysis of the problems and implications of introducing proportional representation, read David Butler's article 'Electoral Reform' in *Cases and Materials* (5.5.1).

5.6.2 THE OPPOSITION

Her Majesty's Opposition is the party with the second largest number of MPs in the House. The importance of the Opposition was recognised by the Ministers of the Crown Act 1937, which authorised the payment of an official salary from public funds to the leader of the opposition. This Act was subsequently consolidated into the Ministerial and Other Salaries Act 1975 (see *Cases and Materials* (5.4)) while the Ministerial and Other Salaries Act 1997 links Parliamentary salaries to those of civil servants. The Opposition leader is therefore paid out of the Consolidated Fund, a common account into which taxes are paid. The role of the Opposition is to provide an alternative government and to challenge and 'oppose' through question and debate. The 'Shadow Cabinet', which includes the leading members of the Opposition, will decide what tactics should be adopted in response to government policies. Each session, 17 days are set aside for the official Opposition and a further three for the second largest Opposition grouping. This provides the Opposition parties with the opportunity to select the subjects for debate on those days. The Prime Minister may consult the leader of the Opposition on major issues, especially defence and foreign affairs, in times of war or public emergency.

It has been said that a government is only as good as its opposition. What does this mean? (On the constitutional duties of the Opposition, see the extract from Brazier in *Cases and Materials* (5.5.2).)

Two obvious ways in which back-bench MPs and the Opposition may hold a government to account are through Parliamentary questions and debates in Parliament.

5.6.2.1 Parliamentary questions

Since the 17th century it has been common practice to question Ministers in Parliament. On Mondays through to Thursdays until 3.30 pm, Ministers may be asked to give oral answers to questions tabled two days in advance. Ministers take questions on a rota basis after consultation with the opposition. The Speaker can authorise private notice questions, if the subject matter is judged urgent and important. These are taken at the end of question time. In the past, the Prime Minister answered questions on Tuesdays and Thursdays, but this has now changed to a single, although longer, session for questions on a Wednesday afternoon. No member may ask more than two questions a day or eight over a period of ten days. Questions may also be tabled for written answers – there is no limit on the number of these and they are normally answered within seven days.

Theoretically, question time is an opportunity for MPs to call Ministers to account and explain actions taken by their departments. In practice this device of providing for Parliamentary control of the executive is limited. Ministers are usually well briefed and answers to questions tabled are comprehensively researched. The author of the question is identified and so answers can be tailored to accommodate the interests of that member.

The use of party 'whips,' who seek to ensure that backbench MPs support the party in power, means that the most difficult questions usually are asked by Opposition Members of Parliament. Notwithstanding the frequent unwillingness of some left-wing and independently minded MPs to toe the party line, Tony Blair's Ministers have, so far, tended to be challenged most often in the Chamber by MPs of other parties. Indeed, in March 1998, the degree of co-operation between some Ministers and backbench Labour MPs was revealed when a question, which press reports suggested was to have been 'planted' by a Junior Minister on a Labour member in the Commons Chamber, was mistakenly faxed to a Conservative MP, who gleefully used this miscommunication to embarrass the Government. Such events are (publicly at least) extremely rare and it must be remembered that Question Time sometimes manages to uncover errors and flaws within the administration. However, perhaps the most serious flaw with Parliamentary questions is the fact that Ministers can refuse to answer questions in a wide range of areas and, in the absence of a statutory or common law power to compel disclosure, there is very little which the person who is asking the question can do about it. For example, a Minister may refuse to provide information on the ground that the issue is outside the Minister's individual responsibilities, or is *sub judice* (e.g. an answer might prejudice the course of justice), or may affect national security. According to a survey carried out in the first three months of 1994 for Channel 4's *Dispatches*, Ministers refused to answer 72 written questions on the grounds of 'commercial confidentiality', 649 written questions for the reason that they were not responsible for the matter raised, 1,226 because it was not in their files and 392 on the ground of cost. These figures suggest that 15 per cent of all the written questions recorded in this period were 'blocked'. More recently, in 1997, Ministers refused to answer 145 Parliamentary questions on a number of matters ranging from access to documents relating to the BSE crisis, the siting of US nuclear weapons and that perennial issue of controversy, the State's tapping of telephones.

For an illustration of the tactics sometimes adopted by Ministers in responding to questions in Parliament, turn to the examples provided by Hillyard and Percy-Smith in *Cases and Materials* (5.5.2).

Philip Norton writes that 'A debate prevents a Government from remaining mute'. (See extract in *Cases and Materials* (5.5.2).) What is meant by this statement?

And according to Griffith and Ryle, what 'significant developments' have they observed from Prime Minister's question time in recent years? (The answer can be found in *Cases and Materials* (5.5.2).)

5.6.2.2 Debates

In addition to debates during the legislative process, there are other opportunities for debate. Half an hour is made available at the end of every sitting day for a back bench MP to raise a topic for debate — this is known as the daily adjournment debate. Advance notice must be given and the Minister is called upon to reply, perhaps where the back-bencher was not satisfied with a response given during question time. MPs may also call for an Emergency Adjournment debate in exceptional circumstances. Standing Order No. 20 permits an emergency debate to be held if the Speaker is satisfied that the issue is one of major importance and urgency; (e.g. the controversial decision of Michael Hesaltine, the former President of the Board of Trade, to close coal mines during the Parliamentary session 1992–93). In addition 20 days are set aside in each session for debating subjects chosen by the opposition parties, while Private Members' motions are allocated 10 Fridays and four other half days for debate.

However, time in Parliament is valuable. Important Bills often eat into the Parliamentary schedule, leaving few opportunities for proper debate. Many hours may be wasted by Parliamentarians adopting delaying tactics. Therefore, in order to save time, Parliamentary debate can be curtailed by the Speaker on the following occasions:

(a) repetitive or irrelevant speeches;

(b) where 100 members vote for a closure motion;

(c) where the Speaker selects those clauses to be discussed ('the kangaroo');

(d) and on 'guillotine motions', when a fixed date is set by which one or more stages of a Bill must be completed. Thus, often quite complex and controversial clauses or amendments must be discussed in only a few hours. When the time limit has expired the 'guillotine' terminates all debate.

The use of the 'guillotine' has significantly increased in recent years. In the 1950s the guillotine was used 8 times; in the 1960s, 13 times; in the 1970s, 29 times; in the 1980s, 51 times; between 1990 and 1994, 26 times and just once between 1995 and 1996. Resorting to the guillotine can prevent valuable critical discussion of legislation and it may mean that legislative amendments are rushed through Parliament without detailed examination.

The use of the guillotine has been likened to 'a dangerous weapon in the hands of the government'.

Explain this statement.

5.6.3 PARLIAMENTARY COMMITTEES

Because it is impossible for the House of Commons to scrutinise all detailed aspects of public administration, a number of specialist committees have been set up. These are Parliamentary Select Committees and Standing Committees.

Select Committees

Following the report of the Select Committee on Procedure (House of Commons Sessional Papers 1977–78), the present Departmental Select Committees were introduced in 1979. Formerly there had been no comprehensive system of select committees and they were established with the aim of strengthening Parliament's control over the executive in terms of its expenditure and policy generally. Apart from the 17 Select Committees each have 11 members selected by a special committee – the House's all-party Committee of Selection. As cross-bench Committees, they tend not to be under the control of any single political party, although party loyalties sometimes create disunity within Select Committees. Parliamentary Select Committees have the power to call individuals to give evidence, such as Ministers and Civil Servants. Since 1989 Select Committee hearings have been televised and Peter Hennessy (see *Cases and Materials* (5.5.3)) says that they are 'a sensitive membrane between the legislature and the executive, capable of transmitting swiftly and efficiently the knowledge, views and insights of each to the other'. There is no doubt that they have been quite successful, although it must be acknowledged that there are limitations to what they can achieve. For example, Select Committees have no legislative or executive powers. Thus, they can only investigate, recommend or report, so their proposals are not legally binding. Publicity is their main weapon, although Select Committee Reports are themselves rarely debated in Parliament. And although Select Committees can demand the attendance of witnesses, these witnesses may resort to silence (e.g. Ian and Kevin Maxwell before the Social Security Committee in 1992 when quizzed about missing pension assets) or refuse to directly answer questions and 'stonewall' (such as former Junior Minister Edwina Currie over the salmonella in eggs controversy in 1988).

Despite these shortcomings, Gavin Drewry (see *Cases and Materials* (5.5.3)) asserts that select committees are now 'an integral and . . . a cherished feature of the parliamentary scene'. Similarly, Lord Nolan, in *The Making and Remaking of the British Constitution* (1997), suggests that the Commons 'now carries out a more direct and less politically charged scrutiny of the detailed work of the executive than ever before', and that even if much of the work of Select Committees is not reported in public, there is no doubt that Government departments are 'significantly influenced by Select Committees'.

What are the strengths and weaknesses of the present system of Select Committees? For an excellent analysis of these turn to the extract from Peter Hennessy's book, *The Hidden Wiring*, in *Cases and Materials* (5.5.3). What are the seven proposals Hennessy suggests would be a 'sensible and achievable agenda for the next state of [their] reform'?

How effective are select committees in controlling the government? Read the extracts from Gavin Drewry and from Harden and Lewis in *Cases and Materials* (5.5.3) for some ideas.

Standing Committees

Standing committees are set up to debate the committee stage of a particular Bill. They operate in a similar way to the full debating chamber of the Commons and are a miniature representation of it. There is no set number of members and the committee may consist of between 16 and 50 members, reflecting party strength in the House. The committees scrutinise individual clauses of Bills and members may propose further amendments. The chairperson decides which amendments are to be discussed. Civil servants can be called to give evidence and the Parliamentary draftsmen may also be present. A Bill can be referred to a committee of the whole House if it is deemed necessary because of its political significance. Standing committees are mainly used to scrutinise statutory instruments, European law and regional issues.

Read the extracts from Kavanagh and Downs in *Cases and Materials* (5.5.3). How do they distinguish between select committees and standing committees?

5.7 Elective Dictatorship

'The liberal model of the Constitution is a statement of how Parliament controls the executive in the sense of holding it accountable' (Professor Dennis Kavanagh). How successful is Parliament in this respect?

Lord Hailsham coined the phrase 'elective dictatorship' to describe a government with a substantial Commons majority. He also added 'I have never suggested that freedom is dead in Britain. But it has diminished, and a principal cause of its impairment has been, in truth, the absolute legislative power confided in Parliament, concentrated in the hands of a government armed with a Parliamentary majority, briefed and served by the professionals of the Civil Service, and given a more than equal share of self-perpetuation by the adroit use of the power of dissolution.' Read the extracts from *The Dilemma of Democracy* and *A Sparrow's Flight* (*Cases and Materials* (5.4)) to understand fully what Lord Hailsham meant by this statement.

Proposals for legislation originate from within government and provided there is a significant majority in the Commons, government Bills usually end up as Acts of Parliament. No majority government has been voted out of office or forced to the polls since 1895. Backbench MPs of the ruling party know that if they are too rebellious, they could jeopardise the government's standing and could lose their seats if an election was forced. The government therefore has an influence in the Commons which in Rodney Brazier's words, 'may be likened to the possession of almost dictatorial powers, albeit powers that are restrained by general elections, [and] by notions of what is generally acceptable in a liberal democracy'.

As a former Lord Chancellor and experienced politician the views of Lord Hailsham on constitutional matters cannot be ignored. Lord Hailsham's term 'elective dictatorship' means that, while the government of the day is elected by the people, a government in office with a significant majority is in a very strong position. It can virtually enact any law it wishes, because of the lack of restraint upon its power.

Goverments with a slim majority are in a much weaker position. Defeat in the Commons may lead to a vote of no confidence which could precipitate their downfall. Minority governments are also more open to defeat during the committee stage of legislation, since standing committees reflect party strength in the Commons.

The Cabinet is the 'power base' where decisions are taken and from whence legislative proposals originate. Bills still have to go through a three-stage process but, as we shall see in **Chapter 6**, the House of Lords is ultimately powerless to stop a Bill becoming law. By convention, the Monarch does not refuse to grant Royal Assent, so the Sovereign is unable to provide much resistance to a determined government wishing to implement its policies through legislation.

5.8 Conclusion

The United Kingdom is often described as a 'Parliamentary democracy'. But what does this phrase mean? The word 'democracy' is defined in the Oxford English Dictionary as 'government by all the people'. Yet to what extent do British citizens enjoy any *real* influence? Obviously the right to vote and the fact that the electorate may decide not to support the party in government at the next election is a power of sorts. However, since the next election may be anything up to five years away, this is not likely to constitute much of a threat to a strong government. And what of referendums? A referendum on Britain's membership of the European Communities was held in 1975 (because of splits within the Labour government Cabinet), while referendums were held in Scotland and Wales in 1979 and in 1997 on the establishment of regional assemblies. It has been claimed that referendums provide 'an extra check against government, [and] an additional protection to that given by Parliament'. (Bogdanor, *The People and the Party System*, p. 69).

Despite the recent referendums in Scotland, Wales and Northern Ireland, as well as Tony Blair's acknowledgement of the possibility in the future of a referendum on Britain signing up for a single European currency, referendums are still rather exceptional in the United Kingdom. As Bradley observes: 'Parliament's importance within British government depends much less upon absolute legislative power, than upon its effectiveness as a political forum in expressing public opinion and in exercising control over government'. You may decide for yourself the extent to which Parliament is successful in this task.

CHAPTER SIX

PARLIAMENT AND THE LAW-MAKING PROCESS – II THE HOUSE OF LORDS

6.1 Objectives

At the end of this Chapter you should be able to:

■ describe the role of the House of Lords;

■ appreciate the relationship between the House of Commons and the House of Lords;

■ explain the present composition of the House of Lords;

■ evaluate the effectiveness of the Lords as a check on the Commons;

■ weigh up the different arguments for reforming the House of Lords.

6.2 Introduction

Having analysed the composition and role of the elected body, the House of Commons, it is now time to turn our attention to the House of Lords. The House has been no stranger to criticism of late with frequent calls made for its reform. Most recently, the Labour Government has announed its intention of removing the voting rights of hereditary peers in the House of Lords. In this Chapter we will examine why the House of Lords is so controversial and consider whether such criticism is justified. We will also look at some of the suggestions for reform.

6.3 Role and Composition of the House of Lords

The House of Lords is one of the oldest legislative bodies in the world. It can be traced back to the *Curia Regis* (King's Court) of the 12th and 13th centuries. The *Curia Regis* later became the King's Council and was composed of the King's tenants-in-chief and barons, as well as the Lords spiritual (archbishops, bishops and abbots) and temporal (earls). If a baron regularly received a summons to attend, a practice evolved that the summons would be issued to his heir. The result was the development of the House of Lords, a body of peers who attended by virtue of their hereditary authority, presided over by the Lord Chancellor. Today, the Lord Chancellor still sits in the House of Lords (as Speaker) while hereditary peers are the largest single group in the Chamber which, with over 1,000 members, is possibly one of the largest legislative assemblies in the world.

The House of Lords consists of four main groups:

(a) **Hereditary peers**

Approximately two thirds of the members are hereditary peers, making it one of the few legislative chambers in the democratic world where membership can be determined by the accident of birth. In March 1998 the Conservative Party had 322 hereditary peers, Labour 17 and the Liberal Democrats 24, while the remaining 200 hereditary peers sit on the cross benches and are not affiliated to a single political party.

(b) **Life peers**

These are men and women who, because of their service to the community, have been awarded titles under the Life Peerages Act 1958. There is no limit to the number of peerages (life or hereditary) which the Queen can create on the advice of the Prime Minister.

(c) **Lords of Appeal in ordinary**

They are the Law Lords, who perform the judicial work of the House of Lords, sitting as the UK's final Appeal Court.

(d) **Lords spiritual**

These are the 26 most senior bishops of the Church of England. Other faiths, (e.g., Catholicism, Islam, Judaism, Buddhism etc.), have no *ex officio* spiritual representatives in the Lords.

SAQ 52

In the Spring of 1998 the Lord Chancellor, Lord Irvine, expressed reservations about the presence of Church of England bishops in the House of Lords. Is is proper that in multi-faith Britain, the only spiritual representatives in the House of Lords should be members of the Anglican faith? Do you agree with the comment of Sir Brian Mawhinney, the former Chairman of the Conservative Party, that it is 'no bad thing for our constitution that the elected Commons has a counterpoint and conscience which does not derive from the same elective process'? (*The Daily Telegraph*, 8 February 1996.)

6.3.1 FUNCTIONS OF THE HOUSE OF LORDS

Many of the functions of the House of Lords resemble those of the House of Commons. However, as we shall soon see, a fundamental difference is that the House of Lords is no longer on a par with the Commons.

In the absence of a written Constitution, the functions of the House of Lords are not officially recorded in any document or statute. However, in 1968, a White Paper on the reform of the House of Lords (Cmnd 3799) was published which listed some of the Upper Chamber's areas of jurisdiction. The White Paper (which was subsequently withdrawn in 1969) suggested that it had six functions. These were that the House of Lords was to:

(a) provide a forum for debate on matters of public interest;

(b) revise public Bills passed by the Commons;

(c) initiate less controversial public Bills;

(d) consider subordinate legislation;

(e) scrutinise the activities of the executive;

(f) consider private legislation.

Over the past 25 years, the House of Lords has been increasingly influential through its Select Committees. A good example is the European Communities Committee, which was set up in 1974 and scrutinises EC legislation.

Read the extract from Bogdanor on the House of Lords Select Committees in *Cases and Materials* (6.1.1). It is important to remember that Lords Select Committees (e.g. the European Communities Committee, the Science and Technology Committee and various ad hoc committees) receive little publicity, but play a significant role in challenging government policies.

6.3.2 ANACHRONISTIC AND ARCHAIC?

Professor Ganz notes that, the 'paradox of the House of Lords is that, as an anachronistic and unelected body, its constitutional justification is to act as a check on the elected House'. The House of Lords is presently composed of approximately 1,200 peers. Of the 'Lords temporal', just under 800 are hereditary peers and nearly 400 are life peers. The Life Peerages Act 1958 allows the Prime Minister to award life peerages to noteworthy individuals who have contributed to public life. Well known appointments include those of Brian Rix (actor and campaigner for MENCAP), P. D. James (author), Sir Richard Attenborough and David Putman (film makers) Helena Kennedy (barrister) and Melvyn Bragg (broadcaster). Frequently retired politicians (such as Lord Tebbit, Lord Jenkins of Hillhead, and Baroness Thatcher) are also honoured with life peerages.

The Peerage Act 1963 (see *Cases and Materials* (6.1)) for both this Act and the Life Peerages Act 1958) enables hereditary peers to renounce their titles. Thus, there is a procedure by which hereditary peers with serious political aspirations can seek election to the House of Commons. The 1963 legislation was initiated by Tony Benn who, on inheriting his father's title (Viscount Stansgate), did not want to be stuck in the House of Lords. Section 3 of the Peerage Act 1963 stipulates that such disclaimers are irrevocable and are binding on a spouse but not on heirs. Sixteen peers have now disclaimed their hereditary titles including Lord James Douglas-Hamilton (Minister for the Scottish Office) who on 28 November 1994 disclaimed the title of the Earl of Selkirk. This enabled him to vote with the Government on the European Communities Finance Bill, a particularly important vote as the former Prime Minister, John Major, had declared that it was to be treated as a vote of confidence in his Government. It is possible that an MP, who has just inherited a peerage, may suddenly become ineligible to belong to the House of Commons because of his or her right to sit in the Lords, so Donald Shell [1995] *Public Law* 551, has suggested that the Peerage Act 1963 should be changed, in order to allow those MPs who inherit titles to continue as full members of the Commons up until they decide either to renounce their peerage or to resign from the House.

As well as hereditary peers, membership includes 26 'Lords Spiritual' (2 archbishops and 24 senior bishops), and 12 'Law Lords' created under the 1876 Appellate Jurisdiction Act. While full members of the upper chamber, the Law Lords normally (by convention) avoid participating in the most politically controversial business of the House. Law Lords retain their membership of the House for life so, at present, the number of Law Lords sitting (including retired Law Lords), is 22. However, in recent years, the Law Lords have increasingly participated in the area of law reform and the Lord Chief Justice, Lord Bingham has, for example, often been prepared to make known his views on legal matters ranging from constitutional reform (see *Cases and Materials* (1.4)) to the treatment of sex offenders (*The Guardian*, 19 March 1998). Similarly, the bishops, who traditionally were disinclined to speak on party political matters, have increasingly participated in controversial debates on immigration, asylum, capital punishment and welfare matters.

Finally, note that aliens, bankrupts and persons under 21 may not become peers. However, s. 6 of the Peerage Act 1963 allows a peeress to take a seat in her own right and s. 1(3) of the Life Peerages Act 1958 allows a life peerage to be granted to a woman. Nevertheless the membership of the House of Lords (like that of the House of Commons) is still overwhelmingly male. As Fay Weldon suggests, 'it is the maleness of the institution which makes the place seem so out of date and ripe for reform' (*The Times*, 16 March 1998).

ACTIVITY 47

When the Bill introducing the Community Charge (Poll Tax) was passed by the House of Lords in 1988, life peers opposed it by 125 votes to 97, but hereditary peers voted 250 to 54 in favour. Should peers have the power to reject financial bills? Read the extract by Brazier on the financial powers of the House of Lords in *Cases and Materials* (6.1.2).

'The idea of hereditary legislators is as inconsistent as that of hereditary judges or hereditary juries' (Thomas Paine, *The Rights of Man*, 1791). On balance, do you think that the House of Lords, as presently composed, is capable of making a valuable contribution to the UK's system of Parliamentary democracy? Give reasons for your answer.

6.4   The Relationship between the Lords and the Commons

Generally it has been assumed and recognised by convention that, in Parliament, the will of the elected House (the Commons) should prevail. (For example, see the statement by Lord Carrington in *Cases and Materials* (6.2).) Prior to 1911 the only means of persuading the Lords to give way was for the Prime Minister to threaten to ask the Sovereign to create enough new peers to enable the Government's Bill to pass through the Lords. For example, in 1832, under such a threat, the Lords abandoned their opposition to the Parliament Reform Bill. However, today, the rules governing the relationship between both Houses are mainly governed by the Parliament Acts 1911 and 1949.

6.4.1   THE PARLIAMENT ACTS

6.4.1.1   The Parliament Act 1911

The Liberal Government, in the early 20th century, faced a number of problems because of the Conservative Party's majority in the House of Lords. In 1909, the Liberal government hoped to initiate a programme of legislation, central to which was a Finance Bill. Its financial proposals were passed by the Commons, but rejected in the Lords, contrary to the convention that the Lords should not oppose a money Bill referred to them by the Commons. A political storm ensued and the Finance Bill was reintroduced. The Prime Minister warned that, unless the Bill was passed by the Lords, he would arrange for the King to create over 400 new Liberal peers to ensure a Liberal majority in the Lords. The Conservative dominated Lords succumbed to this threat and the Finance Bill was passed in 1910. The Liberal government was now concerned that the House of Lords might in the future impede the power of the Commons, by putting obstacles in its way. Therefore, a Bill to curtail the powers of the House of Lords itself was introduced. It was once more made known that King George V was prepared to create over 400 new Liberal peers to ensure a Liberal majority in the Lords. The Lords again compromised and the Parliament Act 1911 was passed. The Parliament Act 1911 did not alter the composition of the Lords but s. 2(1) made three important changes:

(a)   The life of a Parliament was reduced from seven to five years.

(b)   The House of Lords lost its power to veto Money Bills and could not delay them
      for more than one month. (A Money Bill is defined in the Act as a Public Bill
      which 'contains only provisions dealing with the imposition, repeal, remission,
      alteration or regulation of taxation . . . or subordinate matters'.)

(c)   The Lords' power to veto public Bills was abolished and was replaced by a
      delaying power for a maximum of two years, except for any Bill attempting to
      prolong the life of Parliament beyond five years.

Thus, the power of the Lords to frustrate the wishes of the Commons was significantly
diminished, and the Parliament Act 1911 allowed the Welsh Church Act 1914 and the
Government of Ireland Act 1914 to become law.

6.4.1.2   The Parliament Act 1949

A further clash between the Commons and the Lords occurred in 1945 when the Labour
government wished to nationalise the coal and steel industries. Opposition to this came
from the Conservative controlled House of Lords. The Lords suggested a number of
amendments and it was widely believed they would reject the government's Iron and
Steel Bill. Accordingly another Parliament Bill was introduced, designed to reduce the
delaying power of the Lords from two years (as per the Parliament Act 1911) to one year.
The House of Lords predictably rejected the Bill at the second reading but it was
eventually passed by the Commons, after much bitter controversy, under the very
provisions of the Parliament Act 1911 itself.

SAQ 54

What does de Smith mean when he says the Parliament Acts have redefined Parliament?

6.4.2   THE PRESENT POSITION

The effect of the Parliament Acts 1911 and 1949 has been that:

(a)   The maximum life of Parliament has been reduced from seven to five years.

(b)   The House of Lords has only the power to delay legislation. Any public Bill (other
      than a money Bill or one purporting to extend the life of Parliament beyond five
      years), which has been passed by the Commons in two successive sessions but
      rejected by the Lords, may, following the second rejection, be presented to the
      Sovereign for the Royal Assent. It may then become an Act of Parliament **without**
      the consent of the Lords. One year must elapse between the date of the second
      reading in the first session in the Commons and the date of its passing the
      Commons in the second session. When such a Bill is presented to the Sovereign
      for the Royal Assent it must include a certificate signed by the Speaker to the

effect that the provisions of the Parliament Acts have been complied with. This certificate is deemed conclusive for all purposes and shall not be questioned in any court of law.

(c) The House of Lords can delay a 'Money Bill' for up to one month, as long as the Bill is sent to it at least one month before the end of a session. As noted earlier, a 'Money Bill' is a public Bill concerning matters relating to finance (e.g. central government taxation). When presented to the Sovereign for the Royal Assent, a Money Bill must include a certificate signed by the Speaker that it is such a Bill (Parliament Act 1911, s. 3).

The Parliament Acts do not apply to:

(a) local and private legislation,

(b) delegated legislation,

(c) public Bills which confirm provisional orders (these are orders made by a Minister at the request of a local authority under power conferred by an enabling Act), and

(d) Bills to prolong the life of Parliament. Thus the House of Lords has the power to prevent a government from avoiding elections by extending its term beyond five years.

Explain how the Commons can ensure a Bill is enacted when the House of Lords fails to give its approval.

Look up s. 4 of the Parliament Act 1911 in *Cases and Materials* (6.2.1). This section prescribes the enacting words to be used whenever a Bill is presented to the Sovereign under the Parliament Act procedures.

6.4.3 IMPACT OF THE PARLIAMENT ACT PROCEDURES

The 1911 Parliament Act procedure has been used in relation to four Bills which have been subsequently enacted 'over the heads of the Lords'.

The four Acts passed under this provision are:

(a) **The Welsh Church Act 1914**

This Act disestablished the Church in Wales.

(b) **The Government of Ireland Act 1914**

This Act would have permitted home rule in Ireland, but because of the outbreak of the First World War it was never brought into effect and was subsequently replaced by the Government of Ireland Act 1920.

(c) **The Parliament Act 1949**

It reduced the delaying period of the Lords still further. Hood Philips has suggested that the Parliament Act 1949 may not be a valid statute. He takes this view because the Parliament Act 1911 procedure was never intended to be used to amend the 1911 Act itself. It has been argued that, in enacting the 1949 Act, the Queen in Parliament unlawfully delegated its law-making powers to the Queen in Commons. Thus Marshall and Wade claim that any Acts passed by using the Parliament Acts are a form of 'delegated legislation'. De Smith suggests that the Parliament Acts may have redefined Parliament, since laws can be enacted by the 'Queen in Commons' as opposed to the 'Queen in Parliament'.

(d) **The War Crimes Act 1991**

The provisions of the Act allow alleged war criminals to be prosecuted. It applies retrospectively to crimes committed during the Second World War. However, the War Crimes Bill was rejected by 207 votes to 74 in the Lords. Opposition in the House of Lords focused on the difficulties of bringing successful prosecutions, and reservations were expressed that the Bill would create retrospective legislation. Such concerns were not shared by the Commons, which had earlier passed the Bill, on a free vote (273 to 60). When the War Crimes Bill was rejected for a second time by the Lords, the Parliament Act procedures were invoked. Accordingly the Bill became law. Interestingly, the opposition Labour Party backed the government on the principle that the will of the Commons must prevail. The War Crimes Act 1991 is the only time that the Parliament Act procedures have been invoked against a Conservative government. It was also the first time that the House of Lords completely rejected a government measure which had received a second and third reading in the Commons, having attracted overwhelming cross-party support. This raises the question of whether the Lords *should* reject such Bills.

SAQ 56

Ganz says that the passage of the War Crimes Act 1991 has 'highlighted the lack of authority of the House of Lords'. What does she mean by this? For some ideas, turn to her comments on this issue in *Cases and Materials* (6.2.2).

6.4.4 DEFYING THE GOVERNMENT

While the House of Lords has no power to veto Bills presented by the Commons, the Lords can cause the government severe embarrassment by amending government proposals. The first Thatcher administration, (1979–83) was defeated 45 times, but this must be compared to the previous Labour government (1974–9) which suffered 355 defeats in the Lords! A table listing Government defeats in the House of Lords, before Tony Blair came into office, can be found in *Cases and Materials* (**6.2.3**).

In the period from 1 May 1997 to 3 July 1998 (the time of writing), Tony Blair's Government has been defeated 26 times in the House of Lords; ironically this is the number of times that Edward Heath's Conservative administration, in the early 1970s, was defeated during its whole time in office. Notwithstanding the fact that Tony Blair recently increased the number of Labour life peers in the House of Lords, the number of Conservatives in the Lords (495) still massively outweighs those peers who are affiliated to the Labour Party (158) and this imbalance, combined with Labour's proposals to reform the House of Lords, suggests that the present Government is likely to encounter further opposition to a number of its policies.

Look up the Parliament Act 1911 in *Cases and Materials* (**6.2.1**). What is the constitutional safeguard that can be found in s. 2(1)?

6.5 Reform of the House of Lords

Do you agree with the proposition that 'The House of Lords is an ineffectual body which should be abolished or reformed'. If you are struggling for ideas, turn to the extracts from Griffith and Ryle, and from Shell, in *Cases and Materials* (**6.3**).

The question of reform of the House of Lords has been a recurring theme over the years and various proposals and suggestions have been put forward. The preamble to the Parliament Act 1911 (see *Cases and Materials* (**6.2.1**)) stated that it was intended eventually to substitute the existing House of Lords with a second chamber. This would be 'constituted on a popular instead of hereditary basis'. In 1917 a conference under Lord Bryce proposed a House of Lords with:

(a) three quarters of the members elected indirectly by members of the House of Commons on a regional basis, and

(b) one quarter chosen by a joint standing committee of both Houses with prescribed proportions of hereditary peers and bishops.

In 1948 an inter-party conference considered the Parliament Bill and agreed that reform on composition could include:

(a) A second chamber complementary to and not rivalling the lower House, based on a modification of its existing constitution, as opposed to the establishment of a second chamber of a completely new type based on some system of election.

(b) The revised constitution should ensure, as far as possible, that none of the political parties could secure a permanent majority in the second chamber.

(c) The present right to attend and vote in a second chamber based solely on hereditary rights should not by itself be a qualification for admission to a reformed second chamber.

A government White Paper (Cmnd 3799) was issued in November 1968. It followed on from an all-party conference, which had discussed the composition and functions of the House of Lords. This consultative document noted that the present composition of the House of Lords prevented it from effectively performing its complementary role to the Commons. The White Paper recommended that:

(a) The hereditary membership of the Lords should be abolished and that members should be appointed.

(b) The voting rights of members should be dependent on them attending 30 per cent of sittings.

(c) The Lords' power to delay public legislation should be reduced to six months.

(d) The Lords' power to withhold consent to subordinate legislation contrary to the wishes of the Commons should be removed.

These proposals were subsequently introduced by the Labour Government, in the Parliament (No. 2) Bill 1969. However, they were later withdrawn amidst fears that this new legislation would create serious constitutional problems.

What serious constitutional problems might be created by reforming the House of Lords? Do you agree that proposals to remove hereditary peers from the Lords could have repercussions for the Royal Family and ultimately 'pose a threat to our entire constitutional settlement' (Sir Brian Mawhinney)?

'The principal argument for a second chamber in a unitary State is that it is needed to provide a constitutional check on legislation that is oppressive or is damaging to the public interest or to minorities in the community' (Turpin). What are the characteristics of a model second chamber?

In theory a model second chamber should:

(a) have a fixed term of life;

(b) operate as a check on the more powerful House;

(c) provide an opportunity to reconsider proposed legislation; and

(d) be representative of public opinion.

The House of Lords struggles to satisfy these criteria. On the contrary, at least three serious criticisms can be levelled at it. It is (a) socially unrepresentative; (b) has an innate Conservative bias; and (c) is poorly attended.

(a) **Socially unrepresentative?**

As noted earlier, most members are there because of past political service, legal office, ecclesiastical title or the accident of birth. However, critics of the Labour Government have warned of the danger of the Government packing a reformed House of Lords with its supporters and the Conservative Deputy Chairman, Michael Ancram, has claimed that the new life peers recently appointed by Tony Blair all 'have one thing in common . . . they are Tony's cronies' (*The Guardian*, 20 June 1998).

(b) **A Conservative bias?**

Tony Blair has, in the past, claimed that most peers are 'just Tory voting fodder'. Certainly Labour peers constitute a very small proportion of the total membership of the Lords chamber. At the start of 1998 there were 495 Tory peers, 325 cross bench independents, 158 Labour peers, 68 Liberal Democrats as well as Law Lords and bishops. The poor attendance of many peers means that it is important to be aware of the political affiliations of the regular attenders. According to Dick Leonard in the 1988–89 session, 48.2% of regular attenders were Conservative, 13% were Labour, 9% Liberal or Social Democrat and 24.6% were cross bench peers.

If one breaks down these figures, one finds that in 1988–89, 278 attending hereditary peers were affiliated to the Conservatives compared to only 11 hereditary Labour peers. Among the life peers there were 102 Conservatives, 95 Labour supporters, 39 Liberal Democrats (including the SDP) and 74 cross benchers. And what of this last group? Significantly, research by Andrew Adonis ((1988) 41 *Parliamentary Affairs* 382) suggests that cross bench peers tend 'over-whelmingly' to support the Conservatives.

(c) Poor attendance

It is indisputable that many peers fail to attend frequently. Particularly culpable are the hereditary peers. In 1988–89, 43.9% of hereditary life peers were not present at any session of the House, while only 11.3% of life peers failed to attend a session. For this period, the average daily attendance was 316 (out of a membership of over one thousand). Nevertheless, the Government was able to encourage a turn out of more than 500 peers when the Local Government Finance Bill (Poll Tax) passed through the Lords in 1988. Arguably, this has, more than anything else, inspired the Labour Party to reform the House of Lords. Ironically, however, allegations of poor attendance have been made more recently against a number of the 41 Labour life peers appointed by Tony Blair to the House of Lords in the Summer of 1997 and, in an analysis of the voting records of the new Labour peers, *The Times* has claimed that one quarter of these recently appointed peers have voted less than half of the times they could have (*The Times*, 20 April 1998). With membership of the House of Lords not offering any payment (although peers are eligible for a daily subsistence allowance and for accommodation expenses if they normally live outside London), perhaps some of the new peers have been too busy with their full-time jobs to attend more regularly.

How should the House of Lords be reformed both in terms of its composition and function? A number of proposals are put forward by Leonard in *Cases and Materials* (6.3).

How could abolition of the House of Lords be achieved legally? For some ideas, turn to *Cases and Materials* (6.3) and compare Peter Mirfield's article with that of George Winterton. What is the main thrust of their arguments?

In their election manifesto, prior to their victory at the polls in May 1997, the Labour Party promised that 'the right of hereditary peers to sit and vote in the House of Lords will be ended by statute'. Following this, there has been increasing recognition that reform of the House of Lords is not merely inevitable, but is also desirable. Even Lord Cranborne, the Conservative leader in the House of Lords, has conceded that the Government's plans to abolish hereditary peers are 'not worth dying in the ditch over' (*The Independent*, 8 June 1998), while a *Guardian* editorial perhaps caught the public mood for change, in commenting that it was 'almost incredible that, on the eve of the 21st century, hereditary peers still have a role in one half of Britain's legislature' (*The Guardian*, 20 June 1998). Thus, at the time of writing, there seems to be a general recognition that the presence of hereditary peers in the House of Lords is archaic, and incongruous with the principle of democracy, but there is little common ground on exactly *how* the House of Lords should be reformed. There are a number of options which can be considered.

The first, and the least credible option, is simply to abolish the House of Lords and replace it with a single Chamber, the House of Commons. Whilst there are a few other countries in the world which only have one Parliamentary Chamber, it is submitted that the might of the executive, and Britain's lack of a written constitution, are very strong reasons for retaining a bicameral legislature in the United Kingdom.

A second option is to remove the hereditary peers and replace them with selected life peers. If public office holders, such as judges, Ministers, senior civil servants, bishops etc., can be appointed, one could argue that it is really not very different for the members of a reformed House of Lords to be chosen to hold office. Sensitive to possible allegations of political bias in the future nomination of peers, the Government has announced that the Prime Minister will not have exclusive control over such appointments and reports in the press suggest that an independent panel of experts will be established to appoint 'people's peers' (*The Daily Telegraph*, 11 March 1998). However, it is almost inevitable that even if such an appointment committee is set up, its own composition will attract controversy and there are still likely to be allegations of bias.

At the time of writing the Government's plans for reforming the House of Lords should take place in two stages. In the immediate future, stage one will involve the introduction of a Bill in Parliament to deprive the hereditary peers of their powers and privileges. This could take one of the following forms:

(a)   giving some 'hereditary' peers 'life' peerages, thereby permitting them to enjoy their existing rights and enabling the Chamber to benefit from their wisdom and experience;

(b)   depriving hereditary peers of their voting rights, but still allowing them to speak in the reformed chamber; or finally

(c)   simply abolishing the rights and privileges of *all* of the hereditary peers.

It is anticipated that when the Government publishes its Bill to remove the powers of hereditary peers, it will create around 600 life peers to sit in an 'interim' second chamber, and it is then expected to proceed to a more detailed reform of the House of Lords. However, fears have been expressed that these second stage reforms may never happen, and that the Labour Government will be satisfied by having just removed the inherently Conservative hereditary peers (*The Times*, 9 June 1998).

Much of this is political speculation, but it is clear that there is less than universal support for the Government's plans to reform the House of Lords by nomination rather than election, of which the latter is the third possible option we should consider for the reform of the House of Lords. So what is the case for an elected House of Lords? In advocating a directly elected second Chamber, *The Guardian* recently stressed that 'A House of Aristocrats is indefensible, a House of Patronage not much better' (*The Guardian*, 20 June 1998) and even its bitter fleet street rival, *The Times*, has acknowledged that 'there is a case for making the Chamber almost wholly elected' (*The Times*, 9 March 1998).

In the past, the Liberal Democrats have been the strongest advocates for an elected second Chamber, and the main argument for such a proposal is that an elected Upper House would mean that both Chambers of Parliament would have a democratic mandate. It would inject fresh blood into the House of Lords, there would be more women and members of minority groups, and an elected Lords would have greater confidence and moral authority to challenge the executive.

There are at least two ways in which an elected House of Lords could be set up. First, there could be direct elections, with members elected directly to the second Chamber either on a regional basis (such as in the United States) or by proportional representation (perhaps with a single transferable vote, as happened in the June 1998 election for a Northern Ireland Assembly). Alternatively, a less radical option is to have an indirect election, whereby only a proportion of the members of the newly constituted House of Lords would be elected, with the others appointed or chosen (i.e., given life peerages, Bishops, Law Lords). Perhaps an example of this 'mixed' model is the legislative chamber in post-colonial Hong Kong.

Notwithstanding the obvious attraction of having an elected second Chamber, there are a number of problems with this proposal. First, if the members of a second Chamber are to be chosen by vote, which electoral system should be used, proportional representation (PR) or first past the post? The Liberal Democrats are in favour of using a PR model, yet this is likely to be opposed by some because of the anomaly that it would mean the introduction of completely different voting systems for the two Chambers of Parliament.

A second problem might be agreeing when the elections should take place — should they be at the same time as the House of Commons or mid-way through the administration of a particular government? Finally, and perhaps most crucially, an elected House of Lords, with a popular mandate, will probably grow frustrated by its lack of power, so it may seek to win for itself greater powers. The danger is therefore that the constitutional battles of the early 20th century, between the Commons and the Lords, could once more be fought out in the next millennium and this would surely not be in the interests of either Parliament or the country generally.

Thus, it remains to be seen exactly how far Tony Blair's Government will go in reforming the House of Lords. Mindful of the likely opposition of some peers to its reforms, the Government has threatened to invoke the Parliamentary Acts procedures and by-pass the Lords if hereditary peers try to block the Government's legislation in this area. Whilst politically controversial, such a move could be justified on constitutional grounds and, in particular, on the basis of the unwritten Salisbury Convention, whereby peers do not block legislative proposals which have been contained in the manifesto of a newly-elected Government. Thus, at present, it is difficult to predict how the House of Lords will be reformed, but what seems likely is that some fierce political battles lie ahead.

SAQ 62

In 1991/92 the running costs of the Lords were around £19 million and the Commons £58 million. Does the House of Lords offer value for money? Or is it, in the words of Tony Blair (February 1996) 'the most expensive fiasco in fiscal history'? What reasons are there, if any, for the Government to spend more money on radically reforming the House of Lords?

Please read Donald Shell's appraisal of the Labour Party's plans (just before they came into power) to reform the House of Lords in *Cases and Materials* (6.3).

6.6   Conclusion

The extent to which the House of Lords is a safeguard against any abuse of power by the government and the House of Commons is debatable. For example, even an important rule, such as the principle that a Bill to extend the life of Parliament beyond five years (see **Activity 49**) may not be subject to the Parliament Act procedures (s. 2(1), Parliament Act 1911), is not entrenched against future repeal.

We have seen that the House of Lords undertakes a useful role in the legislative process through its scrutiny of proposed legislation. Many complex Bills, which the Commons has not had time to debate or examine fully, have been improved by amendments in the Lords. On the other hand the House of Lords remains socially unrepresentative of the nation it aims to serve, and the Government has pledged to reform this chamber which Tony Blair has described as 'the oddest and least defensible part of the Constitution' (*The Times*, 8 February 1996).

6.7   End of Chapter Assessment Question

The former Deputy leader of the Labour Party, Roy Hattersley, once described the House of Lords as a 'relic of the past – a past built on patronage, privilege and the denial of the basic concept of democracy'.

Is this an accurate description of the House of Lords and is its reform necessary?

(See *Cases and Materials* (6.5) for a specimen answer.)

ENTARY SUPREMACY

7.1 Objectives

By the end of this Chapter you should be:

■ able to define the term 'Parliamentary supremacy';

■ mindful of how the courts look upon legal challenges to Acts of Parliament;

■ in a position to understand what is meant by 'implied' and 'express' repeal;

■ aware of the constitutional significance of the Acts of Union;

■ conscious of the practical restrictions on Parliament.

7.2 Definitions

'The principle of Parliamentary sovereignty means nothing more nor less than this, namely that Parliament has, under the English Constitution, the right to make or unmake any law whatever; and further that no person or body is recognised by the law of England as having a right to override or set aside the legislation of Parliament' (Dicey).

You may be wondering, is it Parliamentary sovereignty or supremecy? Students some-times are unnecessarily alarmed by the interchangeable use of the words 'sovereignty' and 'supremacy'. Dicey himself preferred 'sovereignty' as does de Smith. However, a majority of contemporary constitutional lawyers (e.g. Hood Phillips, Bradley and Ewing) use the term 'supremacy'. The meaning of the words 'supremacy' and 'sovereignty' are explored by Sir Ivor Jennings, extract in *Cases and Materials* (7.1). However, both words are used to express the traditional view that there are no legal limitations on the legislative competence of Parliament. So how is Parliament to be defined in this context? A common mistake students make is to equate Parliament with the House of Commons. It is important to remember that Parliament does not refer individually to either the House of Commons or Lords. Instead it refers to the constitutional phenomenon known as the 'Queen in Parliament': the process by which a Bill requires the consent of the Queen, the House of Commons and the House of Lords before it may become an Act of Parliament.

7.3 Parliamentary Supremacy

Dicey described the legislative supremacy of Parliament as 'the very keystone of the law of the constitution'. Yet the UK constitution is unique in the sense that it is flexible and not formally codified in a single document. Thus, the principle of Parliamentary supremacy distinguishes the UK from most other countries where a written constitution imposes limits on the legislature. Most written constitutions create a constitutional court with the function of deciding whether acts of the legislature are consistent with the constitution. For example, in the United States, in the landmark ruling of *Marbury* v *Madison* (1803) 5 US (1 Cranch) 137, the US Supreme Court held that it had the jurisdiction to decide whether an Act of Congress was or was not in conformity with the US constitution. (For a more detailed comparative analysis see the extract from Bradley in *Cases and Materials* (7.2).) Thus in the United States, if legislation is passed which infringes rights guaranteed by the constitution, it may be held invalid. However, in the United Kingdom, no such restraints are placed on Parliament. In *Madzimbamuto* v *Lardner-Burke* [1969] 1 AC 645, a case which arose out of the unilateral declaration of independence in 1965 by the Rhodesian government, Lord Reid said, at p. 723:

> It is often said that it would be unconstitutional for the United Kingdom to do certain things, meaning that the moral, political and other reasons against doing them are so strong that most people would regard it as highly improper if Parliament did these things. But that does not mean that it is beyond the power of Parliament to do such things. If Parliament chose to do any of them the courts could not hold the Act of Parliament invalid.

Therefore in the UK, the supremacy of Parliament is the fundamental rule of constitutional law. In practice it means that Parliament can legislate on any matter.

SAQ 63

Carefully analyse Lord Reid's comment. Should the courts ever review Acts of Parliament?

SAQ 64

What does T. R. S. Allan mean when he claims that 'The legal doctrine of legislative supremacy articulates the courts' commitment to the current British scheme of Parliamentary democracy?' For an explanation of this, turn to the extract from 'The Limits of Parliamentary Sovereignty' in *Cases and Materials* (7.2).

Examples of Parliamentary supremacy include:

(a)   The Act of Settlement 1700 and His Majesty's Declaration of Abdication Act 1936 which altered the succession to the throne.

(b)   The Septennial Act 1716 which extended the lifetime of a Parliament and delayed a general election. During the First and Second World Wars, Parliament similarly passed legislation which extended its own lifetime.

(c)   The Parliament Acts 1911 and 1949 which substantially reduced the power of the House of Lords.

(d)   Altering the territorial limits of the UK: Island of Rockall Act 1972.

(e)   Membership of the European Community: European Communities Act 1972.

(f)   Reforming the composition of both Houses of Parliament: Representation of the People Act 1832 (Reform Act).

(g)   The passage of retrospective legislation. Notwithstanding the fact that this is usually politically controversial and is contrary to art. 7 of the European Convention on Human Rights, Parliament has altered the law retrospectively: e.g., the War Damages Act 1965, the Northern Ireland Act 1972, the War Crimes Act 1991.

Try to identify other examples of Parliamentary supremacy in addition to those already provided.

7.4   Legal Challenges to Acts of Parliament

Parliament's legislative supremacy has been challenged on a number of occasions, but generally the courts have been reluctant to declare Acts of Parliament invalid. This is illustrated by the following examples:

(a)   **An Act challenged on the ground that when introduced as a Bill into Parliament, notice had not been given as required by the standing orders of the House of Commons**

In *Edinburgh and Dalkeith Railway Co.* v *Wauchope* (1842) 8 Cl & F 710, Lord Campbell said:

All that a court of justice can look to is the parliamentary roll; [if] . . . an Act has passed both Houses of Parliament, and . . . received the royal assent, . . .

no court of justice can inquire into the manner in which it was introduced into Parliament.

(b) **Challenge made on the basis of an alleged procedural irregularity**

In *British Railways Board* v *Pickin* [1974] AC 765, Pickin owned land on either side of a railway line. Private Acts of 1836 and 1845 provided that if the line was ever abandoned, the land on which it was built reverted to the owners of the adjacent land. However, this rule was abolished in 1968, by a private Act which had been sponsored by the Board. Pickin claimed that the Board had fraudulently misled Parliament when the 1968 Act was passed and so the Act should not be relied on. The House of Lords held that once an Act was passed, it must be accepted by the courts. Lord Reid cited Lord Campbell in *Edinburgh and Dalkeith Railway Co.* v *Wauchope* and commented:

> The function of the court is to construe and apply the enactments of Parliament. The court has no concern with the manner in which Parliament or its officers carrying out its Standing Orders perform these functions.

Thus, private Acts such as the Act of 1968 are as fully Acts of Parliament as public Acts and compel acceptance by the courts.

ACTIVITY 51

In *British Railways Board* v *Pickin*, the House of Lords was not prepared to review the conduct of the internal proceedings of Parliament. Why? Compare and contrast the judgments of Lords Reid, Morris, Simon and Wilberforce, extracts in *Cases and Materials* (7.3).

(c) **Challenge based on general principles of human rights**

In *R* v *Jordan* [1967] Crim LR 483, Jordan was imprisoned for inciting racial hatred under the Race Relations Act 1965. He applied for legal aid to enable him to seek habeas corpus on the ground that the Act was invalid, as it violated the principle of freedom of expression. His application was refused.

(d) **Challenge to an Act on the ground that it is inconsistent with public international law**

In *Cheney* v *Conn* [1968] 1 WLR 242, a taxpayer challenged the validity of the Finance Act 1964 arguing that it was in conflict with the international Geneva Conventions on warfare incorporated into UK law as the Geneva Conventions Act 1957. It was claimed that this 1964 Act was contrary to international law, because part of the tax collected would go towards the manufacture of nuclear weapons. Ungoed-Thomas J said that 'What the statute itself enacts cannot be unlawful, because [it is] the highest form of law that is known to this country. It is the law which prevails over every other form of law, and it is not for the court to say that a Parliamentary enactment . . . is illegal'. Thus the Finance Act took precedence over international law. (In this context, note that international law, e.g., rules prohibiting one State using force against another, is completely different from European Community law.)

(e) Act challenged on the ground that it is contrary to the Act of Union 1707

In *Murray* v *Rogers* 1992 SLT 221 it was claimed that the Abolition of Domestic Rates (Scotland) Act 1987 (Scottish community charge legislation) was contrary to art. 18 of the Act of Union 1707. The basis of this argument was the fact that the community charge had been introduced first in Scotland, at a time when there was no equivalent tax in England. The court asserted that it had no power to challenge the validity of the community charge legislation. Thus the complainant had no reasonable excuse for refusing to pay the charge (poll tax). However, rather significantly the court added that the position might be different if it was alleged that the legislation was incompatible with European Community law.

(f) Act challenged on the ground that it is contrary to the European Convention on Human Rights (ECHR)

As we saw in **Chapter 1**, the Human Rights Act 1998 incorporates the ECHR into UK law. However, in the absence of legislation which gave effect to the Convention, British courts in the past rejected suggestions that the ECHR was legally binding. For example, in *Chief Immigration Officer* v *Heathrow Airport, ex parte Salamat Bibi* [1976] 1 WLR 976, Lord Denning stressed that in the event of a conflict between an Act of Parliament and the ECHR, the British statute should prevail. A similar view was also expressed by the House of Lords in *R* v *Secretary of State for the Home Department, ex parte Brind* [1991] 1 AC 696. In *Brind*, the Home Secretary had issued directives under legislation, imposing media restrictions on representatives of Sinn Fein and other proscribed terrorist organisations. Judicial review was sought on a number of grounds, one of which was that the directives violated art. 10 of the ECHR (the principle of freedom of expression). This submission failed and Lord Ackner observed that since the ECHR has not been incorporated into British law, it 'cannot be a source of rights and obligations'. The effect of this ruling is reversed by the Human Rights Act 1998 but, as was noted in earlier in **Chapter 1**, while judges may issue declarations of incompatibility, they may not strike down legislation which is in conflict with the ECHR.

Please turn back to *Cases and Materials* (1.4) and refer to what is written on the Human Rights Act 1998. In your opinion, is this legislation likely to threaten or erode the sovereignty of Parliament?

7.5   Where Two Acts Conflict; the Doctrine of Implied Repeal

Where two Acts conflict the later one should prevail. In *Vauxhall Estates Ltd* v *Liverpool Corporation* [1932] 1 KB 733, it was held that a later statute impliedly overruled an earlier statute, even though that earlier statute had stated that any later inconsistent legislation was to have no effect. Thus, the provisions of a 1925 Act would prevail over a 1919 Act, in so far as they were inconsistent with it. Similarly in *Ellen Street Estates Ltd* v *Minister of Health* [1934] 1 KB 590, Maugham LJ observed: '. . . it is impossible for Parliament to enact that in a subsequent statute dealing with the same subject matter there can be no implied repeal. If in a subsequent Act, Parliament chooses to make it plain that the earlier statute is being to some extent repealed, effect must be given to that intention just because it is the will of the legislature'.

These cases illustrate both the doctrine of implied repeal, and the principle that one Parliament may never bind its successors. Dicey said that 'a sovereign power cannot, while retaining its sovereign character, restrict its own powers by any Parliamentary enactment'. After all if one Parliament could bind its successors a future Parliament would be fettered and lack the freedom of the present Parliament. Thus, the theory is that no limitations may be placed on the legislative competence of Parliament. But what of the practice?

Is the doctrine of implied repeal an example of legislative supremacy or a limitation on it? You will find extracts from *Vauxhall Estates Ltd* v *Liverpool Corporation* [1932] 1 KB 733 and *Ellen Street Estates Ltd* v *Minister of Health* [1934] 1 KB 590 in *Cases and Materials* (7.4).

Read the extracts from Lord Keith's judgment in *Gibson* v *Lord Advocate* 1975 SLT 134 and Lord President Cooper's judgment in *MacCormick* v *Lord Advocate* 1953 SC 396 in *Cases and Materials* (7.4).

7.6   Practical Constraints on Parliamentary Supremacy

7.6.1   ACTS OF UNION

The present UK Parliament is the result of two treaties: the Act of Union with Scotland 1707 and the Act of Union with Ireland 1800. Thus it is debatable whether the modern

UK Parliament was 'born unfree'. In 1800 the Act of Union united the island of Ireland with Great Britain 'forever'. The churches of both countries were also to be 'forever' united. In practice this has not been the case. The Irish Free State (Constitution) Act 1922 facilitated the creation of the Irish Republic while the Church of Ireland was disestablished by the Irish Church Act 1869. Although there are no cases directly on the 1800 Act of Union itself, when a legal challenge was brought against the 1869 statute, the Court held that it had no power to override a statute: *Ex parte Canon Selwyn* (1872) 36 JP 54.

The earlier Act of Union with Scotland (1707) provided for the Union of England and Scotland (art. 1), with the former English and Scottish Parliaments merging to form a British Parliament (art. 3). Guarantees relating to the separate Scottish courts and Church of Scotland were provided and were to be 'observed in all time coming . . . without alteration thereof' (para. 4). Thus the orthodox view is that the English and Scottish Parliaments voluntarily extinguished themselves and this new British Parliament took on the characteristics of the English Parliament, including that of sovereignty.

The fact that Parliamentary sovereignty was a distinctly English characteristic, which had no counterpart in Scottish law, has been noted by Scottish judges. In *MacCormick v Lord Advocate* 1953 SC 396 a declaration was requested that the government was not entitled to publish a proclamation describing the Queen as Elizabeth II of Great Britain, because, as far as Scotland was concerned, there had been no Elizabeth I. Lord Cooper remarked *obiter*: 'The principle of the unlimited sovereignty of Parliament is a distinctively English principle which has no counterpart in Scottish constitutional law'. He added that he had 'difficulty in seeing' why the new British Parliament took 'all the peculiar characteristics of the English Parliament but none of the Scottish Parliament'. Implicit in this was a suggestion that Parliament may be bound by the Act of Union. On the other hand, Lord Cooper appeared to quash such speculation when he added, 'that there is neither precedent nor authority of any kind for the view that the domestic courts of either Scotland or England' have power to 'determine whether a governmental act of the type here . . . conform[s] to the provisions of a Treaty [of Union]'. Thus in Lord Cooper's opinion, violation of the fundamental terms of the union would be unlawful but non-justiciable in a United Kingdom court. Similarly in *Gibson v Lord Advocate* 1975 SLT 134, a case involving EEC fishing regulations, a claim was made in the Scottish Court of Session that membership of the EC was incompatible with the Act of Union. Lord Keith rejected claims that s. 2(1) of the European Communities Act 1972 was null and void. Instead he noted that: 'The making of decisions upon what must essentially be a political matter is no part of the function of the courts, and it is highly undesirable that it should be'.

As de Smith points out, Lord Keith reserved his opinion on the situation which might be created if the United Kingdom had passed an Act purporting to abolish the Court of Session or the Church of Scotland. Were such an Act to be passed it seems that the ultimate decision would have to be taken by the Scottish courts.

Finally, a relevant case was recently decided in the Scottish Court of Session. In *Pringle* 1991 SLT 330, it was claimed that to introduce the community charge (or poll tax) into Scotland a year earlier than England and Wales was contrary to art. 4 of the Treaty of Union. Article 4 stipulates that there should be no difference in the rights and privileges of British citizens. This submission failed. Lord Hope held that the difference in taxation 'would not be sufficient to persuade me, without a much more detailed inquiry into the overall effects of these differences, that there was a failure to do what this part of art. 4 intended should be done'. The words 'detailed inquiry' are unclear. Nevertheless the decision in this case illustrates the general reluctance of Scottish judges to review Acts of Parliament.

7.6.2   GRANTING INDEPENDENCE

Since Parliament is supreme, can it continue to legislate for former British colonies which have been granted independence? This issue was addressed by s. 4 of the Statute of

Westminster 1931. It stated that an Act of the United Kingdom Parliament would not extend to a Dominion (i.e., a former British territory) unless it was expressly stated in the Act that the Dominion consented to and requested it. The question arises, does such an enactment limit the legislative sovereignty of Parliament? Could a future Parliament repeal s. 4 or legislate for a Dominion without its consent?

In *Blackburn* v *Attorney-General* [1971] 1 WLR 1037 Lord Denning MR made the following observations:

> We have all been brought up to believe that, in legal theory, one Parliament cannot bind another and that no Act is irreversible. But legal theory does not always march alongside political reality. Take the Statute of Westminster 1931, which takes away the power of Parliament to legislate for the Dominions. Can anyone imagine that Parliament could or would reverse that Statute? Take the Acts which have granted independence to the Dominions and territories overseas. Can anyone imagine that Parliament could or would reverse those laws and take away their independence? Most clearly not. Freedom once given cannot be taken away. Legal theory must give way to practical politics.

Thus, by granting independence to members or former members of the Commonwealth, the United Kingdom Parliament has surrendered its legislative authority over them. In theory it could pass legislation *claiming* to assert jurisdiction, but in practice this would be most unlikely.

Section 1 of the Northern Ireland Constitution Act 1973 states that 'in no event will Northern Ireland or any part of it cease to be part of Her Majesty's dominions and of the United Kingdom without the consent of the majority of the people of Northern Ireland voting in a poll held for the purposes of this section'. Is s. 1 *legally* binding on a future Parliament, or is it only a *political* guarantee?

7.6.3 JURISDICTIONAL LIMITS

Theoretically Parliament can make any law for any country irrespective of subject matter. However, in practice it would be impossible to enforce (e.g., the often-cited example of Parliament making it an offence to smoke on the streets of Paris) though legally Parliament is competent to pass such legislation.

7.6.4 PUBLIC OPINION

Whilst Parliament may be supreme in theory, in practice it will usually take cognisance of public opinion. Few governments will be foolish enough to initiate legislation contrary to public opinion. This may even be the case where they enjoy a clear majority in the Lords and Commons. The community charge legislation is an excellent example of the power of hostile public opinion. Notwithstanding the successful passage of the poll tax legislation, (Abolition of Domestic Rates (Scotland) Act 1987 and the Local Government Finance Act 1988), the government replaced the community charge with the council tax, in an effort to regain public support.

7.6.5 HUMAN RIGHTS

Lord Scarman has suggested in the past that there is a need for a written constitution because 'No bevy of men, not even Parliament, could always be trusted to safeguard human rights'. Whilst the United Kingdom has yet to codify its constitution in writing, the incorporation of the ECHR into British law goes some way to safeguarding human rights. But to what extent is this an erosion of Parliamentary sovereignty? You should have some ideas on this, having answered **Activity 52**. However, whatever view you take, remember that even with the enactment of the Human Rights Act 1998, individuals living in Britain will still be able to bring complaints under the ECHR to the European Court of Human Rights. Thus, in the meantime, the twin pressures of criticism in the United Kingdom (e.g., in the press and media) and the threat of international censure (e.g., by international organisations such as the Council of Europe, the UN, the EU, etc), seem likely to ensure that Parliament is at least seen as legislating in conformity with its human rights obligations.

Can you think of any other practical limitations on Parliamentary supremacy?

What does T.R.S Allan mean when he says (see *Cases and Materials* (7.2)), that the 'nature and limits of Parliamentary sovereignty are constituted . . . by the political morality which underlies the legal order'?

7.7 Conclusion

Parliamentary supremacy is an important principle of the British Constitution. Since 1700, the courts have recognised the doctrine of the legislative omnipotence of Parliament. Yet there always has been a difference between theory and practice. We have noted the practical limitations on Parliament. In this context, Professor Lasok points out that 'even in Dicey's days absolute sovereignty was not a realistic proposition at least as far as international obligations were concerned since no country exists in isolation' (*Student Law Review* (Autumn 1991), p. 26).

But is Parliament still supreme even in theory? You should have noted that conspicuously absent from this chapter was any mention of the European Community. Professor Mitchell has argued that just as a new legal order was created in 1707 when the Act of Union with Scotland imposed legal restraints on the UK Parliament, so the enactment of the European Communities Act 1972 may have created a new constitutional arrangement. Thus an important question remains to be posed: is the Westminster Parliament still supreme, or has supremacy been transferred to the European Community? The answer will be provided in the next chapter when we examine the influence of the European Community on the British Constitution.

CHAPTER EIGHT

THE UNITED KINGDOM AND EUROPEAN COMMUNITY LAW

8.1 Objectives

At the end of this Chapter you should be:

- familiar with the doctrine of Parliamentary supremacy;

- able to distinguish between different types of Community legislation;

- in a position to appreciate the significance of the European Communities Act 1972;

- aware of the attitude of British courts to Community law;

- mindful of the constitutional implications of closer European ties.

8.2 European Community Law

In 1952 six nations (Belgium, France, Italy, Luxembourg, West Germany and the Netherlands) joined together to regulate their coal and steel industries, signing the Treaty of Paris and creating the European Coal and Steel Community (ECSC). The success of the ECSC led to the formation of the European Atomic Energy Community (EURATOM) and the European Economic Community (EEC) in 1957. These three communities, ECSC, EURATOM and the EEC, were effectively merged in 1965.

The European Economic Community (now renamed the European Community) was established by the Treaty of Rome 1957 (the EC Treaty). The objectives of the EC include the elimination of customs duties and quantitative restrictions on imports and exports within the community, the establishment of common commercial policies towards non-member States, the abolition of obstacles to the free movement of workers and capital within member States, and the creation of common policies in areas such as agriculture and transport (EC Treaty, art. 3). In 1973 three more countries entered the community; the United Kingdom, Denmark and the Republic of Ireland. Greece joined in 1981, and Portugal and Spain in 1986. The former East Germany joined the Community on 3 October 1990 when it became part of a united Germany. At present EC membership stands at 15, with Austria, Finland and Sweden the newest members, joining in January 1995.

The main institutions of the Community are:

(a) The European Parliament.

(b)   The Commission.

(c)   The Council of Ministers.

(d)   The European Court of Justice (ECJ).

8.3   Institutions

8.3.1   THE EUROPEAN PARLIAMENT

The European Parliament usually meets in Strasbourg, France. It has 626 elected representatives or MEPs, of whom 87 are from the UK.

The European Parliament is mainly a consultative forum and not a legislative body such as the Westminster Parliament. Nevertheless, the trend appears to be that the European Parliament is growing in influence and authority. A failure to consult the Parliament can even lead to an instrument being struck down (*Re Road Taxes: European Parliament v EU Council* [1996] 1 CMLR 94). Similarly, in *Roquette Frères v Council* (case 138/79) [1980] ECR 3333, the Court of Justice held that: 'Due consultation of the Parliament in the cases provided for by the Treaty constitutes an essential formality disregard of which means that the measure concerned is void.'

The European Parliament possesses power in at least five respects:

(a)   *The budget*

The Parliament may veto community budget proposals on 'non-compulsory expenditure' but the council has the final say on 'compulsory expenditure'. Although the European Parliament's powers in relation to non-compulsory expenditure relate to less than half of the Community's budget, they are certainly significant and were used to reject budgets in 1980, 1982 and 1985.

(b)   *Accountability*

The Commission is formally accountable to the Parliament. The Parliament may vote by a two-thirds majority to remove the members of the Commission (EC Treaty, art. 144). This has never as yet happened but it is theoretically possible.

(c)   *Enforcement*

The European Parliament may initiate enforcement proceedings in the European Court of Justice (ECJ), if either the Commission or Council of Ministers abdicate their responsibility and fail to meet an obligation to take action. In *Parliament v Council* (case C–70/88) [1990] ECR I–2041, the ECJ held that the European Parliament can bring an annulment action (under art. 173) against an act of the Council or Commission, provided that the action only seeks to defend the Parliament's powers. And in 1986, the Parliament brought an action against the Council for failing to introduce measures to establish a common transport policy in accordance with the relevant provisions of the Treaty of Rome (*Parliament v Council* (case 13/83) [1985] ECR 1513).

(d)   *Supervision*

The European Parliament may establish committees of inquiry to investigate allegations of maladministration or breaches of Community law (art. 138c of the Treaty of Rome as inserted by the Single European Act 1986). The Parliament also appoints the European Ombudsman, who has jurisdiction over allegations of maladministration by EC institutions.

(e) *Conciliation*

Article 189b of the Treaty of Rome, as amended by the Maastricht Treaty has introduced a new co-decision procedure by which a conciliation committee will seek to reconcile any disagreements between the Council and Parliament. As Curtin ((1993) 17 CML Rev 36) notes: '[t]he crux of the new co-decision procedure is that unless Council and Parliament agree on the final text of the legislation, neither is given the last word and the legislation simply falls.'

Thus, to summarise, the European Parliament scrutinises Commission proposals for legislation, votes on amendments, can in theory dismiss the Commission and may reject part of the budget. However, since it lacks any formal power to initiate, or once consulted by the Council, block Community legislation, its influence is in stark contrast to that of most national Parliaments.

ACTIVITY 55

Critically analyse the European Parliament's influence. Should it have powers similar to those of the Westminster Parliament? For some ideas look at what Bogdanor says about the European Parliament and its Westminster equivalent, in the extract from *The Changing Constitution* found in *Cases and Materials* (8.1.1).

8.3.2 THE EUROPEAN COMMISSION

The Commission is based in Brussels, Belgium. With a staff of approximately 9,000 it is the bureaucracy where most of the day-to-day business takes place. There are 20 Commissioners, one from each member State and a second from the 'big five' states, Germany, France, Italy, UK and Spain. Members of the Commission are expected to act independently of their home State (EC Treaty, art. 157) and appointments last for five years. They are appointed, not elected, and one of the 20 is nominated as President.

SAQ 69

In what areas does the European Community claim jurisdiction? A list is provided in art. 3 of the Treaty of Rome (extract in *Cases and Materials* (8.1)).

The functions of the European Commission are two-fold. First the Commission has a legislative role. The Commission proposes new laws and initiates policies to be approved by the Council of Ministers after consultation with the Parliament. It was as President of the European Commission that Jacques Delors was able to formulate proposals for closer European ties and the post is currently held by Jacques Santer, the former Prime Minister of Luxembourg. Secondly, the Commission has an important policing role. In the event of a breach of the Treaty of Rome, the Commission will seek an explanation from the erring State. If the breach continues, the Commission will issue a reasoned opinion, and it may ultimately refer the matter to the European Court. In this respect the Commission is the 'guardian of the Treaties'.

8.3.2.1 Article 169 proceedings by the Commission against a State

If the Commission believes that a member State is in breach of its treaty obligations, it must first prepare a detailed account of the case. This reasoned opinion will call on the member State to correct the alleged breaches. If the State still refuses to obey the Commission, the matter may be referred to the ECJ. Should the ECJ find against the State, it 'shall be required to take the necessary measures to comply with the judgment' (art. 172). Until recently there was no sanction for non-compliance with an ECJ ruling. However, since the Maastricht Treaty, member States which disobey ECJ judgments can be subject to a penalty payment. The UK, for example, was condemned for failing to comply with drinking water standards in 1993, under this procedure.

8.3.2.2 Article 170 Inter-State cases

When one State claims that another is in breach of its Community obligations, the case is first submitted to the Commission for a reasoned opinion. A State which contests the content of the opinion may bring the matter before the ECJ. In the event of intransigence, a political compromise is often the way in which grievances are resolved.

As well as ensuring that Community law is complied with, the Commission also administers EC funds, prepares the Community budget, implements the Common Agricultural Policy, has responsibility over EC competition policy, and may submit legislative proposals to the Council of Ministers. Thus, the Commission is the guardian of the Community Treaties, ensuring the 'fulfilment of the obligations' arising out of the Treaty of Rome (art. 5)

8.3.3 THE COUNCIL OF MINISTERS

The Council of Ministers is the main law-making body of the EC. It takes the most important legislative and executive decisions (EC Treaty, art. 145). Its function is to make policy decisions and to issue Regulations and Directives on the basis of proposals from the Commission. The Council of Ministers is composed of one representative from each member State of the Community. In principle, the representative is the Foreign Minister, but generally speaking, depending on the nature of Council business, it tends to be the appropriate Minister who is sent (e.g., the Health Minister is likely to attend when issues relating to health are on the agenda) so that in 1997, 27 different Ministers represented the UK at its meetings. Unlike the Commission, members of the Council are permitted overtly to represent their national interests, and the Presidency of the Council rotates between the member governments at six-monthly intervals.

EC heads of government also meet twice a year to discuss general and foreign policy, in a body called the European Council. It differs from the Council of Ministers in that it is not referred to in the Treaty of Rome, is essentially a political body and has jurisdiction to examine non-Community matters.

Read the extracts from the Treaty of Rome on the powers of the European Parliament, Commission, Council and Court in *Cases and Materials* (8.1).

8.3.4   THE EUROPEAN COURT OF JUSTICE

The 15 judges of the Court of Justice are appointed by the governments of the member States for a renewable term of six years and they sit in Luxembourg. Their function is to ensure that Community law is observed (EC Treaty, art. 164). The ECJ may deal only with matters relating to Community law. On average the European Court receives 400 new cases each year. Inevitably this has led to delays and an increasing backlog of cases. Therefore a new Court of First Instance ('le Tribunal') was created by the Single European Act 1986, to ease the workload of the existing Court. Fifteen judges sit (in chambers of three or five or seven), and they have jurisdiction to consider three categories of case: EC staff disputes; competition law cases; and actions of judicial review against Community institutions.

It is possible that in the future 'le Tribunal' will relieve much of the European Court's caseload. Certainly this would speed up court proceedings which are based on the Civil law or Continental model. The European Court only gives one judgment (there are no dissenting judgments), from which there is no appeal.

The ECJ's jurisdiction is twofold. A distinction can be drawn between:

(a) cases brought by the Commission or by one member State against another member State which has allegedly violated Community obligations, or by a member State or individuals against the Community (art. 173); and

(b) requests to the ECJ for preliminary rulings on Community law from national courts.

8.3.4.1   Action against the Community or Member States

As mentioned in **8.3.2**, the Commission may initiate proceedings should a member State fail to fulfil a Community obligation. Having invited that State to make its comments, the Commission will issue a reasoned opinion. Should the State not act on the opinion within a specified period, the matter may be referred to the ECJ (similar actions may be instigated by one member State against another member State). If the ECJ considers that the petition is meritorious it will deliver a judgment, with which a member State is expected to comply (EC Treaty, art. 171). For example, in *Commission v UK* (case 165/82) [1984] 1 All ER 353, the ECJ held that the UK had failed to fulfil its Community obligations by not complying with an EC Directive relating to the law on sex equality.

Actions may also be brought by one Community institution against another institution (e.g., *Parliament v Council* (case C–70/88) [1990] ECR I–2041) or by individuals with sufficient *locus standi*. For example, Community institutions are vicariously liable for damage caused by their servants in the course of their official duty. In *Adams v Commission* (case 53/84) [1985] ECR 3595, Adams was an employee of a multinational company being investigated by the Commission in connection with breaches of EC competition rules. He provided the Commission with important information about the company. When his employers discovered this, Adams was sacked, forced into bankruptcy, prosecuted and imprisoned for passing trade secrets to an unauthorised body (the EC Commission). Adams's wife even committed suicide. The ECJ held that the Commission was liable for a breach of confidentiality and Adams was awarded damages for economic loss and mental anguish. In this case Adams clearly had *locus standi*, but in practice this is often a difficult procedural hurdle as the matter must be of 'direct and individual concern' to the potential litigant (EC Treaty, art. 173(2)).

Article 173 also provides that actions may be brought by States or individuals in seeking to challenge or annul Community decisions which are of concern to them. For example, in *UK* v *European Commission, The Times*, 6 May 1998, the European Court held that by banning the export of meat and derived products from the United Kingdom to other States, both in and outside of the European Community, the Commission had not exceeded its discretion, nor had it abused its powers or acted disproportionately.

8.3.4.2 Preliminary rulings

Perhaps the most interesting feature of the Court of Justice is that it can provide preliminary rulings on matters of interpretation of the EC Treaty under art. 177. National courts may submit requests to the ECJ to rule on questions of interpretation and sometimes even on the validity of Community law. British courts have made a number of art. 177 references since Pennycuick VC made the first reference in *Van Duyn* v *Home Office* [1974] 1 WLR 1107 (see extract in *Cases and Materials* (8.1.2.1)). In *H.P. Bulmer Ltd* v *J. Bollinger SA* [1974] Ch 401), Lord Denning MR suggested that a UK court should refer a question of EC law to the ECJ where:

(a)   the decision is necessary to enable the UK court to arrive at its judgment;

(b)   the decision must be conclusive of the case (e.g., it must be relevant to the outcome of the case); and

(c)   the court, where necessary, takes account of factors such as delay, difficulty of the issues, the expense involved and the burden on the court.

Lord Denning's use of the term 'conclusive' created some uncertainty. However, further guidelines were issued by the ECJ in *CILFIT Srl* v *Ministro della Sanità* (case 283/81) [1982] ECR 3415. There the ECJ stipulated that reference is not necessary if:

(a)   the question of Community law raised is irrelevant;

(b)   the point of Community law has already been interpreted by the ECJ;

(c)   and there is no reasonable doubt about how the question should be answered.

The UK Court of Appeal has appeared to encourage art. 177 references. In *R* v *International Stock Exchange of the United Kingdom and the Republic of Ireland Ltd, ex parte Else* [1993] QB 534, it held that British courts and tribunals should not seek to interpret difficult questions of Community law, unless they could themselves answer such questions with 'complete confidence'.

J. Rinze says that the European Court uses art. 177 of the EC Treaty as an 'effective means to guarantee the constitutionality of the laws of the member States' (extract in *Cases and Materials* (8.1.2.1)).

Bearing in mind the jurisdictional remit of the European Community, compile a list of the *areas* in which the court is likely to receive an art. 177 reference.

Article 177 allows a reference to be made by 'any court or tribunal'. In the UK references have been made by the Employment Appeal Tribunal, High Court and magistrates' court, as well as by the superior appellate courts. What are the *advantages* of national courts making art. 177 references?

Preliminary rulings have enabled the European Court to consolidate its influence in areas such as sex discrimination, freedom to receive services, free movement of goods and free movement of people. For example, in answer to **Activity 57** you could have suggested areas such as:

(a) **Sex discrimination**

In *Dekker* v *Stichting Vormingscentrum voor Jong Volwassenen (VJV-Centrum) Plus* (Case C–177/88) [1990] ECR I–3941, a pregnant woman's application for a management post was rejected. Sex discrimination was alleged while Stichting protested that had Mrs Dekker been employed, they would have been obliged to pay her sickness benefit, which they could not afford. On a preliminary ruling the ECJ rejected their defence. The financial consequences to Stichting were irrelevant, as was their lack of intention to discriminate. This decision, following on from *Macarthys Ltd* v *Smith* (case 129/79) [1981] QB 180 and *Garland* v *British Rail Engineering Ltd* (Case 12/81) [1993] 2 AC 751 (see **Cases and Materials (8.1.2.1)**), illustrates the ECJ's considerable influence in the area of sex discrimination law.

(b) **Freedom to receive services**

In *Gravier* v *City of Liège* (case 293/83) [1985] ECR 593, Gravier, a French national, was a student at the Royal Academy in Liège, Belgium. The City of Liège charged only foreign students an enrolment fee to study at the Academy. Gravier refused to pay this sum. On a preliminary ruling the ECJ agreed that the imposition of this fee was tantamount to discrimination, contrary to art. 7 of the EC Treaty.

(c) **Free movement of goods**

In *Conegate Ltd* v *Commissioners of Customs and Excise* (case 121/85) [1987] QB 254, a British company sought to import inflatable dolls from Germany into the UK. A number of these dolls were seized by Customs officials on the ground that they were indecent and obscene. Although legislation prohibited the importation of these dolls, nothing prevented their manufacture in the United Kingdom. The company, in seeking recovery of the dolls, claimed that their seizure contravened the principle of the free movement of goods (EC Treaty, art. 30). In response to an art. 177 reference, the European Court rejected the UK's argument that its measures were justified in order to protect public morality (EC Treaty, art. 36). To allow the UK to prevent the importation of particular goods, while simultaneously allowing its nationals to manufacture such products, would amount to discrimination on the ground of nationality.

(d) **Free movement of persons**

In *Procureur du Roi* v *Royer* (case 48/75) [1976] ECR 497, Royer, a French national, visited his wife in Belgium but failed to comply with the administrative formalities upon entry into the country. He was subsequently convicted of illegal entry. The ECJ in response to a request from a Belgian court for a preliminary ruling, affirmed that Community law guarantees the nationals of one member State the right to enter and reside in another member State (EC Treaty, arts 48, 52 and 59). The European Court added that the failure of a Community national to comply with the administrative formalities upon entry into another member State did not justify expulsion.

(e) **The ECJ's jurisdiction**

Preliminary rulings have been used to assert the jurisdiction of the European Court of Justice. In *Foto-Frost* v *Hauptzollamt Lübeck-Ost* (case 314/85) [1987] ECR 4199, a German court was asked by the applicant to declare a decision of the European Commission invalid. The national court referred the matter to the European Court under art. 177. The ECJ held that it had exclusive authority to declare an act of a Community institution invalid, and that such a power could not be exercised by national courts and tribunals.

The procedure for submitting preliminary references under art. 177 has enabled the European Court to establish itself as arguably the most dynamic of the Community's institutions.

The European Court is also empowered, under art. 228(6) of the EC Treaty, to give an opinion to the EC Council, the Commission or a member State, on whether a particular measure or course of action conforms with Community law. Following such a request from the Council, the Court of Justice considered the question whether the EC would have the competence to accede to the European Convention on Human Rights and, in *Opinion 2/94, The Times*, 29 March 1996, it held that there was no such legal basis for accession.

SAQ 71

Tony Blair has commented: 'As we enlarge [the EC] there is the opportunity for us to reconsider the essential mechanism of political accountability and control. We have had the courage to create the European Union. We must now have the courage to reform it.' (*The Times*, 25 March 1998.) What do you think is meant by this statement?

With this in mind, critically analyse the structure and composition of the Community institutions. How could they be improved? For some ideas you should turn to the views of Bogdanor in *1688–1988 — Time for a New Constitution*, and of the Fabian Society extracts in *Cases and Materials* **(8.1.2.1)**.

SAQ 72

What is the relationship between the four Community institutions? Having clarified the functions of the EC's institutions, you are now in a good position to turn to study the substantive legal issues arising out of Community membership.

8.4   Sources of EC law

There are three main sources of EC law:

(a)   The Community treaties.

(b)   The Legislation of Community institutions.

(c)   Decisions of the European Court of Justice.

8.4.1   THE COMMUNITY TREATIES

The treaties which established the European Communities (the European Coal and Steel Community 1951, the European Atomic Energy Community 1957 and the European Economic Community 1957), as well as the Single European Act (1986), the Maastricht Treaty (1992) and the Treaty of Amsterdam (1997), form the primary source of Community law. The Treaty of Rome is of particular significance. Some (though not all) of its articles create rights and impose duties on individuals and governments. For example, the European Court of Justice has held that art. 30 (the prohibition of quantitative restrictions on imports), art. 48 (the free movement of workers), arts 85, 86 (free competition) and art. 119 (equal pay for equal work for men and women) of the Treaty of Rome are 'directly effective'. This means that they can be invoked by any individual ('vertically' against the government and 'horizontally' against other citizens) in a British court. Thus, these Treaty provisions can be relied upon by individuals as if they were rights guaranteed in an Act of Parliament.

Commenting on the Treaty of Rome, Lord Denning MR in *Schorsch Meier GmbH* v *Hennin* [1975] QB 416, suggested that it 'is by statute part of the law of England'. Similarly, in *Application des Gaz SA* v *Falks Veritas Ltd* [1974] Ch 381 at p. 393, Lord Denning said that 'the Treaty is part of our law. It is equal in force to any statute. It must be applied by our courts'. These statements implied that *all* Treaty provisions are legally binding in the UK. Such a proposition is not strictly accurate and later Lord Denning in *Shields* v *E. Coomes (Holdings) Ltd* [1979] 1 WLR 1408 clarified the situation and expressed the conventional view that only those Treaty articles which have satisfied the conditions for 'direct effect' are binding. These conditions will be examined shortly.

So, to conclude, the Treaties are a primary source of Community law. They are the equivalent of the Community's written constitutions. However, in practice they comprise only the bare bones of Community law. Their real significance perhaps rests in the fact that they grant Community organs the power to make secondary legislation. Of these the most common forms are *Regulations* and *Directives*.

8.4.2 THE SECONDARY LEGISLATION OF COMMUNITY INSTITUTIONS

Article 189 of the Treaty of Rome provides that:

A Regulation shall have general application. It shall be binding in its entirety and directly applicable in all Member States.

A Directive shall be binding, as to the result to be achieved, upon each Member State to which it is addressed, but shall leave to the national authorities the choice of form and methods.

A Decision shall be binding in its entirety upon those to whom it is addressed.

Recommendations and Opinions shall have no binding force.

The two most common forms of Community secondary legislation are Regulations and Directives.

8.4.2.1 Regulations

Under art. 189 of the Treaty of Rome, Regulations are directly binding ('directly applicable'). They are automatically a source of law in the British legal system. Thus, their implementation does not require any further legislation or Parliamentary approval. In the United Kingdom, direct applicability is facilitated by s. 2(1) of the European Communities Act 1972. It states that 'All such rights, powers, liabilities, obligations and restrictions . . . created or arising by or under the Treaties, as in accordance with the Treaties are without further enactment to be given legal effect or used in the United Kingdom shall be recognised and available in law, and be enforced, allowed and followed accordingly'.

The European Court of Justice has held that Regulations prevail over inconsistent national law, even if the conflicting national legislation was enacted after the Regulation (*Amministrazione delle Finanze dello Stato* v *Simmenthal SpA* (case 106/77) [1978] ECR 629). Regulations may also confer rights upon individuals in member States. In *Leonesio* v *Ministero dell'Agricoltura e delle Foreste* (case 93/71) [1972] ECR 287, the ECJ stated: 'a

Regulation produces immediate effects and attributes to individuals, rights which national courts must uphold'. Also, in *Commission* v *UK Re Tachographs* (case 128/78) [1979] ECR 419, the ECJ affirmed that Regulations were directly applicable and could not be applied in an incomplete or selective manner.

8.4.2.2 Directives

As we have already seen, art. 189 of the Treaty of Rome provides that 'A Directive shall be binding, as to the result to be achieved, upon each member State to which it is addressed, but shall leave to the national authorities the choice of form and methods'. Thus, Directives are not automatically binding and member States may choose (usually subject to a time limit) the way in which the aim of a Directive is to be achieved. In the UK this can be done by statutory instrument (European Communities Act 1972, s. 2(2)) or under a specific legislative provision.

Direct effect

Directives may sometimes create rights for individuals, enforceable in national courts. This concept is usually called 'direct effect' and should be distinguished from 'direct applicability' which applies only to Regulations. The difference is that, as noted above, Regulations are automatically part of the domestic legal order in their entirety. On the other hand, the content of a Directive is important in determining whether it is directly effective and creates enforceable individual rights in the national courts. In *Van Duyn* v *Home Office* (case 41/74) [1974] ECR 1337, it was said that a provision of Community law would be directly effective if:

■ there was a clear and precise obligation upon a member State,

■ which was not subject to a condition or limitation, and

■ which left the member State with no real discretion whether to apply the Community rule.

Therefore, in this case (involving a Dutch Scientologist wishing to enter the UK), a Directive which restricted the grounds upon which an EC national could be refused permission to enter another member State could confer rights on the plaintiff in the British courts.

For a Directive to have direct effect, the time limit for implementation must have elapsed or the state must have failed to implement the Directive correctly. In *Pubblico Ministero* v *Ratti* (case 148/78) [1979] ECR 1629, the ECJ held that a Directive relating to products containing dangerous substances could not be invoked by an individual, since the date of its implementation had not passed – however, when the time limit had expired, it might have direct effect.

Horizontal and vertical direct effect

The ECJ has held that an individual cannot invoke the terms of a non-implemented Directive against another individual ('horizontal effect') — that the 'direct effect' of Directives is limited to where an individual is seeking enforcement of rights against an institution of the State ('vertical effect'). This principle was recognised in *Marshall* v *Southampton and South West Hampshire Area Health Authority (Teaching)* (case 152/84) [1986] QB 401 (see *Cases and Materials* (8.2.1.1)). Marshall, who had been dismissed at the age of 62, claimed that the UK's Sex Discrimination Act 1975 contravened Directive 76/207/EEC, by permitting different retirement ages for men and women. The ECJ found evidence of sex discrimination in this case and as her former employer was a State body, Marshall could successfully rely on the Directive. Lord Slynn, noted that 'To give what is called horizontal effect to Directives would totally blur the distinction between Regulations and Directives' and the European Court agreed that 'a Directive may not of itself impose obligations on an individual'.

In *Marshall* the Health Authority was clearly a crown body — but what of other, less obvious, cases? The ECJ provided some guidelines as to what constitutes a State body in *Foster* v *British Gas plc* (case C–188/89) [1991] 1 QB 405. In *Foster* the applicant had been made to retire earlier than her male colleagues. Like Marshall, she sought to invoke the Equal Treatment Directive (76/207/EEC). On the question of what constitutes a State body, the ECJ, responding to an art. 177 reference, held that 'a body, whatever its legal form, which has been made responsible . . . for providing a public service under the control of the State and has for that purpose special powers beyond those which result from normal rules applicable in relations between individuals' could be subject to Directive 76/207/EEC. Applying this test, the House of Lords (*Foster* v *British Gas plc* [1991] 2 AC 306) held that British Gas (then a public corporation) was under the control of the State, so that this created rights capable of having direct effect which could be relied upon by individuals in the national courts.

Indirect effect

The distinction between 'vertical' and 'horizontal' direct effect and the fact that a Directive cannot have horizontal direct effect, so that it may not be invoked against an individual, has been harshly criticised. For example in *Case C-316/93, Vaneetveld* v *SA Le Foyer* [1994] ECR I-763, Jacobs A. G. claimed that 'distortions will obviously result, both between and within member States, if Directives are enforceable, for example, against employers . . . in the public sector but not in the private sector'. He rejected the claim that 'enforcing directives directly against individuals would endanger legal certainty', and responded that 'on the contrary' it would lead 'to greater certainty, and to a more coherent system.' Mindful of such criticism, the ECJ's response has been to develop the principle of 'indirect effect'. In *Von Colson* v *Land Nordrhein-Westfalen* (case 14/83) [1984] ECR 1891, the court held that art. 5 of the Treaty of Rome, which requires that States 'take all appropriate measures . . . to ensure fulfilment of [Community] obligations' meant that 'national courts are required to interpret their national laws in the light of the wording and the purpose of the [relevant] Directive in order to achieve the result referred to in . . . Article 189'. This approach was followed in *Marleasing SA* v *La Comercial Internacional de Alimentación SA* (case C–106/8) [1990] ECR I–4135. There the ECJ held that national courts should interpret national legislation ('as far as possible') so that it conforms with a Directive, regardless of whether the Directive pre- or post-dates that legislation. And most recently in *Faccini Doris* v *Recreb Srl* [1995] All ER (EC) 1, an Italian national sought to invoke against an Italian company, provisions of Directive 85/577, which had not as yet been introduced into Italian law. The ECJ recognised that while the directive could not impose obligations on an individual, the principle in *Marleasing* meant that the Italian court was under an obligation to interpret Italian law as far as possible in accordance with the wording and purpose of the directive.

Commenting on this principle of indirect effect Steiner (*EC Law*, 6th edn) notes that its success 'depends on the extent to which national courts perceive themselves as having a discretion, under their own constitutional rules, to interpret domestic law to comply with Community law'. What then has been the attitude of the British Courts to indirect effect?

In *Duke* v *GEC Reliance Systems Ltd* [1988] 1 AC 618 (see *Cases and Materials* (**8.2.1.1**)), Lord Templeman held that 'Section 2(4) of the European Communities Act 1972 does not . . . enable or constrain a British court to distort the meaning of the British statute in order to enforce against an individual a Community directive which has no direct effect between individuals.' However, in *Litster* v *Forth Dry Dock and Engineering Co. Ltd* [1990] 1 AC 546, the House of Lords cited *Von Colson* when interpreting domestic regulations (the Transfer of Undertakings (Protection of Employment) Regulations 1981 introduced to implement Directive 77/187) so as to comply with an EC Directive (since it had been claimed that the 1981 Regulations had failed adequately to implement Directive 77/187). Lord Templeman explained that 'the courts of the United Kingdom are under a duty to follow the practice of the European Court of Justice by giving a purposive construction to Directives and to Regulations issued for the purpose of complying with Directives.'

The *Litster* decision is significant in that it illustrates that British judges will not merely enforce Community law, but may also give effect to the European Court's interpretation of it. One possible explanation for the House of Lord's ruling in *Litster* is that unlike the case of *Duke*, which concerned an Act of Parliament (i.e. primary legislation), the UK legislation in *Litster* which had been introduced to implement the EC Directive was only a Regulation (a piece of secondary legislation).

The indirect effect model circumvents the vertical/horizontal distinction. However, it remains to be seen how the UK courts will ultimately respond to the *Von Colson* and *Marleasing* principles (extracts of which can be found in *Cases and Materials* (8.2.1.1)). In *Webb* v *EMO Air Cargo* [1992] 4 All ER 929, Lord Keith used the *Marleasing* phrase 'so far as possible' very restrictively when he held that 'a national court must construe a domestic law to accord with the terms of a Directive in the same field only if it is possible to do so.' However, following a preliminary ruling from the European Court in the *Webb* case, which involved a woman who was dismissed by her employer when she discovered that she was pregnant, Lord Keith held that the House of Lords should 'if at all possible' interpret provisions of the Sex Discrimination Act 1975 so as to comply with European law. The question remains, will domestic legislation take precedence over EC law if it is not 'at all possible' to fit domestic legislation into Euopean law? In the absence of any clear answers what can be said is that the domestic courts must interpret National law in accordance with EC law 'if at all possible' or 'as far as possible'.

Why does de Burca claim that, 'For the UK courts to apply the *Marleasing* ruling would certainly mark a change in the traditional role of statutory interpretation within the British constitutional system'? If you are unsure, read her analysis of the *Von Colson* and *Marleasing* decisions in the extract from her article in *Cases and Materials* (8.2.1.1).

Compensation

You may be wondering, if a Directive grants an individual certain rights and a State fails to implement that Directive into its domestic law, is the individual entitled to compensation for the State's omission? The answer is yes.

In *Francovich* v *Italy* (cases 6 & C–9/90) [1991] ECR I–5357 the European Court held that a member State may be obliged to compensate an individual for failing to implement a Directive where three conditions are satisfied. These are:

(a)   that the Directive in question conferred rights on individuals;

(b)   that one could identify these rights from the Directive; and

(c)   that there was 'a causal link' between the government's failure to implement the Directive and the loss suffered by the individual.

Thus the Italian government was required to compensate Francovich, who had suffered financially after his company became bankrupt, because of its failure to implement Directive 80/987, guaranteeing payment of wages in the event of employer insolvency. Following this the ECJ held in *Emmott* v *Minister for Social Welfare* (case C–208/90) [1993] ICR 8, that where a State fails to implement a Directive properly, an individual may sue the State (relying on that Directive if directly effective), until it is correctly implemented.

More recently, the European Court has developed *Francovich* so that a State may be liable, not merely when it fails to incorporate a directive into its national law, but when the state's legislature deliberately passes legislation contrary to EC law. Thus, in *R* v *Secretary of State for Transport, ex parte Factortame Ltd (No. 4)* [1996] QB 404, it was held that there was a right to compensation where:

(a) the rule of law which was breached was intended to confer rights on individuals;

(b) the breach was sufficiently serious; and

(c) there was a direct casual link between the breach of the State's obligation and the damage which was suffered by the injured parties.

Most recently in *R* v *Secretary of State for Transport, ex parte Factortame (No. 5), The Times,* 11 September 1997, the Divisional Court used this test when holding that the Spanish trawler owners and managers who had suffered following the enactment of the Merchant Shipping Act 1988, which was contrary to Community law, would be awarded compensation but that exemplary damages were not available. Commenting on this case. Nigel Gravells suggests that the '*Factortame* litigation has not reached its conclusion yet' and that 'it is difficult to predict the final outcome' ([1998] *Public Law* 8).

What seems clear however is that, post *Francovich*, the state may be responsible irrespective of whether the injury suffered by an individual in these circumstances was attributable to the actions of the state's legislature, judiciary or executive and it can be argued that this, at least to some extent, compensates for the fact that directives do not have horizontal effect.

Why should individuals be entitled to sue to enforce their Community law rights? Some reasons are suggested by Ross in *Cases and Materials* (8.2.1.1).

8.4.2.3 Other legislation

In addition to Regulations and Directives, the Council and Commission can issue 'Decisions'. These may be directed at companies or individuals. Decisions are only binding on those to whom they are addressed, distinguishing them from Regulations. Similarly, the fact that a Decision is ''binding in its entirety' (EC Treaty, art 189) distinguishes it from a Directive. As you may have guessed, Decisions tend to be of less practical significance than Regulations and Directives, although they are quite significant in the area of competition law, under arts 85 and 86.

Provide a definition of the terms *Regulation* and *Directive*. How do *Regulations* and *Directives* differ from *articles* in the Treaty of Rome?

Read the passage from the article by Mancini and Keeling on direct effect in *Cases and Materials* (8.2.1.2). Think about the ECJ's 'judicial creativity'. In view of the ECJ's case law, is there any real difference between a Regulation and a Directive?

8.4.3 CASE LAW OF THE EUROPEAN COURT OF JUSTICE

Decisions of the European Court are a further source of Community law. The court may be influenced by the 'general principles common to the laws of the member States' (EC Treaty, art. 215). Whilst the court is not bound by precedent, it has consistently sought to strengthen and expand the superiority of Community law over national law. The extent to which this has eroded Parliamentary supremacy is now considered.

8.5 The Challenge to Parliamentary Supremacy

The United Kingdom's membership of the European Communities took effect from 1 January 1973. For Community law to be binding in the UK it was necessary for

Parliament to pass legislation incorporating it into domestic law. This was the purpose of the European Communities Act 1972.

It is important that you are familiar with the European Communities Act 1972. You should pay particular attention to ss. 2 and 3 of the Act.

ACTIVITY 59

The best way of understanding the significance of the European Communities Act 1972 is actually to read it. Turn to the extracts from the Act in *Cases and Materials* **(8.3). Study them carefully. What does each section mean? What phrases are particularly difficult to understand or are ambiguous? Then draw up a list of the constitutional effects of the UK's enactment of the Act. Some possible answers are found at the end of this Chapter.**

Section 2(1) of the European Communities Act 1972 is an 'enabling section'. It provides for the direct applicability of Regulations made by the Commission and Council of Ministers. It also requires that Directives shall be binding as to the result to be achieved, although the manner in which that directive is implemented is left to the member States. Section 2(1) therefore provides the mechanism for Community law to be incorporated into the British legal system. Subsections (2) and (4) of s. 2 give wide powers to the government to make delegated legislation to implement community legislation. Section 2(4) also provides for a new principle of interpretation – that UK courts should interpret all UK legislation so as to avoid any possible conflict. Finally, s. 3 of the Act provides that British courts should determine disputes involving Community law in accordance with the principles laid down by the European Court of Justice. The European Court has long held that no member State should legislate inconsistently with Community law.

8.6 Attitude of the European Court of Justice

The approach taken by the European Court of Justice is quite clear: Community law prevails over the inconsistent national laws of member States. Thus member States cannot legislate to change Community law. The ECJ's attitude is illustrated by the following cases:

(a) *Van Gend en Loos* v *Nederlandse Administratie der Belastingen* (case 26/62) [1963] ECR 1

On an art. 177 ruling the ECJ observed that:

the Community constitutes a new order of international law for the benefit of which the States have limited their sovereign rights, albeit within limited fields.

(b) *Costa* v *ENEL* (case 6/64) [1964] ECR 585 (see *Cases and Materials* (8.4))

In *Costa*, the ECJ held that member States 'have restricted their sovereign rights and created a body of law applicable both to their nationals and to themselves'.

(c) *Internationale Handelsgesellschaft mbH* (case 11/70) [1970] ECR 1125

Here the plaintiff company obtained an export licence for maize on payment of a deposit, which was later forfeited when the company failed to export the specified quantity of maize. The company argued that this forfeiture was contrary to the written German Constitution. The European Court of Justice held:

> the validity of a Community measure or its effect within a member state cannot be affected by allegations that it runs counter to either fundamental rights as formulated by the constitution of the State or the principles of a national constitutional structure.

Thus EC law even takes precedence over the key constitutional provisions of member states.

(d) *Re Export Tax on Art Treasures (No. 2)* [1972] CMLR 699

The ECJ stated:

> The grant to the Community by the member States of the rights and powers envisaged by the provisions of the Treaty implies in fact a definitive limitation of their sovereign powers over which no appeal to provisions of international law of any kind whatsoever can prevail.

(e) *Amministrazione delle Finanze dello Stato v Simmenthal SpA* (case 106/77) [1978] ECR 629 (see *Cases and Materials* (8.4))

In this case, an Italian company imported meat from France. A fee was charged for the public health inspection of the meat. Simmenthal, the Italian meat importer, felt that the veterinary inspections of the meat were obstacles to the free movement of goods and were forbidden by Community law. An art. 177 reference was made on the question of how to reconcile the conflict between certain rules of Community law and subsequent inconsistent national legislation. The European Court of Justice held that a national court must itself apply Community law in preference to inconsistent national legislation, 'in its entirety' and 'set aside any proviso of national law which may conflict with it, whether prior or subsequent to the Community rule'.

(f) Even Britain's former judge in the European Court, Sir Gordon Slynn (now Lord Slynn of Hadley), stated that EC law would prevail in the event of a conflict with British legislation. This he claimed was as 'plain as a pikestaff', and if judges found themselves in a conflict between rules of national and Community law, they must set aside the former (*The Guardian*, 19 October 1991).

Therefore, as far as the European Court is concerned, neither the United Kingdom Parliament nor the legislative body of any other member State, can legislate inconsistently with Community law. This applies to both pre and post-accession national legislation.

Whatever the attitude of the European Court, ultimately the application and acceptance of Community law is a matter for the United Kingdom courts. They have the option of referring matters of interpretation to the European Court of Justice and of accepting or rejecting decisions of that court, subject to the EC Treaty's duty of Community loyalty (art. 5).

With the enactment of the European Communities Act 1972, it was assumed that Community law would take precedence over any inconsistent United Kingdom legislation that pre-dated the 1972 Act. Thus any pre-1972 British Statute which conflicts with

Community law is superseded by the relevant Community legislation. This is a clear application of the doctrine of implied repeal.

However, things in this area are not always so simple. Problems exist where there are conflicts between Community law and inconsistent United Kingdom legislation which post-dates the European Communities Act 1972. For example, can a 1998 Act of Parliament overrule a 1993 Community Regulation? According to the European Court of Justice, Community law prevails. So what is the attitude of the UK courts?

Why is the ECJ so unequivocal in its assertion that Community law is supreme in the event of a clash with domestic law?

8.7 Attitude of British Courts

The attitude of the United Kingdom courts is illustrated by the following cases:

(a) *Esso Petroleum Co. Ltd* v *Kingswood Motors (Addlestone) Ltd* **[1974] QB 142 at 151**

Bridge J held that where Community law 'is in conflict with our domestic law the effect of the [European Communities] Act of 1972 is to require that the Community law shall prevail'.

(b) *Aero Zipp Fasteners Ltd* v *YKK Fasteners (UK) Ltd* **[1973] CMLR 819 at 820**

Graham J observed that the European Communities Act 1972 'enacted that relevant Common Market law should be applied in this country and should, where there is a conflict, override English law'.

(c) *Shields* v *E. Coomes (Holdings) Ltd* **[1978] 1 WLR 1408**

Lord Denning MR expressed the view that the United Kingdom courts should interpret any ambiguity in United Kingdom legislation so as to give effect to

British Community obligations – thus where there was a clear inconsistency, Community law should prevail. Lord Denning's explanation for this was the need for consistency within the European Community's economic sphere: 'It would be intolerable if one country interpreted the regulations differently from another'.

(d) *Macarthys Ltd v Smith* **[1981] QB 1804 (see *Cases and Materials* (8.1.2.1))**

In this case, which concerned equal pay, an art. 177 reference was made to the ECJ on the interpretation of art. 119 of the Treaty of Rome (the principle that men and women should receive equal pay for equal work). Lord Denning MR said:

> . . . the provisions of art. 119 of the EEC Treaty take priority over anything in our English statute on equal pay which is inconsistent with art. 119. That priority is given by our own law. It is given by the European Communities Act 1972 itself. . . . whenever there is any inconsistency, Community law has priority. It is not supplanting English law. It is part of our law which overrides any other part which is inconsistent with it.

(e) *Garland v British Rail Engineering Ltd* **(case 12/81) [1983] 2 AC 751 (see *Cases and Materials* 8.1.2.1))**

The female appellant objected to the fact that on retirement, women were ineligible for certain benefits (e.g., travel concessions on trains) enjoyed by former male employees. Since this distinction appeared lawful under domestic law, the House of Lords made an art. 177 reference. The ECJ held that subsidised train travel and other concessions could come within the principle of 'equal pay' under art. 119 of the Treaty. In the House of Lords, Lord Diplock affirmed that the domestic legislation (the Sex Discrimination Act 1975) must be interpreted so as to avoid a conflict with Community law. And even on those occasions where there was a clear conflict, British legislation should be construed so as to conform with Community law, 'no matter how wide a departure from the prima facie meaning may be needed to achieve consistency'.

(f) *Stoke-on-Trent City Council v B & Q plc* **[1990] 3 CMLR 31 at 34**

It was claimed that s. 47 of the Shops Act 1950, which restricted Sunday trading, was incompatible with art. 36 of the EC Treaty. Hoffmann J asserted that:

> The Treaty of Rome is the supreme law of this country, taking precedence over Acts of Parliament.

(g) *R v Secretary of State for Transport, ex parte Factortame Ltd* **(see *Cases and Materials* (8.5))**

This is a very important case. It involved a conflict between EC law and an inconsistent later UK statute. The appellants were companies which owned fishing vessels. The majority of these had first been registered as Spanish, before being re-registered as British vessels. The British government was concerned that the operation of Community quotas would adversely affect the British fishing industry. Parliament therefore passed the Merchant Shipping Act 1988 and Merchant Shipping Regulations 1988 which effectively prevented Spanish ships from being registered as British. Under this legislation, for a ship to be designated as British, the company owning the vessel would have to have its principal place of business in the UK and 75 per cent of its shareholders would have to be British nationals. The appellants (Spanish trawler owners) claimed that this legislation was contrary to provisions of Community law which prohibited discrimination on the grounds of nationality.

When the case came before the Divisional Court, it decided to seek a preliminary ruling from the European Court of Justice. However, in view of the time it would take for this art. 177 reference to be heard, it granted an interim injunction suspending the operation of the legislation, in favour of the shipowners.

The Court of Appeal reversed the decision and quashed the order for interim disapplication of the Act (*R* v *Secretary of State for Transport, ex parte Factortame Ltd* [1989] 2 CMLR 353). Bingham LJ said that such a move was a 'constitutional enormity'. He acknowledged the obligation to give effect to existing enforceable Community rights and was prepared to accept that because of the Community, English law is no longer so inviolable as it once was. However, unless a statute is shown to be inconsistent with Community law, it must remain inviolable (and in saying this he stressed the presumption of validity). Lord Donaldson of Lymington MR agreed and found no authority either in English or Community law for giving such powers to the English courts as the Divisional Court had claimed.

The House of Lords endorsed the Court of Appeal's position with regard to the lack of jurisdiction in the English courts to grant interim relief (*R* v *Secretary of State for Transport, ex parte Factortame Ltd* [1990] 2 AC 85). Lord Bridge of Harwich stated that if the interim injunction was granted and the Spanish fishermen were unsuccessful before the European Court, the applicants would have been unjustly enriched by being able to continue fishing during the litigation. Interim relief could only be obtained if, pending a decision of the European Court of Justice, member States were under a duty to respond to the complaints of litigants that they were being unfairly penalised. It was this question which was then referred under art. 177 to the ECJ.

The Court of Justice held that the Treaty of Rome required the courts of member States to give effect to the directly enforceable provisions of Community law. Any conflicting national law would be inapplicable. Thus where a national court 'in a case before it concerning Community law, considers that the sole obstacle which precludes it from granting interim relief is a rule of national law, it must set aside that rule' (*R* v *Secretary of State for Transport, ex parte Factortame Ltd (No. 2)* (case C–213/89) [1991] 1 AC 603).

In conformity with this ruling, the House of Lords granted the vessel owners interim relief. Lord Bridge said that the European Communities Act 1972 made it clear that 'it was the duty of a United Kingdom court, when delivering final judgment to override any rule of national law found to be in conflict with any directly enforceable rule of Community law' ([1991] 1 AC 603 at p. 659). This decision appears to have considerable constitutional significance, for now the British courts appear to possess the power to order the temporary disapplication of any provision of national law alleged to violate Community law.

The *Factortame* ruling generated controversy in Parliament. The Speaker refused a motion for an emergency debate on the issue, and Sir Teddy Taylor MP claimed that, 'any law which we enact . . . can be repealed in a flash by judges in Luxembourg', while Richard Shepherd MP said that the ruling went to the 'very heart' of Parliament's role.

A less emotive reaction to this judgment was provided by Professor Lasok. He observed that the 'traditional concept of sovereignty which, in the eyes of the positive theory of law as expounded by Dicey, had no limits, cannot be asserted in the EC. Such a truth is hard to swallow by those who in this country believe that ''Britannia rules the waves'', and imagine that Dicey is still walking the corridors of the academy'. (*Student Law Review*, Autumn 1991, p. 26.)

Think back to Dicey's definition of Parliamentary sovereignty? Can it be reconciled with the recent approach of the UK courts to European Community cases?

Nigel Gravells claims that since the *Factortame* decision, 'the British constitutional doctrine of Parliamentary Sovereignty can no longer be relied upon in the British courts to frustrate the application of Community law' ([1991] Public Law 191). Read the extracts from *Factortame* in *Cases and Materials* (8.5). Do you agree with this view? How does the decision in *Factortame* compare with that of the House of Lords in *Equal Opportunities Commission* v *Secretary of State for Employment* [1994] 1 All ER 910 (extract in *Cases and Materials* (8.5)).

De Smith once commented that 'the United Kingdom government has seated Parliament on two horses, one straining towards the preservation of Parliamentary sovereignty, the other galloping in the direction of Community law supremacy'. What is meant by this statement?

8.8 European Union

The European Community has developed far beyond the aims of its founders. Created in 1957 and known as the European Economic Community, it was concerned with only establishing common policies in the areas of agriculture, transport, competition policy, free movement of workers, and the elimination of trade barriers. However, the Community has graduated from exercising an exclusively economic mandate into asserting jurisdiction over a variety of social, financial and political issues.

In 1986 the Single European Act was passed to amend the Treaty of Rome. With its primary aim that of creating a single or internal market, this treaty sought to make 'concrete progress towards European unity'. This process was taken further by the Maastricht Treaty on European Union (1992) which paved the way for full economic and monetary union.

8.8.1 THE MAASTRICHT TREATY

Notwithstanding an unsuccessful challenge to this treaty in the UK Courts (*R v Secretary of State for Foreign and Commonwealth Affairs, ex parte Rees-Mogg* [1994] 2 WLR 115), the Maastricht Treaty was ratified by the UK in 1993 and incorporated into British law by the European Communities (Amendment) Act 1993.

The Maastricht Treaty further amended the Treaty of Rome 1957 in order to achieve the aim of 'ever closer union'. The key elements of the Maastricht Treaty include:

(a) **Institutional changes**

   A significant development was the creation of a major new institution, the European Central Bank (ECB). Other institutions may now sue the ECB for inaction and the art. 177 system of preliminary rulings has been extended to cover the interpretation of ECB actions. Other changes included increasing the influence of the European Parliament, and vesting greater power in the European Court (e.g., power to fine), so as to ensure that member States comply with European law.

(b) **Common foreign and security policy**

   Title V of the Maastricht Treaty provides that member States shall develop a common foreign and security policy. The objectives of this common policy are to safeguard the independence and security of the EC; to strengthen international security in accordance with the principles of the UN charter; and to protect human rights and fundamental freedoms. However, disagreements between European governments during the Gulf and Bosnian conflicts have illustrated the practical difficulties of establishing a Community defence force and of agreeing on a common foreign policy.

(c) **The Social Chapter**

   The Social Chapter of the Maastricht Treaty established minimum working conditions for employees in EC States. John Major's Government chose to 'opt out' of the Social Chapter on the ground that it would erode competitiveness and increase unemployment, but Tony Blair's Labour Government has now signed up to the Social Chapter.

(d)　**Economic and monetary union (EMU)**

The Maastricht Treaty envisaged closer European economic co-operation. It consists of three elements: State membership of the European Exchange Rate Mechanism (ERM); member States converging their economies; and the abolition of national currencies, with the creation of the EURO, as a single European currency.

(e)　**Political union**

Political union refers to the creation of a common policy in the fields of foreign and home affairs, security, education and health. The Maastricht Treaty anticipated that there will be increasing intergovernmental co-operation in the areas of unlawful immigration, terrorism and international crime.

(f)　**Subsidiarity**

Article 3b of the EC Treaty, which has been inserted by art. G(5) of the Maastricht Treaty, defines subsidiarity to mean that the Community is to act 'within the limits of the powers conferred upon it by this Treaty and of the objects assigned to it therein'. Some commentators equate subsidiarity with federalism, since central power would be retained by the European Union and local power retained by member States. This is only one possible interpretation since the Treaty fails to issue clear guidelines on how and when the subsidiarity principle should apply. The views of Sir Leon Brittan (the former Vice-President of the European Commission) on subsidiarity are reproduced in *Cases and Materials* (8.6).

8.8.2　THE TREATY OF AMSTERDAM

The Maastricht Treaty was accused by some of being vague and poorly drafted, but its successor, the voluminous Treaty of Amsterdam which was signed on 2 October 1997, has been subject to many of the same criticisms.

The Amsterdam Treaty has widened the grounds upon which the European Union was founded, to cover the 'principles of liberty, democracy, respect for human rights and fundamental freedoms, and the rule of law' (art. F). The Amsterdam Treaty aims to pave the way for the enlargement of the European Union, making it into an 'area of freedom, security and justice' (art. B). It touches on a wide range of areas and these include: the protection of human rights and the elimination of discrimination on the grounds of 'sex and ethnic origin, religion or belief, disability, age or sexual orientation' (art. 6a); the introduction of measures to tackle unemployment in Europe; the abolition of border controls (although the United Kingdom retains its opt out from this, the Schengen Agreement); the promotion of co-operation in criminal matters, particularly in relation to drug trafficking, offences against children and terrorism; the extension of qualified majority voting; the granting of some additional powers to the European Parliament; extra powers bestowed on the President of the European Commission, including the right to block the appointment of other Commissioners; a greater say for the European Union in defining and implementing a common foreign and defence policy; and finally, the appointment of a Secretary General who will assist the President of the EU's Council in implementing and articulating the Union's foreign policy on the world stage.

Following the Government's ratification of the Amsterdam Treaty, the Opposition claimed that it would further undermine British sovereignty and their spokesman, Michael Howard, claimed that it 'takes power away from democratically elected governments and gives it to an unelected office in Brussels' (*The Daily Telegraph*, 13 November 1997). Nevertheless, the Government has supported the Treaty and it has now been incorporated into British law by the European Communities (Amendment) Act 1998.

European law has, at least to some extent, permeated and influenced almost every area of constitutional and administrative law. An example of this is the correlation between EC law and royal prerogative powers. Please read *R* v *Secretary of State for Foreign and Commonwealth Affairs, ex parte Rees-Mogg* [1994] 1 All ER 457 in *Cases and Materials* (8.6). What was the argument of Lord Rees-Mogg which Lloyd LJ described as 'most interesting jurisprudentially'. How did the court respond to this argument? Are you surprised by the decision?

Robin Cook, the British Foreign Secretary, has said that 'our mission . . . is to create a Europe for the people' (*The Sunday Times*, 14 June 1998). How might this goal be attained?

For some ideas you should look at the views of Sir Leon Brittan in *Cases and Materials* (8.6) on the future development of the European Community.

8.9 Conclusion

In *H.P. Bulmer Ltd* v *J. Bollinger SA* [1974] Ch 401, Lord Denning MR said that the EC treaty 'is like an incoming tide. It flows into the estuaries and up the rivers. It cannot be held back'. Clearly Lord Denning was fond of this imagery. Five years later in *Shields* v *E. Coomes (Holdings) Ltd* [1979] 1 WLR 1408, his lordship observed that: 'the flowing tide of Community law is coming in fast. It has not stopped at the high-water mark. It has broken the dykes and banks. It has submerged the surrounding land. So much so that we have to learn to become amphibious if we wish to keep our heads above water.'

Lord Denning may have retired but the tide of Community law shows no sign of turning. European Community law is indisputably a primary source of the unwritten British

Constitution. The catalyst for this 'flood' was the European Communities Act 1972. As Professor Bradley notes: 'the exercise by Parliament of its legislative supremacy in 1972 has brought about a profound change in the operation of Parliamentary sovereignty'. Thus, in answer to **Activity 59**, it may be said that some of the consequences of the 1972 Act are as follows:

(a) the diminution of Parliamentary supremacy (at least in the Diceyean sense);

(b) the erosion of traditional constitutional principles such as express repeal;

(c) the creation of rights and duties for individuals in Britain as a result of 'directly effective' Community legislation;

(d) the preservation of a future UK Parliament's right to repeal the European Communities Act 1972.

It is theoretically possible that, at some future date, Britain could leave the European Community. Lord Denning MR acknowledged this in *Macarthys Ltd v Smith* [1979] ECR 785 where he commented:

> If the time should come when our Parliament deliberately passes an Act – with the intention of repudiating the Treaty or any provision in it – or intentionally of acting inconsistently with it — and says so in express terms — then I should have thought that it would be the duty of our courts to follow the statute of our Parliament.

Of course any such move would create major political turbulence and economic uncertainty. It is also a moot point whether it would be practically feasible for the UK to leave the Community after nearly a quarter of a century of aligning itself economically, commercially and socially with its Continental European neighbours.

Mindful perhaps of being accused of unwise political speculation, Lord Denning qualified his earlier statement with the proviso: 'I do not however envisage any such situation.' Instead he firmly noted that: 'Unless there is such an intentional and express repudiation of the [EC] Treaty, it is our duty to give priority to the Treaty.'

Therefore, putting it in simple terms, Community membership is akin to one's membership of a club. The club has 'rules' (e.g., rules of etiquette, bans on smoking), which members are obliged to respect. The option to leave always remains. However, the longer one stays, the harder it becomes to sever club ties and leave. So too with the European Community. Thus, Community obligations and the political realities of the late 20th century lead Professor Bradley to conclude that today, 'the orthodox doctrine of the sovereign Parliament is not an immutable part of British constitutional law'.

8.10   End of Chapter Assessment Question

Lord Bridge has acknowledged that the terms of the European Communities Act 1972 mean that 'it was the duty of a United Kingdom Court, when delivering final judgment, to override any rule of national law found to be in conflict with any directly enforceable rule of Community law'. (R v *Secretary of State, ex parte Factortame Ltd* (1991).)

To what extent can this be reconciled with Dicey's theory that Parliamentary Sovereignty was 'the very keystone' of the British Constitution?

(See *Cases and Materials* (8.8) for a specimen answer.)

CHAPTER NINE

THE POLICE: STATUS AND ACCOUNTABILITY

9.1 Objectives

By the end of this Chapter you should be able to:

■ explain the position of the police service within the constitutional framework of the UK;

■ understand the role of the chief constable, local police authority, the Secretary of State, and the relationship between them;

■ comment on the ways in which police officers are held accountable for the exercise of their powers;

■ apply the principles of police accountability to a given scenario.

9.2 Introduction

Knowing where to start a discussion on the police is not easy. Therefore, to put things into an historical context, we will start with the views of a Royal Commission set up to examine policing. The Royal Commission on the Police in 1962 (Cmnd 1728) stated:

24. The police systems in England, Scotland and Wales are the products of a series of compromises between conflicting principles or ideas. Consequently, in contrast to other public services such as health and education, the rationale of the police service does not rest upon any single and definite concept of the public good. Thus it is to the public good that the police should be strong and effective in preserving law and order and preventing crime; but it is equally to the public good that police power should be controlled and confined so as not to interfere arbitrarily with personal freedom. The result is compromise. The police should be powerful but not oppressive, they should be efficient but not officious; they should form an impartial force in the body politic, and yet be subject to a degree of control by persons who are not required to be impartial and who are themselves liable to police supervision.

25. It is not our purpose to describe the history of the police systems of Great Britain in any detail, but these systems cannot be understood without first recognising the main features, or principles, which have moulded their development and which survive to invest them with their modern character. These features are:

1. the local character of the office of constable;

2. the common law origin of the office of constable;

3. the subordination of the constable to justices.

These three principles originated in England in pre-Tudor times, while the remaining two were embodied in 19th century legislation:

4. the organisation of constables into forces;

5. the subjection of police forces to a degree of local democratic supervision.

According to Lord Scarman (extract in *Cases and Materials* (9.1)) what are the two principles of policing a free society?

9.3 Organisation of the Police

9.3.1 HISTORICAL DEVELOPMENT

It has been said that 'the history of the police is the history of the office of constable'. This office had its origins in the village, probably the oldest area of local self-government in England. The constable was an executive agent required to make quarterly reports (presented at courts and later in the 14th century to petty sessions). The reports dealt with the arrest of felons, keeping the peace and also the condition of roads and bridges and many other matters of purely local administration. The latter was extended, after Parliament came into existence, to Popish recusants, persons absenting themselves from their Parish church, profane swearers and cursers. Presentment of these reports survived until as late as 1827.

Every town and local parish had its constable or constables. After the Statute of Westminister 1285 they were helped by watchmen. There was no system of policing, only law enforcement on a local level.

This tradition of local policing persisted and was preserved when constables were established into forces in the 19th century. In the interests of economy and efficiency these small units were enlarged in 1948 by amalgamations of small city and borough forces with the larger county forces. During 1967–68 amalgamations into much larger units took place. This meant that police forces consisted of thousands, rather than hundreds of personnel, covering much larger geographic areas (e.g., the West Mercia Constabulary comprised the old forces of Herefordshire, Worcestershire, Worcester City and Shropshire).

The consequence of the Local Government Act 1972 was that there were fewer combined police forces and most of the police authority areas corresponded to the new county boundaries (e.g., the West Midlands Force).

Even in these larger forces some local identity was retained and there seemed to be no real demand for a national police force. Evidence to the Royal Commission from chief constables suggested that a national force would endanger liberty. Sir Frank Newson, permanent under-secretary at the Home Office 1948–57 said, making a point that should be emphasised in this context, that:

> every police force is under local control, and that there is no danger of the police being used as the servants of the central authority.

However, in 1962 Professor A.L. Goodhart refused to sign the Report of the Royal Commission (Cmnd 1728). He produced a Memorandum of Dissent (p. 157 of the Report) which began:

> I regret that I cannot sign this report. I am convinced that it is essential to establish a centrally controlled police force, administered on a regional basis.

He believed such a force would be more efficient and would not endanger the liberty of the individual. He pointed out that the creation by Sir Robert Peel in 1829 of an organised force of constables in the Metropolitan area, and the consequent abolition of the parish constable, was constitutionally more radical than his own suggestions.

This was in contrast to the views of the Royal Commission which had already endorsed the statement made by a previous Royal Commission of 1929 (Cmd 3297) that:

> The police in this country have never been recognised, either in law or by tradition, as a force distinct from the general body of citizens.

Pause for a moment and think about the two views expressed above. Which view do you think is the more satisfactory, that expressed by Professor Goodhart or that expressed by the Royal Commisson of 1929?

Today some features of policing are organised on a wide regional basis (e.g., regional crime squads), while others operate on a national basis (e.g., the Planning and Research Department at the Home Office). The Police Act 1997 has created two statutory bodies operating nationally within the police service, the National Criminal Intelligence Service and the National Crime Squad. The 1997 Act sets out the structure, functions, safeguards and controls of these bodies.

During the miners' strike in the early 1980s there was something called 'mutual aid'. This enabled constables from different forces around the country to be seconded to work in the areas affected by problems associated with the strike. This was a nationally co-ordinated approach to some localised public disorder problems which overstretched the resources of the local force.

9.3.2 RECENT DEVELOPMENTS

The last few years has seen much Parliamentary and governmental activity relating to policing. In 1993 we saw (a) the publication of the Sheehy Report (Inquiry into Police Responsibilities and Rewards) (Cmnd 2280); (b) a White Paper ('Police Reform: the Government's Proposals for the Police Service in England and Wales') (Cmnd 7781), and (c) proposals introduced by the Home Secretary on 28 October 1993 (Hansard HC, 28 October 1989, cols. 975–89). This was followed by the Police and Magistrates' Courts Act 1994, an Act subject to much debate and criticism. (These criticisms are discussed in the extract from Marshall and Loveday in *Cases and Materials* (9.2.1).) The 1994 Act amended the Police Act 1964. This was followed by the Police Act 1996 which consolidated the changes brought in by the 1994 Act and replaced the 1964 Police Act. So, unless otherwise stated, references to sections and schedules in this Chapter will be to the Police Act 1996.

Read ss. 32 and 33 of the Police Act 1996 in *Cases and Materials* (9.2.1). What does it permit?

By s. 32 of the 1996 Act, the Secretary of State has the power to alter the police areas other than that of the City of London. Such alterations may reduce or increase the number of police areas, but he or she cannot abolish the metropolitan police district. These powers are exercisable, *inter alia*, if 'it appears to him to be expedient to make the alterations in the interests of efficiency or effectiveness'. There are safeguards to prevent the division of, for example, district councils by such alterations. In addition, by s. 33, notice of any alterations has to be given to the relevant authorities. Notwithstanding the fact that the Secretary of State has to consider any subsequent objections, he or she may still make the alterations, and these alterations may contain provisions not referred to in the notice.

We all live in police areas and may think of them as 'local'. But you can see that, potentially, these are sweeping powers to reorganise the geographic areas of police forces.

Think about these powers and answer the following questions.

Could it be that a Home Secretary may feel that, in the interests of efficiency and effectiveness, it is expedient to organise the police on a regional basis? Might this be what Professor Goodhart was referring to in his dissent from the Royal Commission's Report?

Once again there is no definitive answer to the question in **SAQ 81**. It is up to you to express a view after giving it thought.

At present there are 43 police areas in England and Wales including the City of London and the Metropolitan police forces, the latter being the largest (s. 1 and sch. 1 to the 1996 Act). Each area is required to maintain a police force (s. 2) and there must be a police authority for every police area which must be a body corporate (s. 3).

The Government's White Paper which ultimately led through the Police and Magistrates' Courts Act 1994 to the passing of the 1996 Act, promised that its introduction would ensure that 'the bonds between local communities and their police services will be greatly strengthened'. Read the extract from Marshall and Loveday in *Cases and Materials* (9.2.1) to consider whether this has actually been the case.

9.4   Police Authorities

9.4.1   COMPOSITION

Police forces are subject to some degree of local democratic supervision. The Metropolitan Police Act 1829, the City of London Police Act 1839, the Municipal Corporations Act 1835 (which made provision for the creation of police forces in towns) and the County Police Act 1839 (which provided for the creation of police forces in counties) established bodies to supervise police forces. In the boroughs there were watch committees and, in the counties, standing joint committees. The Metropolitan Police were supervised by the Home Secretary. In 1964 the Police Act introduced police authorities. These authorities consisted of two-thirds local councillors and one-third magistrates and were usually referred to as police committees.

By s. 4 of and sch. 2 and 3 to the 1996 Act police authorities now consist of 17 members: 9 from local councils, 3 magistrates and 5 independent members. The independent members are appointed from a short list prepared by the Secretary of State. The chair of the police authority is elected from its members, which by simple arithmetic is likely to be one of the local councillors. This composition was a compromise arrived at as a result of criticism arising out of the legislative proposal from Mr Howard, then Home Secretary, that five members should be appointed by the Secretary of State who should also appoint the chair.

9.4.2 FUNCTIONS

Police authorities have certain functions under the 1996 Act.

Look at ss. 6, 7 and 8 in *Cases and Materials* (9.3.1). What does it require of police authorities?

Section 6 requires a police authority 'to secure the maintenance of an efficient and effective police force for its area'. It must take account of any objectives determined by either the Secretary of State or the authority, performance targets, and any local policing plan. The police authority has to prepare annual force objectives (s. 7) and a local policing plan (s. 8). The Secretary of State also determines objectives and sets performance targets (ss. 37 and 38).

The police authority appoints the chief constable, subject to approval by the Secretary of State (s. 11(1)). Such approval is no mere formality. Several years ago the police authority in Derbyshire wished to appoint their current deputy chief constable to the post of chief, but the Home Secretary refused to approve the appointment. Consequently another person was appointed to the post, with the approval of the Home Secretary. Does this undermine any real power in the local democratic supervison?

Similarly, with the approval of the Secretary of State, the police authority may call upon the chief constable to retire in the interests of efficiency, subject to the chief constable being allowed to make representations beforehand (s. 11(2) and (3)). This provision gives statutory effect to the principle expressed in the case of *Ridge* v *Baldwin* [1964] AC 40. In that case a chief constable was dismissed without being given the opportunity to make representations on his own behalf. This was held to be contrary to the rules of natural justice. He was entitled to make representations.

9.4.3 RELATIONSHIP WITH THE CHIEF CONSTABLE

In 1964 the view of Ministers was that the police authority should not instruct the chief constable in operational matters. This is reflected in the 1996 Act where s. 10 states that the 'police force . . . shall be under the direction and control of the chief constable'.

Approval of this view seems to have been given by the judiciary. In *R v Commissioner of Police of the Metropolis, ex parte Blackburn* [1968] 2 QB 118 Lord Denning MR stated categorically that the Commissioner is not subservient to the Home Secretary in operational matters. The Commissioner's position in such matters is independent and the police authority cannot instruct him or her on his or her duty to enforce the criminal law. That duty is owed to the public and is a duty which could be compelled by mandamus or at the suit of the Attorney-General.

At p. 136 Lord Denning said:

> I hold it to be the duty of the Commissioner of Police of the Metropolis, as it is of every chief constable, to enforce the law of the land. . . . He must decide whether or no suspected persons are to be prosecuted; and, if need be, bring the prosecution or see that it is brought. But in all these things he is not the servant of anyone, save of the law itself. No Minister of the Crown can tell him . . . that he must, or must not, prosecute this man or that one. Nor can any police authority tell him so. The responsibility for law enforcement lies on him. He is answerable to the law and to the law alone.

Lord Denning was speaking before the Crown Prosecution Service was given such a developed role with regard to prosecutions.

A police authority can require reports from the chief constable except where the chief constable thinks they are not needed to enable the authority to discharge its function or that it would not be in the public interest. Once again, this is subject to the approval of the Secretary of State. The authority is also entitled to receive an annual report from the chief constable and it has a duty to keep itself informed about the manner of dealing with complaints against the police.

ACTIVITY 66

Note the composition of and list the functions and powers of a police authority.

The composition of a police authority is 17 people, of which 9 will be councillors, 3 magistrates and 5 independent members. Their functions and powers are:

- to secure the maintenance of an efficient and effective police force for the area;

- to prepare objectives and a local policing plan annually;

- to appoint the chief constable, subject to approval by the Secretary of State;

- and to call upon the chief constable to retire in the interests of efficiency and effectiveness, again subject to the Secretary of State's approval.

Read the extract from Peter Thornton in *Cases and Materials* (9.3.2). Thorton claims that the tripartite structure (the Chief Constable, Home Secretary and the Police Authority) has failed 'to provide true accountability'. What are the three reasons he offers by way of explanation?

9.5 Operational Control

Therefore, subject to what has already been said, the police authority does not have the power to direct the chief constable as to operational matters within the force.

We have already seen that the chief constable has the direction and control of the force, and has to have regard to the local policing plan in discharging those functions. But it is unlikely that this will alter his real independence in day-to-day operational matters.

S.A. de Smith says that the chief constable is an independent officer upon whom powers are directly conferred for the benefit of the populace. However, as Lord Denning MR pointed out in *R v Commissioner of Police of the Metropolis, ex parte Blackburn* [1968] 2 QB 118, the chief constable, while independent in enforcement matters, is answerable to the law for the due performance of his duties.

The 1968 *Blackburn* case concerned a policy decision taken by the Commissioner not to proceed against 'clubs for breach of the gaming laws unless there were complaints of cheating or because they had become haunts of criminals' (per Lord Denning at p. 134). Mr Blackburn sought an order of mandamus to compel the Commissioner to revoke the policy. He did not succeed at first instance and he appealed to the Court of Appeal. During the appeal the Court of Appeal was informed that the Commissioner had undertaken to revoke the policy. Thus no order of mandamus was issued.

However, some illuminating comments were made by the Court of Appeal and without the undertaking from the Commissioner it is arguable that the court would have ordered mandamus. (See the extracts from the judgment of Lord Denning MR in *Cases and Materials* (9.4).)

Later, in *R v Commissioner of Police of the Metropolis, ex parte Blackburn (No. 3)* [1973] QB 241 (extract in *Cases and Materials* (9.4)) another request for mandamus was made by Mr Blackburn this time seeking to compel the Commissioner to enforce the Obscene Publications Act 1959. The Commissioner had allegedly decided not to prosecute under the Obscene Publications Act 1959 without the consent of the Director of Public Prosecutions (DPP). It appeared from the policy statement that the consent of the DPP was a condition precedent to any prosecution. The case failed. The Commissioner argued that the consent of the DPP was not a condition precedent, and the court apparently accepted that statement.

The court seemed to decide that the courts should not interfere with the exercise by a chief officer of his or her discretion unless a chief officer abdicated his or her responsibility over law enforcement.

What do you think might amount to an 'abdication'?

In answer to **SAQ 82** you might have said that a chief constable would abdicate his or her responsibility by refusing to exercise a discretion vested in him or her (by adopting a rigid policy?), or by refusing to enforce a law at all. It would not, it was felt, be an abdication to take decisions of policy to ensure uniformity, nor to seek the DPP's advice, provided it was not a condition precedent.

However, in *Buckoke* v *Greater London Council* [1971] 1 Ch 655 (see **Cases and Materials (9.4)**), an order was given by the London Fire Service permitting its drivers to go through red traffic lights if it was safe. It was a crime at that time to drive through red traffic signals, even if one was driving an emergency vehicle. (Since 1975 a Traffic Regulation Order has allowed emergency vehicles to ignore red traffic signals.) The Court of Appeal held that it was lawful to give such an instruction. Lord Denning said that when the law had become a dead letter, the police need not prosecute and the Commissioner might make a policy decision in proper cases directing his or her men not to prosecute. How does this statement stand alongside the views expressed in the early *Blackburn* case concerning abdication of responsibility?

In 1979 Mr Blackburn brought another action, *R* v *Commissioner of Police of the Metropolis, ex parte Blackburn, The Times*, 1 December 1979. Once again, it concerned obscene publications and a suggestion that the Commissioner had taken a policy decision which divested the police officers of their powers under the 1959 Act. Here too, mandamus was refused. The report reads:

> Apart altogether from the indisputable fact the Commissioner had no authority to divest constables of their lawful powers of arrest and any attempt by him to do so would be of no avail, their lordships were satisfied that the practical effect of the Commissioner's instructions was not to remove their powers of arrest.

Clearly there is power in the courts to control the chief officer but a reluctance to interfere except in extreme circumstances. This is demonstrated by the earlier decisions and the following *CEGB* case.

In *R* v *Chief Constable of Devon and Cornwall, ex parte Central Electricity Generating Board* [1982] QB 458 objectors to nuclear power stations were preventing the survey of a possible nuclear power site at Luxulyan, Cornwall. The objectors were 'passive' and distributed a pamphlet with instructions to the objectors not to breach the peace or commit any criminal act. The Board asked for assistance to remove them. The chief constable said he had no power to do so since there was no likelihood of a breach of the peace. The Board disagreed and sought an order mandamus to compel the police to remove the protestors. The chief constable accepted that if the Court of Appeal held that the police had the power to remove the protesters they would do so. However, the request for an order of mandamus was refused. The chief constable's decision was a policy decision and the courts would not interfere. In this situation the police could lawfully intervene only if they had reasonable cause to suspect a breach of the peace had occurred, was imminent, or that an arrestable offence had been committed.

Could Fred, a member of the police authority, challenge the decision of the chief constable in the following scenarios?

   (a)   None of his officers will take action against prostitutes in the main town in his area because in the opinion of the chief constable they provide a service which reduces the number of sex offences.

   (b)   Cyclists who ignore traffic lights are not to be prosecuted.

   (c)   Officers will not attend incidents of thefts from shops where goods have been stolen of a value less than £200.

From what you have read so far, you should have answered **SAQ 83** as follows:

Fred cannot use his position as a member of the police authority to force the chief constable to change his decision, since the police authority cannot control the chief constable in operational matters. However, Fred could challenge the decisions in the courts so long as he could establish that the chief constable came within the principles of control.

   (a)   If this was a policy decision which prevented the chief constable from carrying out his duty (i.e, being so rigid that it fettered the exercise of his discretion) then the courts may revoke it. This emerges from the judgment of Salmon LJ in the *Blackburn* case of 1968.

   (b)   In the same speech, Salmon LJ gave a similar illustration of where there was a blanket refusal to prosecute. That could be challenged. The chief constable's discretion to make policy decisions is not absolute.

   (c)   This is similar to the example given in the speech of Lord Denning MR and so could also be challenged in the courts.

ACTIVITY 68

Compare and contrast the views of Robertson and Mark in *Cases and Materials* (9.4). Which of these views is the more persuasive?

■ 'Few Western countries permit police forces such organisational independence' (Geoffrey Robertson QC).

■ The British police are 'the least powerful, the most accountable and therefore the most acceptable police in the world' (former Metropolitan Police Commissioner, Sir Robert Mark).

9.6 Secretary of State for the Home Department

In relation to all police forces the Secretary of State has a number of general powers under the Police Act 1996. He or she may call upon a police authority to require a chief constable to retire in the interests of efficiency and effectiveness (s. 42(1)). Before doing so the chief constable must be allowed to make representations and, if representations are made, an inquiry must also be held (s. 42(2) and (3)). He or she can call upon the chief constable to make reports to him or her on any matters which he or she may specify are connected with the policing of any area (s. 44). He or she may also cause a local inquiry to be held into any matter connected with the policing of any area (s. 49). He or she may make regulations as to the government, administration and conditions of service of police forces, including discipline and pay.

The overriding responsibility is that he or she must exercise these powers to promote the efficiency and effectiveness of the police force (s. 36).

The Home Secretary is the police authority for the Metropolitan Police Force (s. 101) and may therefore be equated with provincial police authorities. Marshall in his book, *Police and Government* suggests the Home Secretary has a special relationship with the Metropolitan Police which differs from the relationship between provincial police authorities and their chief constables. The now disbanded Greater London Council (GLC) argued in the early 1980s (unsuccessfully) that the Metropolitan Police Force should be accountable to an elected police authority and not to the Home Secretary.

Being the police authority for the Metropolitan Police the Home Secretary is responsible to Parliament for that force. He or she can be questioned directly in the House on matters concerning the Metropolitan force. However, he or she cannot be questioned directly about individual provincial forces, since he or she is not the police authority for them. Despite not having direct responsibility for each provincial force, the Home Secretary retains some indirect control through the system of finance. (See the comments of former

Metropolitan Police Commissioner Sir David McNee, extract in *Cases and Materials* (**9.5**).) The funding of provincial forces consists in the allocation of grants from the Home Office and revenue from the local authority. This gives the Home Secretary and the Home Office a great deal of indirect influence.

Represent in a diagram, the ways in which the police are held accountable. (Sample diagrams appear in *Cases and Materials* (9.5).)

Pause once again and, in the light of what you have just read, think about the following questions.

Could it be a case of he who pays the piper calls the tune?

Could the threat of withdrawing the Home Office grant be an incentive to follow the suggestions of the Home Secretary?

Could this lead to a loss of independence?

Well what did you think? Once again there are no set answers to any of these questions. They are really points that need to be considered by you but for some ideas you should refer to the views of Thornton, Robertson and Savage extracts of which can be found in *Cases and Materials* (**Chapter 9**).

The relationship between the Home Secretary and the police authority is not an easy one to define. Real power seems to lie with the Secretary of State, since the police authority may exercise its powers only with the approval of the Secretary of State.

The relationship between the Home Secretary and the police authority was raised in the case of *R* v *Secretary of State for the Home Department, ex parte Northumbria Police Authority* [1989] QB 26. The Court of Appeal held that the Home Secretary could supply CS gas and riot equipment to the Chief Constable of Northumbria, from central stores, free of charge, without the consent of the police authority. The police authority objected to the equipment being supplied, but the Home Secretary provided it anyway. The court said he was justified in doing so under s. 41 of the Police Act 1964 (now s. 57 of the 1996 Act). But even without this statutory provision the Home Secretary had the power to make such supplies under the royal prerogative as prerogative powers were not curtailed by s. 4 of the Police Act 1964 (s. 6 of the 1996 Act).

9.7   Her Majesty's Inspectors

Her Majesty's Inspectors of Constabulary make annual inspections of the forces and their annual reports are made public (Police Act 1996, s. 54). Their duty is to report to the Secretary of State on the efficiency and effectiveness of all police forces. There is a Chief Inspector of Constabulary who submits a report to the Home Secretary annually and that report is laid before Parliament.

We have seen the power of the Inspectorate imposed on one force. In 1992 Geoffrey Dear, Her Majesty's Inspector of Constabulary, recommended that Derbyshire Constabulary be refused a certificate of efficiency because of the lack of financial and other resources provided by the police authority. It was agreed that the force be given an extension to improve the situation with the cooperation of the police authority. However, a certificate of efficiency was refused in both 1993 and 1994. Notwithstanding these concerns, the Derbyshire force is of course still in existence. Nevertheless events over the last few years have led to speculation that it may be amalgamated with another larger neighbouring force at some time in the future.

9.8   Status and Accountability of Police Constables

Police constables are part of a hierarchically structured organisation. However, those higher than the constable in the hierarchy cannot direct the constable in any way concerning the exercise of his powers. In *Attorney-General for New South Wales* v *Perpetual Trustee Co. Ltd* [1955] AC 457, a police constable was described as an officer:

> whose authority is original, not delegated, and exercised at his own discretion by virtue of his office. He is a ministerial officer exercising statutory rights independently of contract.

This view was reflected by McCardie J in *Fisher* v *Oldham Corporation* [1930] 2 KB 364 when he quoted a statement made by Griffith CJ in *Enever* v *The King* (1906) 3 CLR 969:

> Now, the powers of a constable, . . . are exercised by him by virtue of his office, and cannot be exercised on the responsibility of any person but himself. . . . A constable, therefore, when acting as a peace officer, is not exercising a delegated authority, but an original authority.

It seems difficult to reconcile this independent, original status with membership of a disciplined, hierarchical body in which the constable is subject to the lawful orders of his or her supervisory officers. Can a police inspector order a constable to arrest an individual? The answer is that he or she can. But it is the constable, not the inspector, who is responsible for that arrest and this is because the powers given to the constable are original, not delegated. If the constable has no reasonable grounds the arrest is unlawful. Thus a dilemma may arise in that a constable may be acting lawfully but in doing so could be committing a disciplinary offence, e.g., by failing to obey an order.

This point was partially examined in *O'Hara* v *Chief Constable of the Royal Ulster Constabulary* [1997] 1 All ER 129. The issue was whether and instruction from a superior officer gave a constable reasonable grounds to arrest. The court accepted responsibility for the exercise of the power lay solely with the officer exercising that power. However, the court seemed to take a pragmatic approach and accepted that there would be circumstances where such an instruction should be obeyed, but only if the officer had sufficient information to give reasonable grounds for suspicion (see discussion at **10.5.3.6**).

The Report of the Royal Commission on the Police (Cmnd 1738) sets out the issue quite clearly.

Please read the extract from the report of this Royal Commission in *Cases and Materials (9.6)*.

What point do you see emerging most clearly from what you have just read?

The answer is that a member of the police force of any rank exercises powers only through the **office of constable**. Hence even the chief constable holds the office of constable.

We need to examine some cases to appreciate more fully the constitutional position and accountability of constables.

In *Fisher* v *Oldham Corporation* [1930] 2 KB 364 Fisher was claiming damages against Oldham Corporation for false imprisonment by a constable of the borough. The judge decided that the watch committee (police authority) had no power to control the constable in the execution of his duties because a master-sevant relationship did not exist between the watch committee and the police. This view was echoed in Scotland in *Muir* v *Hamilton Corporation* 1910 1 SLT 164. The constable is not the servant of the local authority.

In *Attorney-General for New South Wales* v *Perpetual Trustee Co. Ltd* [1955] AC 457 it was decided the Crown could not recover compensation for the loss of the services of a police officer because the relationship of master and servant on which such actions must be founded did not exist between the Crown and the police. The Crown Proceedings Act 1947 does not apply to the police since they are not paid wholly out of central government funds. Thus where a tort was committed against an individual only one person was liable, the police constable himself. The constable is not a servant of the Crown.

From this it would seem that only the constable is liable in law for his or her actions. Since there was no master-servant relationship, vicarious liability did not operate. To remedy this situation s. 88 of the Police Act 1996 made the chief constable liable for torts committed by his police constables in the exercise of their duties. The local authority will pay the damages where a successful action is brought against the chief constable. The local authority may pay damages where a successful action is brought against a police constable personally.

There are both external and internal pressures bearing upon police officers when exercising their powers. A constable is bound to exercise his or her duties within the law and, like any other individual, is himself or herself subject to both civil and criminal law. He or she is also subject to a disciplinary code and a complaints procedure which is now governed by the Police Act 1996.

Why does Savage claim that police accountability is 'a highly complex issue'? If unsure you can find his explanation in *Cases and Materials* (9.5).

9.9   Complaints and Disciplinary Proceedings

If the chief officer of police receives a complaint he or she must determine that it is about the conduct of an officer and it does not relate to the direction or control of the police force. The chief officer must then determine who is the appropriate authority to deal with the complaint. (s. 67 of the 1996 Act) The appropriate authority for senior officers, i.e. chief constables and assistant chief constables, is the police authority, while for lower ranks it is the chief constable (s. 65).

On receipt of a complaint steps must be taken to preserve evidence relating to the complaint (s. 67(1)).

Once the chief constable has decided that he or she is the appropriate authority, the complaint is recorded and the chief constable must decide whether the complaint is suitable for 'informal resolution'. This procedure depends on the consent of the complainant and is available only for minor complaints which will not result in criminal or disciplinary charges. If this procedure is not suitable or fails to resolve the complaint then a formal investigation will take place (s. 69)

Similar provisions apply to complaints against senior officers where the police authority may exercise its discretion in dealing with the complaint informally. This cannot be done unless the authority is satisfied that the complaint would not result in disciplinary or criminal proceedings (s. 68)

If not suitable for informal resolution, the complaint has to be investigated formally. An officer, who has not been involved, must be appointed to investigate the complaint. That investigating officer may be from another force, if the chief officer so requests, and the other force is obliged to comply with such a request. The investigating officer must prepare a report which will be submitted to the chief officer (unless the investigation is being supervised by the Police Complaints Authority) (s. 69).

9.10 Police Complaints Authority

The Police Complaints Authority (PCA) was created by PACE 1984 and replaced the Police Complaints Board which was abolished by the Act. It is now governed by the Police Act 1996. It consists of a chairman, appointed by the Queen and at least eight other members appointed by the Home Secretary. Police officers or former police officers cannot be members of the PCA. Members are appointed for a maximum period of three years and may resign during that period or can be removed by the Home Secretary for a number of reasons including criminal conviction and incompetence. The PCA is neither a servant nor an agent of the Crown. It has regional offices; it must report annually to the Home Secretary and must make annual reports. These reports must be published and laid before Parliament; copies must be sent to police authorities. The Home Secretary may request reports on general matters and the PCA may make a report on matters to which it believes his or her attention should be drawn.

Some complaints **must** be referred to the PCA which must supervise their investigation. Complaints in this category include those alleging conduct resulting in death or serious injury and complaints specified in regulations made by the Secretary of State. So far these have included complaints involving actual bodily harm, corruption and serious arrestable offences. The PCA may also call for a complaint to be referred to it.

Matters may also be referred to the PCA even though not the subject of a complaint. These would be matters which, because of the gravity or exceptional circumstances, should be referred, e.g., a police officer may have committed a criminal offence or a disciplinary offence, but no complaint has been lodged.

Where the PCA supervises an investigation, it can insist on appointing the investigating officer, who must then submit a report to the PCA and send a copy to the appropriate police authority. If practicable, the officer being investigated and the complainant should also receive a copy of the report.

When a chief officer receives the report of an investigation he or she must decide whether a criminal offence may have been committed. If the chief officer decides one may have been committed, he or she must send a copy of the report to the Director of Public Prosecutions for a decision on whether to prefer criminal charges. Following any criminal proceedings, or if no criminal charge was disclosed by the report, the chief officer may bring disciplinary proceedings against the officer, or take no further action. The chief officer must send a memorandum to the PCA specifying what action was taken, and if no disciplinary proceedings were brought, the reasons for that. The PCA may then recommend and, ultimately, direct the chief constable to bring disciplinary proceedings. A chief officer must comply with an order of the PCA to prefer disciplinary charges and must provide any information reasonably required by the PCA.

Disciplinary proceedings may be brought against a police officer without the need for a complaint. If successfully brought punishments include reprimand, fine, reduction in rank, requirement to resign or dismissal. An officer cannot be subject to any of the last three of those punishments unless given the opportunity to be legally represented at the disciplinary hearing.

If an officer is dismissed, required to resign or reduced in rank the officer may appeal to a police appeals' tribunal. In the case of a senior officer the tribunal consists of a lawyer of at least seven years' standing, who will act as the chairman, a member of the PCA and one of HM Inspectors of Constabulary. In the case of other ranks the tribunal still has a legally-qualified chairman, but the other members are a member of the PCA, a chief officer not involved in the proceedings and a retired officer of appropriate rank.

Representation is allowed for the appellant, legal, or serving member of the force. If the tribunal decides to vary the punishment imposed it may do so but only less severely.

What avenues are open to an individual who alleges misconduct by a police officer?

The individual may complain to the chief constable of the officer concerned. The procedures provided by the Police Act 1996 will then come into operation.

The individual might also report that the police officer has committed a criminal offence, or a civil wrong, in which case the legal processes would come into operation.

9.11   Conclusion

The 1996 Police Act confirms a tripartite structure for controlling the police. However, as you will have noticed, power is not equally shared by chief constables, local police authorities and the Home Office. The courts have granted chief constables considerable operational autonomy and neither a Home Secretary nor a local police authority may instruct a chief constable how to deploy his or her resources. Of course, as was earlier noted, a local police authority may call upon a chief constable to resign, but this power can only be exercised with the approval of the Home Secretary. This veto, which the Home Office retains over the appointment and dismissal of senior police officers, adds weight to the claims that, in recent years, power in the British police service has increasingly been centralised. The extent to which this is incongruous with the British tradition of local policing, or can even be considered a threat to individual liberty, remains a political question for you, the reader, to answer.

9.12 End of Chapter Assessment Question

Farmer Giles owns a piece of land in the hills of Wales. One of the fields is being surveyed in order to determine whether uranium can be mined on a commercial basis. The survey is being carried out under statutory authority. It is a summary offence to obstruct the survey and the statute provides that obstructers may be removed and, if necessary, arrested. Anti-nuclear protesters are demonstrating at the site and disrupting the survey. The survey company want the police to keep the protesters away from the site. Instructions have been given by the chief constable that no officer is to enter the land of Farmer Giles and no action is to be taken against the demonstrators unless they are violent. The demonstrators know of this instruction and so have ensured that they are not violent.

Fred, one of the demonstrators, is seen by PC Smith and PC Jones lying in front of one of the surveyor's tractors. They dislike Fred very much, so they go on to the land of Farmer Giles and demand that Fred leaves. Fred remains where he is and calmly says that he has permission from Farmer Giles to be on the land. This is perfectly true because Farmer Giles does not want the mine on his land. PC Smith and PC Jones arrest Fred for obstruction. They lift him from the ground and carry him to a police car parked nearby. As they are going through the gate to the field, they catch Fred's leg on a piece of barbed wire, ripping his trousers and grazing his leg. Inspector Keen has seen PC Smith and PC Jones arresting Fred. He tells them they will be disciplined for disobeying an order from the chief constable by going on to the land and arresting Fred.

Can PC Smith and PC Jones be prevented from arresting Fred and are they liable for a disciplinary offence by failing to obey the order? And who is liable for the damage to Fred's trousers and for the injury to his leg?

See *Cases and Materials* (9.8) for a specimen answer.

CHAPTER TEN

POLICE POWERS

10.1 Objectives

By the end of this Chapter you should be able to:

■ identify the powers of stop and search, entry, search and seizure, arrest and detention, and the safeguards which apply to the exercise of these powers;

■ analyse a given set of facts, apply the legal principles to that set of facts and determine the legality of any police actions;

■ identify the ways in which the courts protect the citizen by the use of exclusionary rules of evidence.

10.2 Introduction

Policing in England and Wales has traditionally been based on consent. The approach has been to give police officers relatively narrow powers but confer on them a wide range of duties. In 1929 the Royal Commission on the Police concluded that the police should have as few powers as possible. To carry out their duties effectively the police would rely on public support and co-operation — consent.

Police powers in England and Wales developed in an 'ad hoc' way and were found in Acts of Parliament, local by-laws, common law and judicial directives, e.g., Judges' Rules. These wide-ranging sources meant that there was often confusion over exactly the nature of police powers and this confusion was compounded by allegations that the police frequently abused their powers.

The Confait affair in 1977 was the trigger which resulted in the Royal Commission on Criminal Procedure 1981 (Cmnd 8092). The Commission aimed to strike a balance between the interests of the community on the one hand and the rights and liberties of the individual and suspect on the other. The recommendations of the Commission formed the basis for the Police and Criminal Evidence Act 1984 (PACE 1984).

As we shall soon see, PACE 1984 was an important catalyst for change. It extended some powers but placed limitations and restrictions on their use and operation; strengthened the safeguards for suspects; provided for the welfare of persons in detention; required that police officers keep full written records; changed laws of evidence and procedure; introduced new complaints procedures; and introduced Codes of Practice to guide police officers while exercising their powers and carrying out their duties.

The Codes of Practice are issued by the Secretary of State under s. 66 of PACE 1984. They are admissible in evidence and any relevant provision must be taken into account by a court (s. 67(11)). (Please note that all statutory sections apply to PACE unless otherwise stated.)

10.3 Stop and Search

10.3.1 INTRODUCTION

We will deal with the powers under PACE 1984 in the order in which they appear in the Act. So let us begin by looking at the powers to stop and search contained in s. 1.

Under s. 1(2) a constable may stop and search a person or vehicle, or anything which is in or on a vehicle, for stolen or prohibited articles, and may detain that person or vehicle for the purpose of making such a search. He may seize any such articles which he discovers (s. 1(6)). But according to s. 1(3) he cannot exercise this power unless he has reasonable grounds for suspecting that he will find stolen or prohibited articles.

This power is of general application and replaces all powers to search for stolen or unlawfully obtained goods which constables had been given under local Acts. There is, therefore, now a general power for a constable to detain a person, short of arrest, to search him for stolen or prohibited articles.

Not all general powers to stop and search have been repealed by the 1984 Act and those still in force include:

■ Misuse of Drugs Act 1971, s. 23;

■ Firearms Act 1968, s. 47;

■ Wildlife and Countryside Act 1981, s. 19;

■ Aviation Security Act 1982, s. 27(1);

■ Prevention of Terrorism (Temporary Provisions) Act 1989, ss. 13A and 13B.

A more complete list can be found in Annex A to Code A, Code of Practice for the Exercise by Police Officers of Statutory Powers of Stop and Search, reproduced in *Cases and Materials* (10.1.1).

Please read s. 1 of PACE 1984 (in *Cases and Materials* (10.1.1)) and answer the following questions.

   (a) Who may exercise the power under s. 1?

   (b) What is the extent of the power and for what purpose may it be exercised?

   (c) What is the major limitation on the exercise of this power?

You should have found the following answers.

(a) A constable may exercise this power in respect of a person or vehicle or anything in a vehicle, although only a constable in uniform may stop a vehicle (s. 2(9)).

(b) To stop and to search for stolen or prohibited articles. To detain any person or vehicle for the purpose of a search and to seize any stolen or prohibited articles.

(c) A constable must have reasonable grounds for suspecting that she or he will find stolen or prohibited articles. The power may be exercised only in a public place.

10.3.2 LIMITATIONS ON STOP AND SEARCH POWER

You probably realise that all powers are limited in some way, otherwise they would be open to abuse. What follows are some of the limitations on the powers of the police to stop and search.

The limitations are found in PACE 1984 and Code A. They apply to the exercise by police officers of **all statutory powers of stop and search** without first making an arrest, not just those found in PACE 1984.

(a) A constable must have reasonable grounds for suspicion. The power exists even where the constable has reasonable grounds to suspect that a person is in innocent possession of a stolen or prohibited article or other item for which he is empowered to search, notwithstanding that there would be no power to arrest (Code A, para. 1.7A). The provisions of Code A, paras 1.6 and 1.7 explain in part what would or would not constitute reasonable grounds. It depends on the circumstances — it requires objective standards. Reasonable suspicion can never be justified on the basis of personal factors alone, e.g., dress, hair-style or general stereotyping. However, where there is 'reliable information . . . that members of a group . . . habitually carry knives unlawfully or weapons or controlled drugs', that can give reasonable grounds (Code A, para. 1.6A). Similarly, where such a group or gang wear a distinctive item of clothing or other means of identification to indicate membership of the group, the members may be identified by means of that distinctive item or other means of identification (Code A 1.7AA).

(b) There is no power to stop and detain a person against his or her will in order to find grounds for search (Code A, para .2.1) but a constable may question a person to eliminate, or confirm a reasonable suspicion and if reasonable grounds cease then no search may take place (Code A, para. 2.2).

(c) The power may be exercised only in a public place (s. 1(1)).

How would you define a public place?

Public place is broadly defined as meaning any place to which the public has access as of right or by virtue of express or implied permission, but which is not a dwelling. However, gardens and yards are included as public places where the constable has reasonable grounds to believe that the person does not reside at the premises or has not the express or implied permission of the resident. So residents and licensees are protected from search under these powers within the curtilage of a dwelling.

(d) A constable may search only for stolen or prohibited articles. *Prohibited articles* include: offensive weapons, articles made or adapted for use in connection with burglary, theft, taking a conveyance, obtaining property by deception, or intended by a person having it for such use and articles that have a blade or are sharply pointed (other than a folding pocket knife with a blade of three inches or less). This last article was introduced by s. 1(8A) and refers to the Criminal Justice Act 1988, s. 139 of which makes it an offence to be in possession of such an article in a public place unless the possessor can show a good reason. A knife which can be locked is such an article even though it is able to be folded when unlocked (*Harris v DPP* [1993] 1 WLR 82). *R v Deegan, The Times*, 17 February 1998, points out the difficulty attached to interpreting s. 139 where there is a locking folding knife with a blade under three inches in length.

(e) Searches in public must be restricted to superficial examination of outer clothing. There is no power to require a person to remove any clothing in public other than an outer coat, jacket or gloves. This applies to **all powers** to detain and search except for a search after arrest (Code A, para. 3.5).

(f) Any search involving removal of more than an outer coat, jacket, gloves, headgear or footwear may be made only by an officer of the same sex as the person searched and must not be made in the presence of anyone of the opposite sex unless the person being searched specifically requests it (Code A, para. 3.5).

(g) What information must be given to the person stopped?

Before beginning the search the constable has a duty to take reasonable steps to bring to the attention of the suspect, if not in uniform, the constable's warrant card, his or her name and police station, the object of and the grounds for the search, and that if a record is made of the search that the suspect is entitled to a copy (s. 2(2) and (3)).

In *R v Fennelley* [1989] Crim LR 142, a heroin addict was charged with possession with intent to supply drugs under s. 5(3) of the Misuse of Drugs Act 1971. The prosecution had not established that Fennelley had been told why he had been stopped, searched and arrested. There had been a breach of s. 2(3) and the Codes. It was held that it would be unfair to admit evidence obtained in this way. The court was not concerned with disciplining the police but with safeguarding the trial of an accused person.

(h) Written records.

Section 3 imposes on the constable a duty to make a written record of the search as soon as practicable. This record must state the object of and grounds for the search, the date, time and place of the search, what was found and any injury to persons or damage to property resulting from the search. A person searched may demand a copy of this record within 12 months of the search. If the constable fails to make a record of a search that failure will not make the search illegal (*Basher v DPP* [1993] COD 372).

However, if ss. 2 and 3 impose a duty upon a constable then a failure to comply with ss. 2 or 3 should mean that the constable is acting unlawfully. In particular, if s. 2 is not followed then, since that precedes the exercise of the power, the constable may be liable for assault, trespass to the person etc.

A person may be detained only for a reasonable time to enable a search to be made at the place of detention or nearby (s. 2(8)). The Codes provide that such a search must be quick, nearby and only as thorough as necessary (Code A, para. 3).

Two points are made in the Codes of Practice notes for guidance about searches which merit consideration.

(a)   Where a person is lawfully detained for the purpose of a search, but no search in the event takes place, the detention will not thereby cease to be lawful (Code A, note for guidance 2A).

(b)   The Code does not affect the power of a police constable to speak to or question a person in the course of the officer's duties without detaining him or her or exercising any compulsion (Code A, note for guidance 1B).

Where an unattended vehicle has been searched the police constable must leave a notice stating the vehicle has been searched and identifying himself or herself and his or her police station (s. 2(6)). Only constables in uniform may stop vehicles (s. 2(9)(b)).

Where any provision of PACE 1984 (a) confers a power on a constable and (b) does not provide that the power may be exercised only with the consent of some person, other than a police officer, the officer may use reasonable force, if necessary, in the exercise of the power (s. 117).

SAQ 89

Read the following and decide whether PC Smith is acting lawfully. If you think not explain why. You should refer to the text above for your information.

(a)   PC Smith sees Bob at 3.00 am in the street and asks Bob to show him what he has in his bag, and to turn out his pockets. Bob does so.

(b)   At 11.00 am PC Smith sees John, a long-haired traveller, who is dressed in hippie-style clothing and who has previous convictions for drug offences, i.e., smoking cannabis, in the garden of the house of Fred, John's friend. PC Smith stops John from going into Fred's house and searches him. When John asks why he is being searched PC Smith says, 'You know very well'. John is told to remove his hat, his jacket and his jumper. He reluctantly does so. Nothing is found.

You should have concluded as follows:

(a)   You probably have said that PC Smith has no power to stop and search Bob because he has no reasonable grounds. Hence the power does not arise and PC

Smith is acting unlawfully. If you thought this unfortunately, you are wrong. However, don't despair, for this is a common mistake. A simple request by PC Smith is *not* the exercise of a power – he is not exercising a power but is simply making a request. The two things are completely different. To make a request is not to exercise a power. So PC Smith cannot be exercising a power unlawfully if he is not exercising a power at all! The fact that Bob complies does not convert the request into an exercise of a power.

(b) This power falls within the Misuse of Drugs Act 1971, s. 23 (see *Cases and Materials* (**10.1.2**)). PC Smith is acting unlawfully. Any one of the following factors would make his actions unlawful. The combination merely compounds the illegality of his actions.

For example, none of the factors which stereotype John can give PC Smith reasonable grounds (Code A, para. 1.7), so PC Smith is acting unlawfully. The stop and search is in Fred's garden; this is not a public place for the purposes of stop-and-search powers unless PC Smith has reasonable grounds to believe that John is not residing there or lacks the express or implied permission of the resident to be there (s. 1(4)). This is unlikely to apply since PC Smith stopped John from going into the house. So PC Smith is acting unlawfully. PC Smith has a duty to take reasonable steps to inform John of his name, station, the object of the search and the grounds for the search (s. 2(2) and (3) and *R* v *Fennelley* [1989] Crim LR 142). He did not do so thus PC Smith is acting unlawfully. Finally, PC Smith cannot require John to remove in public any headgear, nor his pullover. However, he may be required to take off an outer coat, jacket or gloves (s. 1(9) and Code A, para. 3.5).

10.3.3 SECTION 60 OF THE CRIMINAL JUSTICE AND PUBLIC ORDER ACT 1994

The Criminal Justice and Public Order Act 1994 (CJPOA 1994) introduced a number of new powers to deal with various aspects of public order and potential crime. One such power is found in s. 60 (see *Cases and Materials* (**10.1.3**) which provides a power to stop and search in anticipation of violence. As you read this you will see that it differs from the power under s. 1 of PACE 1984.

ACTIVITY 72

Please make a note of the differences because you will be asked to identify them later.

Section 60 of CJPOA 1994 provides that if an officer of the rank of superintendent or above reasonably believes that incidents involving serious violence may take place in any locality in his area and it is expedient to do so to prevent their occurrence, he may authorise in writing the stopping and searching of persons and vehicles within that locality for a period not exceeding 24 hours. That period may be extended by six hours having regard to offences reasonably suspected to have been committed in relation to the incident. (See also Code A, para. 1.8.)

Powers are conferred on constables in uniform to stop and search any person or vehicle, (including drivers and passengers), for offensive weapons or dangerous instruments. These powers may be exercised even though the constable may not have reasonable grounds to suspect that the vehicle or person is carrying any weapon or instrument.

A dangerous instrument is one with a blade or is sharply pointed. 'Offensive weapon' has the same meaning as this term under the Prevention of Crime Act 1953. Any offensive weapon or dangerous instrument may be seized.

Failure to stop is a summary offence punishable with three months' imprisonment and/or a fine.

Where such powers are exercised the person subject to the exercise may make a request for a written statement within 12 months of the incident.

These powers are conferred in addition to and not in derogation from, any powers otherwise conferred.

What do you see as the main differences between the powers to stop and search given by s. 1 of PACE 1984 and the power under s. 60 of CJPOA 1994?

There are several important differences. First, the constable acting under s. 60 must be in uniform, whereas under s. 1 she or he need not be except where a vehicle has to be stopped. Second, under s. 60 she or he can act without reasonable grounds to suspect, whereas under s. 1 she or he requires reasonable grounds. Under s. 60 the superintendent who authorises the stop and search is the only person who needs to have a reasonable belief that serious violence may take place in the area.

10.3.4 ROAD CHECKS

Sometimes you may have seen police road checks in operation. These may operate under different statutory provisions depending upon the purpose for which they are used. PACE 1984 provides one such power.

Section 4 provides that an officer of at least the rank of superintendent may authorise road checks to be set up for a specified period (not exceeding seven days) for the purpose of ascertaining whether a vehicle is carrying:

    (a) a person who has committed an offence for which the officer has reasonable grounds to believe is a serious arrestable offence;

(b)   a person who is a witness to such an offence;

(c)   a person intending to commit such an offence;

(d)   a person who is unlawfully at large.

Only constables in uniform may stop vehicles at the road check.

10.4   Entry, Search and Seizure

We have just looked at stop and search in a public place. In this section we are going to examine entry and search in premises. The first point we need to make is that there is no general power to enter premises without the consent of the owner or occupier. However, entry may be gained with consent, and the powers of entry may be conferred by statute, common law or warrant. We will now examine these.

10.4.1   ENTRY BY CONSENT

As a statement of general law, consent may be given to enter premises and that consent may be either express or implied. Such consent will be said to have created a licence to enter. If the consent is withdrawn then the licence is revoked and the person becomes a trespasser. If consent to enter is refused at the outset then there is clearly no licence to enter premises and the person entering without consent is a trespasser unless that entry can be justified under a legal power. Trespassers can be requested to leave and, if they do not do so, may be physically ejected, but only using reasonable force, and after receiving reasonable time to leave.

In *Davis* v *Lisle* [1936] 2 All ER 213 police officers entered the defendant's garage to make enquiries about a lorry which had been obstructing the highway. The defendant told the officers to leave and then attacked them. It was held that although the police officers were entitled to enter the garage they could not remain there once they had been told to leave. They then became trespassers giving the occupier the right to eject them using reasonable force.

In *Robson* v *Hallett* [1967] 2 QB 939 a police sergeant was told to leave a private house where he was making enquiries. As he walked away he was attacked. Here the sergeant had not become a trespasser as soon as he was asked to leave — he must be given reasonable time to do so. There is an implied licence for anyone to walk up to the front door and here, prior to being told to leave, nothing had been done to revoke that implied licence.

A difficulty may arise where police officers are either instructed to leave premises or refused permission to enter by someone who appears not to be the owner.

In *McArdle* v *Wallace (No. 2)* (1964) 108 SJ 483 a police constable entered a yard to make enquiries. The son of the owner told him to leave and used force to eject him when he refused. The case established that the son had implied authority to eject trespassers and the defendant was acquitted of assaulting a police constable in the execution of his duty.

In *R* v *Thornley* (1980) 72 Cr App R 302 it was held a licence given by a wife to the police to enter premises in the course of a domestic dispute could not be revoked by the husband, who had been the subject of a complaint to the police. This decision was based on the rights of the wife as a co-occupier.

Implied permission to enter will suffice.

In *Faulkner* v *Willetts* [1982] RTR 159 the defendant's wife opened the door to an officer who wished to interview her husband. She did not give him express permission to enter but, having been told why the police were there, turned round and walked back into the house. He followed her into the house and she made him a cup of coffee. You will not be surprised to learn that it was held that this constituted implied permission to enter.

In *Jones* v *Lloyd* [1981] Crim LR 340 L was seen by police officers trying to open a car. He admitted he was not the owner and said the owner was at a party in one of the houses in the street. The police constables asked to see the owner and L invited them into the house. One of the guests at the party told them to leave, but having discovered that she did not own the house, they refused. The constables satisfied themselves that L was entitled to have the car keys and were leaving when they were assaulted by two guests at the party. The Divisional Court held that the police officers were not trespassers. This was a broad view of the scope of the implied licence doctrine but since the owner neither knew of nor objected to the presence of police officers, the guests could not be said to be acting on the owner's behalf.

In *Riley* v *DPP* (1989) 91 Cr App R 14 Watkins LJ said, at p. 22:

> If police officers are invited onto premises by an occupier or other person authorised so to do, who has been told by them the reason for their entry, as was undoubtedly the fact here, then in our view they are lawfully on the premises. . . . [The provisions of PACE 1984, s. 17] give a right to police officers to enter and search a house in the absence of consent by the occupier, subject of course to compliance with the terms of that section by the police officers concerned.

The facts of *Riley* were that officers went to the defendant's address to search for and arrest his brother. The defendant admitted them after they explained their purpose. The entry was lawful, but the arrest could not be proved to be lawful.

However, as far as the police are concerned, Code of Practice B applies to **entries with consent** for the purposes of conducting a **search.** The consent must be given in writing on a special notice. Before seeking consent a constable must state the purpose of the search and inform the person concerned that she or he is not obliged to consent. This procedure is not necessary in circumstances where the seeking of consent would cause disproportionate inconvenience to the person concerned, (e.g., a brief search of a garden very late at night to see whether stolen articles were discarded during pursuit of a thief). So is this an implied licence to enter?

10.4.2   ENTRY WITHOUT CONSENT

10.4.2.1   Statute

Section 17 of PACE 1984 (see *Cases and Materials* (**10.2.1.1**)) gives a constable power to enter and search any premises for the following purposes:

(a)   To execute a warrant of arrest or commitment.

(b)   To arrest a person for an arrestable offence.

(c)   To arrest a person for an offence under:

   (i)   s. 1 of the Public Order Act 1936 (uniforms); or

   (ii)   s. 4 of the Public Order Act 1986 (causing fear or provocation of violence); or

   (iii)   if in uniform, ss. 6, 7, 8 or 10 of the Criminal Law Act 1977 (offences relating to entering and remaining on property); or

      (iv) s. 76 of the CJPOA 1994 (failure to comply with interim possession order).

(d) To arrest any child or young person who has been remanded or committed to local authority accommodation under s. 23(1) of the Children and Young Persons Act 1969.

(e) To recapture a person unlawfully at large and whom he is pursuing.

In *D'Souza* v *DPP* [1992] 1 WLR 1073 the House of Lords decided that this power is available only when the police are 'in pursuit'. A woman, who had been detained under the Mental Health Act 1983, discharged herself from hospital and returned home. More than three hours later the police went to her home and were prevented from entering by the woman's husband and daughter. This was not an assault on police officers in the execution of their duty because the police had no power to enter under s. 17. Even though the woman might have been unlawfully at large there was no pursuit involved.

In such cases the constable must have reasonable grounds to believe that the person she or he is seeking is on the premises. Where the premises consist of two or more dwellings she or he can enter and search only that part of the premises which is used in common by the occupiers. Any search made must be restricted to that which is necessary to achieve the object of the search.

(f) To save life or limb or to prevent serious damage to property. Reasonable grounds are not needed here.

We will not deal with powers of entry under other statutory provisions.

10.4.2.2 Entry and search following an arrest

Please look at s. 18(1) of PACE 1984 in *Cases and Materials* (10.2.1.2) and make a note of its provisions.

Did you notice that under s. 18 authorisation in writing by an officer of at least the rank of inspector is required for such a search? This written authorisation can be taken to the premises which are to be searched and shown to anyone on the premises (*R* v *Badham* [1987] Crim LR 202). However, such a search may take place without authorisation and without first taking the suspect to the police station if that person's presence is necessary at another place for the effective investigation of the offence (e.g., recovery of property). If this form of search takes place an officer of at least the rank of inspector must be informed as soon as practicable. A written record must be made of any search, the grounds for the search and the nature of the evidence sought.

Section 32 of PACE 1984 gives a constable the power to enter and search any premises in which a person was arrested, or in which she or he was immediately before arrest. The word 'immediately' might suggest that the power should be exercised as soon as the arrest takes place. However, no time limit is placed upon when the power should be exercised. Nevertheless, in *R v Badham* [1987] Crim LR 202 the Crown Court said that an entry and search four hours after the arrest could not be a legitimate use of the power.

However, where the arrest takes place in the street, the police are entitled to enter and search premises in which the arrested person was known to have been shortly before the arrest (*R v Beckford* (1991) 94 Cr App R 43). It is a question for the jury, not the judge, whether the genuine purpose of the police officer's search was to search for evidence to support the reason for the arrest.

This power under s. 32 (see *Cases and Materials* (**10.2.1.2**)) is not limited to the premises controlled or occupied by the person arrested (as in s. 18), nor is it restricted to an arrest for an arrestable offence (as is s. 18).

However, the power to search under s. 32 is limited to that which is reasonably required for the purpose of discovering evidence relating to the offence and will only arise unless the constable has reasonable grounds for believing that there is evidence for which a search is permitted. So the power is narrower than s. 18 in this respect.

The word 'premises' includes 'any vehicle' (s. 23). However, in *R v Churchill* [1989] Crim LR 226 it was held that the police acted beyond their powers under s. 32(2)(a)(ii) in requiring a suspected burglar to hand over his car keys for the purpose of taking his car to the police station to be searched and also for safe keeping. The keys were not 'evidence relating to an offence'.

This power is an extension of the principle established in *Dillon* v *O'Brien and Davies* (1887) that there was a power to search the room in which a person was arrested. There are limitations where the 'premises' concerned are, for example, a dwelling divided into flats. In such a case only the flat of the person arrested (and any communal areas) may be searched.

10.4.2.3   Common law

Section 17(5) abolishes all rules of common law under which a constable has power to enter premises without a warrant. However, s. 17(6) preserves any power of entry to deal with or prevent a breach of the peace. (Breach of the peace will be discussed more fully in the arrest section.)

Thomas v *Sawkins* [1935] 2 KB 249 established that the police are entitled to enter and remain on premises to prevent a breach of the peace, i.e., to prevent it from starting and to prevent it from continuing.

The power extends to public meetings (including those held on private premises) and private homes. In *Lamb* v *DPP* (1989) 154 JP 381 a woman, who was removing her possessions from a house in which she had been living with a man, feared violence and so requested the presence of a police officer. The man told the officer to leave yet before the officer could do so the woman was attacked. The police officer intervened. His continuing presence on the premises to intervene was held lawful.

Citizens' common law powers of entry have not been repealed by PACE 1984. The Royal Commission at para. 40 summarised them as powers: 'To save life or limb, or to prevent serious damage to property'. In *Swales* v *Cox* [1981] QB 849 Donaldson LJ said that at common law a constable and a citizen had the right to enter in order to prevent murder, or if a felony (sic) had been, or was about to be committed. The constable's powers are now covered by s. 17.

ACTIVITY 74

List the various powers in PACE 1984 and at common law given to the police to enter premises without a warrant.

Your answer should look something like this.

(a) Under s. 17 in order to execute a warrant; to arrest a person for an arrestable offence or other specified offences; to recapture a person unlawfully at large and whom an officer is pursuing; to save life or limb or to prevent serious damage to property.

(b) Under s. 18 where the occupier or controller of premises is under arrest for an arrestable offence and there are reasonable grounds for suspecting that there is evidence on the premises relating to that offence or some other arrestable offence connected with or similar to that offence.

(c) Under s. 32 where the person was arrested or where the person was immediately before his or her arrest.

(d) The common law power to deal with or to prevent a breach of the peace.

Did you include entry with consent? If so then you are incorrect because consent is *not* a power. If consent is given, whether expressly or impliedly, then the police do not need to exercise any power.

10.4.3 ENTRY AND SEARCH UNDER WARRANT

The next provisions of PACE 1984 will be discussed only in outline so that you can appreciate the need for powers to search for evidence. Here we will concentrate on the provisions found in PACE 1984.

10.4.3.1 Justices of the Peace

Section 8(1) of PACE 1984 provides that, on an application by a constable, a justice of the peace may issue a warrant to a constable to enter and search premises if the justice has reasonable grounds for believing that a serious arrestable offence has been committed and that there is material on the specified premises which is likely to be of substantial value to the investigation of the offence and is likely to be admissible at a trial for the offence. Such material must not consist of or include items subject to legal privilege, excluded material or special procedure material (see later).

Before a justice issues a warrant he or she must be satisfied independently, and based upon the information supplied, that the material sought is neither subject to legal privilege nor is it special procedure material (*R v Guildhall Magistrates' Court, ex parte Primlaks Holdings Co.* (1988) 89 Cr App R 215).

No such warrant may be issued unless any one of the following conditions is satisfied:

(a)   it is not practicable to communicate with any person entitled to grant entry to the premises; or

(b)   if it is, it is not practicable to communicate with any person entitled to grant access to the evidence; or

(c)   that entry to the premises will not be granted unless a warrant is produced; or

(d)   that the purpose of a search may be frustrated or seriously prejudiced unless a constable arriving at the premises can secure immediate entry to them (s. 8(3)).

A constable may seize and retain anything for which a search has been authorised under such a warrant (s. 8(2)).

In all provisions of PACE 1984, 'premises' includes any place and, in particular, includes any vehicle, vessels, aircraft or hovercraft, any offshore installation and any tent or movable structure. It is not therefore restricted to buildings.

The PACE 1984 power is in addition to existing powers provided in other statutes, e.g., Misuse of Drugs Act 1971, s. 23(3), Obscene Publications Act 1959, s. 3 and Theft Act 1968, s. 26.

So what does the PACE 1984 power do? It fills a gap where one existed previously. This was well identified in *Ghani v Jones* [1970] 1 QB 693 where Lord Denning MR said, 'No magistrate — no judge even — has any power to issue a search warrant for murder'.

10.4.3.2   Material for which a warrant cannot be issued.

(a)   **Items subject to legal privilege** (s. 10): e.g., lawyer–client communications.

However, items held with the intention of furthering a criminal purpose are not to be regarded as items subject to legal privilege. This is so even if the items are in the possession of a solicitor who is innocent (*R v Central Criminal Court, ex parte Francis and Francis* [1989] AC 346).

But not every lawyer–client communication will be subject to legal privilege. It must relate to giving advice or legal proceedings (*R v Inner London Crown Court, ex parte Baines and Baines* [1988] QB 579).

Items held by a solicitor which are not legally privileged will be special procedure material (see *Norwich Crown Court, ex parte Chethams* [1991] COD 271).

(b)   **Excluded material** (s. 11): certain material, if held in confidence, is excluded.

(i)   **Personal records** acquired or created in a trade, business, profession or other occupation or for the purpose of any office, paid or unpaid.

Records are personal if they relate to an individual's physical or mental health or to counselling etc., and the individual may be identified from them, e.g., probation report, clergyman's papers.

(ii)   **Human tissue or fluid** taken for purposes of diagnosis or treatment.

Materials in (1) and (2) will be held in confidence if there is an express or implied undertaking to that effect, or a statutory requirement to restrict disclosure.

(iii) **Journalistic material** consisting of documents or records acquired or created for the purposes of journalism, in the possession of the creator or acquirer.

Material of this type must be held in confidence and must have been so held since it was first acquired or created for the purpose of journalism. It cannot acquire the status of excluded material at a later time just to avoid a search and seizure.

(c) **Special procedure material**

(i) Journalistic material other than excluded material. It does not have to be held in confidence.

(ii) Material (other than items subject to legal privilege or excluded material acquired or created in a trade, business, profession or occupation, or for the purpose of any office paid or unpaid), *where it is held in confidence* subject to an express or implied undertaking to that effect or to a statutory requirement to restrict disclosure or maintain secrecy e.g., bank accounts (*R* v *Leicester Crown Court, ex parte DPP* [1987] 1 WLR 1371), or accounts of a youth association (*R* v *Central Criminal Court, ex parte Adegbesan* [1986] 1 WLR 1292). Note that solicitor/client material is not subject to legal privilege as mentioned above.

10.4.3.3 Circuit judges – orders to produce

Access to excluded material and special procedure material for the purpose of a criminal investigation may be obtained if the procedures set out in sch. 1 to PACE 1984 are satisfied (s. 9). An application is made to a circuit judge who may make an order requiring the person in possession of the material to produce it to a constable for him to take away, or give a constable access to it, within a specified period, normally seven days.

10.4.4 SAFEGUARDS

You will remember, when we discussed the safeguards in relation to the powers of stop and search earlier, that those safeguards applied to all powers of stop and search, not just those under PACE 1984. Similarly, s. 15 of PACE 1984 provides that 'an entry on or search of premises under a warrant is unlawful unless **it** complies with this section and section 16 below'. These provisions relate to the issuing of the warrant, the content of it and its execution (see *Cases and Materials* (**10.2.2**)).

The Code of Practice for entry and search, Code B, includes some general rules devised mainly for the protection of the occupier. For example:

- the search must be at a reasonable hour;

- it may be carried out only to the extent necessary to achieve the object having regard to the size and nature of what is sought – for example, you would not look in drawers for a fridge!

- the search must be carried out with due consideration for the property and privacy of the occupier and with no more disturbance than is necessary;

- the person concerned may have a friend present as a witness unless the officer in charge considers this would seriously hinder the investigation, the officer is not obliged to wait for the friend to arrive;

- records must be made of the location of the premises, the date, the authority for the search, the names of officers, the articles seized, and finally, if force was used and damage caused;

■ the officer must provide the occupier with a copy of a notice explaining the rights of the occupier and the officer's authority for the search.

You may think, on reading these safeguards, that the police would have their hands tied when executing a warrant but the courts may take a 'common-sense' approach when dealing with the Codes. Let us consider a case which illustrates this approach.

In *R v Longman* [1988] 1 WLR 619 police officers had obtained a warrant under s. 23 of the Misuse of Drugs Act 1971 to enter and search the appellant's premises for drugs. They knew that almost certainly there would be difficulties in obtaining entry. In fact, they obtained entry by a subterfuge. It was argued that s. 15 and s. 16 required the constable executing the warrant to announce his identity, produce his warrant card and search warrant, and serve a copy of the search warrant upon the occupier who was present before the entry took place. The court rejected this argument. An officer executing a warrant might effect entry to occupied premises before identifying himself or producing the search warrant if the circumstances were such that he had reasonable grounds for believing that alerting the occupier by attempting to communicate with him would frustrate the object of the search or endanger the officer or others (Code B, para. 5.4.(iii)).

Paragraph 5.5 of the Code made it clear that the time when those formalities had to be observed, in the circumstances of this case, was *after* entry. The requirement was that at the very earliest opportunity the constable should, *after* entry and *before* search, announce his identity, produce his warrant card and the search warrant and, at the first reasonable opportunity, give the occupier a copy of the search warrant.

There has been some difficulty in determining to what the word 'it' in s. 15 relates. In *Longman* the Court of Appeal, when interpreting s. 15, thought *the* word 'it' referred to the warrant rather than the entry or search, and that the entry and search must comply with s. 16. Nevertheless, they deliberately left the point unresolved.

However, in *R v Central Criminal Court, ex parte AJD Holdings Ltd* [1992] Crim LR 669 the Divisional Court refused to accept that *Longman* left it open to the court to hold that the invalidity of the warrant did not render the search unlawful:

Whilst it was accepted that s. 15(1) was not altogether easy to understand, where there was a warrant which on its face was clearly not justified by the information upon which it was based, it was impossible to construe the section as saying that the warrant can legitimise what would otherwise be an unlawful action.

Also, in *R v Chief Constable for Lancashire, ex parte Parker* [1993] Crim LR 204 the Divisional Court held that, although the original warrants had been lawfully issued, due to breaches of s. 16(5) the entry and search had been unlawful. The breaches in this case were that copies of the warrant and schedules were not given to the occupier, the schedules having become detached, and the original schedules were not shown to the occupier, but only copies.

10.4.5 SEIZURE OF PROPERTY

You would be right in thinking that there is little point in being able to enter premises and search for items unless there is then the power to seize those items. Provision is made for that in s. 19 of PACE 1984 (see *Cases and Materials* (**10.2.3**)) under which a constable who is lawfully on any premises has power:

(a) to seize anything which is on the premises if she or he has reasonable grounds to believe that it has been obtained in relation to an offence, and that it is necessary to seize it in order to prevent it being concealed, lost, altered or destroyed;

(b) where she or he has similar reasonable grounds, to require that information which is contained in a computer, and is accessible from the premises, be produced in a visible and legible form which can be taken away.

This power is in addition to any power otherwise conferred. However, no power to seize, given under any statute applies to items which the constable has reasonable grounds to suspect are subject to legal privilege.

This section gives statutory authority to seize property which the courts had previously decided at common law could be seized, i.e., material evidence of a crime, and the fruit of a crime. But you will note that it does not apply to items which a constable has reasonable grounds to believe are subject to legal privilege.

Section 19 applies whenever a constable is lawfully on any premises, i.e., following entry by consent, by warrant, under statutory powers or at common law. But what would be the position in the following case?

SAQ 91

A constable is on premises with consent and begins to look around. Before he finds anything he is asked to leave. He continues to look for a little while and finds something which he believes is evidence.

If the constable was on the premises only by consent then, after being requested to leave, is he a trespasser? Any search or seizure would not be within the statute and therefore unlawful. So far so good, but what about the evidence he has seized? You may think that, since he has seized it unlawfully, it cannot be used as evidence. However this is not necessarily the case. The courts may be willing to allow evidence to be adduced even though it has been obtained unlawfully (*R* v *Sang* [1989] AC 402).

The power to seize property is somewhat similar to the power to freeze assets which the courts have. By way of illustration, in *West Mercia Constabulary* v *Wagener* [1982] 1 WLR 127 the accused was arrested for fraud. His accomplice had a bank account containing money believed to be the proceeds of the fraud. The police applied for an injunction to restrain the accomplice from making any withdrawals on the account. The High Court decided that, although the magistrates' court had no such power, the High Court could fill the gap. It had power to grant an injunction to seize the proceeds of an alleged crime. The court said that the police had a common law power to seize property which is the subject of a crime for the purpose of preserving material evidence.

The courts also have powers of confiscation and forfeiture and there are provisions that relate to these in, e.g., the Drug Trafficking Offences Act 1986, the Criminal Justice Act 1988, and the Prevention of Terrorism (Temporary Provisions) Act 1989.

Sometimes it is not possible to seize the exact item, e.g., s. 20 of PACE deals with computerised information. Finally, note that s. 21 provides that records of items seized must be provided to the occupier of premises, or person who had custody or control of the premises, immediately before the seizure.

10.4.6   RETENTION OF PROPERTY

Section 22 of PACE 1984 provides that anything seized by a constable under a statutory power may be retained for as long as is necessary in all the circumstances. In particular anything seized for the purposes of a criminal investigation may be kept for use as evidence at a trial, for forensic examination or for further investigation unless a copy or photograph would suffice.

Items which were seized because they could have been used to cause physical injury, or damage to property, or to interfere with evidence or assist an escape from lawful custody, cannot be retained once the person from whom they were taken is no longer in police detention, or the custody of the court, or has been released on bail. This provision echoes the principles established in *Ghani* v *Jones* [1970] 1 QB 693 and reiterated in cases such as *Frank Truman Export Ltd* v *Metropolitan Police Commissioner* [1977] QB 952.

10.5   Arrest

The next power we shall examine is that of arrest. You will need to understand the constituent elements of a lawful arrest. The material which follows will cover the powers of the police and citizens.

So what is an arrest? An arrest is the beginning of imprisonment (per Lord Simonds in *Christie* v *Leachinsky* [1947] AC 573). It is preventing a person from going about his or her business. In *Hart* v *Chief Constable of Kent* [1983] RTR 484 an arrest was said to consist of seizing and touching a person's body and that person need not submit or be brought under control. Older cases suggest that any touching will suffice, so there is no need to use handcuffs (*Nicholl* v *Darley* (1828) 2 Y & J 399).

The mere use of words is not enough to effect an arrest unless the suspect submits (*R* v *Jones, ex parte Moore* [1965] Crim LR 222) in which case there will of course be an arrest.

The words spoken by a police officer are important and as you will see, an arrest is not lawful unless certain information has been given to the person arrested.

10.5.1   INFORMATION TO BE GIVEN ON ARREST – SECTION 28 PACE 1984

A person who is arrested must be informed of the fact of arrest and the ground for it either at that time, or as soon as practicable thereafter (s. 28 — see *Cases and Materials* (**10.3.1**)). Where the arrest is made by a police officer this information must be given even if the fact of and the grounds for arrest are obvious. If this is not done, the arrest is unlawful. Perhaps the only times when it is not reasonably practicable to comply with s. 28 is when a person escapes from arrest before the information can be given (s. 28(5)) or is so drunk that it is not possible to inform him or her at the time.

The following cases illustrate these principles.

In *DPP* v *Hawkins* [1988] 1 WLR 1165 the defendant violently resisted arrest. He was taken to a police station and was still not told of the grounds for his arrest. Even though it was not practicable to tell him at the time of his arrest he should have been told as soon as practicable afterwards. The arrest was therefore unlawful. The police officers were not, however, acting outside the execution of their duty when they arrested the suspect and took him to the police station.

In *Edwards* v *DPP* (1993) 97 Cr App R 301 the prosecution cited *DPP* v *Hawkins* as an authority for the proposition that an arrest is lawful as long as the arresting officer is acting in the execution of his or her duty, even though insufficient reasons are given for the arrest. However, Evans LJ refused to go as far as that, and observed that in *Edwards* the reason given for the arrest was invalid and so the arrest was unlawful. Giving the correct information for the arrest is therefore extremely important.

In *Edwards* the defendant had appealed against a conviction for obstructing an officer in the execution of his duty. He had intervened to try to prevent the police officer arresting a friend. It was imperative to determine whether the arrest of the friend was lawful. The officer told Edwards that he was 'nicked for obstruction'. There is no power of arrest for obstruction (unless accompanied by a breach of the peace) and, since it was not possible to infer the officer had anything else in his mind, the arrest was unlawful under s. 25 of PACE 1984 (see **Cases and Materials (10.3.1)**). We shall consider the general arrest conditions later.

The *matter* of informing the detained person arose in *Dawes* v *DPP* [1994] RTR 209. Police had set a trap in which a car automatically locked and detained Dawes. It was held on appeal that the arrest took place at the moment he was trapped in the car. It was then that the police had the duty to inform him of the fact of, and grounds for the arrest, as soon as practicable. Once that duty was discharged, the arrest was made lawful. The police had done this, but the court recommended that the police install a device which in future would automatically tell the offender he or she had been arrested and why.

It is worth comparing *DPP* v *Hawkins* with *Lewis* v *Chief Constable for South Wales* [1991] 1 All ER 206. This was a civil case in which damages were claimed. L was arrested on reasonable suspicion of burglary, but not informed of the reasons for his arrest — contrary to s. 28(3). He was given the reasons 10 or 20 minutes later. The Court of Appeal said that L was entitled to damages only for the period until he had been informed. Arrest was a continuing act so the detention became lawful once reasons had been given.

The result is that these requirements apply to all arrests in all circumstances and to police constables and citizens.

Ordinary language can be used to convey the information as long as it is clear why the person is being arrested. In *Alderson* v *Booth* [1969] 2 QB 216 Lord Parker CJ suggested that the best words to use were 'I arrest you'. The court held that a request to a motorist to accompany a police officer to the police station for further tests did not indicate to the motorist that he was under arrest. However, in *R* v *Brosch* [1988] Crim LR 743 it was held that these words were not a necessary prerequisite of a lawful arrest. It was held to be enough where a manager of a restaurant grabbed the shoulder of the person and said, 'Stay there. . . . You're on drugs aren't you.' The same court approved the statement from the earlier decision of *R* v *Inwood* [1973] 1 WLR 647 that 'there is no magic formula; only the obligation to make it plain to the suspect by what is said and done that he is no longer a free man'.

The reason given may describe more than one offence so long as it covers the offence for which the arrest was made. In *Abbassy* v *Metropolitan Police Commissioner* [1990] 1 All ER 193, the Court of Appeal said in respect of a civil action for damages for wrongful arrest and false imprisonment:

> Although a police officer exercising his power of arrest without warrant was required by common law to inform the person being arrested of the grounds on which the arrest was being made, he was not required to specify a particular crime or to give a technical definition of the offence or refer to his power of arrest, since it was sufficient if by using commonplace language the police officer informed the person being arrested of the offence or type of offence for which he was being arrested so that the person being arrested had the opportunity of volunteering information which would avoid the arrest.

In *Abbassy* the plaintiff had driven in an inconsiderate manner and, when stopped by the police, became rude and offensive and refused to give any information as to the ownership of the vehicle. The officer told the plaintiff that unless he gave the information he would be arrested 'for unlawful possession' of a vehicle. He was arrested. The plaintiff did, in fact, have authority to use the vehicle and was subsequently charged with obstruction of the police in the execution of their duty. The trial judge decided that this made the arrest unlawful. The Court of Appeal thought that decision should have been left to be determined by the jury.

When an arrest is made a caution must be given to the person arrested unless a caution was given immediately before arrest (Code C, para. 10). Originally the caution was to remind the person that he or she was not obliged to say anything but what was said might be given in evidence. However, the caution now has a broader significance as can be seen from the new provisions in ss. 34 to 39 of the CJPOA 1994. The Codes of Practice have been amended to take account of these new provisions. The new caution is 37 words long and reads:

> You do not have to say anything. But it may harm your defence if you do not mention when questioned something which you later rely on in court. Anything you do say may be given in evidence.

From this wording you should be able to see quite plainly that the accused could be in a difficult position if he or she wished to rely on something in court which he or she had not mentioned when questioned. Sections 34 to 39 allow a court or jury to draw inferences from the fact that a person does not answer questions put by the police or does not give evidence in court. Further details of ss. 34 to 37 can be found in *Cases and Materials* (**10.3.1**).

SAQ 92

What must a person be told when being arrested? What are the consequences of a failure to convey this information?

The person arrested must be told the fact of and the grounds for the arrest as soon as practicable (s. 28). Failure to do so renders the arrest unlawful. In addition the person arrested must be cautioned under the new caution. Failure to caution will not render the arrest unlawful but it will be a breach of the Codes. That may lead the courts to declare any admissions made by the accused inadmissible; we will return to this later.

10.5.2 ARREST UNDER WARRANT

A warrant may be issued for the arrest of a person who has committed or is suspected of having committed an indictable offence. Warrants are issued by magistrates. PACE 1984 amends the Magistrates' Courts Act 1980 and provides that in some circumstances a warrant may be executed by a constable even though it is not in his or her possession at the time. The warrant must be shown to the arrested person as soon as practicable if he or she asks to see it.

10.5.3 ARREST WITHOUT A WARRANT

10.5.3.1 Statutory powers

PACE 1984 gives powers of summary arrest to citizens and police constables in respect of **arrestable offences**. That is a term of art and has a specific meaning. It is used to describe those offences to which the powers of summary arrest apply. Those powers apply only to arrestable offences and nothing else.

Arrestable offences are defined in s. 24(1) as:

(a) offences for which the sentence is fixed by law, for example, murder;

(b) offences for which a person, 21 years of age or over and not previously convicted, may be sentenced to imprisonment for a term of five years;

(c) offences specifically listed in the Act, e.g., customs amd excise offences, Official Secrets Acts offences, indecent assault on a woman, taking a motor vehicle without authority (s. 12 of the Theft Act 1968), going equipped to commit burglary or theft (s. 25 of the Theft Act 1968), publishing material intended to stir up racial hatred (s. 19 of the Public Order Act 1986), ticket touting in respect of designated football matches (s. 166 of the CJPOA 1994), having obscene articles for publication for gain (s. 2 of the Obscene Publications Act 1959), taking, having or publishing indecent photographs of children (s. 1 of the Protection of Children Act 1978); an offence under s. 2 of the Protection from Harassment Act 1997; carrying an offensive weapon in a public place (s. 1 of the Prevention of Crime Act 1957; carrying an article with a blade or point in a public place (s. 139(1) of the Criminal Justice Act 1988); and having such an article on school premises (s. 139A of the Criminal Justice Act 1988) (the last three offences were brought within s. 24 by s. 1 of the Offensive Weapons Act 1996);

(d) conspiring to, and attempting to, commit any of these offences.

(See also *Cases and Materials* (10.3.2.1).)

10.5.3.2 Citizens

You will doubtless have heard the expression 'citizen's arrest'. Well this can be used to describe the statutory powers given to citizens in PACE 1984.

Section 24(4) of PACE 1984 provides that any person may arrest without warrant anyone who is in the act of committing an arrestable offence, or anyone whom he has reasonable grounds for suspecting to be committing such an offence.

This may be referrd to as the 'there and then' power as it is limited in time and is exercisable only when a person is, or is suspected to be, committing the offence. Thus an arrest must be made neither too soon nor too late.

This power may be exercised even though an arrested person is not committing an arrestable offence himself since the power arises if the citizen has reasonable grounds to suspect a person is committing an arrestable offence. Although a suspicion may be mistaken, the arrest will be lawful if it was based on reasonable grounds.

Section 24(5) provides that where an arrestable offence has been committed, any person may arrest without warrant anyone who is guilty of the offence or anyone whom he has reasonable grounds for suspecting to be guilty of it.

The valid exercise of this power by a citizen is dependent on the fact that an arrestable offence has actually been committed. This enacts the principle established in *Walters* v *W.H. Smith and Son Ltd* [1914] 1 KB 595. A clear illustration of this limitation is found in *R v Self* [1992] 1 WLR 657. The defendant was seen to take a bar of chocolate from a shop. He was chased by an assistant and a store detective. He was seen to discard the chocolate. A citizen assisted in detaining him. The defendant was acquitted of the theft of the chocolate. He was also acquitted of assault whilst resisting arrest because when he assaulted those trying to detain him the purported arrest was not lawful. There was no power to arrest by virtue of the limitation in s. 24(5) – no arrestable offence had been committed. The Court of Appeal felt bound to decide the case in this way even though it recognised that such an interpretation could lead to absurdity.

Other statutes give citizens powers of arrest, e.g., s. 25(4) of the Theft Act 1968 (going equipped) and s. 3(4) of the Theft Act 1978 (making off without payment). They are both 'there and then' powers.

If a private citizen makes an arrest he 'must, as soon as he reasonably can, hand over the n to a constable or take him to the police station or take him before a magistrate' (per Lord Denning MR in *Dallison* v *Caffery* [1965] 1 QB 348 at pp. 366–7). There is no requirement that this be done immediately – a reasonable delay is allowed (*John Lewis and Co. Ltd* v *Tims* [1952] AC 676).

10.5.3.3 Police

The powers given to constables under PACE 1984 are much broader than those given to citizens. The powers in relation to arrestable offences are discussed in **10.5.3.4** and powers in relation to other offences in **10.5.3.5**.

10.5.3.4 Arrestable offences

Section 24(6) provides that where a constable has reasonable grounds for suspecting that an arrestable offence has been committed he may arrest without warrant anyone whom he has reasonable grounds for suspecting of being guilty of that offence.

This power involves two tests of reasonableness. First there must be reasonable grounds to suspect an arrestable offence has been committed; and secondly, reasonable grounds to suspect that the person being arrested is guilty of the offence.

There is no requirement that an arrestable offence must have been committed.

Section 24(7) provides that a constable may arrest without warrant anyone who is about to commit an arrestable offence, or anyone whom he has reasonable grounds for suspecting to be about to commit an arrestable offence.

SAQ 93

Compare this with the citizen's power of arrest. How does it differ?

The answer is, of course, that this power arises much earlier than the powers of the citizen.

10.5.3.5 Non-arrestable offences

Section 25 provides that where a constable has reasonable grounds for suspecting any offence which is not an arrestable offence has been or is being committed or attempted, he or she may arrest the 'relevant person' if it appears that service of a summons is impracticable or inappropriate because any of the 'general arrest conditions' are satisfied.

Potentially this is an extremely wide power because it applies to all offences other than arrestable offences, including attempts to commit any non-arrestable offences.

The general arrest conditions fall into five different groups. The first three relate to the name and address of the relevant person:

(a)   The name of the relevant person is unknown and cannot be readily ascertained by the constable (e.g., a suspect refuses to give it). In *Nicholas* v *Parsonage* [1987] RTR 199 a constable said, 'What is your name?' and later said, 'What is your address?' The person refused to answer. It was held that, in such circumstances, where a person whose name was unknown to a constable was reasonably suspected by him of having committed an offence (not an arrestable offence), s. 25(1) and (3) were satisfied.

In that case a police officer had warned the defendant about riding his bicycle with no hands. The applicant responded with an obscene gesture. The constable told him of the power of arrest and asked for his name and address. The defendant was convicted of assault on the constable in the execution of his duty under s. 51 of the Police Act 1964 (now s. 89 of the Police Act 1996 — see *Cases and Materials* (**10.3.2.2**)) and the conviction was upheld.

(b)   The constable has reasonable grounds for doubting that the name given by the relevant person is his or her real name. This should require something more than a mere 'hunch'.

G v *DPP* [1989] Crim LR 150 decided that the reason given by a police officer for doubting the name and address of the person arrested being that 'suspects usually give false names and addresses' was not enough.

(c)   (i)   The relevant person has failed to furnish a satisfactory address for service, or

(ii)   the constable has reasonable grounds for doubting whether an address furnished by the relevant person is a satisfactory address for service (e.g., a temporary address or box number is not satisfactory).

Can you see how this provision might cause difficulties in the wider sphere of constitutional law?

It could cause problems if the practical effect is to impose an obligation on a suspect to provide his or her name and address even though this is not a legal obligation. The common law position in *Rice* v *Connolly* [1966] 2 QB 414, that a person is not under a legal obligation to answer questions put by the police, is not affected.

Even if the name and address of a suspect are known he or she may still be arrested if:

  (d) The constable has reasonable grounds to believe the arrest is necessary to prevent the suspect:

      (i)   causing physical injury to himself or any other person;

      (ii)   suffering physical injury;

      (iii) causing loss of or damage to property;

      (iv)   committing an offence against public decency;

      (v)   causing an unlawful obstruction of the highway.

  (e) The constable has reasonable grounds for believing that an arrest is necessary to protect a child or other vulnerable person from the suspect.

Please see the earlier reference to *Edwards* v *DPP* (1993) 97 Cr App R 301, in which an arrest under s. 25 of PACE 1984 was regarded as unlawful.

PACE 1984 specifically preserves some powers of arrest which are listed in s. 26.

 SAQ 95

What powers of arrest without a warrant are given to the police under PACE 1984? Please try to compile a list.

Your list should have looked something like this.

  (a) Where a constable has reasonable grounds for suspecting that an arrestable offence has been committed he may arrest anyone whom he has reasonable grounds for suspecting to be guilty of it (s. 24(6)).

  (b) He may arrest anyone who is about to commit an arrestable offence, or anyone whom he has reasonable grounds for suspecting to be about to commit an arrestable offence (s. 24(7)).

  (c) Under s. 25 where he has reasonable grounds to suspect that a non-arrestable offence has been committed or attempted, or is being committed or attempted, he may arrest that person if it appears to him that service of a summons is impracticable or inappropriate because any of the general arrest conditions are satisfied.

10.5.3.6   Reasonable grounds

You will have seen that all these powers of arrest are subject to the existence of 'reasonable grounds' and if such grounds do not exist the arrest will not be lawful. Without reasonable grounds the power of arrest does not arise. In *Chapman* v *DPP* (1988) 89 Cr App R 190, Bingham LJ said, at p. 197, 'Reasonable suspicion is the source from which all police constables' powers of summary arrest flow.'

He continued 'He [the police officer] must, in my judgment, reasonably suspect the existence of facts amounting to an arrestable offence of a kind which he has in mind. Unless he can do that he cannot comply with s. 28(3) of the Act by informing the suspect of grounds which justify the arrest.'

In the past a constable's action has rarely been challenged on the basis that 'reasonable grounds' did not exist. In cases where the question has arisen it has been held to be an objective rather than a subjective test and in *Lister* v *Perryman* (1879) LR 4 HL 521 it was treated as a matter of law for the judge. *Dumbell* v *Roberts* [1944] 1 All ER 326 decided that 'the police are not called upon before acting to have anything like a prima facie case for convicting'. They may, where a person is likely to escape, have to act on the spur of the moment, but where practicable should make enquiries before acting.

Reasonable grounds will only exist if a reasonable man in the position of the officer at the time of arrest would have thought that the accused was probably guilty of the offence (*Dallison* v *Caffery* [1965] 1 QB 348; *Wiltshire* v *Barrett* [1966] 1 QB 312). In *Hussien* v *Chong Fook Kam* [1970] AC 942 it was accepted that a failure to ask relevant questions before arrest could mean that the officer did not have reasonable grounds.

The following cases illustrate these principles.

In *Ware* v *Matthews* [1982] LR 476 police constables stopped a car using their powers under the Road Traffic Acts. The driver, Ware, and the passenger, his father, demanded to know why they had been stopped. Reluctantly Ware gave his name and address after initially refusing. They had no means of identification and no proof they were in lawful possession of the car. When requested to get out of the car they locked the doors and wound the windows up. The sergeant had refused to check Ware's ownership of the car on the computer and arrested them on suspicion of theft. It was held that there were no 'reasonable grounds' for suspicion of theft. The judge thought it unwise to establish principles concerning 'reasonable grounds' although he felt a refusal to give a name and address might suffice in some circumstances. Here, there was no reason why the computer should not be checked. Ware and his father were awarded £250 in damages.

In *Holtham* v *MPC*, *The Times*, 28 November 1987 the police were found on appeal to have had reasonable grounds to make an arrest. In an investigation of a murder, the plaintiffs were the parents of the suspect who had been arrested. Their house was searched for goods which had been stolen from the murder victim. The plaintiffs were cooperative and the only grounds for their subsequent arrest (for doing acts to impede the son's prosecution under s. 4 of the Criminal Law Act 1967) were (a) that the loft was surprisingly clean and (b) a statement that their son had not visited them in July or August had been contradicted by a neighbour. This was enough to give reasonable suspicion.

Castorina v *Chief Constable of Surrey* (1988) 138 NLJ 180 concerned a burglary thought to have been an 'inside job'. The police arrested and held for nearly four hours the plaintiff who had recently been dismissed by the managing director from the company concerned. There were no grounds to believe she was responsible for the offence. She was awarded £4,500 compensation on the grounds that the police lacked reasonable cause for the arrest.

In assessing whether or not the arresting officer has 'reasonable cause to suspect', the court must look at both what the officer knew and what he ought to have known at the time of the arrest. The officer should carry out such further inquiries as would enable him to have reasonable confidence in the evidence on which he relies.

In *Chapman* v *DPP* (1988) 89 Cr App R 190 the plaintiff's arrest for assault was found to be unlawful because there was no evidence to suggest that the arresting officer suspected an arrestable offence has been committed.

In *Holgate-Mohammed* v *Duke* [1984] AC 437 the House of Lords decided that a police constable exercising his discretion whether or not to arrest a person was entitled to take into consideration as a relevant ground the fact that the suspect would be more likely to tell the truth (confess) if questioned at a police station rather than at home. But this was not a substitute for the reasonable grounds test, only a relevant consideration **after** the power to arrest had arisen. An attempt had been made to challenge the arrest under judicial review alleging *ultra vires* under the '*Wednesbury* principles', by alleging that the officer had acted on some irrelevant considerations or for an improper purpose when arresting Holgate-Mohammed.

It is worth comparing this case with *Plange* v *Chief Constable of South Humberside Police*, *The Times*, 23 March 1992 in which the Court of Appeal (Civil Division) held that where a constable arrested a person on reasonable suspicion that he had committed an arrestable offence and the arrested person could prove that the arresting officer knew (at the time of the arrest) that there was no possibility of a charge being made, then the arrest would be unlawful because the arresting officer had acted on some irrelevant consideration or for some improper purpose.

According to *O'Hara* v *Chief Constable of the Royal Ulster Constabulary* [1997] 1 All ER 129, the 'mere fact that an arresting officer had been instructed by a superior officer to make an arrest was not capable of amounting to reasonable grounds for the necessary suspicion'. Neither would a request from an officer of inferior or equal rank. Obviously if the arresting officer had been given sufficient information by another officer that might provide reasonable grounds. It would depend on the circumstances, but such a police officer should not be in a worse position simply because the information comes from another officer rather than a civilian informant.

10.5.4 COMMON LAW POWERS

The common law power to arrest for a breach of the peace is unaffected by s. 26 of PACE 1984. The common law was examined by the Court of Appeal in *R* v *Howell* [1982] QB 416 where Watkins LJ stated at p. 426:

> We hold that there is power of arrest for breach of the peace where: (1) a breach of the peace is committed in the presence of the person making the arrest or (2) the arrestor reasonably believes that such a breach will be committed in the immediate future by the person arrested although he has not yet committed any breach or (3) where a breach has been committed and it is reasonably believed that a renewal of it is threatened.

These powers are not restricted to police officers. In *Albert* v *Lavin* [1982] AC 546, Lord Diplock said:

> . . . every citizen in whose presence a breach of the peace is being, or reasonably appears to be about to be, committed has the right to take reasonable steps to make the person who is breaking or threatening to break the peace refrain from doing so;

and those reasonable steps in appropriate cases will include detaining him against his will. At common law this is not only the right of every citizen, it is also his duty, although, except in the case of a citizen who is a constable, it is a duty of imperfect obligation.

This would sanction a detention short of arrest so long as it was a reasonable step in preventing a breach of the peace.

So the next question is: what is a breach of the peace?

In *R v Chief Constable of Devon and Cornwall, ex parte Central Electricity Generating Board* [1982] QB 458, Lord Denning MR defined breach of the peace as 'whenever a person who is lawfully carrying out his work is unlawfully and physically prevented by another from doing it'.

However, in *R v Howell* Watkins LJ said at p. 426:

> Nevertheless, even in these days when affrays, riotous behaviour and other disturbances happen all too frequently, we cannot accept that there can be a breach of the peace unless there has been an act done or threatened to be done which either actually harms a person, or in his presence his property, or is likely to cause such harm, or which puts someone in fear of such harm being done. There is nothing more likely to arouse resentment and anger in him, and a desire to take instant revenge, than attacks or threatened attacks upon a person's body or property.

It is submitted that the better view is that expressed in *R v Howell* and it was preferred in *Parkin v Norman* [1983] QB 93. The justices were in error in thinking that mere disturbance not involving violence or a threat of violence could amount to a breach of the peace, and felt that the remarks of Watkins LJ in *R v Howell* had put the matter beyond doubt.

Further comment was made in the case of *Moss v McLachlan* (1984) 149 JP 167. The police stopped convoys of vehicles containing striking miners and tried to persuade them not to take part in any demonstaration or mass picket. If persuasion failed they were ordered to turn round thereby preventing them from going to working mines. Those who refused to turn back were arrested and some were convicted of obstructing the police in the execution of their duty. The justices decided that anyone aware of the current strike would realise there was a substantial risk of an outbreak of violence. Provided the police honestly and reasonably decided that there was a real risk of a breach of the peace then reasonable preventive action could be taken. The possibility of a breach of the peace must be real to justify preventive action. The imminence or immediacy of the threat to the peace determined what action was reasonable.

The case of *Wershof* v *Commissioner of Police of the Metropolis* [1978] 3 All ER 540 demonstrates how the presence of a breach of the peace may create a power to arrest where one does not normally exist. It was held that a police officer had a power to arrest for obstruction of police in the execution of duty, but only if:

(a)   the nature of the obstruction was such that the offender actually caused or was likely to cause a breach of the peace or it was calculated to prevent the lawful arrest of another person, or

(b)   at the relevant time the constable was acting in the execution of his duty and honestly believed, on reasonable grounds, that the offender was wilfully obstructing him and that the obstruction was likely to cause a breach of the peace.

Note that obstructing the police in the execution of their duty is a non-arrestable offence (s. 89 of the Police Act 1996) and so could fall within the scope of s. 25 of PACE 1984.

10.5.5   PROCEDURE FOLLOWING ARREST

Let us suppose that a person has been arrested by a police officer. What is that officer allowed to do with that person after the arrest? Depending on the circumstances, it is likely that the officer will want to search the person. Provision is made in PACE 1984 for that to take place.

10.5.5.1   Search on arrest

The provisions relating to some aspects of search and arrest have already been dealt with in **10.4.2.2** above. There we looked at s. 18, which allowed entry to the premises of an occupier or controller who had been arrested for an arrestable offence, and s. 32, which allowed entry and search of the premises where the person was either when arrested, or immediately before arrest.

But s. 32 goes further. It provides for constables to search a person on arrest where the arrest is made at a place other than a police station:

(a)   if the constable has reasonable grounds for believing that the arrested person may present a danger to himself or others, e.g., where the person was arrested for an arrestable offence involving violence or threats of violence; or

(b)   where the constable has reasonable grounds for believing the arrested person has concealed on him anything which:

   (i)   he might use to assist him to escape from lawful custody; or

   (ii)   might be evidence relating to an offence.

In *Lindley* v *Rutter* [1981] QB 128 a woman police constable removed the bra of a woman who had been arrested for being drunk and disorderly. Would this be lawful under s. 32?

The Divisional Court decided the constable had not considered whether or not she had lawful grounds for searching the accused or whether the removal of the bra was necessary for the defendant's own protection and it was therefore impossible to justify her conduct. This would not be within the provisions of s. 32. Prior to PACE 1984 the courts took a similar line to s. 32.

You will see that there is a limitation attached to this power, i.e., the requirement for reasonable grounds. Any such search is limited to doing only what is reasonably required for the purposes of discovering the object of the search. So, where there are no reasonable grounds, there is no power to search. In reality it is likely that a police officer will effect a quick search whenever the officer feels the need.

The courts have commented upon such searches and the following cases illustrate some of the points made.

In *R v Badham* [1987] Crim LR 202 it was held that such a search must be made at the time of arrest and not several hours later.

In *R v Churchill* [1989] Crim LR 226 it was held that the police acted beyond their powers under s. 32(2)(a)(ii) in requiring a suspected burglar to hand over his car keys for the purpose of taking his car to the police station to be searched and also for safe keeping. The keys were not 'evidence relating to an offence'.

A constable carrying out such a search may seize and retain any articles he finds that may be used to cause physical injury to the arrested person or to any other person, that might be used to escape lawful custody or that are evidence of an offence or have been obtained through the commission of any offence (ss. 32(8) and (9)).

Do you remember what the police must do when stopping and searching?

Hopefully, you will have remembered that police officers must give certain information to the person stopped — otherwise the exercise of this power is unlawful (ss. 2 and 3 of PACE 1984). At common law there may be a requirement to inform a person being searched after his or her arrest of the reason for the search. In *Brazil v Chief Constable of Surrey* [1983] 1 WLR 1155 it was held that a personal search by police officers imposes a restraint on a person's freedom to which he should not be required to submit unless he knew in substance the reason for it, and that a police officer who had decided to carry out a search should inform the person concerned of the reason for it unless the circumstances rendered the giving of reasons unneccessary or impracticable.

If the person to be searched is arrested at a police station, or is detained at a police station following arrest, such searches will be undertaken by, or authorised by, the custody officer at the police station (ss. 54 and 55 of PACE 1984 — see *Cases and Materials* (10.3.3.1)).

10.5.5.2   Removal of arrested persons to a police station

So we are at the stage where a person has been arrested and probably searched. What next?

The person who is arrested by a police constable, or who is taken into custody by a police constable having been arrested by someone else, must be taken to a police station as soon as practicable (s. 30(1) of PACE 1984). The main reason for this is so that the safeguards regarding detention and treatment of persons in custody cannot be avoided (e.g., the length of time in custody is controlled and the custody officer has particular responsibilities). We will deal with this in **10.5.8** below. Generally the police station must be a designated police station, i.e., one which is to be used for the purpose of detaining arrested persons (s. 35(1)), and, of course, at which there is a custody officer. But there are exceptions to this rule:

(a)   It may be any police station unless it appears necessary that the arrested person will be detained for more than six hours (s. 30(3)).

(b)   Where a constable is on his own and no assistance is available and injury may occur if the longer journey to a designated police station were undertaken then the constable may take an arrested person to **any** police station (s. 30(5)).

When an arrested person is taken to a police station which is not a designated police station he must be taken to a designated police station within six hours of his arrival at the first station if he is to be kept in detention. But PACE 1984 does allow a delay under s. 30(10) if the presence of the arrested person is necessary elsewhere in order to carry out such investigations as it is reasonable to carry out immediately, e.g., to help with the recovery of stolen property or to ensure the arrest of accomplices. The reason for any delay must be recorded when the arrested person first arrives at the police station.

You can see from this that the general principle is that an arrested person is to be taken to a designated police station. The occasions when such a person is not taken to a designated police station should be exceptional. But what happens if an arrested person is not taken to a designated police station? Are there any consequences?

Why have the courts decided that evidence obtained in breach of PACE 1984 and/or the Codes will not always be excluded?

It is generally accepted that it is not the function of the courts to discipline the police — they simply are not equipped for it nor do they employ the police. The focus should therefore be on the rights of the suspect and unfairness in the trial process. One other thought. If you start to exclude evidence for minor breaches by the police, does that mean all subsequent evidence — however crucial — must be excluded? From a purely pragmatic point of view, that cure seems worse than the disease!

Let us look at a couple of cases and see how the courts have approached the matter.

In *R v Keane* [1992] Crim LR 306 there was a breach of s. 30(1). The police interviewed the defendant at the flat where he was arrested and did not take him to a police station 'as soon as practicable after the arrest'. There was also a breach of s. 30(11) — not recording the reasons for the delay. His alleged confession during the interview was admitted by the judge and conviction followed. He appealed, alleging that the confession should be excluded under s. 78(1) of PACE 1984 because of the breaches of PACE 1984 and the Codes. But his conviction was upheld because the judge had correctly addressed his mind to s. 78(1) and the exercise of his discretion. (For a fuller discussion of s. 78(1) see **10.5.8.9** below.)

In *R v Khan* [1993] Crim LR 54, the Court of Appeal warned police and customs officers that, even if they were justified in delaying taking a subject to a police station in order to carry out a search, they should not abuse the opportunity by asking a lengthy series of questions to circumvent the Codes and that, if they did, they risked having the admissions excluded under s. 78(1). This is not so much a threat from the courts that sanctions may apply (i.e., evidence obtained in breach could be excluded) but more a recognition of the rights of a suspect under the due process of law. However, from the facts of the case you will see that the result was that the evidence was not excluded.

Customs officers arrested Khan and took him to two flats while they searched for money and drugs. During the searches they asked him questions. It was held by the court that, although the officers were entitled to keep Khan away from the customs office, this did not give them carte blanche to circumvent the Codes by asking questions during the search which should normally be asked at a designated police station. Although some of the questions went beyond what was strictly necessary, the judge's decision to admit the part objected to was not unreasonable.

The principle from *Khan* was applied in the case of *R v Raphaie* [1996] Crim LR 812.

One final point to note is that where an arrest has been made at a place other than a police station, the arrested person shall be released before reaching a police station if there are no grounds for keeping him or her under arrest (s. 30(7)).

Is PC Smith acting lawfully in the following circumstances?

PC Smith arrests John for criminal damage to a shop window. He sees a bulge in John's inside coat pocket and automatically searches John. He finds a large hammer. PC Smith then takes John into the shop where he interviews John at length.

Your answer should address the following issues. PC Smith may be able to arrest John lawfully if he has reasonable grounds to believe that John committed the criminal damage (s. 24(6)). Criminal damage is an arrestable offence. He would be able to search John on arrest if he had reasonable grounds to believe that John had concealed on him anything which he might use to assist him to escape from lawful custody or which might be evidence relating to the offence (s. 32). The hammer could fall within either or both of these categories.

But PC Smith has searched John automatically and so has not given any thought to whether reasonable grounds exist. So, technically the search would be unlawful, but how could we establish this, if at all? It seems unlikely that we could. No sanctions would therefore be imposed on PC Smith for this search.

Finally, John should have been taken to a police station as soon as practicable after the arrest: s. 30(1). He should not have been taken into the shop to be interviewed at length. PC Smith was acting unlawfully because he had no legitimate reason not to take John directly to a police station.

10.5.5.3   Arrest for a further offence

Sometimes you will find that a person who is under arrest for one offence may confess to others. It used to be possible to release that person and then, perhaps just as he was leaving the police station, to arrest him again for that other offence. That clearly would have a strong psychological effect upon the individual. However, under s. 31 PACE 1984, where a person has been arrested and detained at a police station in connection with an offence and it appears to a constable that were he to be released he would be liable to arrest for some other offence, he may be arrested for that other offence.

In *R* v *Samuel* [1988] QB 615, Hodgson J said (*obiter*), 'It seems to this court that the obvious purpose of that section is to prevent the release and immediate rearrest of an alleged offender. Nor does the section impose any duty on the constable to arrest immediately. We see nothing in the section which would prevent the constable delaying arresting him until the time (if it ever arrived) when his release was imminent'.

Clearly the view of the courts is that this provision is designed to prevent the police from using rearrest to bring psychological pressure on a suspect.

10.5.6   VOLUNTARY ATTENDANCE AT POLICE STATION

Not every suspect who attends at a police station is there following arrest. Very often a person will attend at a police station voluntarily. If that is the case then the provisions of s. 29 of PACE 1984 cover the situation. It reads:

> Where for the purpose of assisting with an investigation a person attends voluntarily at a police station or at any other place where a constable is present or accompanies a constable to a police station or any such other place without having been arrested —
> (a)   he shall be entitled to leave at will unless he is placed under arrest;
> (b)   he shall be informed at once that he is under arrest if a decision is taken by a constable to prevent him from leaving at will.

Such a person is not under detention and so the time constraints on detention etc., do not apply. The person is entitled to leave at any time unless arrested, and it is only an arrest which can lawfully prevent that person from leaving. This leads us nicely on to the next point for discussion. We often hear that someone is helping the police with their enquiries. So what is meant by this term?

10.5.7   'HELPING THE POLICE WITH THEIR ENQUIRIES'?

First, the general rule is that there is no power of detention short of arrest. As Viscount Simon commented in *Christie* v *Leachinsky* [1947] AC 573, 'The matter is a matter of substance and turns on the elementary proposition that in this country a person is, prima facie, entitled to his freedom'. Arrests and detentions must therefore be justified by some legal authority, either under common law or statute.

The principle is well illustrated by the case of *Kenlin* v *Gardiner* [1967] 2 QB 510 in which police constables stopped two youths because it was thought that they may have been involved in a burglary. There was a slight scuffle as the youths tried to get away. The youths were held to be not guilty of an assault on the police in the execution of their duty because, as the police constables had not arrested the youths, their actions were unlawful. There was no power to detain for questioning so the youths were entitled to resist.

Let us contrast *Donnelly* v *Jackman* [1970] 1 WLR 562 where a constable, wishing to talk to the accused, tapped him on the shoulder to attract his attention. The accused assaulted the constable and was charged with assault on a police officer in the execution of his duty contrary to s. 51 of the Police Act 1964. The court decided he was guilty because not every trivial interference with the liberty of a subject will amount to conduct taking a police constable outside the execution of his duty, and here there had been no attempt to detain the accused.

Whether any interference with a person's liberty is unlawful is a matter of degree dependent on the circumstances (*Collins* v *Wilcock* [1984] 1 WLR 1172).

In *Bentley* v *Brudzinski* (1982) 75 Cr App R 217 the defendant and his brother were stopped and questioned at 03.30 by a police constable. They answered his questions truthfully and identified themselves. After waiting for about 10 minutes, while the constable tried unsuccessfully to confirm their identities by radio, they walked away. Another constable stopped the defendant by putting his hand on his shoulder and the constable was punched in the face.

Suppose you were acting for the defence. What would be your main argument?

It was argued (and held) that this was more than a trivial interference with the defendant's liberty and was an unlawful attempt to stop and detain him. The respondent was not guilty of assaulting a police constable in the execution of his duty.

There is no general power to detain for questioning and a person who has been unlawfully detained may use reasonable force to escape (*Kenlin* v *Gardiner* [1967] 2 QB 510 above). Another well known case that illustrates this point is *R* v *Inwood* [1973] 1 WLR 647. The defendant had only been asked to accompany the police constable to the police station for further tests concerning a possible drink-driving offence. No arrest had been made. He was therefore entitled to leave the police station at any time and could not be prevented from doing so. His use of force to prevent the police from stopping him leaving was not an assault on a police officer under s. 51 of the Police Act 1964 (now s. 89 of the Police Act 1996). You will realise that this sort of situation is now covered by s. 29 of PACE 1984 which we just discussed.

Some of you are probably thinking, 'If there is no general power to detain for questioning, how is that the police often do detain for the purpose of asking questions?' The answer is that there are some statutory powers which allow the police to detain a person for a specific purpose (e.g., Road Traffic Acts allow the police, in certain circumstances, to require the name and address of a motorist). That clearly does and must involve a detention short of arrest.

The point is illustrated by the case of *Squires* v *Botwright* [1973] Crim LR 106. A plain-clothes police constable followed Squires in her car because he suspected her of drinking and driving. He stopped her in her driveway and asked her to wait for a police constable in uniform to administer a breath test. He also asked for her name, address and driving licence. She hit him with her handbag and he barred her way. The court said that although Squires had not been arrested the police constable had the right to detain her to require her name and driving licence. He was acting lawfully so she was guilty of an assault on a police officer in the execution of his duty under s. 51.

On a more general note, the police remain entitled to ask questions of anyone. Simply to ask a question is not the exercise of a power and should not be confused with one. Of course, there is no obligation to answer any of the questions which the police may put to you (*Rice* v *Connolly* [1966] 2 QB 414). However, you should remember the power of arrest and the general arrest conditions relating to name and address under s. 25 of PACE 1984. In those circumstances refusal to give your name and/or address could lead to one of the general arrest conditions being satisfied and to you being arrested.

Read the following facts and determine whether the police are acting lawfully.

John has gone to the police station in response to a telephone call requesting his attendance. The police have told him that they need to speak to him to eliminate him from their enquiries. When he arrives he is taken by PC Smith and PC Kean to an interview room and subjected to some fierce questioning. During the questioning he gets up to leave. The police officers grab hold of him and push him back into his seat telling him that they have not yet finished with the interview. John pushes them both aside and runs off.

You should have concluded that since John has attended the police station voluntarily, he is entitled to leave whenever he wishes. The only way in which he can be prevented from leaving is for the police to arrest him (s. 29). There is no indication that he has been arrested. So when he is pushed back into the seat the police are acting unlawfully. He is entitled to use reasonable force in order to escape from unlawful detention.

Let us now recap, for the sake of completion and to reinforce the point. When you are invited to the police station, or you voluntarily attend, that is not a detention. If you decide to leave and are then prevented from doing so, that becomes a detention. Such a detention would be unlawful unless there had been an arrest. This is clearly illustrated from the previous discussions on s. 29 and the case of *R v Inwood*.

10.5.8   DETENTION AT A POLICE STATION

Earlier we talked about the fact that persons under arrest should be taken to a designated police station (see **10.5.5.2**). One of the reasons for this was that the safeguards written into PACE 1984 and the Codes with respect to the length of time of custody and the responsibility of the custody officer only operate at the police station. So the next part of our discussion involves the custody officer's responsibilities.

10.5.8.1   The custody officer

Quite simply, the custody officer (CO) has responsibility for persons in custody. This position was created by s. 36 of PACE 1984 (see *Cases and Materials* (**10.3.5.1**)). A CO must be of the rank of sergeant or above, is appointed by the chief constable (or his or her delegate), and there must be one at every designated police station.

The role of the CO is part judicial and part administrative. It is his or her responsibility to ensure compliance with all of the detailed provisions relating to the treatment of suspects set out in PACE 1984 and Code C. The CO must be independent of the officers investigating a crime and questioning a suspect (s. 36(5)). This detaches the CO from the individual case and ensures that he or she acts independently.

The CO must compile and ensure the accuracy and completeness of the custody record (s. 37(4)). This is a record of all the major events of the suspect's detention including the reasons for initial detention, reasons for continued detention, times of interview, meals, refreshments etc. The purpose of the record is to ensure that the suspect is treated in accordance with the letter and spirit of PACE 1984. It is also a safeguard against police misconduct. A suspect is entitled to a copy of the custody record. The custody record is admissible in court. Failure to insert accurate entries in the custody record will amount to a disciplinary offence by the CO.

Let us look more closely at the responsibilities of the CO in relation to detention of suspects.

10.5.8.2   Detention

When an arrested person is brought to the police station he or she should be taken to the CO. It is then for the CO to determine whether there is sufficient evidence to charge that person with the offence for which he or she was arrested (s. 37(1)). This has to be determined as soon as practicable after the person has been brought to the police station, or, if arrested at the police station, as soon as practicable after that arrest (s. 36(10)). Authorisation of detention is not automatic. Time for detention (known as the 'clock') begins to run from this point.

Where the CO does not have enough evidence to charge the arrested person he or she must order that person to be released unless the CO has reasonable grounds for believing that detention before charge is necessary:

 (a)   to secure or preserve evidence relating to an offence for which that person is under arrest: or

 (b)   to obtain such evidence by questioning him or her (s. 37(2)).

This was the first occasion on which a statute had conferred a right to detain a person for questioning. It has been criticised for being inconsistent with the right to silence. We have seen the effects of s. 34 of CJPOA 1994 which allows inferences to be drawn from a failure to reply to questions (**10.5.1** above).

A review must be made of a suspect's detention, no later than six hours after the detention was first authorised by the custody officer (s. 40). Thereafter there must be further reviews every nine hours to check that the criteria for detention are still satisfied and, if they are not, the suspect must be released immediately. Reviews may be postponed where it is 'not practicable' to carry them out at the precise time they are due.

Normally an arrested person detained without charge may be detained for up to 24 hours and must then be released or charged (s. 41).

Detention without charge beyond 24 hours and up to 36 hours will be allowed only where a police officer of at least the rank of superintendent authorises it (s. 42). Such detention may be authorised only if there are reasonable grounds for believing that:

(a)   it is necessary to detain that person without charge in order to secure or preserve evidence, or to obtain such evidence by questioning him;

(b)   the offence is a serious arrestable offence; and

(c)   the investigation is being conducted diligently and expeditiously.

We have now come across the term 'serious arrestable offence'. Please look at s. 116 in *Cases and Materials* (10.3.5.2) and familiarise yourself with the definition.

Did you notice:

■   that there are some offences which are always serious;

■   that others are serious if intended to have specified consequences;

■   paragraph (e) and (f) on substantial gain and loss?

R v Smith [1987] Crim LR 579 concerned a robbery at Woolworths of two video recorders valued at £800 plus £116 cash. How would you decide the issue of serious arrestable offence on these facts?

It was held not to be a serious arrestable offence. It seems that the financial gain to the robbers was not substantial and it was not a serious loss to the store. Did you decide that? What about stealing £20 from a pensioner who is on very limited income with limited means?

To return to detention, should the police wish to detain a person beyond 36 hours they must apply on oath and by way of information to a magistrates' court for a warrant of further detention (s. 43). The detained person must be present at the hearing, have a copy of the information laid on oath by the police, and has the right to be legally represented.

The magistrates can issue a warrant of further detention for up to another 36 hours, provided the absolute maximum period for which a person can be detained without charge is no longer than 96 hours (s. 44). Thus within this maximum period a person's detention must be reviewed at least twice by the magistrates. After 96 hours a person must be released unless charged.

If we recap for a moment we will see how the picture might be emerging in a simple scenario.

A person (X) is arrested and brought to a police station. The custody officer determines that X will be detained. He will probably be interviewed. The detention will be reviewed. That detention may be extended, perhaps while further evidence is obtained. Then if there is sufficient evidence X is charged. When X has been charged by the police then, normally, he must be released.

This is where the provisions of s. 38 of PACE 1984 come into operation. They provide that once X is charged he must be released unless:

(a)   his name and address cannot be ascertained or verified; or

(b)   the CO has reasonable grounds to believe that detention is:

   (i)   necessary for his own protection; or

   (ii)   to prevent him causing physical injury to persons or damage to property; or

   (iii)   he will fail to answer bail, if granted; or

   (iv)   he will interfere with witnesses or obstruct the course of justice.

These criteria for continuing detention are similar to those matters generally considered by the courts as grounds for refusing applications for bail under the Bail Act 1976.

10.5.8.3   Rights of detained person

We have already discussed, in part, the responsibilities of the CO. There are further responsibilities which must be performed.

Please look at Code C, para. 3.1 (*Cases and Materials* (10.3.5.3)) on the duties of the CO and make a list.

Your list should have included:

(a) The right to have someone informed of the arrest.

(b) The right to legal advice (free of charge).

(c) The right to consult the Codes of Practice.

Did you also notice that these rights can be exercised at any time? The CO must also give the person a written notice which sets out the above rights, the right to a copy of the custody record and the caution. The notice must also explain the arrangements for obtaining legal advice. The person must be asked to sign the custody record to acknowledge receipt of these notices and any refusal to sign must be recorded on the custody record.

These rights are very important and need to be examined a little more closely.

10.5.8.4 Right to have person informed of detention and access to legal advice

These two rights are covered by ss. 56 and 58 of PACE 1984 respectively. (See also the extracts from Code C in *Cases and Materials* (10.3.5.3).)

The first thing that has to be observed is that these rights are exercisable only if requested by the detained person. If the detained person does not request them then they will not be provided. Even if a request is made there may be a delay in providing the rights.

However, the maximum permitted delay is 36 hours. Delay may be permitted only where an officer of at least the rank of superintendent authorises it (s. 56(2) or s. 58(6) and (8) respectively). In each case rights can be delayed only where the person is detained for a serious arrestable offence.

Authorisation may be given only where there are reasonable grounds to believe that certain consequences will follow. Please read the respective sections in *Cases and Materials* (10.3.5.4) and make a note of the consequences.

Did you notice that each of the consequences is prefaced by the word 'will'? This was, presumably, deliberate. It could have been 'might' or 'may' or 'could' but it was not. Please bear this in mind when reading the following case on the validity of delays.

In *R v Samuel* [1988] QB 615 the police suspected that the defendant had been involved in a serious armed robbery at a building society. A cashier thought she recognised him and on that basis he was arrested. A search of his house revealed incriminating evidence – two face masks, a building society passbook hidden under the carpet, lots of property from some other burglaries, and photographs of the defendant kissing bundles of banknotes. The defendant admitted the burglaries but not the robbery. The police were anxious to charge him with this as well. When he first arrived at the police station at 14.00 he said that he did not want a solicitor. But at 20.30 he asked for his lawyer. The superintendent refused access, recording that it was a serious arrestable offence and that there was a 'likelihood of other suspects to be arrested being inadvertently warned'. The defendant was kept in custody overnight and questioned in more detail. At 11.00 the following day his mother was told of his detention. She managed to get the services of a highly respected solicitor, but the police refused to let him near the defendant. At 16.00 the defendant was charged with the burglaries, but questioning about the armed robbery continued. The solicitor was still refused access. A new police questioner was brought in and the defendant now faced three officers whereas before he had faced only two. At about 17.30, over 27 hours into his detention and after four extended bouts of questioning, he confessed to the robbery. At 18.20 he was charged and at 19.25 he finally saw his solicitor.

On appeal against his conviction, the Court of Appeal condemned this sequence of events. A suspect should always be able to see a solicitor after being charged and Samuel was charged with burglary at 16.30. Access should be denied before charge only in very rare circumstances. Mistrust of a solicitor must be based on fact, and could not simply reflect a suspicion of the legal profession in general. Here, the defendant's mother knew he was in police custody and could have tipped off any alleged accomplices long before a solicitor could do it inadvertently. Denying access because the solicitor might advise his client to keep quiet was 'wholly unsustainable'. Time was running out before the defendant would have to be allowed access to his solicitor (36 hours) and the court concluded that whoever decided to refuse the defendant access to his solicitor at 16.45 was probably motivated by the desire to have one last chance of interviewing him in the absence of his solicitor. The court concluded the confession was wrongly obtained and quashed the conviction for armed robbery.

Others charged with serious crimes have had their convictions quashed because their admissions had been obtained after being wrongly denied access to a solicitor. In R v Davison [1988] Crim LR 422 the accused was acquitted of the murder of a police sergeant and the attempted murder of a constable. In R v Vernon [1988] Crim LR 445 a confession to two murders was disallowed.

However, the picture is not as clear-cut as it might at first sight appear. There are cases where access has been denied in breach of s. 58, but the conviction has stood.

In R v Alladice (1988) 87 Cr App R 380 the accused, a youth, confessed to armed robbery after the police had denied his request for access to a solicitor. The interview was conducted with propriety and the solicitor would have added nothing to the knowledge the detainee already had about his rights. The confession was admissible. Lord Lane CJ accepted that the refusal to allow access was quite improper and a clear breach of s. 58 but it did not follow from this that the confession should be excluded. According to his lordship:

> The result [of legal advice] is that in many cases a detainee, who would otherwise have answered proper questioning by the police, will be advised to remain silent. Weeks later, at his trial, such a person not infrequently produces an explanation of, or a defence to the charge the truthfulness of which the police have had no chance to check.

> . . . The effect of s. 58 is such that the balance of fairness between prosecution and defence cannot be maintained unless proper comment is permitted on the defendant's silence in such circumstances. It is high time that such comment should be permitted together with the necessary alteration to the words of the caution.

You will remember, of course, that the words of the caution have now been changed and provisions have been made to allow the court to draw proper inferences where the accused seeks to rely on explanations which he or she had not given at an earlier time: we discussed this at **10.5.1** above.

In R v *Chief Constable of South Wales, ex parte Merrick* [1994] 1 WLR 663 it was stated that the right of access to a solicitor under s. 58(1) of PACE 1984 does not extend to a person on remand in custody at a magistrates' court. However, there is a right of access at common law which was not abrogated by the Act. The right is, on request, to be permitted to consult a solicitor as soon as is reasonably practicable. Thus a police policy of refusing a person in custody at court access to a solicitor on the sole ground that the request was made after 10.00 am without reference to whether it was reasonably practicable to allow access at once or within a reasonable time, was unlawful.

You will have noticed that in the cases of R v *Samuel* and R v *Alladice* the issue was whether the confession was admissible. Confessions and admissions will normally arise as a result of police questioning. If such questioning is not conducted within PACE 1984 and Code C any admissions resulting therefrom may be challenged as being inadmissible. So we need to examine the provisions relating to police questioning.

10.5.8.5 Questioning

As we have already seen, a police officer may make enquiries of any person. However, when the officer has grounds to suspect that the person being questioned has committed an offence the officer must caution. The caution informs the person that he need not say anything but it might harm his defence if he does not mention when questioned something he later relies on in court, and that anything he says may be given in evidence (Code C, para. 10.1). When there are reasonable grounds to suspect that the person has committed an arrestable offence that person may be arrested. On arrest the person arrested must be cautioned unless the caution has been given immediately before the arrest (Code C, para. 10.3).

A person who has been arrested may not be interviewed except at a police station or other authorised place of detention unless delay is likely to interfere with or harm evidence or cause physical harm to others, alert persons not yet arrested or hinder the recovery of property (Code C, para. 11.1).

Where a person is interviewed, whether in police custody or not, an accurate record must be kept. A written record must be made during the course of the interview unless, in the investigating officer's view, this would not be practicable or would interfere with the conduct of the interview (Code C, para. 11.5). Any interview or inquiry of a detained person can only be with the CO's permission (Code C, para. 12.1).

Interviews should, as far as possible, take place in interview rooms which must be adequately heated, lit and ventilated (Code C, para. 12.4). In any 24-hour period a detained person must be allowed at least eight hours rest free from questioning (Code C, para. 12.2). There must be breaks from interviewing for refreshments at approximately two-hour intervals as well as breaks at recognised mealtimes. But the interviewing officer may decide not to allow a break if there are reasonable grounds for believing that it would involve risk of harm to people or serious loss of, or damage to property, delay unnecessarily the person's release, or otherwise prejudice the outcome of the investigation (Code C, para. 12.7). Finally, the Codes of Practice provide that interviews at a police station must be tape-recorded in respect of indictable or either-way offences.

One of the main purposes of an interview is to obtain a confession from the suspected person. Many convictions are obtained as a result of confessions. It is therefore important that there are protections for the suspect in custody. This is where PACE and the Codes were intended to protect the suspect from improper pressure by the police during an interview. If there has been a breach of the Codes of Practice one needs to know what will be the likely consequence of such a breach.

A failure to comply with the Codes is not a criminal offence, nor is it actionable in civil proceedings (s. 67(1)). However, the Codes are admissible as evidence when a court is determining any question to which the Codes are relevant (s. 67(11)). Thus, failure to comply with the Codes of Practice may be taken into account when a trial judge has to decide whether or not to exclude as evidence any confession made in breach of the Codes.

10.5.8.6 Exclusion of confessions

Please look at ss. 82(1) and 76(1) of PACE 1984 in *Cases and Materials* (10.3.5.5) and note their meanings.

You should have noticed that a confession includes any statement wholly or partly adverse to the person who made it, whether made to a person in authority or not and whether made in words or otherwise (s. 82(1)); and that confessions are, generally, admissible (s. 76(1)).

Now let us look at s. 76(2) in *Cases and Materials* (10.3.5.5) to see what is provided there.

Section 76(2) ensures that a confession must be excluded by the court unless the prosecution proves beyond reasonable doubt that the confession was not obtained by oppression or in consequence of anything said or done which was likely to render it unreliable.

10.5.8.7 Oppression

What amounts to oppression is a question of law. Section 76(8) contains a partial definition that oppression includes torture, inhuman or degrading treatment, and the use or threat of violence. Let us look at some cases to see how the judges have dealt with oppression.

In *R v Fulling* [1987] QB 426 the court said that PACE 1984 was a codifying statute and that according to the principles set out in *Bank of England* v *Vagliano* [1891] AC 107 the meaning had to be ascertained by interpreting the language of the statute uninfluenced by previous decisions. Oppression was thus to be given its ordinary dictionary meaning of the 'exercise of authority or power in a burdensome, harsh, or wrongful manner; or cruel treatment of subjects, inferiors etc. or the imposition of unreasonable or unjust burdens'. Lord Lane CJ said: 'We find it hard to envisage any circumstances in which such oppression would not entail some impropriety on the part of the interrogator.'

'Rude and discourteous' questioning, with a raised voice and some bad language, giving the impression of 'impatience and intimidation' was not considered to amount to oppression (*R v Emmerson* (1991) 92 Cr App R 284). Neither was raising voices slightly with no shouting or oppressive hostility (*R v Heaton* [1993] Crim LR 593).

But where the police shouted at a suspect what they wanted him to say after he had denied involvement in the offence charged over 300 times, the Court of Appeal held they had behaved oppressively (*R v Paris, Abdullahi and Miller* (1992) 97 Cr App Rep 99). The court criticised the defence solicitor for sitting passively during the majority of the interview. Lord Taylor of Gosforth CJ also commented that 'short of physical violence, it is hard to conceive of a more hostile and intimidating approach by officers to a suspect'.

In *R v Davison* [1988] Crim LR 422 the defendant was arrested at 06.00 for handling stolen goods. No evidence had come to light by 11.00 and he had not confessed. He was then interviewed about a gold robbery to which he did confess. It was held that he had been unlawfully detained. The detention was oppressive because the police had used their authority in a wrongful manner. They had arrested him for handling stolen goods to give them more time to talk to him about the gold robbery when they had no real grounds to do so. His confession was inadmissible.

In *R v Beales* [1991] Crim LR 118 oppression was present and a confession was ruled inadmissible. There had been hectoring and bullying right through the interview. There had also been deliberate misstatements by the interviewing officer to put pressure on B.

10.5.8.8   Unreliability

Where does the burden of proof lie when confessions are excluded?

When one examines the authorities in this area, it becomes clear that all sorts of issues may affect reliability — the age or mental condition of the suspect, the bona fides of the police, breaches of PACE 1984 and the Codes of Practice (especially legal access) etc. There are no hard and fast rules so the courts decide every case on its facts.

The following are some cases used as examples to illustrate the courts' approach.

In *R v Everett* [1988] Crim LR 826 the defendant had a mental age of eight. If the police had realised this they should have ensured the presence of an independent and mature person. The confession was inadmissible.

In *R v Cox* [1991] Crim LR 276 interviewing a juvenile in the absence of an appropriate adult rendered the confession inadmissible.

In *R v Harvey* [1988] Crim LR 241 the defendant's confession to murdering a man in the presence of her lesbian lover was held to be unreliable because she was of a low IQ and suffered from a psychopathic disorder.

However, in *R v Goldenberg* [1988] Crim LR 678, the confession of a heroin addict who said that he had confessed because he was anxious to be released as he needed another fix, was held not to be unreliable. It was the defendant's own conduct here, not that of the police.

Failure to caution before interview under Code C (*R v Doolan* [1988] Crim LR 747) and failure to allow access to solicitor (*R v Chung* (1991) 92 Cr App R 314) have led to exclusion of evidence under this head.

The case of *R v Silcott, Braithwaite and Raghip, The Times*, 9 December 1991, gives a good illustration of unreliable confessions, including interviews without solicitors, without appropriate adults in the case of juveniles and a mentally-disordered person, and failure to record interviews contemporaneously.

In *R v Marshall, The Times*, 28 December 1992, a confession was held unreliable on appeal. The Court of Appeal said that police officers are seldom justified in re-interviewing a suspect in his solicitor's absence who, in an earlier interview, at which the solicitor was present had made no admissions. The re-interview was particularly unreliable in the circumstances because the defendant was on the borderline of subnormality and his admission did not square with the objective facts. It is not clear from the case whether the appeal was allowed under s. 76 or s. 78 of PACE 1984.

10.5.8.9 Discretion to exclude evidence

In addition to the duty under s. 76(2) to exclude confessions, the court has a discretion to exclude admissible evidence under s. 78(1) of PACE.

ACTIVITY 80

Please read s. 78(1) of PACE in *Cases and Materials* (10.3.5.6) and make a list of the points which you consider to be important.

The important issues are:

- it applies to all admissible evidence, not just confessions;

- it applies to evidence 'on which the prosecution proposes to rely';

- it creates a discretion;

- the way in which evidence was obtained is relevant;

- the seminal issue is 'such' unfairness to the accused at trial that the evidence should be excluded.

At common law the courts had a discretion to disallow admissible evidence but its basis and scope were unclear. The common law position seems to have been retained by virtue of s. 82(3) of PACE 1984. This provides that nothing in Part VIII of the Act shall prejudice any power of a court to exclude evidence, whether by preventing questions from being put or otherwise, at its discretion.

However, s. 78(1) is on its wording, and has in practice been interpreted to be, much wider in scope than the common law. The decision in *R v Samuel* [1988] QB 615, considered in **10.5.8.4**, confirms this and shows that if there have been significant and substantial breaches of PACE 1984 or the Codes, then judges are increasingly prepared to exclude evidence by virtue of s. 78(1).

In *R v Parris, The Daily Telegraph*, 21 November 1988, the Court of Appeal ruled that evidence of an interview with the accused was inadmissible because he had been denied access to his solicitor (in breach of s. 58), that he had not been allowed to have someone informed of his arrest (in breach of s. 56), and that the interview was the only evidence offered by the prosecution.

The discretion to exclude evidence under s. 78 applies to any evidence the prosecution would seek to adduce according to the Court of Appeal in *R v Mason* [1988] Crim LR 141 where police officers deliberately lied in telling the defendant and his solicitor that fingerprints had been found on a bottle used in arson. The police admitted, 'We set about conning the defendant'. It was held this had an adverse effect on the fairness of the proceedings and the evidence was therefore excluded.

In *R v Walsh* [1989] Crim LR 822 bad faith on the part of the police was held to be a significant consideration.

One can see that the provisions in s. 78 have been invoked successfully, and quite frequently, to exclude evidence and, as a result quash convictions.

10.5.8.10   Agents provocateur and entrapment

One aspect of unfairness may be where the police, or other agency, seem to instigate the commission of a criminal offence by being agents provocateur or trying to entrap the accused. Where this has been alleged the courts have taken a particular view depending upon the circumstances of the case and whether the device is used to avoid the safeguards found in PACE 1984 and the Codes of Practice.

The starting point must be the case of *R v Sang* [1980] AC 402. In this case the House of Lords recognised the discretion to exclude evidence on the grounds of unfairness. On the facts of the case itself they refused to exclude evidence which had been obtained as a result of an agent provocateur's activities. From this case the common law position is that there is no defence in English criminal law of agent provocateur or entrapment.

However, some movement may be taking place by using the provisions of s. 78 of PACE 1984. In *R v Smurthwaite, R v Gill* (1994) 98 Cr App R 437 the Court of Appeal held that

s. 78 has not changed the rule of law, as clarified in *Sang*, that entrapment or use of an agent provocateur does not *per se* afford a defence in law to a criminal charge. However, evidence obtained by entrapment etc. may be excluded under s. 78 if it has an adverse effect on the fairness of the proceedings.

Lord Taylor CJ gave a list of some factors the judge might take into account:

■ Was the agent provocateur enticing the defendant to commit an offence he would not otherwise have committed?

■ What was the nature of the entrapment?

■ How active or passive was the officer's role in obtaining the evidence?

■ Had the undercover agent abused his role to ask questions which ought properly to have been asked by a police officer in accordance with the Codes? (See *R v Bryce* below.)

On the facts of the actual case the appeals were dismissed (S and G had been convicted of soliciting an undercover police officer to murder their spouses).

For the police to leave an unattended van containing a load of cigarettes, which were visible, was not entrapment (*Williams & Others v DPP* [1993] 3 All ER 365). The defendants were arrested removing the cigarettes.

It was also not entrapment where two undercover agents lured a heroin smuggler from Pakistan into the UK, one of the agents posing as a buyer (*R v Latif and Shahzad* [1996] Crim LR 414).

However, a couple of recent cases may have qualified this area.

In *R v Christou & Wright* [1992] 3 WLR 228 the Court of Appeal stated that it would be wrong for the police to adopt an undercover pose or disguise to enable them to ask questions about offences in order to circumvent the Codes of Practice.

In the case *R v Bryce* (1992) 95 Cr App R 320 an undercover police officer, posing as a potential buyer, questioned the suspect who was selling a car. The officer asked how long had the car been stolen. The reply was, 'two or three days'. The court held that this was inadmissible evidence.

The present situation appears to be:

■ The admissibility of confessions can be challenged under s. 78 as well as under s. 76. (and see s. 82(3)).

■ If s. 76 is satisfied the court **will** exclude the confessions, i.e., unless the prosecution can prove that a confession was not obtained by oppression or in circumstances which render it unreliable.

■ If s. 78 applies the court **may** exclude the evidence, i.e., on the grounds of fairness.

■ Evidence is not to be excluded simply as a means of punishing the police.

10.6 Conclusion

In a democracy, a balance must be struck between the rights of the citizen and the powers of the police. The law on police powers in Britain reflects this approach. When reading through PACE 1984 and the Codes of Practice (extracts in *Cases and Materials* (**Chapter 10**)) you will probably have been struck by how often a police officer is given power subject to a proviso that it may only be exercised if there are 'reasonable grounds' for doing so. As Reiner and Leigh point out, 'while the powers of the police have expanded considerably in the last two decades', PACE 'attempts to erect a network of safeguards'. For an indication of the effectiveness of these PACE safeguards, you should turn to the extract from Reiner and Leigh in *Cases and Materials* (**10.4**).

10.7 End of Chapter Assessment Question

PC Smith arrests Bob on suspicion of theft. He drives Bob to the police station. At the police station he immediately takes Bob into an interview room and starts to question him. After two hours Bob is really angry and asks to see a solicitor and also have his wife informed of his whereabouts. PC Smith simply ignores the request and continues questioning Bob. After another hour Bob admits the theft. He is then charged and released to appear at court.

Explain whether the actions of the police are lawful. What would be the attitude of the courts to the confession made by Bob?

See *Cases and Materials* (10.6) for a specimen answer.

CHAPTER ELEVEN

PUBLIC ORDER LAW — FREEDOM OF ASSEMBLY AND ASSOCIATION

11.1 Objectives

By the end of this Chapter you should be able to:

- explain the powers the police enjoy to maintain order in society;

- outline the legal obligations on those wishing to assemble publicly in the United Kingdom;

- identify the public order offences committed in a given fact situation;

- assess the extent to which a proper balance is struck between the need to respect the individuals right to protest and the preservation of public order.

11.2 Introduction

In **Chapter 10** we looked at general powers available to the police in relation to the investigation and detection of crime. In this Chapter we shall narrow our focus to the law relating to public order. The liberty of citizens to protest publicly has long been regarded as an important characteristic of a democratic and free society and it distinguishes a liberal democracy from a totalitarian State. In this Chapter we will examine the extent of the individual's right to assemble and protest in public.

11.3 The 'Right' to Protest

Read *The Abuse of Power* extract in *Cases and Materials* (11.1). What does Patricia Hewitt mean when she claims that 'the characterization of demonstrations and other forms of public protest as a threat to normal community living obscures the basic fact that protest is a *part* of normal community life and serves a vital function in a democratic system of government?'

It is often assumed that there exists in this country a right to gather together for the purpose of holding a public meeting or procession. You may be surprised to learn that until the Human Rights Act 1998 comes into force in England and Wales, there is no such legal right of peaceful assembly or procession. In the absence of a statutory right to hold public meetings Article 11 of the European Convention on Human Rights (ECHR) is the only safeguard in this area, as it provides that:

(a)   Everyone has the right to freedom of peaceful assembly and to freedom of association with others . . .

(b)   No restrictions shall be placed on the exercise of these rights other than those such as are prescribed by law and are necessary in a democratic society in the interests of national security or public safety, for the prevention of disorder or crime, for the protection of health or morals or for the protection of the rights and freedoms of others . . . .

The fact that the Human Rights Act 1998, when it comes into force, will incorporate the ECHR which guarantee in express terms that everyone has the 'right to freedom of peaceful assembly' is a significant development. The traditional British approach in this area and to civil liberties generally was that one may do anything unless there is a law preventing or restricting that activity. Freedoms, such as that of assembly or that of expression, are by their very nature *residual*. People may gather anywhere they wish or say anything they want, subject to restrictions imposed by the State.

Thus, according to this residual approach, if you wish to arrange a demonstration about, say, a new road-building programme near your home, you are entitled to do so, but problems will arise if your demonstration conflicts with any existing laws. Factors which might render a meeting or procession unlawful or even prevent it from being held include the number of people likely to attend, its location and the duration of the event.

In *Duncan* v *Jones* [1936] 1 KB 218 (see *Cases and Materials* (**11.1**)) Lord Hewart CJ said:

'English law does not recognise any special right of public meeting for political or other purposes. The right of assembly . . . is nothing more than a view taken by the court of the individual liberty of the subject.'

ACTIVITY 82

Read the extract from Lord Scarman's report on the Red Lion Square Disorders (1975) in the *Cases and Materials* (11.1). Compare and contrast Lord Scarman's comments with those of Lord Hewart in *Duncan* v *Jones*.

SAQ 105

To what extent is freedom of assembly protected by law in the United Kingdom?

As was noted earlier, the law in Britain aims to strike a balance between legitimate protest and generally maintaining the peace. The problem which arises is that one individual's form of protest may well impinge upon another's freedom of movement. The result must inevitably be some form of compromise whereby freedom of assembly is limited in the interests of an ordered and non-violent society. One illustration of this is the legal regulation of the highway.

11.3.1 REASONABLE USE OF THE HIGHWAY

There is a traditional right to pass along a public highway provided the highway is not physically obstructed. Obstruction of the highway constitutes an offence under the Highways Act 1980, s. 137. This provides that an offence is committed '[i]f a person without lawful authority or excuse, in any way wilfully obstructs the free passage along a highway' (s. 137(1)). The power of arrest for this offence is now found in the Police and Criminal Evidence Act 1984, s.25, and a police constable can arrest without warrant anyone seen committing the offence.

The Court of Appeal has held that stationary peaceful picketing is not a reasonable use of the highway (*Hubbard* v *Pitt* [1976] QB 142, see *Cases and Materials* (**11.1.1**)). In this case, a community action group gathered outside estate agents' offices in Islington, protesting against affluent outsiders moving into their area to buy the houses of local residents. They distributed leaflets and displayed placards outside these estate agents' offices. The Court of Appeal granted the estate agents an interlocutory injunction, in favour of the picketing being stopped. However, Lord Denning MR (dissenting) held that the use of the highway in these circumstances was not unreasonable and did not constitute a nuisance at common law. He considered that picketing other than for trade disputes was lawful as long as its purpose was to communicate information or peacefully persuade others.

The use of the highway for public meetings and processions is also restricted by the tort of trespass. In *Harrison* v *Duke of Rutland* [1893] 1 QB 142, it was held that use of the highway for an improper purpose may constitute a trespass against the owners of adjoining property in whom 'the soil of the highway is vested'.

The offence of wilful obstruction of the highway (s. 137 of the Highways Act 1980) requires the prosecution must prove three elements for the offence of obstruction:

(a) The fact of obstruction (i.e., the physical obstruction).

(b) That it was wilful (i.e., it was done with intent).

(c)   That is was without lawful excuse (i.e. it was not a *reasonable use of* the highway).

In *Arrowsmith* v *Jenkins* [1963] 2 QB 561 (see *Cases and Materials* (**11.1.1**)), Pat Arrowsmith addressed a meeting in Nelson Street, Bootle, which linked two main roads. She spoke for half an hour, and for five minutes the road was completely blocked. The police had to clear a way for a fire engine and were assisted by the defendant with the means of a loud-hailer, but the carriageway remained partially obstructed until she had finished her speech. Arrowsmith was convicted of committing the offence of wilful obstruction but argued that an element of intention was necessary to commit this offence and that the assistance she gave the police indicated that she had not deliberately intended to cause an obstruction of the highway. The Divisional Court held that although Arrowsmith had co-operated with the police, she had caused the highway to be obstructed and had been rightly convicted.

ACTIVITY 83

Read the extract from the judgment of Glidewell LJ in *Hirst and Agu* v *CC of West Yorkshire* in *Cases and Materials* (**11.1.1**). What is the test for the offence of wilful obstruction of the highway?

In *Nagy* v *Weston* [1965] 1 WLR 280, Lord Parker CJ commented that reasonable use of the highway 'depends upon all of the circumstances, including the length of time the obstruction was caused, the place, the purpose for which it is done, and whether it does in fact cause an actual obstruction as opposed to a potential obstruction'. On the facts of this case, Nagy's decision to park his hot-dog van in a lay-by where there was a bus stop was not reasonable. Even though the road was wide, the time was 10.15 p.m. and with heavy traffic passing by it was not a suitable place from which to sell hot dogs.

As you should have seen in **Activity 83**, guidance as to what constitutes a reasonable use of the highway is also found in *Hirst and Agu* v *Chief Constable of West Yorkshire* (1986) 85 Cr App Rep 143. Six members of a group of animal rights supporters were convicted by magistrates of obstructing the highway. They had protested outside a shop which sold furs in Bradford Shopping Centre. It was a spacious but busy pedestrian precinct. The defendants claimed that their conduct constituted reasonable use of the highway. The Divisional Court allowed their appeal on the grounds that the spacious location was a relevant consideration and that the prosecution had not successfully proved that the appellants were obstructing the highway without lawful excuse. In reaching this conclusion, Otton J quoted Lord Denning in *Hubbard* v *Pitt*, that 'so long as good order is maintained, the right to demonstrate must be preserved.'

In *DPP* v *Jones* [1997] Crim LR 599, a demonstration had taken place within an area in which trespassory assemblies had been prohibited by an order made under s. 14A of the

Public Order Act 1986. Counsel for the defendants argued that as long as an assembly on the highway was peaceful and non-obstructive it was lawful. This argument was rejected by the court and Collins J stated that 'the holding of a demonstration on the highway, however peaceful, had nothing to do with the right of passage', and that there was no right to hold an assembly on the highway.

Why does Geoffrey Robertson QC in *Freedom, the Individual and the Law* claim that 'Cars and horses have more legal rights on the highway than people?'

11.3.2   THE PUBLIC ORDER ACT 1986

Some of the most important provisions governing organised processions and assemblies are to be found in the Public Order Act 1986. The Act redefined the powers of the police to deal with processions and assemblies, as well as replacing certain common law offences (e.g. riot) with clearer statutory offences. The Public Order Act 1986 followed a government White Paper, *Review of Public Order Law*, published in May 1985 (Cmnd 9510), and a Law Commission report, *Criminal Law: Offences Relating to Public Order* (Law Com. No. 123) (1983). These proposals for reform had been triggered by a number of public order incidents which occured in the early 1980s.

Think back over the past two decades. Can you identify those incidents of serious public disorder which led to the enactment of the Public Order Act 1986?

See *Cases and Materials* (11.1.2) for some examples.

The powers of the police have been further extended by the Criminal Justice and Public Order Act 1994 which contains a number of new provisions giving the police power to deal with 'raves' and mass trespass. We shall return to these later on in this Chapter.

11.4   Processions and Assemblies

11.4.1 PROCESSIONS

We have seen that political processions are prima facie lawful provided that they do not infringe upon the rights of others to use the highway. However, the Public Order Act 1986 introduced a series of new rules relating to the holding of processions, demonstrations and assemblies.

How would you define a public procession? Now turn to s. 11 of the Public Order Act 1986 in *Cases and Materials* **(11.2.1). For what types of procession is advance written notice required?**

1.

2.

3.

And for what kinds of procession is advance notice not required?

11.4.1.1   Advance notice

As you will have seen from s. 11 of the Public Order Act 1986, the reason why it is important to know what constitutes a public procession is because s. 11 requires that the organisers of certain marches must give six clear days written notice to the police. Unless it is not 'reasonably practicable', advance written notice must be given for any proposal to hold a public procession intended to:

(a)   'demonstrate support for or opposition to the views or actions of any person or body or persons,

(b)   to publicise a cause or campaign, or

(c)   to mark or commemorate an event' (s. 11(1)).

The organisers of the march may be guilty of an offence if they fail to give the police the required notice or fail to comply with the date, time or route specified in the advanced notice (s. 11(7)). However, it is a defence for a march organiser if he or she can show that they were unaware that they had failed to comply with the notice requirements (s. 11(8)) or if the failure for doing so arose from circumstances beyond their control (s. 11(9)).

Section 16 of the Public Order Act 1986 defines a 'public procession' as a procession in a 'public place'. This may cover a highway or 'any place to which . . . the public or any section of the public has access, on payment or otherwise, as of right or by virtue of express or implied permission.' Not withstanding this definition, the powers in the Public Order Act 1986 relating to the advance notice requirements for processions lack detail in three respects: first, the definition of procession in s. 16 does not stipulate the number of participants needed for a procession to be designated as a 'public procession', secondly, no examples of marches where it 'is not reasonably practicable to give any advance notice', are given in the Act; and thirdly, the Public Order Act 1986 fails to provide a test as to who is the organiser of a march.

Sensitive policing of processions may remedy the alleged first two omissions, while case law provides valuable assistance in dealing with the third. Thus, in *Flockhart* v *Robinson* [1950] 2 KB 498 (see *Cases and Materials* (**11.2.1.1**)), Lord Goddard CJ, stated that a procession 'is a body of persons moving along a route' and that 'the person who organizes the route is the person who organizes the procession.'

11.4.1.2 Imposing conditions on public processions

Under s. 12 of the Public Order Act 1986, the senior police officer at the scene may impose conditions on the march if he or she 'reasonably believes' that it:

(a) 'may result in serious public disorder, serious damage to property or serious disruption to the life of the community, or

(b) the purpose of the persons organising it is the intimidation of others with a view to compelling them not to do an act they have a right to do, or to do an act they have a right not to do.'

The conditions which may be imposed will be in directions given to the organisers and participants, and may include prohibiting marchers from entering a specified public place or the police imposing a certain route. It is an offence if organisers and participants knowingly fail to comply with these conditions, but it is a defence for them if they can prove that this failure arose from circumstances beyong their control (s. 12(4) and (5)).

However, what if the conditions which may be imposed under s. 12 are not enough to prevent public disorder? Then in these circumstances the police may have the power to ban a march.

11.4.2 BANNING PROCESSIONS

In the past, under the Public Order Act 1936, the police had the power to ban certain marches. Today, s. 13 of the 1986 Act retains this power, and the chief officer of police may prohibit public processions being held in a district or part of a district if she or he reasonably believes that the holding of a public procession will result in serious public disorder. Outside London the chief police officer must apply to a district council for an order prohibiting the holding of all public processions (or those of a specified class) for a period not exceeding three months. To make such an order the council must have the consent of the Home Secretary. Similarly, in London, the Commissioner of Police for the City of London or the Metropolitan Police Commissioner, may, with the consent of the Secretary of State, make an order for a period not exceeding three months, banning all public processions or those of a specified class (e.g. marches about nuclear weapons). Anyone who organises a march during such a period, commits a criminal offence.

In *Kent* v *MPC, The Times*, 15 May 1981, a CND procession was banned as a result of a 'blanket ban' on marches imposed by the Metropolitan Police Commissioner which affected the whole of the London Metropolitan area. CND challenged this on the ground that the Metropolitan Police Commissioner had failed to take into consideration all relevant matters. The Court of Appeal rejected CND's claim and held that the Metropolitan Police Commissioner was entitled to conclude that such a march carried a risk of the police or the participants being attacked. The effect of the ban was that no processions could be held within the 786 square miles of the Metropolitan Police district 'except those traditionally held on May 1st to celebrate May Day and those of a religious nature customarily held'.

Where conditions are imposed by the police on marches (Public Order Act 1986, s. 12), or if the march is banned (s. 13), the organizers of the procession may seek judicial review of the police orders. However, such a remedy has two obvious disadvanges. First, by the time the application for judicial review may have been heard, the date of the march is likely to have passed. Thus judicial review is only an *ex post facto* check. Secondly, the courts tend to be reluctant to challenge operational policy decisions of chief constables (*Kent* v *MPC*), so that the individual's chances of succeeding in such a case are rather slim.

What steps should the organisers of a procession take to ensure compliance with the law?

11.4.3 ASSEMBLIES

Until the Public Order Act 1986 there were no statutory provisions governing public assemblies. The main reason why s. 14 of the Act was introduced was to curb the sort of mass picketing which had occurred during the 1984 miners' strike and the News International dispute at Wapping in 1986. The introduction of the new measures caused controversy. Geoffrey Robertson QC, has called it 'a recipe for conflict and confusion at demonstrations', while Gerald Kaufman (Shadow Home Secretary from 1983 to 1987) described s. 14 as the 'most objectionable provision of the Act'. So what are 'public assemblies', and how are they controlled by the police?

Section 16 of the 1986 Act defines a public assembly as 'an assembly of 20 or more persons in a public place which is wholly or partly open to the air'. This would include pickets, pop festivals, football crowds, and any other form of outdoor public meeting in excess of 20 participants. Conditons may be imposed if the senior police officer present reasonably believes that serious public disorder, serious damage to property or serious disruption to the life of the community is likely, or that the purpose of the organisers is one of intimidation. Only three conditions may be imposed on assemblies — these are conditions as to the:

(a) *Place* at which the assembly may be or continue to be held.

(b) Maximum *duration*.

(c) Maximum *number* of persons.

Senior police officers can impose conditions which, in practice, largely defeat the purpose of the meeting (e.g. ordering the protest to be held at another less inflamatory location).

Challenges may again be brought against such conditions by means of judicial review, but of course this takes time, so that the application may not be heard until after the event.

Failure to comply with a condition is an offence subject to the defence that the failure arose from circumstances beyond the control of the person confined (s. 14(4) and (5)) and a police officer in uniform has the power to arrest on suspicion that an offence is being committed (s. 14(7)).

In *Police* v *Reid* [1987] Crim LR 702 the defendant and 20 others were demonstrating outside South Africa House in Trafalgar Square against apartheid. Reid and others shouted slogans through a microphone at arriving guests such as 'Apartheid murderers get out of Britain' and 'You are a dying breed'. The senior police officer at the scene — a chief inspector — responded by purporting to impose a condition because he regarded their action as intimidatory. He also shouted through a megaphone — 'This is a police message. You are required to go to the mouth of Duncannon Street, north of the tree.' The defendant refused to move but eventually retreated to the tree when reinforcements were called. At the tree she refused to go further and told an officer 'I am going back to where I came from'. She was arrested and charged with failing to comply with a condition under s. 14. Her appeal was allowed because the chief inspector was not justified in concluding that it was the purpose of the organisers to intimidate others — other than to cause them discomfort. The necessary element of the offence was not present, so there were no grounds for imposing this condition.

SAQ 109

Summarise the main differences between a procession and an assembly.

Procession   *Assembly*

Section 14 of the 1986 Act has been amended by the Criminal Justice and Public Order Act 1994 which inserts new ss. 14A, 14B and 14C (see *Cases and Materials* (**11.2.2**)). These changes relate to new police powers to deal with *trespassory public assemblies*. In your comparison of the main differences between processions and assemblies you should have noted that there is no power to ban assemblies. However, by virtue of ss. 70 and 71 of the Criminal Justice and Public Order Act 1994, which amends s. 14, there is a power to ban *trespassory assemblies only* an on application by the chief officer of police to the local council where the assembly is to be held and subject to the approval of the Secretary of State. The effect of a ban under s. 14A is that the holding of all trespassory assemblies in that district shall be prohibited. The order may last no longer than four days and may apply only within a five mile radius of the specified point of assembly (s. 14A(6)).

A chief officer of police may apply for such an order to be made where he or she reasonably believes that an assembly of 20 persons or more is intended to be held at a place or land in the open air to which the public either have no right, or a limited right, of access. Two further conditions must be satisfied:

(a)   that the assembly is likely to be held without the permission of the occupier, or to exceed that permission or exceed the public's right of access (s. 14A(1)(a)), **and**

(b)   that it may result in either serious disruption to the life of the community, or in significant damage to the land, or any building or monument upon that land, where any of these is of historical, architectural, archaeological or scientific importance (s. 14A(1)(b)).

Under s. 14B it is an offence to organise such a prohibited assembly, or take part in, or incite others to take part in, any such assembly. A police officer in uniform may arrest without warrant anyone reasonably suspected of committing these offences and in addition, under s. 14C, may stop anyone reasonably believed to be on route to such an assembly and direct them not to so proceed. This power may only be used within the area covered by the ban (s. 14C(2)).

Read ss. 14A, 14B and 14C of the Public Order Act 1986 in *Cases and Materials* (11.2.2). What sort of 'trespassory assemblies' do you think these provisions were introduced to cover? For some assistance you can turn to the section on trespassory assemblies in the extract by A.T.H. Smith in *Cases and Materials* (11.2.2).

11.4.4   THE PUBLIC ORDER ACT 1936

The bulk of the Public Order Act 1936 was replaced by the Public Order Act 1986 but two offences have been retained.

First, under s. 1 of the 1936 Act, it is an offence to wear in a public place or at a public meeting, uniforms signifying association with a political organisation. In *O'Moran* v *DPP* [1975] QB 864 mourners at an IRA funeral wearing dark sweaters, trousers and berets were held to have committed this offence. Secondly, under s. 2 of the 1936 Act it is an offence to organise, train and equip persons for the purpose of enabling them to usurp the functions of the police and armed forces. For example, in 1963, organisers of a neo-Nazi group called Spearhead were convicted under this section, because of the uniforms they wore and their practice of exchanging Nazi salutes. It is not necessary to show that such groups actively train their members – only that the way in which they are organised may arouse a reasonable apprehension that they are either trained or equipped for the specified purpose (see *R* v *Jordan* [1963] Crim LR 124).

ACTIVITY 86

According to Lord Widgery CJ in *O'Moran* v *DPP* [1975] QB 864 in *Cases and Materials* (11.2.3), what does 'wearing' mean for the purposes of the Public Order Act 1936?

11.5   Public Order Offences

If serious public disorder occurs while a procession or an open-air meeting is actually taking place there are several offences with which the persons concerned may be charged. These offences are now defined in the Public Order Act 1986 and replace the old common law offences of riot, affray and unlawful assembly. The Public Order Act 1986 introduced the following statutory offences in a hierarchy of severity:

Section 1 Riot
Section 2 Violent disorder
Section 3 Affray
Section 4 Fear or Provocation of Violence
Section 5 Harassment, alarm or distress

We shall look at each of these offences in turn. Some of the clauses appear in more than one offence so you will need to be aware of both the similarities and differences between the five offences. It is also recommended that you refer to the relevant sections of the Public Order Act 1986 as we go through these offences (see *Cases and Materials* (11.3)).

11.5.1   RIOT

This is the most serious offence, as reflected in the punishment (10 years' imprisonment, or a fine, or both), but it is rarely charged. Any prosecution requires the consent of the Director of Public Prosecutions. Moreover under the Riot (Damages) Act 1886 (see *Cases and Materials* (11.3.1)), compensation can be claimed for damage caused by a riot, payable by the local police authority. This might be one reason why riot is rarely charged, but it is not necessary to prove that someone has been charged or convicted of the offence of riot for compensation to be available — only that the offence of riot was committed and the conduct was 'tumultuous' as well as 'riotous' (*DH Edwards Ltd* v *East Sussex Police Authority*, *The Times*, 15 July 1988). For example, after the Handsworth riots in 1985, £2 million was paid out in damages to shopkeepers and householders.

In the period prior to the enactment of the Public Order Act 1986, the offence of riot was charged on a number of occasions (e.g. after the 1981 inner city riots and 1984–5 miners' strike) but virtually all of these prosecutions were unsuccessful. For example at the height of the miners' dispute, 273 arrests were made at Orgreave with 232 police officers and 107 miners injured, but all of the prosecutions for riot were withdrawn after 48 days, because of inconsistencies in the evidence, and doubt which had been cast on the police version of events by video-recordings of the events.

Section 1 of the Public Order Act 1986 stipulates that:

> Where 12 or more persons who are present together use or threaten unlawful violence for a common purpose and the conduct of them (taken together) is such as would cause a person of reasonable firmness present at the scene to fear for his personal safety, each of the persons using unlawful violence for the common purpose is guilty of riot.

11.5.1.1   Twelve or more are present

At common law only three or more were required, but this has now been increased to 12 and the prosecution must prove that all 12 were using or threatening violence if anyone is to be charged with riot.

11.5.1.2   'Use of unlawful violence'

Only those within the group of 12 or more who actually use violence commit the offence. Simply threatening violence is not sufficient. Nor is it enough to encourage others to use violence, since there must be some evidence that violence was used (*R* v *Jefferson* [1994] 1 All ER 270).

However, if one of the 12 is *using* violence and all of the others are merely threatening violence, that one using violence would commit riot and the other 11 would only be guilty as accomplices: 'Anyone who fails to dissociate himself effectively and rapidly when a riot develops will run the risk of conviction' (de Smith). Violence includes **any violent conduct** (not just towards people but also to property), and injury or damage need not result, so long as the actions themselves are violent (e.g. it covers throwing missiles which miss: s. 8). Two groups advancing towards each other would not be regarded as engaging in violent conduct unless they started attacking each other.

11.5.1.3   'Common purpose'

All 12 must act in *pursuance of a common purpose* or goal – the nature of the purpose, its legality, and any individual motives, are of no relevance or significance provided there is the common intent (e.g. to destroy shops, or to attack the police). A common purpose can be inferred from members of the group uttering the same threatening chants or by making the same gestures (e.g. Hitler style salutes). In *R* v *Tyler* (1993) 96 Cr App Rep 332, the common purpose was 'demonstrating against the poll tax', while in *R* v *Jefferson* [1994] 1 All ER 270 it was 'celebrating the victory of England over Egypt in their World Cup match.'

11.5.1.4   'Conduct such as would cause fear'

The conduct must be such as to cause fear, alarm or apprehension, but it need not go so far as to cover extreme terror. The test is an objective one — the hypothetical bystander test. The conduct must be such as would cause a person of reasonable firmness present to fear for his or her personal safety. Such a person need not actually be present at the scene, but if there, the conduct must have been such that he or she would have feared for his or her personal safety.

Turn to s. 1 of the Public Order Act 1986 in *Cases and Materials* (11.2.3). Having analysed the component parts of the offence, why do you think that the number found guilty or cautioned each year for riot (e.g., 31 in 1992, 18 in 1993) is so small?

List the differences between ss. 1 and 2 of the Public Order Act 1986.

11.5.2   VIOLENT DISORDER

Section 2(1) of the 1986 Act states that:

> Where three or more persons who are present together use or threaten unlawful violence and the conduct of them (taken together) is such as would cause a person of reasonable firmness present at the scene to fear for his personal safety, each is guilty of violent disorder.

This is an arrestable offence, punishable by five years' imprisonment, and it may be committed in public or private. The word 'unlawful' in s. 2(1) preserves the defences of self defence and the reasonable defence of others (R v *Rothwell and Barton* [1993] Crim LR 626).

11.5.2.1   Three or more

There must be at least three persons present together but there is no need to establish any common purpose, only that those guilty of violent disorder are using or threatening violence (R v *Mahroof* (1988) 88 Cr App R 317).

In R v *Fleming* (1989) 153 JP 517 the Court of Appeal held that three or more includes the accused and if two out of the four men accused of violent disorder are acquitted or discharged, then the remaining two cannot be guilty. In this case the conviction for violent disorder was quashed, and in its place a conviction for affray was substituted.

11.5.2.2   Use or threaten violence

This is wider than riot as it includes those who threaten violence and is not restricted to its actual use. The hypothetical bystander test again applies. As violent disorder is triable either on indictment or summarily, less serious cases may be tried more speedily in the magistrates' courts. The flexibility of this offence makes it particularly suitable for dealing with group violence. It is also much easier to prove than riot, since there is no need to prove a common purpose. Thus being present at the scene of a fight where bottles were being thrown at the police and threats were being made, was enough to convict (*R v Hebron* [1989] Crim LR 389).

In answer to **SAQ 110**, you should have noticed three differences between riot (s. 1) and violent disorder (s. 2):

■   for s. 1, 12 or more people must be involved, while for s. 2, the number is only 3;

■   there is a requirement for a common purpose under s. 1, but not under s. 2;

■   for s. 1 (but not s. 2), the defendant must be shown to have *used* unlawful violence.

ACTIVITY 88

Read the extract in *Cases and Materials* (11.3.2.1) from Bonner and Stone. Do you agree that the changes introduced by ss. 1 to 4 of the Public Order Act 1986 'constitute steps down a route that is potentially damaging to police community relations'?

11.5.3   AFFRAY

Section 3 of the 1986 Act defines affray:

A person is guilty of affray if he uses or threatens unlawful violence towards another and his conduct is such as would cause a person of reasonable firmness present at the scene to fear for his personal safety.

This offence may be committed in public or private (s. 3(5)) and is punishable by three years' imprisonment. A police constable may arrest anyone reasonably suspected of committing it (s. 3(6)).

11.5.3.1   Use or threaten unlawful violence

As with s. 2, threats will suffice, but note that the violence or threats must be directed towards another person. For the offence of affray, violence to property is not in itself enough.

Section 3(3) states that threats made by words alone will not suffice. They must be accompanied by some other threatening actions or gestures. In *R v Robinson* [1993] Crim

LR 581, an aggressive tone of voice was not enough, but in *R v Dixon* [1993] Crim LR 579, Dixon's setting his dog on police officers with the words, 'Go on, Go on', was sufficient to fall within s. 3(3).

11.5.3.2　One person only

The offence of affray may be committed by only one person. However s. 3(2) states that where two or more persons use or threaten the unlawful violence, it is the effect of their combined conduct that must be considered. Affray is the normal charge brought in cases of fights in the street, outside public houses and clubs etc. The hypothetical bystander test must again be satisfied. In *DPP v Cotcher and Cotcher* [1993] COD 181, the Court of Appeal stated that account could be taken of the nature of the premises and the scene where an affray took place, when considering the test that a person of reasonableness firmness had to fear for his or her own safety.

Finally, note the common elements in ss. 1 to 3. All may be committed in public and in private, and no person of reasonable firmness need actually be (or likely to be) present at the scene.

11.5.4　FEAR OR PROVOCATION OF VIOLENCE

Section 4 of the Public Order Act 1986 provides that a person is guilty of this offence:

> . . . if he or she—
> (a) 'uses towards another person threatening, abusive or insulting words or behaviour, or
> (b) distributes or displays to another person any writing, sign or other visible representation which is threatening, abusive or insulting,
> with intent to cause that person to believe that immediate unlawful violence will be used against him or another by any person, or to provoke the immediate use of unlawful violence by that person or another, or whereby that person is likely to believe that such violence will be used or it is likely that such violence will be provoked'.

This offence may be committed in both public and private (s. 4(2)) and a constable may arrest anyone reasonably suspected of committing it (s. 4(3)).

Therefore s. 4 prohibits words, behaviour or other visible representations which are either threatening, abusive or insulting, in circumstances where violence is likely to occur.

How would you define 'threatening, abusive or insulting words or behaviour'? For some ideas, turn to the extract from *Brutus v Cozens* [1973] AC 854 in *Cases and Materials* (11.3.3).

Threatening, Abusive or Insulting

In *Brutus* v *Cozens* [1973] AC 854, Brutus, an anti-apartheid protester stepped on to No. 2 court at Wimbledon, while Drysdale, a South African, was playing tennis. Brutus blew a whistle, threw around some leaflets, sat down on the court and play was disrupted. He was charged with using insulting behaviour contrary to s. 5 of the Public Order Act 1936 (the equivalent of s. 4 of the 1986 Act). It was held in the House of Lords that since 'insulting' has an ordinary meaning in the English language, its meaning here was a question of fact and not a question of law. As Lord Kilbrandon said, 'It would be unwise . . . to attempt to lay down any positive rules for the recognition of insulting behaviour as such, since the circumstances in which the application of the rules would be called for are almost infinitely variable . . .'. Thus on the facts, whilst Brutus's behaviour was 'deplorable', it was not insulting.

Likelihood

In *Parkin* v *Norman* [1983] QB 92, it was held that behaviour does not lose its insulting nature simply because the person who witnessed it was not actually insulted (in this case police officers approached by a male importuning in public toilets). Thus the words 'likely to' do not mean 'liable to'. However, neither will behaviour be insulting simply because it gives rise to anger, disgust or distress. In *R* v *Ambrose* (1973) 57 Cr App R 538, the defendant was alleged to have shouted at a 12-year-old girl: 'If a girl and boy go out together and have a bunk up, what does it mean?' The Court of Appeal held that words which are rude or offensive are not necessarily insulting, and the words alleged to have been used were incapable of amounting to insulting behaviour.

Towards another

The threatening, insulting or abusive behaviour must be directed towards another person. In *Masterson* v *Holden* [1986] 1 WLR 1017 the actions of two gay men kissing at a bus stop in a busy London street were held to be 'insulting'. The case arose prior to the 1986 Act, but today such conduct could not be brought within s. 4 because it was not deliberately aimed at a particular person or persons. The court in *Masterson* accepted that while the men were kissing, they were unaware of the fact that other people nearby were offended by their actions.

Section 4(2) specifically excludes the use of words or behaviour inside a dwelling house. Thus domestic disputes are not covered unless one of the parties is outside the house. The victim must also perceive the threat personally and it is not enough that the existence of a threat was relayed by a third party (*Atkin* v *DPP* (1989) 89 Cr App R 199, in *Cases and Materials* (11.3.3)). Thus the term 'uses towards' connotes physical presence, so if the 'other person' is out of earshot, there is no offence within this section.

Immediacy of violence

There must be a likelihood of immediate violence. In *R* v *Horseferry Magistrates' Court, ex parte Siadatan* [1991] 1 All ER 324 the court upheld a refusal by the magistrate to issue a summons against Penguin Books Ltd for an offence under s. 4 of the 1986 Act. Penguin Books Ltd had published and distributed Salman Rushdie's book, *The Satanic Verses*. Regarded as offensive by almost all Muslims, its publication had resulted in firebomb attacks on a number of bookshops stocking the book. The Divisional Court decided that publication of the book did not come within s. 4 as the threat of violence was not immediate, so that the words 'such violence' meant 'immediate unlawful violence.'

ACTIVITY 89

Read the extract from *Siadatan* in *Cases and Materials* (**11.3.3**). What three reasons did Watkins LJ give for this interpretation of s. 4(1) of the Public Order Act 1986?

11.5.5   INTENTIONAL HARASSMENT, ALARM OR DISTRESS

As a result of an increase of complaints about racial abuse and harassment, a new offence was introduced by s. 154 of the Criminal Justice and Public Order Act 1994. This has now become s. 4A of the Public Order Act 1986. In the hierarchy of offences, it sits between ss. 4 and 5. The offence requires that the prosecution must prove 2 things: that the defendant intended to cause harassment, alarm or distress; and that the victim suffered accordingly. (See the actual wording of s. 4A in *Cases and Materials* (**11.3.4**).)

At one stage it was proposed that this offence should be limited to cases where the defendant had acted 'on racial grounds', but this was rejected; thus it can now apply in any appropriate situation. The offence carries a maximum of six months' imprisonment and may be committed in public or private. However, under s. 4(2) no offence is committed where the relevant conduct is perpetrated by:

(a)   a person inside a dwelling house;

(b)   and the person who is harrassed, alarmed or distressed is also inside that or another dwelling.

There is a defence if it can be shown that:

(a)   the defendant's conduct at the relevant times was reasonable (s. 4A(3)(b)), or

(b)   that the defendant was inside a dwelling and there was no reason to believe that anyone outside the dwelling would hear or see the relevant conduct (s. 4A(3)(a)).

11.5.6   HARRASSMENT, ALARM OR DISTRESS

Section 5 is arguably the most controversial provision in the Public Order Act 1986. When first proposed it was heavily criticised by many civil liberties pressure groups, on the ground that since it gave police officers so much discretion it might be abused. Now that s. 5 is law, Peter Thornton has claimed that it has been 'used quite indiscriminately' against youths throwing fake snowballs, men kissing in the street, nudists on the beach and in their own home, and students putting up a satirical poster of the Prime Minister. (See the extract in *Cases and Materials* (**11.3.5**).)

Under s. 5 a person is guilty of an offence if he or she:

(a)   uses threatening, abusive or insulting words or behaviour, or disorderly behaviour, or

(b)   displays any writing, sign or other visible representation which is threatening, abusive or insulting,

within the hearing or sight of a person likely to be caused harassment, alarm or distress thereby.

It can be seen that the wording is very similar to both s. 4 and s. 4A.

As with ss. 4 and 4A, the offence can be committed in public or private, but not if both the offender and the other person are inside a dwelling house. This offence is punishable by a fine and the power of arrest only arises where the offensive conduct is repeated after a warning from a police officer. Section 5 was intended to deal with annoying or aggravating behaviour which was not sufficiently serious to fall within s. 4 of the 1986 Act.

Recently s. 5 was relevant in *Vigon* v *DPP, The Times*, 9 December 1997, where a market stall holder selling female swimwear, who had installed a hidden video camera in a changing room, was convicted of insulting behaviour likely to cause harassment, alarm or distress under s. 5.

11.5.6.1   Within hearing or sight

The conduct must occur within the hearing or sight of a person likely to be caused harassment, alarm or distress. There is no requirement that a victim actually gives evidence, or that anyone was caused harassment etc., provided the conduct did in fact occur within the sight or hearing of a person and that person was *likely* to be caused harassment, alarm or distress.

The prosecution will have to identify that person, even if they are not called as a witness. It is a defence if the defendant can prove that he or she had no reason to believe that there was any person within their hearing or sight who was likely to be harassed etc., or if he or she can prove that his or her conduct was reasonable: (s. 6; s. 5(3)). In *Poku* v *DPP* [1993] Crim LR 705, the Divisional Court held that the defendant's response to the police unlawfully seizing his van ('you're not taking my fucking van') was reasonable.

11.5.6.2   Harassment, alarm, distress

These words are not defined by the Act. However, a police officer is capable of being a person likely to be caused harassment, alarm or distress (*DPP* v *Orum* [1989] 1 WLR 88). In this case the defendant had an argument in the street with his girlfriend, in the early hours of the morning. Two police officers arrived. One of them told him to be quiet to which the defendant responded 'Fuck off' and threatened to hit the officer. His conviction under s. 5 was upheld, so that a police officer may be harrassed, alarmed, etc.

In the case of alarm being caused, this need not necessarily be personal alarm, and alarm about the safety of a third person will suffice. In *Lodge* v *DPP, The Times*, 26 October 1988, a police officer was concerned that an accident might occur because the defendant was shouting in the middle of the road and a car was approaching. The offence was committed because of the danger and risk to traffic and the alarm caused to others.

In *DPP* v *Clarke* (1991) 94 Cr App R 359, pictures of aborted foetuses displayed by anti-abortion campaigners outside an abortion clinic caused harassment, alarm or distress. However, it was not proved that the defendants either intended, or were aware of, the likelihood of this effect; accordingly they were therefore acquitted of any offences under s. 5.

Finally, it is important to note that under s. 5, the power of arrest is essentially a preventative measure, conditional on the police officer warning anyone engaging in offensive conduct to desist. If the suspect then continues to engage in further offensive conduct immediately or shortly after the warning he or she may be arrested (s. 5(4)).

However, the power of arrest under s. 5(4) is only exercisable by the actual police officer who had earlier administered the warning (*DPP* v *Hancock and Tuttle* [1995] Crim LR 139).

What kind of fact situations was s. 5 of the Public Order Act 1986 designed to cover? For an illustration of how it operates, turn to the extract from *DPP* v *Orum* **[1989] 1 WLR 88**, in *Cases and Materials* **(11.3.5)**.

Remember that because there is hierarchy of public order offences, if the one originally charged is not successfully proven in court, the defendant may be found guilty of a lesser offence on the scale. For example, if a person charged with violent disorder or affray is found not guilty by the court, an alternative verdict of a s. 4 offence may be substituted.

Read ss. 1 to 5 of the Public Order Act 1986 in *Cases and Materials* **(11.3)**. You will notice that these offences are quite similar, yet they also have some distinctive elements. Compile your own chart to illustrate both the similarities and differences. You could include the number of persons required to commit the offence, the kind of behaviour or conduct covered, the available penalties, etc. (See *Cases and Materials* **(11.3.5)** for some ideas.)

The problem of stalking recently led to the enactment of the Protection from Harassment Act 1997. It provides that a person must not engage in conduct which amounts to harassment of another and which he or she knows, or should know, constitutes harassment (s. 1). Harassment is not fully defined but it will 'include alarming the person or causing the person distress' (s. 7(2)). The potential for the 1997 Act being used to cover activities which are at present lawful was illustrated in *Huntingdon Life Sciences and Another* v *Curtin and Others*, *The Times*, 11 December 1997, when HLF, a large animal testing laboratory, tried to gain injunctions under the Act to curb the activities of animal rights activists. They were unsuccessful and Eady J stated that the 1997 Act was 'clearly not intended by Parliament to be used to clamp down on the discussion of matters of public interest or upon the rights of political protest and public demonstration which are so much part of our democratic tradition'. It remains to be seen whether this liberal approach is adopted by other judges, when interpreting the Act.

11.5.7 RACIAL HATRED

The Public Order Act 1986 introduced measures to protect individuals from racial hatred. Sections 18 and 19 create two similar offences related to behaviour *intended* to stir up racial hatred, or which (having regard to all the circumstances) is *likely* to have that effect. Section 18 is phrased like s. 4, so that anyone who uses threatening, abusive or insulting words or behaviour to incite racial hatred, commits an offence. Section 19 creates an offence of publishing or distributing written material which is threatening, abusive or insulting, with intent to stir up racial hatred, or in circumstances where it is likely to be stirred up. In addition there is a further offence of being in *possession* of racially inflammatory material (including visual recordings or sounds), with a view to its publication, distribution, showing or broadcasting (s. 23), and the police are given powers to search for and seize racially inflammatory material (s. 24).

Read ss. 17 to 19, 23 to 24 and 27 of the Public Order Act 1986 in *Cases and Materials* (11.3.6). Very few prosecutions are brought under these sections. Why is this so? Turn to the extracts from Geoffrey Bindman and W.J. Wolfe in *Cases and Materials* (11.3.6) for some ideas.

11.6   Preventative Measures

In certain circumstances the most effective means of maintaining public order may be by measures likely to stop or dissuade agitators from continuing their activity. Such measures were often used during the 1985 miners' strike to stop striking miners from picketing working mines. These powers often derive from the traditional and long-established common law duty of the police to maintain the peace.

11.6.1   BREACH OF THE PEACE

Section 40(4) of the Public Order Act 1986 specifically declares that nothing in the Act 'affects the common law powers of the police in England and Wales to deal with or prevent a breach of the peace'. So what is meant by a 'breach of the peace'?

ACTIVITY 92

Read the extract from the Justices of the Peace Act 1361 in *Cases and Materials* (11.4.1). What should happen to individuals who do not keep the 'King's peace'?

In *R v Howell* [1982] QB 416 (see *Cases and Materials* (11.4.1)), the Court of Appeal held that a breach of the peace occurs whenever harm is actually done or is likely to be done to a person or, in his presence, his property, or a person is in fear of being so harmed through an assault, an affray, a riot or some other disturbance.

A breach of the peace would therefore include the offences of riot, affray, violent disorder, but it would not necessarily be threatening behaviour or disorderly conduct, unless it is likely that this would lead to the use of violence.

Unlawful conduct which is neither violent nor an incitement to violence is not a breach of the peace. In *R v Chief Constable of Devon and Cornwall, ex parte Central Electricity Generating Board* [1982] QB 458, a group of protestors occupied private land. They sought to prevent employees of the Central Electricity Generating Board (CEGB) from carrying out a survey to assess the suitability of the land for the construction of a nuclear power station. The protest was intended to be peaceful but the protestors did in fact cause an obstructon. The CEGB asked the chief constable to help remove the protestors but he refused on the following grounds:

(a) that no power of arrest was available for the obstruction;

(b) that the common law power of arrest could not be used as there was no breach of the peace;

(c) that there was no unlawful assembly or anticipated breach of the peace.

The Board then sought an order of mandamus from the Court of Appeal, ordering the chief constable to remove the protesters.

ACTIVITY 93

Turn to the extract from the *CEGB* case in *Cases and Materials* (11.4.1). Was the chief constable correct in asserting that no power of arrest extended to the three grounds given?

The judges of the Court of Appeal observed that the chief constable could have intervened:

(a) to assist the CEGB in exercising its right of self-help (Templeman LJ);

(b) to deal with an actual breach of the peace. 'There is a breach of the peace whenever a person who is lawfully carrying out his work is unlawfully and physically prevented from doing so' (Lord Denning MR);

(c) to prevent a reasonably apprehended breach of the peace. If the CEGB staff sought to remove 'passive resisters' by force, this would prevent an anticipated breach of the peace (Lord Denning, but not supported by Lawton LJ);

(d) to prevent an unlawful assembly (this offence was repealed by the Public Order Act 1986 and would probably not be covered by violent disorder);

(e) to prevent the crime of obstruction. 'It is within the authority of the police to intervene to prevent any criminal offence being committed in their presence, even though it is only a summary offence where the offender fails or refuses or avoids giving his name and address' (Lord Denning).

Thus, on the facts, the Court of Appeal refused a request for an order of mandamus.

Do you think the chief constable should have taken a more robust approach? What are the implications of this case for police accountability and the relationship between the police and the courts? (Remember what was discussed in Chapter 9.)

A breach of the peace may occur in private. In *McConnell v Chief Constable of Greater Manchester Police* [1990] WLR 364, the police were called to a carpet store in Oldham and found the plaintiff in the manager's office refusing to leave. He was escorted outside, but when he tried to re-enter, he was arrested on the basis that it was likely that a breach of the peace would occur. The plaintiff subsequently claimed damages for false imprisonment. This action failed because it was held that events occurring on private premises (where no member of the public is affected) could constitute a breach of the peace. In *R v Lamb* [1990] Crim LR 58, police assistance was sought by S who wished to collect her belongings from the house she shared with Lamb. S had falsely told the police that she was the joint owner of the house. At the house, Lamb ordered them all to leave and there was a violent struggle between Lamb and S. A police constable intervened and was assaulted. The court held that the anticipated breach of the peace justified the police officer remaining on the premises, even though he had been told to leave by Lamb.

The power of the police to arrest for breach of the peace is a common law power which has not been affected by PACE 1984 and was outlined in the case of *R v Howell* [1982] QB 416. A constable or any other person may arrest:

(a)   anyone who is committing a breach of the peace in his or her presence; or

(b)   where it is believed that such a breach of the peace will be committed in the immediate future by the person arrested, although he or she has not yet committed any breach; or

(c)   where a breach has been committed and it is reasonably believed that a reoccurence of it is threatened.

In *Albert* v *Lavin* [1982] AC 546, Lord Diplock said that 'Every citizen in whose presence a breach of the police is being, or reasonably appears about to be, committed has the right to take reasonable steps to make the person who is breaking or threatening to break the peace refrain from doing so.'

In theory, any passer-by may be called upon to assist a constable where there is a breach of the peace, or where a constable has been assaulted or obstructed in the course of making an arrest. Refusal to assist is technically an offence, unless a lawful excuse can be shown, or it would be physically impossible to help (*R* v *Brown* (1841) Car & M 314).

11.6.2   DEALING WITH DISTURBANCES

Problems sometimes arise as to who is actually responsible for provoking public disorder in a particular situation and what should be the appropriate police response. In *Beatty* v *Gillbanks* (1882) 9 QBD 308, Beatty was a Captain in the Salvation Army, which was accustomed to holding processions through Weston-Super-Mare. These processions were in themselves peaceful, but a rival group, the Skeleton Army, would march at the same time creating disorder. The police prohibited marches by the Salvation Army because of the trouble they caused (albeit indirectly), but when Beatty persisted in holding processions, the police arrested him for unlawful assembly. Justices found Beatty guilty on the ground that he knew the Skeleton Army would cause disruption and had still held his meetings. However, the Court of Appeal quashed his conviction because Beatty had done nothing unlawful. The reasoning behind the decision is unclear but in effect the court instructed the police that they could not disperse an otherwise lawful assembly simply because of opposition from another body and that they should direct their attention to dealing with the counter-demonstration.

Despite this it seem that the police can, in certain circumstances, take action against an 'innocent' person in relation to public disorder. In *Humphries* v *Connor* (1864) 17 ICLR 1, the removal by a police officer of an orange lily (a flower of political significance) from the jacket lapel of a Protestant woman who was walking through a crowd of Roman Catholics in a Nationalist area of Ireland was not an assault, as it was necessary to prevent a breach of the peace.

More recently, however, in *Foulkes* v *Chief Constable of Merseyside Police, The Times*, 26 June 1998, Bedlam LJ held that '[t]here must be a sufficient real and present threat to the peace to justify the extreme step of depriving of his liberty a citizen who was not at the time acting unlawfully'.

Could the wearing of an orange lily constitute a uniform or emblem for the purposes of the Public Order Act 1936 (see 11.4.4)?

In *Wise* v *Dunning* [1902] 1 KB 167, Wise, a Protestant zealot who frequently publicly attacked the Roman Catholic faith, was held to have been properly bound over to keep the peace, after one of his mass meetings in Liverpool resulted in riots among the audience. There was, however, no doubt that if charged with unlawful assembly, he, together with his active supporters at the meetings, could have been convicted of that offence. This case was distinguished from *Beatty* v *Gillbanks* because a criminal offence had been committed. However, in *Duncan* v *Jones* [1936] 1 KB 218, Duncan was about to hold a meeting outside a training centre for the unemployed. The Chief Constable directed her to hold it around the corner from the centre. She began her speech without moving as directed and was arrested and charged with wilfully obstructing a police officer in the execution of his duty. The Divisional Court confirmed her conviction, since she had previously held meetings in the same place which had resulted in disturbances and the court found that she was aware of the probable consequences of organising such a meeting. The police had reasonably apprehended a breach of the peace and were under a duty to prevent the meeting; by attempting to hold it, Duncan had obstructed them.

According to *Thomas* v *Sawkins* [1935] 2 KB 434, police officers may enter a public meeting on private premises if they have reasonable grounds for believing that, if they were not present, a breach of the peace would occur. Finally, one should not forget the Public Meeting Act 1908, where a person acting in a disorderly manner at a public meeting may be ejected (see *Cases and Materials* (11.4.2)).

What exactly is a breach of the peace?

Summarise the main elements of this offence.

You may find the extracts from *Duncan* v *Jones* [1936] 1 KB 218, *Thomas* v *Sawkins* [1935] 2 KB 434 and *Beatty* v *Gillbanks* (1892) 9 QBD 308 in *Cases and Materials* (11.4.2) useful in this task.

11.6.3 POWERS TO PREVENT DISORDER

Most of the preventative powers to deal with public disorder are associated with breach of the peace. However, there are other miscellaneous powers.

11.6.3.1 Bind over

As you may have read in *Cases and Materials*, magistrates have the ancient power under the Justices of the Peace Act 1361 to bind persons over to be of 'good behaviour or to keep the peace'. If they refuse, such persons may be imprisoned for up to six months. Section 115 of the Magistrates' Courts Act 1980 preserves this power but it must be shown that violence, or the threat of violence, occurred before someone can be bound over (*Percy* v *DPP, The Times*, 13 December 1994). In this case the complainant entered an

RAF air base as a trespasser to protest peacefully. There was no evidence to suggest that violence was the natural consequence of her actions, so the 14 days commital to custody for refusing to be bound over to keep the peace was not justified, as only a civil trespass had been perpetrated.

11.6.3.2 Breach of the peace

The police have a common law duty to take reasonable steps to prevent a breach of the peace. This power was often used during the NUM miners' strike in 1984, when it was estimated that a total of 164,508 'presumed pickets' were turned away at roadblocks in Nottinghamshire during the first six months of the strike to prevent them getting near the Nottinghamshire collieries. Many cars were stopped at strategic points on the M1 motorway and pickets were forced to turn back from as far away as the Dartford Tunnel. The legality of this police action was tested in *Moss* v *McLachlan* (1984) 149 JP 167. The Divisional Court held that police officers were entitled to order pickets travelling to collieries in Nottingham to return home, as the likelihood of a breach of the peace occurring was imminent in both time and place. In this case the roadblock was within five miles of various collieries. This power should be compared with that now given by s. 14C of the Public Order Act 1986 (see **11.4.3** and *Cases and Materials* (**11.2.2**)).

11.6.3.3 Bail conditions

During the 1984 miners' strike the courts also imposed conditions of bail on 'flying pickets', when arrested for public offences, preventing them from picketing at their own or others' places of work. In *R* v *Mansfield Justices, ex parte Sharkey* [1985] QB 613, the Divisional Court approved the application of bail conditions accepting police evidence that mass picketing was likely to lead to violence or intimidation, so there was a real risk that the defendants would commit further offences.

Bail conditions can therefore be used to put restrictions on those charged with public order offences.

11.6.3.4 Injunctions

An injunction may be imposed by a court to prevent an individual from carrying out a particular form of action. In *Department of Transport* v *Williams, The Times,* 7 December 1993, a judge granted injunctions against protestors who had violently disrupted the building of a motorway authorised by a statutory instrument. One of the injunctions restrained the defendant from 'preventing or interfering with . . . the carrying out of work on the said land'.

ACTIVITY 94

Compare and contrast the decisions of *Piddington* v *Bates* [1961] 1 WLR 162 and *Moss* v *McLachlan* (1984) 149 JP 167 in *Cases and Materials* (11.4.3.1).

SAQ 116

'The law of public order is a compromise. It seeks to balance the competing demands of freedom of speech and assembly on the one hand with the preservation of the Queen's peace on the other.'

How satisfactory is the balance which is attained?

11.7   Additional Public Order Provisions

The Public Order Act 1986 and the Criminal Justice and Public Order Act 1994, Part V, contain a number of new powers relating to football matches, the contamination of goods and mass trespass.

11.7.1   FOOTBALL GROUNDS

Part IV of the Public Order Act 1986 introduced a new exclusion order scheme aimed at tackling the root of soccer hooliganism by excluding trouble makers from football matches. The courts can impose an order on anyone found guilty of a football-related offence prohibiting attendance at prescribed football matches. The court may impose such an order where it believes that it will help to prevent violence or disorder at, or in connection with, prescribed football matches. The offences which bring into operation the power to make an exclusion order include any offence committed inside a football ground and any offence of violence committed by the offender on the way to or from a football match. Powers have also been given to the courts to order a person to have a photograph taken for the purposes of the exclusion order. Anyone defying an exclusion order commits an offence and may be imprisoned for one month. Schedule 1 to the 1986 Act also amended the Sporting Events (Control of Alcohol etc.) Act 1985, to make possession of smoke bombs or fireworks at, or on entry to, a football ground, an offence.

11.7.2   CONTAMINATION OF GOODS

Part V of the 1986 Act created new offences connected with the contamination of, or the interference with goods, with the intention of causing public alarm or injury, or economic loss to any person as a result of that action. It is an offence to contaminate products, to make it appear that they have been interfered with or to claim that this has been done. It is also an offence to be in possession of the materials with which this may be done. The maximum penalty for this offence is 10 years' imprisonment, a fine, or both. This section was introduced to deal with the growing problem of deliberate tampering, where glass was found in baby foods and poison in drinks.

11.7.3 MASS TRESPASS

In the years immediately preceding the Public Order Act 1986, several incidents occurred involving mass trespass committed by groups such as Hell's Angels and New Age travellers. This led to the enactment of s. 39 of the Public Order Act 1986. Under s. 39 of the 1986 Act, a senior police officer could direct trespassers to leave land provided a number of conditions were satisfied. These were that:

(a) there was reason to believe two or more peope had entered the land as trespassers;

(b) the occupier had taken reasonable steps to ask them to leave;

(c) and that either 12 or more vehicles had been brought onto the land, and damage had been caused, or that threatening, abusive or insulting language had been used towards the occupier or his or her family.

This section has now been repealed and replaced by s. 61 of the Criminal Justice and Public Order Act 1994. While civil proceedings can be brought against trespassers, this is likely to be slow and expensive. Therefore criminalisation would seem to be Parliament's response to landowners' complaints of 'New Age travellers' and 'hippy convoys' descending on their land.

Only six vehicles are required to be on the land instead of 12, and there is no need to prove that persons intended to trespass on the land, only that they are physically present. Section 61 now states that the senior police officer present at the scene of the incident must reasonably believe:

(a) that two or more people are trespassing on land for the common purpose of residing there; and

(b) that the occupier has taken reasonable steps to ask them to leave.

Section 61 does not apply to a highway unless it comes within s. 54 of the Wildlife and Countryside Act 1984, (footpath, bridleway or byway open to all traffic or road used as a public path) or is a cycle track.

In *Krumpa* v *DPP* [1989] Crim LR 295, squatters on some vacant land belonging to Tesco had been warned in December that the land was being redeveloped and that the bulldozers would arrive after Christmas. In January the senior police officer told them to leave but they successfully challenged the direction because the warning given by the owner (i.e., Tesco) was not a 'request to leave'.

If such belief exists then a further condition must be satisfied. This is that either:

(a) damage to the land or property on the land has been caused by the trespassers or alternatively there has been threatening, abusive, insulting words or behaviour towards the occupier or the occupier's family; or

(b) the trespassers have six or more vehicles on the land with them.

If all the above are satisfied the officer may direct those persons to leave the land and remove any vehicles or property they have with them.

Anyone who fails to leave the land when so directed commits an offence punishable with up to three months' imprisonment (and/or a fine) and may be arrested on reasonable suspicion (s. 61(4)). It is also an offence to re-enter the land within three months of such a direction. Local authorities are also given extended powers to direct people to leave land. Non-compliance with a direction allows a magistrates' court to make orders allowing the authority to clear the land. No period of notice is required. The duty of local authorities to provide traveller sites is also abolished and replaced with discretionary power to provide sites (ss. 77 to 80).

Neil and the Young Ones, who between them have four caravans, and are given permission by Farmer Giles to camp in one of his fields. Six weeks later he changes his mind and tells them to leave.

Read s. 61 of the Criminal Justice and Public Order Act 1994 in *Cases and Materials* (11.5.1)) and advise Neil.

11.7.4   AGGRAVATED TRESPASS

Section 68 of the Criminal Justice and Public Order Act 1994 created the new offence of aggravated trespass. Aimed at groups such as hunt saboteurs, a person may commit this offence by trespassing on land in the open air and acting in a way which is intended to intimidate, obstruct or disrupt other persons engaging in a lawful activity. So what is meant by a lawful activity?

A lawful activity is any activity which may be carried out on the land without committing a criminal offence or trespass. Thus, in *Winder and others* v *DPP, The Times*, 14 August 1996, the defendants were trespassing on land with the intention of disrupting a hunt. The offence of criminal trespass under s. 68 covers a situation where a trespasser 'does there anything' which is intended to intimidate, obstruct or disrupt a lawful activity. The Divisional Court held that even 'running' in these circumstances could fall within the words 'does there anything'. Moreover, in *Nelder and Ors* v *DPP, The Independent*, 8 June 1998, it was held that the words in s. 68, deterring, disrupting and obstructing were overlapping concepts, and that an accused would not need to be charged separately with each.

Read ss. 68 and 69 of the Criminal Justice and Public Order Act 1994 in *Cases and Materials* (11.5.2). Ask yourself, might s. 68 be relevant to some of the cases on public order we have already covered? Think back to some of the cases on ss. 4 and 5 of the Public Order Act 1986 and those on breach of the peace.

There is a power of arrest on reasonable suspicion that the offence is being committed, but in addition the police also have the power to act *before* any intimidation or obstruction occurs, by directing persons to leave the land (s. 69). Failure to leave or re-entry is an offence subject to the defence of reasonable excuse or proof that the person was not in fact trespassing.

If you stand on the steps of your local town hall to protest against proposed new road developments in your area, would you be committing an aggravated trespass?

11.7.5   RAVES

Sections 63 to 67 of the Criminal Justice and Public Order Act 1994 relate to 'raves'. These provisions are intended to deal with large gatherings, which cause a nuisance to local residents because of noise. The police are given wide powers to direct people to leave and may also seize vehicles and sound equipment, which may be forfeited by order of a court on conviction. Seized vehicles may be retained until all charges for removal and retention have been paid (ss. 66 and 67).

Section 63(2) provides that a police officer of the rank of superintendent or above may direct anyone to leave a rave, taking vehicles and property with them, where he or she has a reasonable belief that:

(a)   two or more persons are making preparations for the holding of a gathering to which the section applies;

(b)   10 or more persons are waiting for such a gathering to begin; or

(c)   10 or more persons are attending such a gathering which is in progress.

Such a direction may be communicated by a police constable, and an officer of the rank of superintendent or above may also authorise a constable to enter any land to ascertain whether the necessary circumstances exist to justify a direction being made (s. 63(3)). It is an offence to fail to leave the land as soon as reasonably practicable, knowing that such a direction has been made, or to re-enter the land within seven days (s. 63(6)). This is subject to a defence of reasonable excuse (s. 63(7)). Finally, note that the police have a power to stop people travelling to a rave, within a five-mile radius of the gathering (s. 65).

Section 63 applies to gatherings which meet the following conditions:

■   the gathering is on land in the open air, or partly open to the air; and

■   100 or more persons are in attendance; and

■   amplified music is played during the night; and

■   this is likely to cause serious distress to the inhabitants of the locality.

'Music' is defined as including 'sounds wholly or predominantly characterised by the emission of a succession of repetitive beats' (s. 63(1)(b)). This broad definition was deliberately employed to cover the wide range of sounds usually associated with raves.

SAQ 118

The provisions in the Criminal Justice and Public Order Act 1994 relating to public order have been described by A. T. H. Smith as 'a mean-spirited, intolerant, ungenerous piece of work that may, if equally ungenerously implemented, lay trouble in store for years to come' ([1995] Crim LR 27). Is this a fair comment? For an explanation of these sentiments see the extract from Puddephatt in *Cases and Materials* (11.5.3).

The Criminal Justice and Public Order Act 1994 has received a mixed reception. On the one hand supporters of the legislation maintain that its measures are necessary to maintain law and order. On the other, critics claim that it has eroded civil liberties. Michael Mansfield QC calls it 'the most draconian act this government has put through' since there is 'no effective right to assemble', as 'it's at the discretion of police officers.'

Michael Mansfield's conclusion is that '[t]he democratic right to demonstrate in this country is going down the chute.' The extent to which you agree with this statement is a political question, which only you can answer. However, it is undeniable that in recent years the police have acquired a wide range of new statutory public order powers. For example, consider your answer to **SAQ 117**. Standing on the town hall steps to protest might constitute an aggravated trespass under s. 68 of the 1994 Act, because standing on the steps is not using them to enter or leave the building. If approaches were made to employees or representatives at the town hall going about their daily business one could also have disrupted or obstructed their lawful activity! The concept of 5-mile zones within which the police can turn back persons travelling to an assembly or musical gathering has also been heavily criticised as putting into a statutory format the controversial decision of *Moss* v *McLachlan* (1984) 149 JP 167. Ironically this legislation precipitated a number of mass demonstrations, culminating in a rally in London on 9 October 1994, when approximately 20,000 demonstrators protested about the measures introduced by the Criminal Justice and Public Order Act 1994.

11.8   Conclusion

The protection of individual and group rights is an essential prerequisite of a democratic society. Difficulties, however, arise where the protection of civil liberties for some is obtained at the expense of others. The subject matter of this chapter provides a graphic illustration of such problems. The law relating to public order is concerned with ensuring that the correct balance is struck between providing the police with the powers they need to maintain law and order while protecting the right of the individual to protest publicly.

11.9   End of Chapter Assessment Question

The regional branch of RAM, Racists Against Minorities, wish to hold a meeting in a public park in the centre of Nottingley. The meeting has been publicised in advance and the organisers plan to march on a Saturday afternoon to the park. Approximately 150 members are expected to attend and the organisers have notified the Chief Constable of Nottingley. Local residents in this cosmopolitan area have also written to the Chief Constable asking him to ban the meeting. The Chief Constable responds that it will be adequately policed. On the day of the meeting the police are heavily outnumbered as over 1,000 supporters of RAM congregate in the park.

Some anti-RAM protesters also turn up but are stopped by the police from entering the park. Roy, a heavily tattooed man with long hair, who appears to be leading the anti-RAM protest, is taken aside by PC Keith and asked to turn out his pockets and remove his baseball cap. He refuses but his pockets are searched anyway. During the search his hat is knocked off. A small paper packet falls from within his hat, which contains a white powdery substance. PC Keith then arrests him, while Roy protests that this is only talcum powder which he plans to put on later to 'freshen himself up'.

The arrest and speeches inflame the anti-RAM protesters who overturn and smash some of the wooden benches at the entrance of the park. One of the local residents, Percy, who has been walking his dog in the park, is mistakenly arrested by WPC Gray after Inspector Bean told her to arrest him for causing criminal damage.

In retaliation a large group of RAM supporters led by Sid storm down Nottingley High Street and attack a local anti-racist bookshop. They damage the stock and threaten the staff, punching one of the assistants in the face. The owners of the shop are disgusted with the lack of police protection and wish to take the matter further.

Discuss the legality of the actions taken by the police and advise them on their legal responsibilities in respect of these incidents.

(See *Cases and Materials* (11.7) for a specimen answer.)

CHAPTER TWELVE

THE RULE OF LAW

12.1 Objectives

By the end of this Chapter you should be able to:

■ explain what is meant by the phrase 'the rule of law';

■ describe and evaluate Dicey's three principles of the rule of law;

■ recognise the limitations of Dicey's three principles;

■ appreciate the contemporary significance of the rule of law.

12.2 Introduction

The rule of law is the principle that those exercising a governmental function should be subject to legal controls. As de Smith puts it: 'powers exercised by politicians and officials must have a legitimate foundation . . . based on authority conferred by law'. Described by Jeffrey Jowell as a 'principle of institutional morality', adherence to the rule of law means that the rights of individuals are protected from erosion or interference by those governing the State. Thus, Sir John Laws suggests (see *Cases and Materials* (**12.1**)) that the rule of law is based on three ideas: freedom, certainty and fairness.

12.3 History

The principle of the rule of law can be traced back to the writings of philosophers in ancient Rome and Greece. For example, the maxim, 'the rule of law is preferable to that of any individual', has been attributed to the Greek philosopher Aristotle. Traditionally it was thought that over and above all man-made law ('positive law'), there is a universal law ('natural law') which applies to all men everywhere and at all times (based on rules ordained by God). In the 17th century, Coke CJ identified natural law with the common law of England. Since human reason was given by God, the principles of natural law were deducible by the use of reason.

The theory of the rule of law became particularly important in England following the struggle between Parliament and the Crown in the 17th century. During this conflict, Coke CJ claimed that the common law was above the King and the executive (King's Ministers). In this power struggle Coke CJ and other common law judges joined forces with Parliament. As we know, Parliament was victorious, and the supremacy of Parliament over the Sovereign was eventually reflected by the Bill of Rights 1689.

The British model of the rule of law owes much to Dicey. According to Ian Harden and Norman Lewis ('The Noble Lie', 1986), Dicey provided the 'standard against which to judge constitutional propriety' and his work 'still occupies the high ground of British constitutional theory.' In his book *Introduction to the Study of the Law of the Constitution* (1885), Dicey suggested that the rule of law has three meanings:

(a) 'It means the absolute supremacy or predominance of regular law as opposed to the influence of arbitrary power, and excludes the existence of arbitrariness, of prerogative, or even of wide discretionary authority on the part of the government. Englishmen are ruled by the law, and by the law alone; a man may with us be punished for a breach of the law, but he may be punished for nothing else.'

(b) 'It means, again, equality before the law, or the equal subjection of all classes to the ordinary law of the land as administered by the ordinary law courts.'

(c) 'The 'rule of law', lastly . . . [means] . . . that with us the law of the constitution . . . [is] . . . not the source but the consequence of the rights of individuals, as defined and enforced by the courts . . . the constitution is the result of the ordinary law of the land.'

Briefly summarise Dicey's three main headings. What do they each mean in plain English? Keep a separate record of their meanings. Then return to it at the end of this Chapter. You may surprise yourself by finding that your answers are quite accurate.

Read the extract from Raz (see *Cases and Materials* (12.2)) on the meaning of the rule of law. Also, according to Jowell (extract in *Cases and Materials* (12.2)), what two functions does the rule of law serve?

12.4   Absolute Supremacy of Regular Law

Dicey's three headings will be considered individually beginning with the first proposition that there should be:

12.4.1   SUPREMACY OF THE REGULAR LAW AND ABSENCE OF ARBITRARY AND EVEN WIDE DISCRETIONARY POWERS

If this proposition is true then any decisions made by those in authority must be made in accordance with the law. For example, a police officer or anyone else making an arrest, may not proceed unless he or she is acting lawfully. Punishments can be imposed only by reference to the law. However, where alternative forms of punishment are available, this will involve the exercise of discretionary powers by the courts, although the judges are expected to act within the law.

The government of the day must also respect the law. This is illustrated by *Entick* v *Carrington* (1765) 19 St Tr 1030 (see *Cases and Materials* (12.3.1)), which has been described as 'perhaps the central case in the English constitutional law' (Keir and Lawson). The defendant had broken into the plaintiff's premises and seized some papers. The plaintiff brought an action for trespass, but the defendant argued that he had a warrant issued by the government authorising the trespass and seizure of the papers. The court refused to accept this and decided that as the government lacked any authority to issue these warrants, the warrant was illegal. Thus, today, a police officer cannot enter one's house unless he or she has the owner's/occupier's consent or a lawful power to do so.

Dicey believed that individuals should not be subject to wide discretionary powers. He felt that wherever there is discretion, there is room for arbitrariness. However, in contemporary Britain, Ministers (and other executive bodies) are often given wide discretionary powers. The proliferation of delegated legislation means that typically a Minister may be empowered 'to act as he thinks fit' or 'if he is satisfied'. During situations of crisis (e.g., war, civil unrest, epidemics), much wider powers tend to be given by law to the executive, and it seems that such discretionary powers are often virtually unreviewable.

In *Liversidge* v *Anderson* [1942] AC 206, the Home Secretary was empowered under Defence Regulations (issued under the Emergency Powers (Defence) Act 1939) to imprison any person if he had 'reasonable cause to believe' such a person had hostile associations. Liversidge was detained without trial under the Defence Regulations and sued the Home Secretary for false imprisonment. The House of Lords (4–1) held that the court could not inquire into the grounds for the detention, as long as there was no evidence to suggest that he had acted other than in good faith. Thus the Home Secretary's decision would not be challenged and he could not be compelled to disclose his reasons.

ACTIVITY 98

Read and compare the extract from the opinions of Lord Wright and Lord Atkin in *Liversidge* v *Anderson* (see *Cases and Materials* (12.3.1)). How do they differ? Which of these judgments is the more persuasive? And why do you think J. A. G. Griffith (*The Politics of The Judiciary*, 4th edn) refers to Lord Atkin's speech as 'the most highly influential minority opinion in the English courts of the 20th century'?

Liversidge v *Anderson* was a case decided during the Second World War. However, the courts still remain loath to challenge the executive's wide discretionary powers when considerations of national security are an issue. For example, in *R* v *Secretary of State for Home Affairs, ex parte Hosenball* [1977] 1 WLR 766, the Court of Appeal was unwilling to prevent the deportation of an American journalist by the Home Secretary. The appellant (Hosenball) claimed that the decision to deport him had breached the rules of natural justice, because the Home Secretary had not revealed the grounds on which he considered Hosenball to be a security risk. However Lord Denning noted: 'There is a conflict between the interests of national security on the one hand and the freedom of the individual on the other. The balance between these two is not for a court of law. It is for the Home Secretary.' (See *Cases and Materials* (**12.3.1**) for a more detailed extract from this judgment.) And during the Gulf conflict in 1990, the courts showed that they were similarly reluctant to intervene. In *R* v *Secretary of State for the Home Department, ex parte Cheblak* [1991] 1 WLR 890, 'national security' was given by the Home Secretary as the reason to deport Cheblak, a Palestinian national living in the UK. Since national security was 'exclusively the responsibility of the executive', the court would not inquire into the facts upon which the Minister had relied. As Lord Donaldson of Lymington MR noted: 'the jurisdiction of the courts in cases involving national security is necessarily restricted, not by any unwillingness to act in the protection of the rights of individuals or any lack of independence from the executive, but by the nature of the subject matter'.

What does Lord Donaldson mean when he uses the phrase 'nature of the subject matter'?

The meaning of this phrase and the attitude of the courts to the executive in times of national or public emergency, is well illustrated by the reluctance of the courts to challenge 'exclusion orders' which have often, in the past, restricted the access of people from Northern Ireland to Britain. For example, in *R* v *Secretary of State for the Home Department, ex parte Gallagher* (1994) *The Times*, 16 February 1994, an 'exclusion order' was issued against an Irish citizen, Gallagher which prohibited him from residing in Great Britain and effectively banished him to Ireland. Although Gallagher had not been provided with reasons for the decision, the Court of Appeal rejected his protests. Since the Home Secretary had been given the widest possible discretion under the relevant statute (the Prevention of Terrorism (Temporary Provisions) Act 1989) he or she was not obliged to give specific reasons for the order where the case involved matters of national security. The approach of the European Court of Justice was much less deferential to the executive, following an art. 177 reference in this case (*R* v *Secretary of State, ex parte Gallagher, The Times*, 13 December 1995). However, the attitude of British judges to exclusion orders (see also *R* v *Secretary of State, ex parte Adams* [1995] 1 All ER 177, where the President of Sinn Fein unsuccessfully challenged an exclusion order which was only lifted following the IRA cease fire in 1994) is symptomatic of their reluctance to scrutinise the government closely in times of crisis. Even basic rights, such as one's access to a lawyer, have been held to be restricted by anti-terrorist and emergency legislation, so in *R v Chief Constable of the RUC, ex parte Begley* [1997] 1 WLR 1475, the House of Lords rejected an appeal against a murder conviction on the ground that the appellant had been lawfully refused access to his solicitor during police interviews under the Prevention of Terrorism (Temporary Provisions) Act 1989. Thus, as Lord Diplock pointed out in *CCSU v Minister for the Civil Service* [1984] 3 All ER 935, 'National security is the responsibility of the executive government; what action is needed to protect its interests is . . . a matter on which those on whom the responsibility rests . . . [which is] . . . not the courts of justice, must have the last word.'

Do you consider that the courts have abdicated their constitutional responsibilty for controlling the executive in times of crisis or public emergency? Read the extract from *R v Secretary of State for the Home Department, ex parte Cheblak* in *Cases and Materials* (12.3.1). Bear in mind the political context in which it was decided. To what extent *should* such background factors be relevant?

Dicey's ideal was that State officials should be prevented from exercising wide discretionary powers. As noted earlier, Dicey equated discretion with arbitrary government and thought that discretionary decision-making powers could be abused since the limits of such powers are not fixed by law (i.e. rules) so to return to Lord Acton's famous phrase (see **Chapter 3**) 'absolute power corrupts'. Thus, Dicey favoured a system of government based on laws (rules) and not men (discretion), and Geoffrey Wilson (see *Cases and Materials* (12.4.2.2)) claims that this principle that 'government should not have arbitrary power' gives the rule of law 'real force today'.

Dicey's ideas were heavily influenced by the 'laissez-faire' political philosophy of the 19th century, which emphasised individual liberties. However, the 20th century has witnessed increasing State intervention and today the State regulates national life in a number of ways which would have been completely unimaginable to Dicey. An obvious example has been the post-war British welfare state.

In calculating a person's entitlement to a welfare benefit, the discretion of a welfare assessment officer is often decisive (e.g., does the fact that a claimant owns an expensive new yacht disqualify him/her from a welfare benefit?). Dicey would probably have regarded as arbitrary many of the powers of contemporary government, relating to the provision of social welfare. Therefore, few would still subscribe to Dicey's view that to comply fully with the rule of law, it is necessary to have legislative rules and judicial decisions ('absolute supremacy of regular law') replacing discretion ('arbitrary action').

Does the existence of rules ensure that the law is obeyed? In order to answer this question read the extracts from K. C. Davis's *Discretionary Justice* and Smith and Gray's 'Police and People in London' in *Cases and Materials* (12.3.2).

In answer to **Activity 99** it is likely that you concluded that the executive requires additional power in some circumstances. Yet in reality, wide discretionary powers are not confined to periods of crisis or national emergency. Dicey's ideal therefore seems incongruous with examples such as:

(a)   The proliferation of delegated legislation and the danger of it being abused.

The number of statutory instruments which have been passed has increased from 1,770 in 1979, to over 3,300 in 1994. Thus, it is now common for discretionary power to be bestowed on a Minister by Parliament (e.g., 'to act as he thinks fit'). The proliferation of delegated legislation increases the chances of it being abused. Of particular concern are Henry VIII clauses which, in the words of the House of Lords Select Committee on the Scrutiny of Delegated Powers (1992–93), 'enable primary legislation to be amended without further scrutiny'. We will look at Henry VIII clauses, and delegated legislation generally, in more detail in **Chapter 13**.

(b)   The development, by the judiciary, of some common law offences which are rather uncertain in scope.

It is expected that judges will, in general, define the law in a way which is clear and certain. However, in *Shaw* v *DPP* [1992] AC 220, the House of Lords effectively resurrected the offence of conspiracy to corrupt public morals. In that case (involving the publication of a directory listing prostitutes and their services), Shaw was convicted of conspiracy to corrupt public morals. He claimed that there was no such offence. The House of Lords rejected this submission. Instead Viscount Simonds (expressing the view of the majority) stated that 'In the sphere of criminal law, I entertain no doubt that there remains in the courts of law a residual power to enforce the supreme and fundamental purpose of the law, to conserve not only the safety and the order but also the moral welfare of the State, and that it is their duty to guard it against attacks which may be the more insidious because they are novel and unprepared for'. Although public mischief offences had in the past been expanded to include matters such as outraging public decency, perverting the course of justice and conspiracy to defraud, many felt the categories were closed. Nevertheless in *R* v *Knuller (Publishing, Printing and Promotions) Ltd* v *DPP* [1973] AC 435, the House of Lords actually affirmed the decision in the *Shaw* case. Lord Simon of Glaisdale held that: 'What the courts can and should do . . . is to recognise the applicability of established offences to new circumstances to which they are relevant.' More recently, in *R* v *Gibson* [1990]

2 QB 619, the common law offence of outraging public decency, was resurrected to cover the display of two ear-rings in an art gallery, each made from a freeze-dried human foetus.

In 1976, the Law Commission (in a report entitled 'Criminal Law') recommended that the offence of outraging public decency should be abolished, because of the difficulties of defining this offence. Thus, it would appear that such vague common law offences seem difficult to reconcile with the principle of the rule of law, of which certainty is an essential prerequisite.

(c)   The possibility of Parliament passing retrospective legislation.

Retrospective legislation is legislation which relates to a situation which occurred prior to its enactment. Remember that Parliament is supreme, so it has the power to pass retrospective legislation. In *Burmah Oil Co. Ltd* v *Lord Advocate* [1965] AC 75, compensation was awarded to an oil company whose installations had been destroyed to prevent them falling into enemy hands. However, no compensation was paid due to the retrospective effect of the War Damages Act 1965. This statute, which was passed following the House of Lords decision, abolished any right at common law to compensation from the Crown in respect of the destruction of property on the authority of the Crown during or in contemplation of war. Another more recent example of retrospective legislation is the War Crimes Act 1991. It empowers the UK courts to punish war crimes committed by persons who were not subject to British jurisdiction at the time when the crimes were committed.

Retrospective legislation is always politically controversial. An aversion to it in principle led many peers to reject the War Crimes Bill when it was debated in the House of Lords. Retrospective legislation is also prohibited by art. 7 of the European Convention on Human Rights 1950 and art. 11(2) of the UN Universal Declaration of Human Rights 1948. However, since neither of these international documents have been incorporated into British law, political rather than legal factors ensure that retrospective legislation is seldom introduced in the United Kingdom.

Compile a list making the case for the elimination of discretion (pro-Dicey). Compare it to a separate list noting the disadvantages of rules (or the advantages of retaining discretionary powers).

12.4.2   RULES v DISCRETION

In **SAQ 121**, you were asked to compile a list, noting the arguments for and against Dicey's interpretation of his first meaning of the rule of law. Your list should look something like this:

(a)   **The case for eliminating discretionary law making (pro-Dicey)**

    (i)   **Certainty**

        The main virtue of rules is that individuals are aware of the rules to which they are subject, e.g., it's fairer to a person prosecuted for a tax offence to have been made aware of the precise tax required than for the levels to have been determined at the discretion of an official.

    (ii)   **Uniformity**

        Since rules tend to be formally published standards, they may entail uniformity of treatment, with 'like' cases being treated alike, e.g., a tax regulation which stipulates that everyone who earns £30,000 per annum must pay income tax at a rate of 40 per cent will apply to all who qualify, without bias on grounds of race, colour and religion.

    (iii)   **Accountability**

        Rules provide for the accountability of those who administer them. Therefore, rules expose agents of government to greater accountability than the 'cloak' of discretion.

(b)   **The disadvantages of rules; and advantages of discretion**

    (i)   **Inflexibility**

        Whilst rules tend to be objective and even-handed, they may lack flexibility. Thus the virtue of rules to the administrator (routine treatment) may be a defect to the client with a special case. For example, if it was a rule that no-one owning a car could receive unemployment benefit, then an unemployed person who had an old car for his disabled wife would be penalised harshly if the rule was automatically or rigidly obeyed.

    (ii)   **Implementation**

        The existence of rules does not necessarily ensure their implementation. The existence of a rule specifying a maximum town speed limit of 30 m.p.h. will not necessarily mean that speeding motorists are prosecuted. For example, the case of an ambulance rushing to an emergency, or fire engines answering a call. Similarly, assault laws are sometimes not enforced against feuding members of a family, because the police may be unwilling to exacerbate further existing family tensions.

Perhaps the Diceyean approach, which is wary of subjecting individuals to the discretionary powers of the State, is no longer relevant in the late 20th century, since discretionary authority in most spheres of government is inevitable. In *The State and the Rule of Law in a Mixed Economy*, (1971), at p. 95, W. Friedmann noted that:

    The proposition that the rule of law in modern democracy is incompatible with any kind of economic planning by the State . . . is of course incompatible with the reality of any contemporary democracy. It would be a useless exercise for us to attempt to define the rule of law in a way that bears no relation to the minimum functions of social welfare, urban planning, regulatory controls, entrepreneurship and other essential functions of the State in a mixed economy.

As K.C. Davis (see *Cases and Materials* (**12.3.2**)) observes:

the elimination of all discretionary power is both impossible and undesirable. The sensible goal is development of a proper balance between rule and discretion.

A similar conclusion is reached by Jeffrey Jowell (see *Cases and Materials* (**12.3.2**)). He suggests that both rules and other adjudicative procedures have distinct qualities which protect individuals against excesses of official power. Thus, rather than attacking the existence of discretionary powers, it would seem wiser to concentrate on establishing a system of legal and political safeguards by which discretionary powers may be controlled. The main legal safeguard (i.e., judicial review) will be examined later (**Chapter 15**) while we covered the relevant political safeguards earlier in **Chapters 2** and **3**.

How does the use of positive legal rules eliminate the exercise of discretion? In what circumstances may the exercise of discretionary power be advantageous?

12.5 Equality before the Law

In his explanation of this proposition Dicey claimed that in Britain 'every official, from the Prime Minister down to a constable or a collector of taxes, is under the same responsibility for every act done without legal justification as any other citizen'. Thus, Dicey felt that a strength of the British constitution was that no-one (irrespective of rank, title, sex or race) was exempt from the jurisdiction of the law.

12.5.1 THE PRINCIPLE OF EQUALITY

Dicey suggested that all citizens should be treated equally before the law. Therefore, as long as laws were applied equally, without irrational bias or unreasonable distinction, this aspect of the rule of law would be complied with. However, before we critically analyse his theory of equality, spend a few minutes on **SAQ 123**.

SAQ 23

In *Francome* v *Mirror Group Newspapers Ltd* [1984] 1 WLR 892 at p. 897, Lord Donaldson MR stated: 'Parliamentary democracy as we know it is based upon the rule of law. That requires all citizens to obey the law, unless and until it can be changed by due process. There are no privileged classes to whom it does not apply.' What does this mean? Are there any circumstances in which discrimination may be permissible?

No matter how attractive Dicey's theory of equality before the law may appear in theory, there are obvious exceptions to it in practice. Some of these exceptions include:

(a)　**The powers of the Queen**

The Queen cannot be sued personally in her own courts. Before the Crown Proceedings Act 1947, the Crown was immune from litigation. Although the Crown may now be liable in tort and contract in certain circumstances, the 1947 Act does not affect the personal immunity of the Sovereign.

(b)　**Diplomatic immunity**

Foreign sovereigns, ambassadors and diplomats enjoy a special immunity from the civil and criminal law of the country to which they are officially posted (the Diplomatic Immunities Act 1961 and the State Immunity Act 1978).

(c)　**High Court judges**

Judges are immune from civil litigation for actions falling within their official jurisdiction. Even the terms and conditions of all judges are not equal. For example, as noted in **Chapter 3**, the Lord Chancellor is exempt from the compulsory age for the retirement of judges under the Judicial Pensions and Retirement Act 1993.

(d)　**Parliamentary privilege**

An MP cannot be sued for defamation in respect of proceedings in Parliament (Bill of Rights 1689, art. 9). Parliament has the exclusive right to regulate its own composition and procedure (*Bradlaugh* v *Gossett* (1884) 12 QBD 271). Similarly, Members of Parliament are immune from civil arrest. In *Stourton* v *Stourton* [1963] P 302, a wife applied to have her husband arrested for civil contempt but the husband, a member of the House of Lords, pleaded privilege and freedom from civil arrest. The court accepted his argument, although this immunity does not extend to criminal arrest.

(e)　**Extra duties**

Some rules impose greater duties or a higher standard of behaviour on some members of the community as opposed to others. For example, clergymen are subject to both the law of the land and to ecclesiastical law, while members of the armed forces are subject to both civil law and to the disciplinary regulations of their service.

(f) Special powers

Certain officials (e.g., the police, public health inspectors, customs officers etc.), are in possession of special powers which are not enjoyed by ordinary members of the public.

(g) Blasphemy

The Church of England (and accordingly other Christian denominations which share its theological beliefs) is uniquely protected against vilification by the law of blasphemy (*R* v *Chief Metropolitan Stipendiary Magistrate, ex parte Choudhury* [1991] 1 All ER 306 — see *Cases and Materials* (**12.4.1**)).

Although there is UK legislation prohibiting discrimination on the grounds of race (the Race Relations Act 1976) and sex (the Sex Discrimination Act 1975), discrimination on religious grounds is not prohibited by law in Great Britain (although equivalent legislation exists in Northern Ireland) (Fair Employment (NI) Acts 1976 and 1989).

(h) Homosexuality

The age of consent for heterosexual intercourse is 16 in the UK, but it is 18 for homosexual intercourse. The Court of Appeal has also upheld the policy that homosexuality is incompatible with service in the armed forces (*R* v *Secretary of State for Defence, ex parte Smith* [1996] 1 All ER 257).

(i) Practical differences

Some may dispute whether 'in practice' there is equality before the law in the UK. Arguably the extent to which one may obtain legal redress may be limited to one's age, sex, race, education, profession or social status. For example, the National Association for the Care and Resettlement of Offenders (NACRO) has claimed that young blacks have a greater chance of being prosecuted and sent to prison than their white counterparts. Similarly, claims are often made that police powers to stop and search suspects are exercised disproportionately against ethnic minorities. For example, in a recent report commissioned by the Metropolitan Police, it was found that black people are more than four times as likely to be stopped and searched in the street by police officers than whites (*The Independent*, 8 June 1998).

Can you think of any permissible exceptions to the principle of equality before the law?

Obviously the law must treat certain groups of people differently. For example, rules which specifically relate to children (e.g., laws governing the age of criminal responsibility) have an objective and rational justification.

As we can see, even a stable democracy such as the United Kingdom struggles to comply with the principle of equality before the law. Dicey was aware of these limitations, but he was putting forward a 'general' rule. His was a principle that there should be equality, unless there was some justification for according certain people special privileges. Dicey's theory sets standards which nations should strive to attain. In practice, few are likely to succeed. As George Orwell observed of the animal society in *Animal Farm*: 'All animals are equal, but some animals are more equal than others'!

12.5.2 EQUALITY BEFORE THE LAW, DICEY AND FRENCH ADMINISTRATIVE COURTS

In explaining what he meant by equality before the law, Dicey contrasted the British court structure with that on the Continent, particularly France. In England there was no separate system of administrative law, while in France the legal system distinguished between ordinary legal actions between individuals and disputes between individuals and State officials. With regard to the latter, State officials in France were not responsible for their official actions to the ordinary courts. Instead, they were subject to special administrative tribunals ('*tribunaux administratifs*') which administered a special law ('*droit administratif*').

Dicey felt that 'equality before the law' required that *all* citizens, including public officials, should be subject to the jurisdiction of the ordinary courts. Therefore, he assumed that the administrative courts in France were biased in favour of public officials. Dicey argued that because there were no special courts in England to deal with claims against government officials, the 'ordinary' courts in England offered individuals greater protection than in France. This view can be criticised on two grounds. First, a number of academics have suggested that perhaps Dicey's view of French administrative tribunals was mistaken. Secondly, the last two decades have witnessed the creation of a number of specialised British administrative tribunals, which have operated fairly and efficiently.

12.5.2.1 Academic criticisms

(a) Brown and Garner, *French Administrative Law*.

They assert that the administrative tribunals which Dicey distrusted, have often been more rigorous in controlling administrative abuses than the courts in common law countries.

They also point out that in the modern State there has been an enormous growth in the number of administrative tribunals which deal with matters such as, employment, social security and compensation for the acquisition of land. Like the French administrative tribunals, the British tribunals are separate from the ordinary courts, are impartial, adhere to the rules of natural justice and possess considerable specialised knowledge.

(b) W Friedmann, *The State and the Rule of Law in a Mixed Economy* (see **Cases and Materials (12.4.2.1)**).

He claims that Dicey was mistaken, because the aim of French administrative courts was not to exempt officials from the law, but rather to enable experts in public administration to determine the extent of official liability. Therefore, the French themselves saw their administrative courts as protecting individuals and not unfairly benefiting the government's employees.

12.5.2.2 Adminstrative tribunals in the UK

The credibility of Dicey's theory is further eroded when one considers the contemporary importance of administrative tribunals. Administrative tribunals deal with a number of issues such as social security, taxation, immigration, the National Health Service, education and employment. Some disciplinary bodies may take the form of a tribunal (e.g., the General Dental Council and the General Medical Council). For others (such as the Civil Aviation Authority), licensing is an important role. Thus, it has been noted that there are 'a multiplicity of tribunals each operating within the bounds of a confined jurisdiction and each directed toward disposing of claims and arguments arising out of a particular statutory scheme' (Hendry (1982) 1 CJQ 253).

Garner and Jones (*Administrative Law*) suggest that the five hallmarks of a tribunal are:

(a)   independence from the administration;

(b)   a capacity to reach a binding decision;

(c)   decisions taken by a panel of members (as opposed to a single judge);

(d)   a simpler procedure than that of a court; and

(e)   a permanent existence.

Although separate from ordinary courts of law, tribunals are not contrary to the rule of law as long as they are impartial, independent and observe the rules of natural justice. In *Ridge* v *Baldwin* [1964] AC 40, the House of Lords held that the rules of natural justice should extend to bodies which have the power to determine matters which affect individuals. Thus, these rules of natural justice (see **Chapter 15**) have been extended to the disciplinary hearings of doctors, dentists, prisoners and students.

Legal representation is usually permitted at tribunals, although it is not an absolute right (*R* v *Board of Visitors of HM Prison the Maze, ex parte Hone* [1988] AC 379). Similarly tribunal hearings tend to be held in public (subject to considerations such as national security, confidentiality etc.), and this is consistent with the 1957 Franks Committee's recommendations of 'openness, fairness and impartiality'.

Far from abusing their power, as Dicey would have feared, it could be argued that administrative tribunals in the UK have been more rigorous in controlling administrative abuses than the courts. Much of their success can be attributed to their speed, technical expertise and relatively low cost (tribunal decisions tend to be cheaper than those of courts). As the Franks Committee (1957) noted:

> the continuing extension of governmental activity . . . has greatly multiplied the occasions on which an individual may be at issue with the administration . . . as to his rights and the post-war years have seen a substantial growth in the importance and activities of tribunals.

Explain why Dicey believed that the English system, where officials are held accountable to the ordinary courts, was preferable to the French system, which distinguishes between ordinary legal actions and those involving State officials. For a criticism of this aspect of Dicey's theory, you may turn to the extract from Heuston in *Cases and Materials* (12.4.2.2).

Explain Professor Geoffrey Wilson's claim that 'the rule of law is not in fact a rule of law' but rather 'a conventional obligation which lies . . . on government and the legislature'.

For some assistance, look at his views in *Cases and Materials* (12.4.2.2).

12.6   The Constitution — the Result of the Ordinary Law of the Land

At the beginning of this book, it was pointed out that the UK is unusual in that its Constitution is unwritten. In most other States which possess a written constitution, the rights and duties of citizens are expressly codified in written form. Dicey expressed the British position as follows: 'with us the constitution is the consequence of the rights of the individual as defined in the courts of law'. Dicey said that the unwritten British constitution is a product of the ordinary law of the land, and that (subject to a few exceptions such as statutes) the rights and duties of the citizen can be found in common law.

Thus, anyone wanting to know their constitutional rights must look at the various statutes and decided cases relating to those rights which are not (as in other countries) embodied in a single document. Dicey saw two advantages in this the British position:

(a)   For every right enjoyed by an English citizen there is a corresponding remedy. For example, since the law provides that there is freedom from arbitrary arrest, if a police officer seeks to arrest an individual arbitrarily, a court will provide a remedy — compensation in the form of damages in a civil action for false imprisonment.

However, critics of Dicey might argue that there is no apparent reason why this corollary between individuals' rights and remedies would cease to exist, if the British Constitution was to be codified.

(b)   Dicey felt that a strength of the British Constitution was that any citizen could ascertain his or her rights from past legal cases and from statutes. He also felt that should a director or tyrant come to power in this country, the 'ordinary law of the land' (in other words the citizens' rights as embodied in statute and case law) would be harder to set aside than a written constitution. After all, a written constitution in Germany in the 1930s failed to stop Hitler from coming to power; the same is true with Idi Amin in Uganda and Saddam Hussein in Iraq. A written constitution is merely a piece of paper, which is only as strong as the way it is interpreted. On the other hand, it should not be forgotten that most written constitutions have a special 'legal sanctity' and great symbolic value. A dictator may think twice before tearing up a constitution, in view of the public loyalty which many written constitutions attract.

Turn to Chapter 1 of this book and examine the Government's method of incorporating the European Convention on Human Rights into British law. Do you consider that it is harder to set aside 'the ordinary law of the land' than a written constitution, as Dicey claimed? How might Dicey have regarded the Human Rights Act 1998?

What did Dicey mean when he claimed that a strength of the British Constitution is the common law's effectiveness 'in controlling the exercise of arbitrary or discretionary power which could interfere with individual liberty'? You may also find the comments of P.P. Craig on the third limb of the rule of law in *Cases and Materials* (12.5) of some assistance.

12.7   The Rule of Law in the Late 20th Century

Certain features of the rule of law which have been adopted and applied in the 20th century, are now of universal application. For example, in 1957, a colloquium was held at Chicago under the general title of 'The Rule of Law as Understood in the West'. Here it was agreed 'that even if the recognition of fundamental rights formed an element in the rule of law, it was only one element. The other two were concerned with the institutions and with the procedures whereby these rights were given effect.' It was also noted that 'a fair hearing with an independent judge was essential as the ideal of the rule of law'.

At this time Europe was divided by the 'cold war'. Yet notwithstanding these political and ideological differences, Communist nations held their own rule of law conference in Warsaw the following year. It met to consider the meaning of the rule of law in Communist countries. Certain 'elemental matters of human dignity' were recognised but it was noted that freedom of speech and of association must conform with 'the interests of the workers'. Thus whilst the Western democracies emphasised the civil and political rights of the individual (e.g., freedoms of expression, assembly, religion) and the Eastern European states prioritised economic and social rights (e.g., the right to work, the right to shelter), each power bloc (at least in theory) recognised the principle of the rule of law.

The meaning of the rule of law was further discussed in January 1959, when the International Commission of Jurists issued the 'Declaration of Delhi'. The declaration has no legislative force, creating only moral obligations. However the International Commission concluded that the rule of law relates to: (a) the legislature; (b) the executive; (c) the judiciary; and (d) the criminal process.

(a) **The legislature**

There is a right to representative and reasonable government. The legislature must not pass discriminatory laws with reference to individuals or minority groups. For example, in *Oppheimer* v *Cattermole* [1976] AC 249, a majority in the House of Lords agreed (*obiter*) that they would refuse to recognise a Nazi decree depriving Jews of land. Lord Cross of Chelsea said: '. . . legislation which takes away without compensation from a section of the citizen body singled out on racial grounds all their property on which the State passing the legislation can lay its hands and, in addition, deprives them of their citizenship . . . constitutes so grave an infringement of human rights that the courts of this country ought to refuse to recognise it as a law at all' (p. 278). More recently, Lord Bridge, in *X* v *Morgan-Grampian Ltd* [1991] AC 1, established a link between the legislature and the rule of law when he commented: 'In our society the rule of law rests upon two foundations: the sovereignty of the Queen in Parliament in making the law and the sovereignty of the Queen's courts in interpreting and applying the law.'

Read the extract from E. Barendt's 'Dicey and Civil Liberties' in *Cases and Materials* (12.6). Then ask yourself, what is the legal basis of Lord Cross's statement? How does one reconcile this view with the traditional principle of Parliamentary supremacy?

(b) **The executive**

There is a need for adequate controls to prevent an abuse of power by the executive. All governments should be subject to independent judicial control (see **Chapter 4**) and this is illustrated by cases which we have looked at earlier, such as *M* v *Home Office* [1994] 1 AC 377, where Lord Templeman stressed the powers of the courts 'for the purpose of enforcing the law against *all* [author's emphasis] peoples and institutions'. In the UK remember that, in addition to legal controls, there are also political checks (e.g., constitutional conventions, select committees, questions in Parliament etc.) which operate to limit the powers of the executive.

(c)   **The judiciary and the legal profession**

The judiciary should be independent. There should be proper grounds and procedures for the removal of judges. In the UK judges are appointed by the executive and appointments to the most senior positions are made by the Crown on the advice of the Prime Minister. The Lord Chancellor advises the Crown on the appointment of High Court and circuit judges, as well as recorders. However, there is no requirement that these nominees must be scrutinised by the legislature, and judges of the High Court, Court of Appeal and Lords of Appeal in Ordinary can only be removed by the Queen, following a resolution passed by both Houses of Parliament. The last 'superior' court judge to be removed by a motion in Parliament was Jonah Barrington, an Irish judge in 1830 who was found to have misappropriated litigants' money. (See also **Chapter 4** on the independence of the judiciary.)

Finally, in this connection, the International Commission of Justice has stated that the rule of law also means that there should be an organised, responsible and autonomous, legal profession.

(d)   **The criminal process**

The right to a 'fair trial' includes: certainty of the criminal law, the presumption of innocence, restrictive powers of arrest, and rights of appeal. On the internationally recognised standards for a fair trial look at art. 6 of the European Convention on Human Rights and art. 14 of the International Covenant on Civil and Political Rights 1966 (see *Cases and Materials* (**12.6**)).

Following **Activity 102** you may be wondering how the rule of law can be reconciled with Parliamentary Supremacy? Remember that for Dicey, Parliamentary Sovereignty (Supremacy) meant the right of Parliament 'to make or unmake any law whatever' (see **Chapter 7**). Thus on a strict legal interpretation it might appear that Parliament is not bound by the rule of law. For example, since it is supreme, Parliament has the right to confer wide discretionary powers on Ministers and government officials. Dicey explained this apparent conflict as follows: if the highest body in the State is in practice an elective and deliberative body then it is not going to act contrary to the rule of law without some good reason. Therefore in times of war, Parliament can take Draconian measures in order to respond to the emergency situation, restoring the rule of law when the crisis is over. For example, during both world wars, Parliament passed legislation to extend its life, to avoid calling a general election which would disrupt the national war effort. However, at the end of hostilities, Parliament reverted back to the usual system (i.e., with the maximum duration of a single Parliament being five years). Thus for Dicey, the rule of law 'operated to prevent a substitution of the despotism of Parliament for the unbridled prerogative of the Crown.' (T.R.S. Allan (1985) 44 *Cambridge Law Journal* 112).

12.7.1   CONTEMPORARY ILLUSTRATIONS OF THE RULE OF LAW

(a)   The ideals of freedom and justice underpinning the rule of law are expected to influence legislators.

Thus, in *R* v *Secretary of State for the Home Department, ex parte Pierson* [1997] 3 WLR 522, the House of Lords accepted that, 'Unless there is clearest provision to the contrary, Parliament must be presumed not to legislate contrary to the rule of law.'

(b) The principles of the rule of law should be of assistance to judges in the area of statutory interpretation.

Thus, the rule of law may encourage courts to lean in favour of the liberty of the citizen, as perhaps illustrated by the presumption of innocence (*Woolmington* v *DPP* [1935] AC 462) and the common law right to silence (*Rice* v *Connolly* [1966] 2 All ER 649).

(c) The rule of law may be used as a rule of evidence.

An example of this is the principle that everyone is, prima facie, equal before the law. Thus, Lord Wilmot CJ's statement, in *Wilkes* v *Lord Halifax* (1769) 19 St Tr 1406, that 'the law makes no difference between great and petty officers . . . they are all amenable to justice', is as valid today, as it was when originally made more than 200 years ago.

(d) The development of international human rights law bears testimony to the recognition of the rule of law by the international community.

It is significant that the world's first specialised international human rights document, the Universal Declaration of Human Rights 1948, states that: 'It is essential, if man is not to be compelled to have recourse, as a last resort, to rebellion against tyranny and oppression, that human rights should be protected by the rule of law.' The Universal Declaration was the catalyst for a number of other human rights Treaties, Conventions and Documents which recognise and protect both civil and political, as well as economic, social and cultural rights; and today, it is difficult to think of a contemporary international State which has not signed or ratified at least one of these human rights treaties. Finally, the War Crimes Tribunals, which have been set up to investigate and punish the perpetrators of atrocities in the former Yugoslavia and Rwanda, as well as recent moves to ban land mines and to establish a permanent international criminal court, would seem to illustrate the relevance of the rule of law, even under international law.

12.8   Conclusion

Dicey's theory of the rule of law was clearly influenced by the contemporary political 'laissez faire' philosophy which focused on individual liberties. During the 20th century the emphasis has been more on social justice, rather than on strictly enforced private rights. In pursuit of this goal, successive governments have chosen to take measures which are seemingly incompatible with Dicey's interpretation of the rule of law: e.g., by the implementation of social legislation resulting in the granting of wide discretionary powers to Ministers and the creation of administrative tribunals.

Since Dicey discussed it, the 'rule of law' has become a commonly used term. As has been seen, it is susceptible to a variety of different interpretations. Whilst this gives it flexibility, it invariably leads to uncertainty. The rule of law may mean 'all things to all men', and like that other indefinable word 'democracy', it is a principle which many accept in theory, but disagree upon in practice.

CHAPTER THIRTEEN

DELEGATED LEGISLATION

13.1 Objectives

By the end of this Chapter you should be able to:

- identify the sources of administrative power;

- list the different types of delegated legislation;

- evaluate the role of delegated legislation within the law-making framework;

- consider what measures are available to check and control the possible abuse of delegated powers.

13.2 Introduction

A century ago the government was mainly concerned with foreign affairs, defence and public order. In accordance with the policy of 'laissez-faire', the state played a limited role in the life of the individual. This is no longer the case. The government in contemporary Britain is concerned with a wide variety of issues. These include education, transport, welfare, public health and housing. The government has assumed such functions as a matter of policy, although overall supervision remains with Parliament. Execution of these policies often leads to disputes and it is with these that administrative law is concerned.

The role of the courts in this area is only to determine the *legality* of administrative action. The *policy* which underpins a decision may not be challenged. The questions which arise are frequently technical and tend to involve the interpretation of statutory provisions. Apart from certain prerogative powers, legislation (including delegated legislation) is almost exclusively the source of administrative power. The principle of Parliamentary supremacy ensures the primacy of Acts of Parliament. As we noted earlier, statutes are not generally subject to judicial review unless in direct conflict with European Community law (see the extracts from *R* v *Secretary of State for Transport, ex parte Factortame Ltd (No. 2)* [1991] AC 603, and *Equal Opportunities Commission* v *Secretary of State for Employment* [1994] 1 All ER 910 in **Cases and Materials (8.5)**). However, delegated legislation may be challenged in a court of law. It receives its authority from statute and power is conferred under a 'parent Act' which delegates power to executive bodies for defined purposes. Delegated legislation is therefore a form of subordinate legislation. In this Chapter we will consider the manner and form of delegated legislation and the checks and controls which may be imposed on it.

What did the Select Committee on Procedure mean when it claimed in 1977/78, that the 'very concept of delegated legislative powers . . . involves an uneasy confusion between executive and legislative authority'? You should turn to the extract from the Select Committee's First Report in *Cases and Materials* (13.1) for the answer.

13.3   Types of Delegated Legislation

The Statutory Instruments Act 1946 controls the publication and procedural requirements to be followed in the making of delegated legislation. Orders in Council and Regulations made by Ministers are published as statutory instruments under the provisions of the Act. Statutory instruments are published in documentary form by Her Majesty's Stationery Office (HMSO).

(a)   **Orders in Council**

Here force of law is given to acts of the government. Effectively the order is made by the appropriate Minister, with the formal assent of the Crown. Orders in Council are a useful tool for formalising matters of constitutional importance – (e.g., the fixing of the date for the referendum in 1975 on Britain's continued membership of the European Community). Powers to make Orders in Council tend to be authorised by statute (e.g., orders to issue regulations in times of emergency under the Emergency Powers Act 1920). However, it is important to note that some Orders in Council are derived from the Royal prerogative. An example of this is *Council of Civil Service Unions* v *Minister for the Civil Service* [1985] AC 374, where the House of Lords reviewed, but would not interfere with, the government's decision banning employees at GCHQ from membership of trade unions.

An Order in Council made under a statute is a statutory instrument, whereas prerogative Orders in Council (as their name suggests) have as their source the Royal prerogative. In both cases the order will be prepared by the Minister responsible to Parliament and they each require the assent of the Monarch in the Privy Council.

(b)   **Regulations made by Ministers**

Here authority is conferred by statute on the Minister in person to make regulations. For example, the Local Government Finance Act 1988 enabled the

Secretary of State for the Environment to control expenditure by local authorities. A wide range of powers is conferred on Ministers by Parliament, allowing the Minister to make regulations, orders, rules etc. Under the Police and Criminal Evidence Act 1984 the Home Secretary is given the power to make regulations which can be found in the Codes of Practice.

(c) **By-laws**

Delegated authority may be conferred on public authorities (e.g., local authorities) to make by-laws. Thus, the Local Government Act 1972 (see *Cases and Materials* **(13.2)**) empowered district councils and London boroughs to make by-laws for 'the good rule and government' of their area.

(d) **Other types of delegated legislation**

Many other bodies are authorised to make delegated legislation. Groups such as the National Trust may create by-laws. Similarly, the legislation of the General Synod of the Church of England ('measures') is a form of delegated legislation.

What criticisms can be made of this form of law making? You should turn to the extract from S.A. Walkland in *Cases and Materials* **(13.2)** for one explanation of why there is often suspicion of delegated legislation.

13.4 The Need for Delegated Legislation

In April 1932 the Committee on Ministers' Powers (Cmd 4060) presented a report to Parliament concerning the powers exercised by, or under the discretion of, Ministers of the Crown. The aim of the report was to consider which safeguards were necessary to secure the constitutional principles of Parliamentary sovereignty and the supremacy of the law. The Committee reported that:

we do not agree with those critics who think the practice is wholly bad. We see in it definite advantages, provided that the statutory powers are exercised and the statutory functions performed in the right way. But risks of abuse are incidental to it, and we believe that safeguards are required, if the country is to continue to enjoy the advantages of the practice without suffering from its inherent dangers. But in truth whether good or bad the development of the practice is inevitable.

The Committee on Ministers' Powers 1932 (see in *Cases and Materials* (13.3)) identified six reasons in support of the need for delegation. What are these six reasons? Which of them are the most important and why?

The volume of delegated legislation produced far exceeds the number of statutes enacted annually. In 1989, 2,510 statutory instruments were published and by 1995 the annual figure had risen to 3,345. Since then the number has remained close to this total, and in their first report (1995–96), the Joint Committee on Statutory Instruments pointed out that 'the overall volume of statutory instruments has increased markedly . . . [and they] take up approximately 2 feet, 6 inches in bookshelf'. This can be contrasted with the number of Acts of Parliament (on average just over 50) which are passed annually.

13.4.1   THE ADVANTAGES OF DELEGATED LEGISLATION

It has generally come to be accepted that some degree of delegation is essential in modern government, not merely to relieve pressure on Parliamentary time. In addition to this, other advantages include:

(a)   **The technical nature of subject matter**

Through a consultative process, technical regulations may be made in areas where a high degree of technical knowledge is required. In an age of advancing technology, few members of Parliament can be expected to have a detailed knowledge of highly specialised areas, such as safety standards in coal mines. Parliament can enact the principles and delegate responsibility for the detailed application of these principles in delegated legislation. As Lord Alexander, Chairman of the Delegated Powers Scrutiny Committee observed, when giving evidence to a Commons Select Committee on Procedure (1995–96); 'Neither Parliament nor the executive could cope if changes to the law could only be made by primary legislation: there would not be enough time and acts would be impossibly long and detailed.'

(b)   **Flexibility**

Formal change to the law results in a slow and cumbersome process – this will be inappropriate in situations where frequent change is experienced. For example, regulations relating to road traffic matters and changes in social conditions may require corresponding changes through the detailed application of new rules. New regulations that prove unsatisfactory may be withdrawn quickly and replaced with others. Delegated legislation can also be used to authorise the delay or implementation of certain statutes, e.g., the Football Spectators Act 1989. This allows any changing circumstances to be taken account of, such as safety improvements to football stadiums.

(c) **Emergency powers**

In the wake of a public emergency (e.g., a war, famine, epidemic, civil unrest), a government will need power to act quickly and decisively. Such powers may be granted by Parliament in an 'enabling Act'. This will include the power to make detailed regulations appropriate to the particular emergency. For example, the Emergency Powers (Defence) Act 1939 allowed such regulations as appeared necessary to secure public safety, defence of the realm and the maintenance of public order.

A good example of the delegation of powers is *McEldowney* v *Forde* [1971] AC 632 where the House of Lords upheld a widely phrased ban on Republican clubs imposed by the Northern Ireland Minister for Home Affairs. Read the extracts from the ruling of Lord Hodson in this case (see *Cases and Materials* (13.3.1)).

Since the suspension of local government in Northern Ireland (the old Stormont administration) and the introduction of 'direct rule' from Westminster, the bulk of legislation introduced in Northern Ireland has been of a 'secondary' rather than 'primary' nature. This has allowed London to run the Province reasonably smoothly, but the lack of scrutiny of many of the measures which have been introduced has incurred the wrath of a number of Ulster's politicians. For example, David Trimble, the leader of the Official Unionist party, in a Commons debate on 13 November 1997, complained that 'Acres of Northern Ireland legislation have passed through the House without being debated or examined' and that this was 'a crying disgrace'. The creation of a New Northern Ireland Assembly, with Mr Trimble as its First Minister, may lead to greater scrutiny of legislation, but many of the criticisms made of secondary legislation in Northern Ireland apply equally to the rest of the UK.

13.4.2 CRITICISM OF DELEGATED LEGISLATION

Generally it would seem that any criticism of delegated legislation emanates not from its existence, but from the possibility of the abuse of delegated power. The main disadvantages that have been suggested are as follows:

(a) **Usurping the role of Parliament**

Delegated legislation may involve legislation on matters of principle which should only be considered by Parliament. The delegation of such powers could lead to the erosion of the legislative supremacy of Parliament. This may allow laws to be enacted without the extensive public debate which takes place at each stage of the legislative process in Parliament.

Acts of Parliament can be passed in skeleton form containing only basic principles. Procedures and detail are left to the relevant department to implement by means of regulations. The use of delegated legislation to 'flesh out' such skeleton Bills was criticised in the Committee on Ministers' Powers Report (Cmd 4060, 1932):

The extent of its adoption is . . . excessive, and leads not only to widespread suspicion and distrust of the machinery of government, but actually endangers our civil and personal liberties.

The creation of the much-maligned Child Support Agency in 1993 was introduced by means of a skeleton Bill. The Child Support Act 1991 provided the bare bones of the legislation, but details of the payment schemes and other provisions were all included in the accompanying regulations. The danger of this is that, as the

Joint Committee on Statutory Instruments pointed out in 1986, statutory instruments can sometimes be used to alter a government's policy 'in ways that were not envisaged when the enabling legislation was passed'.

(b) **Henry VIII clause**

Henry VIII clauses enable a Minister to alter or repeal an Act of Parliament by a statutory instrument. They are so called because it was that Monarch who claimed the right to modify Acts of Parliament by Proclamation. Acts may be repealed in whole or part and such modification is contrary to the principle that there should be a proper discussion in Parliament when an Act of Parliament is altered. The Factories Act 1961 provided that the Secretary of State may, by regulation, amend the provisions of that Act relating to welfare. The Health and Safety at Work etc. Act 1974 and the Deregulation and Contracting Out Act 1994 also contain similar provisions. Henry VIII clauses have been one of the main concerns of the Delegated Powers Scrutiny Committee, and you will find details of some of their concerns in the extract from Himsworth's article (see *Cases and Materials* (**13.3.2**)).

(c) **Possibility of sub-delegation**

This is objectionable because it leads to a loss of control over the exercise of legislative power. There is also the possibility that the Statutory Instruments Act 1946 will not be applicable as it only applies to orders made by the Monarch or a Minister. Sub-delegation was strongly criticised in *Patchett* v *Leathem* (1949) 65 TLR 69 where Streatfeild J said:

Whereas ordinary legislation, by passing through both Houses of Parliament or, at least, lying on the table of both Houses, is thus twice blessed, this type of so-called legislation is at least four times cursed. First, it has seen neither House of Parliament; secondly, it is unpublished and is inaccessible even to those whose valuable rights of property may be affected; thirdly, it is a jumble of provisions, legislative, administrative or directive in character, and sometimes difficult to disentangle one from the other; and, fourthly, it is expressed not in the precise language of an Act of Parliament or an Order in Council but in the more colloquial language of correspondence, which is not always susceptible of the ordinary canons of construction.

(d) **European Community law**

Delegated legislation is commonly used to incorporate European Community Directives into British law. This is provided for in s. 2(2) of the European Communities Act 1972. However, by using a statutory instrument to implement a European Directive, important legislation may be passed without detailed prior discussion in Parliament.

SAQ 130

Why has delegated legislation been described as a 'necessary evil'? For some ideas, you should return to the extract from the Report of the Committee on Ministers' Powers (1932) in *Cases and Materials* (**13.3**).

13.5 Control of Delegated Legislation

Although delegated legislation may be necessary, it is also clear that there must be mechanisms in place for preventing any possible abuse of delegated powers. Therefore we must now turn to: (a) Parliamentary safeguards; (b) political controls; (c) judicial checks.

13.5.1 PARLIAMENTARY SAFEGUARDS

There are a number of methods which can be employed to curb the possible abuse of delegated power. The most obvious way is to ensure that the Parent Act is not itself drafted so as to devolve wide delegated powers which may be difficult to control. Thus de Smith calls this the 'contraceptive' approach, making sure that all necessary precautions are taken!

As with primary legislation there is an opportunity for the extent and purpose of the delegated legislation to be discussed, both in Parliament and at the committee stage. The usual procedures of both Houses may be employed (e.g., Parliamentary question time, adjournment motions etc.). However, the very pressure on Parliamentary time which in the first place necessitates delegation may actually prevent any really effective consideration at this stage in the first place. Instead control may be exercised through procedural requirements for laying the instrument before Parliament or through scrutiny by the Select Committees on Statutory Instruments.

13.5.1.1 Laying before Parliament

Whether or not an instrument must be laid before Parliament will depend on the provisions of the Parent Act (see *Cases and Materials* (**13.4.1.1**) for the relevant provisions of the Statutory Instruments Act 1946). An instrument is usually presented before both Houses, with the exception of financial matters, which are only laid before the Commons. Laying before Parliament may take one of the following forms:

(a) **Laying** *simpliciter*

   The parent Act may do no more than make it obligatory for the instrument to be laid on the table of both Houses for the information of members. No resolution is necessary for the instrument to become effective.

(b) **Laying subject to a negative resolution**

   In this case the instrument will automatically come into force after 40 days, *unless* before the expiry of that time either House passes a resolution that the order be annulled. An order may also be laid in draft form subject to a similar resolution that no further proceedings be taken. No amendments can be made so it can only be accepted or rejected. The 40 days excludes any time during which Parliament is dissolved. As the Minister concerned will usually be able to count on a government majority, it is unlikely that such an instrument would be annulled. Thus, the Commons Select Committee on Procedure, in its Fourth Report on Delegated Legislation (1995–96) (see *Cases and Materials* (**13.4.1.1**)) has criticised the 'negative' procedure as being 'palpably unsatisfactory' and for giving the House of Commons 'scarcely any opportunity for constructive and purposeful discussion'.

(c) **Laying subject to an affirmative resolution**

   By this procedure an instrument which is not approved within 40 days of its being laid before the House will not come into effect. The Minister concerned must therefore present the instrument for approval and government time must be found to deal with it. Usually amendments are not possible. An instrument may also be laid in draft subject to an affirmative resolution before it can be 'made'. It is questionable whether the 40 day limit is a sufficiently long period of time and the Commons Procedure Committee has suggested that the period of 40 days for scrutiny should be increased to 60, to comply with the Deregulation Committee. The main reason for this is the growth of delegated legislation in recent years. The Select Committee on Procedure (1995–96) has suggested that, over the past 15 years, there has been an increase by 50 per cent of instruments subject to the 'affirmative' procedure, while the number of instruments subject to the 'negative' procedure has also doubled in this time, from 700 to over 1,300. Thus, this rapid growth increases the need for close scrutiny of such secondary legislation.

13.5.1.2   Scrutiny

A Joint Committee of both Houses of Parliament scrutinises statutory instruments and draft instruments where appropriate. The Joint Select Committee on Statutory Instruments is required to consider whether the attention of each House should be drawn to any instrument. The department concerned should first be given the opportunity to forward its case. The Committee consists of seven members of each House, Counsel to the Speaker and Counsel to the Lord Chairman of Committees. It is a convention that the chairperson is from the opposition.

The terms of reference of the Joint Select Committee on Statutory Instruments are to be found in the House of Commons Standing Orders (see *Cases and Materials* (13.4.1.2)). Every statutory instrument of a general character should be considered by the Committee with a view to determining whether or not it should be brought to the attention of the House if any of the eight listed grounds apply. What are these eight grounds?

In the light of these guidelines why might it be said that the Parliamentary scrutiny of delegated legislation is not an effective democratic control?

Write a short summary of the Parliamentary safeguards on delegated legislation. Then compare your answer to the extract from Griffith and Ryle on Parliamentary controls on secondary legislation in *Cases and Materials* (13.4.1.2).

The most important aspect of the Joint Select Committee on Statutory Instruments is that it submits regulations for Parliamentary debate and scrutiny. Government departments are aware of its 'critical eye'. Adverse reports from the Committee can lead to a prayer for annulment or force a department to revoke or amend a particular instrument. However less than 2 per cent of the instruments scrutinised by the Committee are reported to the House even though the Committee reports on every instrument.

13.5.2 POLITICAL CONTROLS

In addition to the scrutiny of subordinate legislation by Parliament and the Joint Select Committee, other 'political' controls exist:

(a) **Prior consultation**

Acts of Parliament sometimes provide that the Minister *may* or *shall* consult with interested bodies or advisory committees before issuing regulations. The Parent Act may therefore stipulate that there must be consultation in either general or specific terms. Consultation with interested parties is now common for reasons of political expediency as well as legal necessity. Such bodies may be specified in the Act or chosen at the Minister's discretion but, while Ministers may be obliged to consult, they are not normally bound to follow the advice offered. The House of Commons Liaison Committee, in its First Report on the work of Select Committees in 1997, has recommended that 'whenever a draft Bill or draft clauses are published, the Department concerned should include the relevant Select Committee among those to whom documents are sent for consultation'.

(b) **Publication**

Delegated legislation usually comes into force when it is made unless some other date is specified in the Parent Act. Twenty-one days are usually allowed from the date it was laid before Parliament. Section 2 of the Statutory Instruments Act 1946 provides that after a statutory instrument has been made, it shall be sent to the Queen's Printer of Acts of Parliament. There it is printed, numbered and made available to the public at Her Majesty's Stationery Office as soon as possible (although s. 8(1) of the 1946 Act does provide for some exceptions — see *Cases and Materials* (**13.4.1.1**)).

According to s. 3, if an instrument creates an offence, it shall be a defence for any person accused to show either:

(a) that at the date of the alleged offence the instrument had not been 'issued' by the Stationery Office; or

(b) that in cases of non-publication it was not sufficiently publicised.

In *Simmonds* v *Newell* [1953] 1 WLR 826 a conviction for an offence of selling in contravention of an Iron and Steel Prices Order 1951, was quashed by the Divisional Court because of insufficient publicity of the order. However, in *R* v *Sheer Metalcraft Ltd* [1954] 1 QB 586 a conviction was ordered for buying in contravention of the same order, even though the instrument had not been published. This was because the prosecution successfully established that the contents of the instrument had been extensively advertised in relevant trade journals.

The basis of the requirement of publication is that if every person is to be presumed to know the law, then the contents of the law must be accessible to them. However, as Lord Hewart pointedly asked in *The New Despotism* (1929) 'Does any human being read through this mass of departmental legislation?'

ACTIVITY 107

Read the extract from *R* v *Sheer Metalcraft Ltd* [1954] 1 QB 586 in *Cases and Materials* (13.4.2).

13.5.3 JUDICIAL CHECKS

The power of the courts in relation to statutes is confined to interpretation. In respect of statutory instruments their powers are wider as the court must first be satisfied that the provisions of the Parent Act have been complied with. If not, the resulting instrument will be *ultra vires* and void. An instrument may be declared void for the following reasons:

(a) **On substantive grounds**

A statutory instrument may be held to be *ultra vires* if no power to make that particular instrument is conferred by the Parent Act.

In *Chester* v *Bateson* [1920] 1 KB 829 (see *Cases and Materials* (13.4.3)) a regulation provided that no action could be taken before the courts to recover the possession of a munition worker's home without the consent of a Minister. The court held that this regulation was void, as such a requirement could only be imposed by an express enactment, because it affected a fundamental right. In *Commissioners of Customs and Excise* v *Cure and Deeley Ltd* [1962] 1 QB 340 (see *Cases and Materials* (13.4.3)), Sachs J ruled that a tax regulation made by the Commissioners, purporting to give them an unchallengeable right to determine the amount of tax due from the taxpayer, was void because it ousted the jurisdiction of the courts to adjudicate on such matters.

(b) **On procedural grounds**

Where the exact procedure as laid down in the Parent Act has not been complied with, the secondary legislation which has been created may be struck down. The likelihood of the court intervening will largely depend on whether the procedures are mandatory or directory. If mandatory, non-compliance is likely to make the instrument defective. If directory, the courts may take the view that non-compliance does not affect its validity (see **Chapter 15** on judicial review). The problem is that the enabling section of the Parent Act is not always clearly expressed. However, the courts will adopt a stricter approach where the exercise of delegated legislation interferes with the liberty of the individual, excludes the citizen from access to the courts, imposes taxation or removes property rights without consultation or compensation.

In *Rollo* v *Minister of Town and Country Planning* [1948] 1 All ER 13, the relevant Act required the Minister to consult 'with any local authorities who appear to him to be concerned'. The court held that this requirement meant that the Minister should give the authority sufficient information to enable it to give advice and allow an opportunity for that advice to be tendered. It was found therefore that the precise procedures in the Parent Act had not been followed. As a general rule, a failure to consult with all appropriate bodies in the relevant field may render any subsequent statutory instrument invalid. In *Agricultural, Horticultural and Forestry Industry Training Board* v *Aylesbury Mushrooms Ltd* [1972] 1 WLR 190, the Minister consulted with the Farmers' Union about a new agricultural scheme, but failed to consult with the Mushroom Growers' Association. The court held that he had not consulted widely enough and the statutory procedures had not been properly observed.

Read the extract from the *Aylesbury Mushrooms* case in *Cases and Materials* (13.4.3).

(c)   **Unreasonableness (irrationality)**

Delegated legislation may also be declared void on the grounds of unreasonableness under the principle in *Associated Provincial Picture Houses Ltd* v *Wednesbury Corporation* [1948] 1 KB 223 (now referred to as 'irrationality' by virtue of Lord Diplock's comments in the *GCHQ* case — see **Chapter 15** on judicial review). Unreasonableness applies particularly to by-laws. In *Kruse* v *Johnson* [1898] 2 QB 91, Lord Russell of Killowen CJ held that a by-law which is unequal in its operation as between different classes, or which is an 'oppressive or gratuitous interference with the rights of the subjects' would be void.

In *Kruse* v *Johnson* (1898) a by-law forbidding singing within 50 yards of a dwelling house was found not to be unreasonable and was therefore valid. However, in *Munro* v *Watson* (1887) 57 LT 366, a by-law forbade the playing of music, singing, or preaching in any street without the express licence of the mayor and was declared void for unreasonableness. Nevertheless, the courts tend to construe by-laws benevolently and will normally uphold them if possible.

Why are the courts usually reluctant to strike down by-laws? For an illustration of the judicial scrutiny of by-laws, turn to the extract from *Kruse* v *Johnsson* (1898) in *Cases and Materials* (13.4.3).

13.6 Conclusion

Dicey once said that the British Constitution is based on two principles: the sovereignty of Parliament (see **Chapter 7**) and the rule of law (see **Chapter 12**). However, by concentrating power in the hands of the executive, delegated legislation clearly rests uneasily with these two principles. And by giving Ministers the power to 'make law' (albeit subject to the provisions of the Parent Act), delegated legislation appears to infringe the notion of a strict separation of powers (see **Chapter 3**).

Therefore, the use of delegated legislation creates a constitutional dilemma. Parliament is the supreme law-maker, but its ability to legislate is severely limited by the practical considerations noted earlier. Lord Hewart CJ, writing in 1929 (*The New Despotism*), considered that delegated legislation was an abdication by Parliament of its main constitutional role (law making). However, times have changed. The State has grown in power and the skills required for modern government are increasingly technical. The smooth running of Parliament would cease if all reforms had to be introduced in the form of primary legislation. Thus, the use of delegated, or subordinate legislation is a necessary characteristic of the governance of Britain in the late 20th century. As the Committee on Ministers' Powers once observed:

> In a modern State there are many occasions when there is a sudden need of legislative active. For many such needs delegated legislation is the only convenient or even possible remedy.

Notwithstanding its potential for abuse, delegated legislation is necessary (a necessary evil?) for the effective management of the contemporary British State.

CHAPTER FOURTEEN

PREROGATIVE POWERS

14.1 Objectives

At the end of this Chapter you should be able to:

- understand what is meant by the Royal prerogative;

- describe the courts' attitude to the exercise of prerogative powers;

- assess the importance of prerogative powers;

- appreciate the significance of the *GCHQ* decision in this area.

14.2 Introduction

Historically the Sovereign was vested with special powers and privileges. As chief feudal Lord in medieval times, the King could not be sued in his own courts. He enjoyed a wide variety of powers which could be used in protecting the State from external and hostile forces. The King was the fountain of justice and could adjudicate in legal disputes. Through his council he had the power to decide other matters, such as the pardoning of criminals, the granting of peerages and the taking of measures to deal with emergencies. These were known as the Royal prerogative powers.

As a result of the struggle for power between the Crown and Parliament in the 17th century, the Bill of Rights 1688 rationalised the use of these prerogative powers. It provided that statutes could expressly abolish or restrict the existence and exercise of the Crown's prerogative powers. Over the years statutes have gradually whittled away these powers. For example, the Crown Proceedings Act 1947 abolished the immunity of the Crown in respect of actions in tort and contract, although it retained the personal immunity of the Sovereign.

In this chapter we shall analyse those prerogative powers which still exist, the ways in which they may be exercised and the extent to which the courts are prepared to review their exercise.

According to Tony Benn MP, 'To understand how we're governed, and hence the power of the Prime Minister, you have to understand the power of the Crown. It's like the Trinity: God the Father is the Queen — she's just there and nobody knows very much about her; God the son is the Prime Minister — who exercises all the patronage and has all the real power; and God the Holy Ghost is the Crown — the Royal Prerogative — and the Crown is a State-within-a-State, surrounded by barbed wire and covered in secrecy.' What does he mean by this statement? (Think back to Chapters 1 to 6 for some ideas.)

14.3   The Queen in Council

The powers of the Crown may be exercised in three ways:

(a)   at the personal discretion of the Sovereign;

(b)   by the Sovereign on the advice of Ministers;

(c)   by Ministers alone, through statutory powers conferred on them, but exercised on behalf of the Crown.

At one time the Monarch was the lone source of executive power, acting on the advice of an inner council of advisers — the Privy Council. History shows a decline in the advisory and judicial functions of the Privy Council. Acts of the Privy Council nowadays tend to involve the formal sanctioning of Orders in Council without any prior discussion. To do this usually only four or five of the 300 members are summoned.

Responsibility for the content of these Orders rests with the government department concerned. Such Orders in Council are a form of delegated legislation. Members of the Privy Council include Cabinet Ministers, senior members of the Royal Family, Archbishops and Law Lords (who constitute the Judicial Committee of the Privy Council). The prefix 'Right Honourable' signifies membership of the Privy Council and although all Cabinet Ministers are Privy Councillors, the Cabinet and the Privy Council are entirely separate. In practice the Cabinet deliberates and the Privy Council gives formal approval. Members of the Cabinet meet as Crown servants (not as a committee of the Privy Council) and are summoned by the Prime Minister. The Privy Council is convened by the Clerk to the Council.

Members of the Privy Council take an oath of secrecy (this includes members of the Cabinet) on appointment. This is not to reveal anything said or done in Council without the consent of the Sovereign. It was felt that this oath would also bind the members of the Cabinet, not to disclose matters therein.

SAQ 133

The duration and extent of this oath was considered in which case relating to the publication of the Crossman Diaries? (See Chapter 2 and the section on the convention of ministerial responsibility for the answer.)

Although the Privy Council's importance has decreased, it does retain some important functions. The Judicial Committee of the Privy Council is the last avenue for appeals from some Commonwealth countries. Recent rulings of the Privy Council have had particularly important implications for capital punishment. In *Guerra* v *Baptiste* [1996] 1 AC 397, it was suggested that where a State operates a system of capital punishment, the execution must follow as swiftly as possible after sentencing, while allowing a reasonable time for appeal. Similarly, in *Pratt* v *A-G for Jamaica* [1994] 2 AC 1, the Privy Council found that since there had been a substantial delay between the prisoner's conviction for murder and the date of his execution (five years), his sentence should be commuted to life imprisonment. However, in *Reckley* v *Minister of Public Safety and Immigration (No. 2)* [1996] AC 527, the Judicial Committee of the Privy Council ruled that, under the Constitution of the Bahamas, the prerogative of mercy was not subject to judicial review.

Finally, the Privy Council may also give advice, and ad hoc committees have been set up in the past to examine matters such as telephone tapping and the Falklands conflict.

14.4 The Royal Prerogative

In 1765 Blackstone referred to the Royal Prerogative as that 'special pre-eminence which the King hath, over and above all other persons, and out of the ordinary course of the common law, in right of his regal dignity'. However, Dicey defined prerogative powers, as 'the residue of discretionary or arbitrary authority which at any given time is legally left in the hands of the Crown'. Since the 20th century has witnessed the diminishing influence of prerogative powers, Dicey's description would today appear to be more accurate.

Prerogatives are residual Royal powers rather than common law creations and de Smith regards them as 'inherent legal attributes' unique to the Crown. **Inherent** because they originate from custom and the common law; **legal**, because they are recognised by the courts; and **attributes**, because they include not merely powers but also rights and duties.

SAQ 134

In what kinds of public law areas would you imagine prerogative powers to be relevant?

Before we proceed any further it would be useful to be aware of the sorts of issues governed by prerogative powers. We will now look at some of the main powers by dividing them under the following headings: personal prerogatives of the sovereign; political or ministerial prerogatives; judicial prerogatives; prerogatives relevant to the defence of the realm; and finally, prerogatives in the area of foreign affairs.

14.4.1 PERSONAL PREROGATIVES OF THE SOVEREIGN

The Sovereign still retains certain powers inherited from medieval times when the Sovereign was all-powerful. These include:

- The prerogative that the Sovereign never dies — i.e., there is no interregnum at common law since, when one monarch dies, there is an automatic succession.

- The person of the Sovereign is inviolable — it is high treason to assault or attempt to assassinate the Sovereign — this crime is punishable by death.

- The Sovereign can do no wrong — this is based on the old feudal system that a lord could not be tried in his own court. As all the courts are the Sovereign's courts it followed that he or she could not be tried by them. Prior to 1947 and the enactment of the Crown Proceedings Act, individuals could rarely sue the Crown.

Which Minister tried unsuccessfully to advance the argument that, as a Minister of the Crown, he was not subject to the court's jurisdiction, when accused of being in contempt of court? (See Chapter 2.)

- The Sovereign is the commander-in-chief of the armed forces and may declare war or make peace under the Royal prerogative. Of course this, in practice, is done on the advice of the Prime Minister. Whilst war was neither formally declared during the Falklands conflict (1981), nor on Iraq during the Gulf crisis (1990), it was the Prime Minister who authorised the British use of force on each occasion.

- Whilst it is the Prime Minister who has the authority to award most honours, a few are still dispensed personally by the Sovereign.

14.4.2 POLITICAL PREROGATIVES

In addition to the personal prerogatives of the Sovereign, there exist a number of 'political prerogatives', exercisable in theory by the Sovereign but in practice (by convention) through government Ministers. As we saw in **Chapter 2,** two of the most important prerogatives that the Sovereign may exercise are the appointment of Ministers (including the Prime Minister) and the summoning and dissolution of Parliament. These are exercised by convention, as are prerogative powers relating to the dismissal of Ministers and the Royal Assent. A list of the Sovereign's prerogative powers are provided by Peter Hennessy in *Cases and Materials* (**14.1.1**) and he claims to 'have long been worried about the lack of public and political knowledge about the principles that have shaped any exercise of the Queen's personal prerogatives' (*The Guardian*, 27 February 1997).

What is the 'advice' which the Sovereign receives from her Ministers? For some ideas turn to the views of Vernon Bogdanor in *Cases and Materials* (14.1.1).

14.4.3 JUDICIAL PREROGATIVES

The Crown may no longer use prerogative powers to establish new courts, (*Re Lord Bishop of Natal* (1864) 3 Moo PC), since this is now governed by statute. However, the Crown can stop a prosecution through the Attorney-General, who can enter the seldom used *nolle prosequi*, while some prosecutions may only be initiated by the Attorney-General (e.g. certain offences under the Official Secrets Acts 1911 and 1989). The appointment of judges by the Crown (on the advice of the Lord Chancellor) is by virtue of the Royal prerogative while the source of the Home Secretary's power to grant pardons is the prerogative of mercy.

14.4.4 DEFENCE OF THE REALM

The Sovereign is commander-in-chief of the armed forces. (The Navy is the only force maintained without direct statutory authority, though its recruitment and discipline are now governed by statute since it did not come within the prohibition of a standing army in peacetime as required by the Bill of Rights 1688.) Officers in the armed forces hold their commission from the Sovereign and, since the control of troops comes within the prerogative, it cannot be legally challenged (*Chandler* v *DPP* [1964] AC 763). Whilst declarations of war and peace are at the behest of the Sovereign, the dispositon of troops requires the agreement of the Commons, because only Parliament can supply the necessary finance.

Obviously, in times of emergency, there is a need for decisions to be taken quickly without having to go through lengthy Parliamentary procedures. Thus, while it is impossible to define the extent of the prerogative in times of emergency, it would appear that:

■ The Crown is responsible for the defence of the realm and is the only judge of how that defence should be effected (*R* v *Hampden* (1637) 3 St Tr 826 (the Ship Money case)).

- The land of any individual may be entered to erect fortifications for the nation's defence (*Case of the King's Prerogative in Saltpetre* (1607) 12 Co Rep 12) subject to the safeguard that they must be removed when the danger is past.

- British ships in territorial waters may be requisitioned in times of national crisis (as occurred during the Falklands conflict with the Requisitioning of Ships Order 1982).

- The Crown, when necessary in time of war, may appropriate property within the realm, which belongs to a neutral person (*Commercial and Estates Co. of Egypt* v *Board of Trade* [1925] 1 KB 271).

Compensation may be payable at common law following the requisition or destruction of property through the exercise of prerogative powers. In *Burmah Oil Co. Ltd* v *Lord Advocate* [1965] AC 75, the House of Lords considered this issue. Following the Japanese invasion of Burma in 1942, a number of oil installations in that territory were destroyed by British soldiers, in order to prevent them later being of use to the enemy. Burmah Oil claimed compensation and argued that the State was responsible for these actions, as the demolitions had been ordered under a prerogative power. The House of Lords held that a subject could receive compensation where a prerogative power has been used in order to deprive them of property in a time of war. However, following this decision of the House of Lords to award compensation, Parliament overturned it by passing the War Damage Act 1965. This legislation prevented compensation from being paid, retrospectively, for damage to, or destruction of, property by lawful acts of the Crown 'during or in contemplation of the outbreak of a war in which the Sovereign is or was engaged'.

Read the extract from Lord Reid's opinion in *Burmah Oil Co. Ltd* v *Lord Advocate* [1965] AC 75 in *Cases and Materials* (14.1.2). What justification does Lord Reid provide for the use of the prerogative in emergency situations?

14.4.5 THE PREROGATIVE IN FOREIGN AFFAIRS

The making of treaties is a prerogative power of the Crown. Once a treaty has been signed by the United Kingdom, international law regards the UK as being bound by that treaty. However, the United Kingdom's courts will not enforce a treaty unless incorporated into British law by legislation (*The Parliament Belge* (1879) 4 PD 129).

Although the signing of a treaty is a prerogative act, and Parliamentary approval is not always necessary, in some cases Parliamentary confirmation is required. This is necessary for:

- treaties expressly made subject to confirmation by Parliament (e.g., the European Communities Act 1972);

- treaties involving an alteration of English law on taxation; and

- treaties affecting private rights.

Compare Viscount Radcliffe's dissenting judgment to that of Lord Reid in *Burmah Oil Co. Ltd* v *Lord Advocate* in *Cases and Materials* **(14.1.3). Why do they disagree and which view do you find more persuasive?**

14.5 Determining the Existence and Extent of Prerogative Powers

Prerogative powers have been recognised by the courts since the *Case of Proclamations* (1611) 12 Co Rep 74. There it was held that the Crown could not create new criminal offences and that the King could only act through Parliament if he wished to make new laws. As Lord Reid observed in *Burmah Oil Co. Ltd* v *Lord Advocate* [1965] AC 75: '[i]t is not easy to discover and decide the law regarding the Royal prerogative and the consequence of its exercise'.

Therefore, the courts have adopted a number of rules to determine the existence and extent of prerogative powers.

14.5.1 NO NEW PREROGATIVE POWERS MAY BE CREATED

As the prerogative is derived from the common law, no new prerogatives may be claimed under this authority. In *British Broadcasting Corporation* v *Johns* [1965] Ch 32, it was held that the British Broadcasting Corporation (BBC) was not entitled to benefit from the Crown's immunity from taxation, as it was not a central government department. Diplock LJ said:

> . . . it is 350 years and a civil war too late for the Queen's courts to broaden the prerogative. The limits within which the government may impose obligations or restraints upon citizens of the United Kingdom without any statutory authority are now well settled and incapable of extension.

Similarly, in *Burmah Oil Co. Ltd* v *Lord Advocate* [1965] AC 75, Lord Reid said that: '. . . the way to recognise a prerogative power is to delve back in history . . . a power does not come to be extinct because of disuse, just more difficult to identify'.

Thus, for any residual prerogative power to be claimed, it must be shown that it can be traced back to before the 'Glorious Revolution'.

14.5.2 CONFLICTS BETWEEN STATUTORY PROVISIONS AND PREROGATIVE POWERS

Statutory powers will generally take precedence over prerogative powers and may preserve or abolish prerogative powers. Difficulty may arise where the effect of a statutory power upon a prerogative power is not clearly expressed.

A statute may, by implication, replace a prerogative, (e.g., where the statute covers the same ground as the prerogative). In *Attorney-General* v *De Keyser's Royal Hotel Ltd* [1920] AC 508, De Keyser's Royal Hotel was taken over by the War Office during the First World War to house the Royal Flying Corps. The Army offered to pay rent for the accommodation but negotiations broke down and the hotel was requisitioned under the Defence of the Realm Regulations. The company, which owned the hotel, claimed full compensation under these Regulations. The Crown argued that a prerogative right existed to requisition property in times of emergency, under which compensation was not payable – that this power could be used, despite the existence of a statute covering the same ground. De Keyser claimed that the Crown had taken possession under the statute and so could not fall back on its prerogative power to refuse compensation. The House of Lords agreed with the hotel owner, that the Crown had taken possession under statutory powers, and the statute took precedence over the prerogative power.

Read the extracts from *Attorney-General* v *De Keyser's Royal Hotel* in *Cases and Materials* (14.2.1). What differences were there in the decisions of Lords Atkinson, Moulton and Parmoor?

14.5.3 ANCIENT PREROGATIVES MAY BE REVIVED IF RELEVANT TO CONTEMPORARY CONDITIONS

Unlike conventions, prerogative powers do not lapse through any lack of use. This is because of the common law principle of desuetude. It would also seem that ancient prerogatives can be revived to apply to contemporary conditions. In *Malone* v *Metropolitan Police Commissioner* [1979] Ch 344, the practice of telephone tapping was authorised under the ancient prerogative power of the Crown to intercept the subject's mail.

In *R* v *Secretary of State for the Home Department, ex parte Northumbria Police Authority* [1988] 1 All ER 556 (see **Cases and Materials** (14.2.2)), the court also recognised the existence of an ancient prerogative as being relevant to a contemporary situation. The

Home Secretary had sought to provide a chief police officer in Northumbria with CS gas, without the approval of his local police authority. Section 4 of the Police Act 1964 (now s. 6 of the Police Act 1996) empowered each local police authority to equip its force to respond to public emergencies. The Court of Appeal held that the Home Secretary's action was justified under the ancient prerogative power to keep the peace, a power which had not been replaced by any statutory provision. However, the Court of Appeal added that, if a prerogative power is superseded by statute and that statute is later replaced, the prerogative should not be revived normally, unless it is particularly relevant to the contemporary situation.

What happens when a statutory provision and a prerogative power cover a similar issue? Do you think that the outcome is acceptable from a constitutional point of view? In order to develop your ideas, turn to the extracts from the judgments of Croom-Johnson and Nourse LJJ from *R* **v** *Secretary of State for the Home Department, ex parte Northumbria Police Authority* **[1988] 1 All ER 536 in** *Cases and Materials* **(14.2.2).**

14.6   Judicial Control of Prerogative Powers

Although the courts have always been willing to determine whether or not a prerogative power exists, they were traditionally reluctant to question the way in which it was exercised. They tended to adopt the approach that questions relating to the exercise of prerogative powers were essentially political, rather than judicial.

The catalyst for change was the *GCHQ* case (*Council of Civil Service Unions* v *Minister for the Civil Service* [1985] AC 374). Before we examine this landmark decision, we shall first consider its predecessors, so that it can be properly seen in its legal context.

In *Chandler* v *DPP* [1964] AC 763, an attempt was made by nuclear demonstrators to enter and gather on land at an RAF airbase. This was contrary to the Official Secrets Act 1911. Armed forces were dispatched to remove them and Lord Devlin commented: 'The courts will not review the proper exercise of discretionary power but they will intervene to correct excess or abuse.' Thus, the courts could determine the limits of the prerogative powers, but would not review their exercise, unless there was some suggestion of abuse or misuse. This principle was reaffirmed in *Gouriet* v *Union of Post Office Workers* [1977] QB 729, where Lord Denning MR, in the Court of Appeal, held that the Attorney-General's refusal to give consent to relator proceedings (thereby exercising his discretion) could be reviewed by the courts.

Lord Denning went on to comment: 'The Attorney-General has no prerogative to suspend or dispense with the laws of England.' However, the House of Lords unanimously allowed the Attorney-General's appeal and refused to review the exercise of his discretion (*Gouriet* v *Union of Post Office Workers* [1978] AC 435).

Notwithstanding this, in the earlier case of *R v Criminal Injuries Compensation Board, ex parte Lain* [1967] 2 QB 864, the High Court had held that it had the power to review decisions taken by the Criminal Injuries Compensation Board (a body set up under the auspices of the Royal prerogative to deal with claims from victims of crime seeking compensation).

Another breakthrough came in *Laker Airways Ltd v Department of Trade* [1977] QB 643 (see *Cases and Materials* (**14.3**)). The Court of Appeal decided that the Labour government's decision to revoke a licence providing for the low-cost Laker transatlantic 'Skytrain' service was unlawful. The Crown had a prerogative right to designate airlines for specified routes under the Bermuda Agreement 1946, a treaty between the United Kingdom and the United States. However, this had been superseded by the Civil Aviation Act 1971. The government claimed that, despite this Act (which created a statutory scheme for licensing scheduled air services), the designation had been authorised using the prerogative and could not be reviewed by the courts. The Court of Appeal rejected this claim. Rather controversially Lord Denning MR declared (*obiter*) that the use of a prerogative power was justiciable, and might be examined by the courts just like any other discretionary power which was vested in the executive.

14.6.1   THE *GCHQ* CASE

Lord Denning's view subsequently influenced the House of Lords in the leading case of *Council of Civil Service Unions v Minister for the Civil Service* [1985] AC 374 — the *GCHQ* case. Staff at the Government Communications Headquarters (GCHQ) had, since 1947, been permitted to join trade unions. In December 1983, without consultation, their conditions of service were altered. Instructions were issued under an Order in Council, prohibiting GCHQ staff from holding trade union membership. The appellants sought judicial review on the ground of unfairness, due to a failure to consult with the relevant unions. The House of Lords had to consider whether the courts had the power to review an instruction, in an Order in Council, issued under the Royal prerogative on the ground of procedural irregularity (failure to consult).

In the *GCHQ* case, the House of Lords considered Lord Denning's earlier claim (in *Laker Airways Ltd v Department of Trade*), that the prerogative is a discretionary power which must be exercised for the public good. Lords Diplock, Scarman and Roskill were of the opinion that acts directly authorised under the Royal prerogative were subject to judicial review, where the issues involved were **justiciable**. Rather than seek to define those issues which are justiciable, Lord Roskill cited six prerogative powers which are non-justiciable (i.e., not appropriate for judicial review) (see **Activity 113**). Lord Roskill also criticised Lord Denning's assertion that the courts may examine the exercise of discretionary powers under the prerogative to ensure that they are not used improperly or mistakenly. Nevertheless, the House of Lords in the *GCHQ* case questioned the traditional doctrine of judicial non-intervention and set the law on a new footing.

Read the extract from Lord Diplock's opinion in the *GCHQ* case in *Cases and Materials* (14.3.1). What does he mean in the final sentence when he says, '. . . I see no reason why simply because a decision-making power is derived from common law and not a statutory source, it should *for that reason only* be immune from judicial review'.

According to Lord Diplock, what should be the correct approach of the courts towards the judicial review of prerogative powers?

Now read the extract from Lord Roskill's opinion in *Cases and Materials* (14.3.1). On what basis does he criticise Lord Denning's comments in *Laker Airways Ltd* v *Department of Trade*?

To what extent does Lord Roskill agree with Lord Diplock, that all prerogative powers are now potentially reviewable by the courts?

Why does C. Walker [1987] *Public Law* 62, describe the decision of the House of Lords in *GCHQ* as a 'landmark' ruling?

14.7 Developments since the *GCHQ* Case

As a result of the decision in the *GCHQ* case, the law has become more settled. According to Lord Diplock, the exercise of all prerogative powers is now potentially reviewable by the courts. However, some prerogative powers may still be excluded from judicial review because of the nature of their subject matter. Lord Diplock's assertion has, therefore, been somewhat circumscribed by Lord Roskill who qualifies such a wide remit on the grounds that certain prerogative powers, because of their subject matter, would not be appropriate for judicial scrutiny.

Look at the extract in *Cases and Materials* (14.3.1) where Lord Roskill cites six prerogative powers which he considers are not justiciable (appropriate for review by the courts). What are they and what is the justification for their exclusion from judicial review.

Since the *GCHQ* case, the courts have become increasingly willing to review the exercise of prerogative powers. For example, in *R v Secretary of State for Foreign and Commonwealth Affairs, ex parte Everett* [1989] QB 811 (see *Cases and Materials* (**14.4**)), it was decided that the prerogative power to issue passports is reviewable. Everett, a British citizen, was living in Spain. He applied for a British passport, but was refused because a warrant for his arrest had been issued in the United Kingdom. The Court of Appeal accepted that whether there should be judicial review of the prerogative power depends on its subject matter. Non-justiciable matters would include the making of treaties, the dissolution of Parliament, and the mobilisation of the armed forces, but the issuing of or refusal to grant a passport was different. It was only an administrative decision and, as such, was reviewable unless it had national security implications.

To test the extent to which the courts have extended the boundaries of judicial review of prerogative powers we shall consider Lord Roskill's six exceptions.

14.7.1   THE MAKING OF TREATIES

It would seem that this is perhaps an area that the courts would prefer to leave to the government and politicians. In *Ex parte Molyneaux* [1986] 1 WLR 331, the Hillsborough Agreement negotiated by the governments of the United Kingdom and the Irish Republic, relating to the future of Northern Ireland, was challenged by four Ulster Unionist MPs. It was claimed that the Agreement would fetter the statutory functions of the Secretary of State for Northern Ireland and threaten the rights of Northern Ireland's citizens. The application was dismissed because the agreement fell within the field of international relations and was therefore 'akin to a treaty'. Similarly, in *Re International Tin Council* [1987] Ch 419, the court decided that it had no jurisdiction to deal with treaty obligations arising from the creation of an international organisation, the International Tin Council.

The courts have also been unwilling to consider treaties relating to the UK's membership of the European Union. In *Blackburn v Attorney General* [1971] 1 WLR 1037, Lord Denning MR considered that it was not an appropriate matter for the courts. Lord Denning noted that when Ministers 'negiotate and sign a treaty . . . they act on behalf of the country as a whole. They exercise the prerogative of the Crown'. Therefore, such Ministerial actions 'cannot be challenged or questioned in these courts'. The matter was also debated more recently in *R v Secretary of State for Foreign and Commonwealth Affairs, ex parte Rees-Mogg* [1994] 2 WLR 115 (see *Cases and Materials* (**14.4.1**)). Lord Rees-Mogg claimed that, by ratifying the provisions of the European Union Treaty which established a common European foreign and security policy, the government would be transferring some of its Royal prerogative powers (e.g., those relating to national security and foreign policy) to European institutions. He also protested that this had been effected without any statutory authority.

However, the Queen's Bench Divisional Court rejected these submissions. Lloyd LJ held that the part of the European Union Treaty establishing a common foreign and security policy (Title V) was an exercise and not an abandonment or transfer of the Crown's prerogative powers relating to foreign affairs.

14.7.2 THE DEFENCE OF THE REALM

As in the *GCHQ* case, this is another area where the courts have been reluctant to assert their jurisdiction. In *R v Secretary of State for the Home Department, ex parte Ruddock* [1987] 1 WLR 1482, members of CND (Campaign for Nuclear Disarmament) alleged that their telephones had been tapped contrary to published guidelines. The Minister refused to comment on the grounds of national security. Taylor J held that, despite the issues relating to national security, he was prepared to exercise his jurisdiction. However, having declared himself competent to decide the issue, he found that the Home Secretary had not acted unreasonably, nor had he broken any guidelines with regard to the warrant which authorised the phone tapping.

The *Ruddock* decision is perhaps unusual, since the courts tend to show much greater deference where issues involve national security. Remember that in the *GCHQ* case, the House of Lords had, on the facts, agreed that the Order in Council, which had been issued, was justifiable on the grounds of national security. Also, in *R v Secretary of State for Foreign and Commonwealth Affairs, ex parte Everett* [1989] QB 811, the court had qualified its judgment by adding that a decision to issue or withdraw a passport may be unreviewable where national security is involved. Thus, the courts are particularly loath to review decisions taken on the ground of national security, particularly in times of war or public emergency (e.g., see *R v Secretary of State for the Home Department, ex parte Cheblak* [1991] 1 WLR 890 discussed in **Chapter 12**).

14.7.3 THE PREROGATIVE OF MERCY

Pardons may be granted to convicted criminals by the Home Secretary under the prerogative of mercy. Until 1965 this included the power to commute the death penalty to life imprisonment. Whilst Lord Roskill included this as one of his six exceptions in the *GCHQ* case, this prerogative has more recently been reviewed by the courts.

In *R v Secretary of State for the Home Department, ex parte Bentley* [1994] QB 349, Iris Bentley sought judicial review of the Home Secretary's decision not to recommend a posthumous pardon for her brother Derek Bentley. The Divisional Court held that the Royal prerogative of mercy was a flexible power capable of being exercised in many different ways. Thus the court would 'invite' the Home Secretary to re-examine the matter and consider whether it would be just to exercise the prerogative of mercy and give recognition to the commonly held belief that Bentley should have been reprieved. In November 1997, it was announced that the case of *ex parte Bentley* would be referred to the Court of Appeal following a recommendation of the Criminal Cases Review Commission which had been set up to investigate alleged miscarriages of justice, and in July 1998 Derek Bentley's conviction for murder was finally overturned by the Court of Appeal.

However, a different approach was adopted by the Privy Council in *Reckley v Minister of Public Safety and Immigration (No. 2)* [1996] AC 527. Reckley had been sentenced to death but challenged this on the ground that he had a right to make representations to a

Bahamian Advisory Committee on the Prerogative of Mercy, which advised on whether the final execution warrant should be issued. He sought to rely on *R* v *Secretary of State for the Home Department, ex parte Doody* [1994] 1 AC 531, where it had been held that a Minister had a duty to provide a prisoner with reasons for the term of his life sentence, but the Privy Council distinguished *Doody* from Reckley's case on the ground that only the latter concerned mercy. Thus, it was held that the prerogative of mercy was not reviewable and Reckley was subsequently executed.

(a) **What was the rationale behind the decision of Watkins LJ in *ex parte Bentley* to extend the courts' jurisdiction to review the prerogative of mercy? For some ideas you should turn to the extract from his judgment and the comment on this case by I. Hare in *Cases and Materials* (14.4.2)**

(b) **David Pannick claims that the decision in *Reckley* v *Minister of Public Safety and Immigration (No. 2)* 'is a very regrettable and unjustified abdication of judicial responsibility' (*Cases and Materials* (see 14.4.2)). Do you agree?**

14.7.4 THE GRANTING OF HONOURS

The conferment of honours is a matter solely for the Prime Minister and the Sovereign. This is a clear example of a non-justiciable issue which is not an appropriate matter for review by a court.

14.7.5 THE DISSOLUTION OF PARLIAMENT

As we have already seen this prerogative lies with the Crown but, by convention, is exercised at the behest of the Prime Minister — a practice that has been adhered to for over 100 years. If a government is defeated on a vote of confidence, and refuses to leave office, the Sovereign retains the prerogative power to dismiss that government. This has not happened since 1783 and the Queen would need first to call a meeting of the Privy Council.

14.7.6 THE APPOINTMENT OF THE PRIME MINISTER AND DISMISSAL OF MINISTERS

By convention the leader of the majority party should be invited to form a government. However, if there is no outright victor, there may be a hung Parliament. In such circumstances the Queen could exercise her personal choice. Yet problems may arise if none of the parties has a majority and an agreement cannot be reached between them on the formation of a coalition government. For example, in 1931 Prime Minister Mac-Donald, following a disagreement within his own Cabinet, resigned. He was immediately invited by the King to form a national government. This action was criticised because MacDonald had lost the support of his own party and it was claimed that the King was appointing an individual who did not have the support of the Commons as Prime Minister.

What do you think the post-GCHQ cases tell us about the attitudes of the courts towards the Royal prerogative?

14.7.7   RECENT DECISIONS

In answer to **SAQ 140** you probably observed that, since the *GCHQ* decision, the courts have been increasingly willing to challenge the exercise of prerogative powers. Perhaps the best example of this is the decision of the House of Lords in *R v Secretary of State for the Home Department, ex parte Fire Brigades Union* [1995] 2 All ER 244. The background to this case was that the Criminal Justice Act 1988 had been passed to replace the existing non-statutory criminal injuries compensation scheme for the payment of compensation to the victims of violent crime. Section 171(1) of the 1988 Act provided that, 'this Act shall come into force on such day as the Secretary of State may by order made by statutory instrument appoint'. However, because of the escalating costs of providing compensation, the Home Secretary announced that the Government had chosen not to implement the provisions of the Criminal Justice Act 1988 which dealt with compensation — that, instead, it intended to introduce a new (and less generous) tariff-based scheme under which compensation, which was to be paid, would not take account of the loss of earnings or other similar expenses. The Fire Brigade's Union, and a number of other unions whose members were particularly at risk from crimes of violence, complained that they would be unfairly affected by these changes and challenged the Home Secretary's decision by way of judicial review.

The House of Lords held (3–2) that the Home Secretary had acted unlawfully because he had exceeded his powers in introducing the new tariff-based criminal injuries compensation scheme without reference to Parliament. On the powers of the court, Lord Browne-Wilkinson pointed out that, subject to the non-justiciability of certain prerogative powers (and he gave the example of treaty-making powers), 'judicial review is as applicable to decisions taken under prerogative powers as to decisions taken under statutory powers'. Thus, having asserted this general principle, Lord Browne-Wilkinson suggested that on the facts of the case:

> the fact that a scheme approved by Parliament was on the statute book and would come into force as law if and when the Secretary of State so determined . . . [was] directly relevant to the question whether the Secretary of State could in the lawful exercise of prerogative powers both decide to bring in the tariff scheme and refuse properly to exercise his discretion under s. 171(1) . . .. The Secretary of State could only validly exercise the prerogative power to abandon the old scheme and introduce the tariff scheme if, at the same time, he could validly resolve never to bring the statutory provisions and the inconsistent statutory scheme into effect.

Since the Home Secretary was, in practice, seeking to use a prerogative power to repeal provisions in an Act of Parliament, his actions were unlawful and they amounted to 'an abuse of the prerogative power' (Lord Browne-Wilkinson).

ACTIVITY 114

Read the extract from Eric Barendt on the *ex parte Fire Brigades Union* case in *Cases and Materials* (14.4.3).

14.8 Conclusion

The significance of the use of prerogative powers in the British Constitution cannot be underestimated. These non-statutory powers of the Crown still have considerable significance, even as we approach the new millennium. However, to what extent are prerogative powers appropriate in a modern Parliamentary democracy? For example, surely the most momentous decision for any country to make is a declaration of war. Yet, as we discovered earlier, decisions to declare war are not taken by the United Kingdom's Parliament, but rather by the government using its prerogative powers. Thus, when British troops were sent to the Gulf to liberate Kuwait, early in 1991, Tony Benn MP commented: 'This is the first time in the history of this country that British troops have been sent into battle under foreign command using the Royal prerogative on war making, without the House having had an opportunity to express its view on any matter other than the adjournment of the house' (*The Guardian*, 15 January 1991). Parliament's exclusion from, and its lack of involvement in, the making of crucial decisions such as these certainly appears to be rather incongruous with the traditional view that Parliament is 'supreme' or 'sovereign'.

The waging of war (which is seldom formally declared today by combatant States) is an extreme example of the use of a prerogative power, and few governments would be so politically naïve as to drag this country into a full scale armed conflict without considerable support in both Parliament and the country at large. But what of less emotive prerogative powers? The danger of a government abusing its prerogative powers have always been real though, until the *GCHQ* decision, the courts were unwilling to review the exercise of such powers. Even now, post-*GCHQ*, there are still limits to judicial scrutiny, and the courts remain reluctant to assert jurisdiction over prerogative powers relating to non-justiciable matters such as national security, foreign policy matters, the granting of honours, the appointment of Ministers and the dissolution of Parliament.

These examples, which were given by Lord Roskill in *GCHQ*, are essentially *political* rather than *legal* prerogative powers and it is arguable that they are quite properly outside the remit of the courts. After all, political rather than legal considerations would appear to be the appropriate determinants in the event of a hung Parliament or if there is a Commons vote of no confidence in the government and the Prime Minister refuses to resign. The role of the Monarch and exercise of the Royal or personal prerogatives could therefore be crucial in such a constitutional crisis, a prospect which has, in the past at least, concerned some present members of the Government. In 1993, perhaps significantly while still in opposition, the current Secretary of State for Northern Ireland, Mo Mowlan, suggested that it was time to review the Sovereign's power to decide who should be the head of the government in the event of a hung Parliament. She argued that it was wrong that 'it should be the Queen's role effectively to decide who should govern', while her present Cabinet colleague, Jack Straw (the Home Secretary) also called for 'a more limited role for the Monarch' (*The Independent*, 21 January 1993).

Referring to the Royal prerogative, Colin Munro (*Studies in Constitutional Law*, 1987, p. 183) has pointed out that 'there are deficiencies in political accountability' and '[p]erhaps the answer lies in a return to the 1688 solution: legislation to abolish or reform'. In 1991, the Institute for Public Policy Research, in *The Constitution of the United*

Kingdom, advocated abolition as an option, but there is no evidence that such a radical proposal is either workable or has any support in the Cabinet or the country. Reform, however, cannot be ruled out as a possible future option. Press reports suggest that Tony Blair's administration is proposing to remove much of the pomp and ceremony which is normally associated with the annual State Opening of Parliament (*The Sunday Times*, 8 March 1998), so it remains to be seen whether the Government will go any further and reform the Monarch's powers which some defend as a symbolic legacy of Britain's regal past and others view as undemocratic and anachronistic.

CHAPTER FIFTEEN

JUDICIAL REVIEW

15.1 Objectives

By the end of this Chapter you should be able to:

■ identify when a decision will be amenable to judicial review;

■ recognise grounds for an application for judicial review;

■ select appropriate remedies;

■ explain the procedure for an application for judicial review;

■ appreciate the significance of judicial review in the UK Constitution.

15.2 Introduction

Judicial review is concerned with the power of the court to check and control activities and decisions of governmental bodies and agencies, tribunals and inferior courts (and, as we shall see, decisions of some private bodies that affect the public).

Judicial review provides a way of keeping control over people or bodies whose actions and decisions affect the public.

In its reviewing capacity the court is basically looking to see whether a decision-making body has acted '*ultra vires*' or '*intra vires*'. The term '*ultra vires*' means 'without power'; '*intra vires*' means 'within power'. If a decision-making body acts *ultra vires* the reviewing court has the discretion to intervene.

We will look later at the remedies available in judicial review — for present purposes it will assist you to have basic knowledge of the types of court orders available to the reviewing court and their consequences:

(a) **certiorari** will quash, i.e., nullify the decision in question;

(b) **mandamus** compels a decision-maker to carry out a duty;

(c) **prohibition** prevents the decision-maker engaging in *ultra vires* activities;

(d) **declaration** is a statement by the court of what the particular legal issues are;

(e) **injunction** can be either negative, to prevent an action, or mandatory, to compel an action;

(f) **damages** (but rarely applicable).

Unlike appeal cases, the reviewing court is not concerned with the merits of a decision or activity, only with whether the decision or activity is *ultra vires*. Further, it cannot substitute its own decision for that of the decision-making body.

15.3   Preliminary Hurdles

15.3.1   LEAVE TO APPLY

Judicial review is governed by s. 31 of the Supreme Court Act 1981, and Order 53 of the Rules of the Supreme Court 1965 which you will find in the *Supreme Court Practice*, commonly known to practitioners as 'the White book'. We will look into the procedure for applying for judicial review in more detail later. It is essential at this stage, however, to understand the concept of 'applying for leave to apply for judicial review'.

Try and summarise your own definition of the term 'judicial review'.

You might have ventured something along the lines of: 'examination by the courts of activities and decisions of public bodies'. Before a court will review a decision or activity the applicant (either the person actually affected or a pressure group acting on such a person's behalf) has to apply for **leave** to apply for judicial review. This is not as strange as it seems. The application for leave is a way of filtering out those cases which are not amenable to judicial review for one reason or another.

On application for leave to apply for judicial review the court will consider the following factors:

(a) Is the decision itself amenable to judicial review?

(b) Has the right to judicial review been excluded?

(c) Has the applicant sufficient interest in the issue (*locus standi*)?

(d) Do grounds for review exist?

Distinguish between the role of the court in its reviewing capacity with that in its appellate capacity.

In appeal cases, the Court of Appeal (or House of Lords) is looking at the **merits** of the decision under appeal and has the power to substitute another decision if so minded. In judicial review, the court is examining the **decision-making process** itself, rather than the merits of the decision. If that decision-making process is flawed, then the reviewing court can, *inter alia*, quash, that is nullify, the decision under review and thus return the parties to the original, pre-decision position.

Let us consider each of the above factors separately.

15.3.2 IS THE DECISION ITSELF AMENABLE TO JUDICIAL REVIEW?

Basically, only public law issues are amenable to judicial review.

Sometimes it will be obvious that the issue is amenable to judicial review, e.g. a public body making a public law decision.

Difficulties arise when the matter in issue concerns an activity/decision emanating from a private body.

The Court of Appeal decision in *R v Panel on Take-overs and Mergers, ex parte Datafin plc* [1987] QB 815 was warmly welcomed as it stated that a decision emanating from a private body would be reviewable if that body had powers to take decisions that affected the public.

However, two recent cases have seen the courts retreating from *Datafin*. In *R v Disciplinary Committee of the Jockey Club, ex parte Aga Khan* [1993] 1 WLR 909 (see *Cases and Materials* (**15.1.1**)) the Court of Appeal held that a decision of the Jockey Club was not amenable to judicial review because its powers were not governmental in nature and also because the members had agreed to be bound by its rules (i.e., a voluntary contract). However, the Master of the Rolls indicated that Jockey Club decisions may be amenable to judicial review if the applicant was not in a contractual relationship with it. This might include members of the general public, as well as jockeys and trainers etc., who choose not to be bound by the Jockey Club rules.

In *R v Insurance Ombudsman Bureau, ex parte Aegon Life* [1994] COD 426, the Divisional Court held that decisions were not amenable to judicial review if the decision-maker's power was contractual in nature.

The current position is therefore that the decision of a private body can be amenable to judicial review, providing its powers are:

(a)   governmental in nature; and

(b)   those affected are not in a contractual relationship with the decision-making body.

15.3.3 THE RULE ON 'EXCLUSIVITY OF PROCEEDINGS'

The problem facing lawyers when presented with a new case is to decide whether to commence proceedings by writ, summons or judicial review. Private law actions are commenced by writ or summons, public law actions are commenced by way of judicial review. Because of this 'exclusivity' rule, the court has the power to 'strike out' an action if the wrong procedure is used on the grounds that there has been an abuse of process.

O'Reilly v *Mackman* [1983] 2 AC 237 (see *Cases and Materials* (**15.1.2**)) demonstrates the importance of correctly identifying whether you are dealing with a public or private law issue. The case concerned prisoners whose remission had been forfeited by the Board of Visitors. They commenced proceedings by way of private action, i.e., by writ. The House of Lords held that they did not have any private law rights. Their only rights lay in public law and any action should have been commenced by way of judicial review.

Why was the fact that the prisoner's lawyers had commenced by way of private action rather than judicial review so disastrous for the prisoners in *O'Reilly* v *Mackman*?

The prisoners should have commenced by way of Ord. 53. To commence by writ was said to be an abuse of process. Unfortunately, the three-month time limit for applying for judicial review had expired and, consequently, review was no longer available. It is crucial to get it right!

In *R* v *Birmingham City Council, ex parte Dredger* (1993) 91 LGR 532, the Divisional Court took a pragmatic view. The local authority claimed that the matter concerned private law issues. The Divisional Court rejected this, and were influenced greatly by the fact that a denial of judicial review would have left the applicant without alternative remedy.

However, it will not be an abuse of process for someone who is the defendant in private law proceedings taken against them by a public body (i.e., local authority suing a tenant for rent arrears) to make a counter-claim on the basis of public law. *Wandsworth London Borough Council* v *Winder* [1975] AC 461 is an example of such a case.

See also *Roy* v *Kensington and Chelsea and Westminster Family Practitioner Committee* [1992] 1 AC 624. This case concerned a GP suing the FPC for money withheld on the grounds that he had not devoted sufficient time to the NHS, spending too much time on private patients. He commenced an action in private law. The FPC applied for the action to be struck out as an abuse of process, arguing that public law issues arose and judicial review was the correct procedure. The House of Lords decided that there was no abuse of process. Dr Roy had private law rights and the fact that the case also contained public law issues was irrelevant.

The approach in *Roy* has become known as a 'broad approach'. If a person has private law rights as well as public law rights, it is not always necessary to commence by judicial review. In contrast the 'narrow' approach assumes that judicial review is the appropriate forum for all issues involving an public element. Defining these two approaches in *Roy*,

Lord Lowry admitted that it was not always easy to decide which approach should be taken.

A step forward can be seen in the case of *Mercury Communications Ltd* v *Director General of Telecommunication* [1996] 1 All ER 575. The House of Lords, reversing the decision of the Court of Appeal, held that it was important to be flexible in the distinction between public and private law. The important question to bear in mind was whether commencing an action other than by judicial review was **in fact** an abuse of process. In *Mercury*, their Lordships held that the plaintiff's procedure (of originating summons rather than judicial review) was at least as well suited to the determination of the issues as judicial review. They held, therefore, that there was no abuse of process.

15.3.4 HAS JUDICIAL REVIEW BEEN EXCLUDED EITHER EXPRESSLY OR IMPLIEDLY?

15.3.4.1 Express exclusion

Sometimes a clause in a statute will attempt to exclude the right to judicial review. For example, the Act may state, 'The decision of the Minister shall not be called into question'.

The reviewing courts do not like their jurisdiction to be excluded and so when faced with such a clause the court will decide whether in fact it was really Parliament's intention that they would not be able to intervene in any decision made under the Act; or whether Parliament's intention was to restrict rights of appeal rather than access to judicial review.

Some attempts at exclusion will never oust the court's jurisdiction as the following cases demonstrate. In *R* v *Medical Appeal Tribunal, ex parte Gilmore* [1957] 1 QB 574 it was held that a clause stating that a decision 'shall be final' will never exclude the court's jurisdiction to review. Again in *Anisminic Ltd* v *Foreign Compensation Commission* [1969] 2 AC 147 it was held that a clause stating that a decision 'shall not be questioned' will not exclude the court's jurisdiction to review where the decision-maker has made an error of law that affects their power to decide (see later).

The court may decide, however, that its power to review has been effectively excluded by the wording of a statute. In the case of *R* v *Registrar of Companies, ex parte Central Bank of India* [1968] QB 1114 a clause stated that if the Registrar of Companies issued a certificate to the effect that he had complied with all necessary procedure this would 'be conclusive evidence' that all conditions had been complied with. The court decided that this effectively precluded it from examining any evidence, preventing it from examining whether the decision-maker had been *ultra vires* (see below).

Is it possible to reconcile *R* v *Registrar of Companies, ex parte Central Bank of India* with *Anisminic Ltd* v *Foreign Compensation Commission*? If not, do you think the former case was wrongly decided?

If you found it impossible to reconcile *Central Bank of India* with *Anisminic* do not despair! You are not alone. Many academics point to the potential absurdity that would occur where a decision-maker has been *ultra vires* — but the courts being prevented from reviewing the decision as the result of the kind of exclusion in *R* v *Registrar of Companies, ex parte Central Bank of India*.

15.3.4.2 Implied exclusion

Even where there is no express attempt in a statute to exclude judicial review the courts may decide they are impliedly excluded where an alternative remedy exists. However, the court will have discretion to review even where there is an alternative remedy available if the case involves (*inter alia*) serious illegalities or would lead to serious delay or an unsatisfactory outcome for the applicant.

15.3.5 HAS THE APPLICANT THE NECESSARY SUFFICIENT INTEREST (*LOCUS STANDI*)?

RSC, Ord. 53, r. 3(7), states:

> The Court shall not grant leave unless it considers that the applicant has sufficient interest in the matter to which the application relates.

15.3.5.1 Individual applicants

The leading case is *Inland Revenue Commissioners* v *National Federation of Self-Employed and Small Businesses Ltd* [1982] AC 617 — commonly known as the Fleet Street casuals case. The NFSSB was attempting to challenge the Revenue's grant of a tax amnesty to Fleet Street casual workers on the grounds that it was illegal. The House of Lords held that NFSSB did not have *locus standi* to challenge the Revenue's decision with regard to another group of taxpayers.

Importantly, the House of Lords stated that the question of *locus standi* should be looked at in two stages:

(a) at the application for leave to apply for judicial review; and

(b) at the hearing itself.

At the first stage, only cases where the applicant clearly does not have sufficient interest would be rejected. At the second stage, however, a more detailed look at the applicant's 'standing' should take place — it then becomes important to examine the merits of the case on the basis that the clearer it was that the applicants had good grounds for review, the more likely it was that the applicant had the necessary *locus standi*.

Each case must therefore be considered on its own particular legal and factual issues. But there are some guidelines offered by *Cane* [1992].

(a) Look at case law — does the applicant fall into a category of persons previously been held to have sufficient interest?

(b) Look at the statute in question — this might state which people can challenge decisions;

(c) Look at the nature of the complaint — it might be patently obvious that the applicant does or does not have sufficient interest.

(d) How serious is the 'wrong'? The more serious, the more likely the applicant will be held to have sufficient interest.

(e) The courts do not like the possibility of there being a lacuna in the legal system — if there is a chance that an aggrieved person will not have an alternative means of challenging the decision in question, the more likely the courts will find that person to have *locus standi*.

SAQ 144

What is the purpose of the standing requirements?

Their purpose is simply to 'filter out' unmeritorious, frivolous or trivial applications and thereby to save the court time.

15.3.5.2 Pressure groups as applicants

What is the position with regard to pressure groups applying for judicial review on another's behalf? Clearly a pressure group may not fulfil the criteria of being personally affected by the decision or activity in question.

In *R v Secretary of State for the Environment, ex parte Rose Theatre Trust Co.* [1990] 1 QB 504 it was held that the Trust did not have *locus standi* as the question of standing should be determined on the basis of whether the applicant has personal interest.

This case concerned the unearthing by builders of the remains of the 17th century Rose Theatre, famous for its productions of Shakespeare's plays. The Trust Co. was formed by people who wished the Secretary of State for the Environment to schedule the site as a monument of national importance and thus protect the site from the builders. The Secretary of State refused to do so. The court held that the act of forming a company did not in itself give the members *locus standi*. If the individual members did not have standing, neither, then, did the company.

The Minister's powers emanated from discretionary powers given to him under the Ancient Monuments and Archaeological Areas Act 1979 and it was held that there was nothing in this statute that gave an ordinary individual sufficient interest. Paul Craig (1994) suggests that this is one area of Ministerial decision that is not reviewable.

The Rose Theatre case was seen as a setback to other pressure groups. More recent cases, however, have seen the courts taking what Richard Gordon QC calls an expansionist view towards pressure groups having standing.

In *R v Her Majesty's Inspectorate of Pollution, ex parte Greenpeace Ltd* [1994] 1 WLR 570, Greenpeace was challenging the decision of Her Majesty's Inspectorate of Pollution's decision to allow a 'variation' of British Nuclear Fuel's Sellafield licence on the grounds of illegality and irrationality (see later). Judicial review was refused as the grounds were not substantiated. However, Otton J held that Greenpeace did actually have standing to apply for review. He took into account the fact that Greenpeace is a responsible, well-resourced public-interest group, committed to broad public interests. Greenpeace International has almost 5 million supporters world-wide. Greenpeace UK has over 400,000 supporters, about 2,500 of these living in the Cumbrian region where the THORP plant was situated — the local element being very significant. Account was also taken of the fact that Greenpeace International had been given consultative status by several UN bodies and had observer status with many international organisations. It was therefore in a much better position to present a case than an ordinary individual.

The House of Lords case *R* v *Secretary of State for Employment, ex parte Equal Opportunities Commission* [1995] 1 AC 1 concerned equal opportunities. The applicants alleged that the Employment Protection (Consolidation) Act 1978 was discriminatory (albeit indirectly) against female employees in that it offered less protection to part-time workers (who tend to be women) than to full-time workers.

The person affected would not ordinarily have been entitled to judicial review because the statute provides that challenges should be dealt with by the Employment Appeal Tribunal and judicial review is not normally available in cases where an alternative remedy exists.

The Secretary of State argued, *inter alia*, that the EOC did not have *locus standi*.

However, Lord Keith pointed out that under s. 53(1) of the Sex Discrimination Act 1975 the Commission had a duty to work towards eliminating discrimination. In applying for judicial review the EOC was carrying out its duty and purpose under the 1975 Act and this gave it sufficient interest.

In *R* v *Secretary of State for Foreign and Commonwealth Affairs, ex parte World Development Movement Ltd* [1995] 1 WLR 386, the WDM successfully challenged Douglas Hurd's authorisation of £234 million aid for the Pergau dam project in Malaysia on the grounds that the project was 'economically unsound' and therefore a misuse of funds from the Overseas Development Administration budget.

The Foreign Secretary's power was derived from the Overseas Development and Co-operation Act 1980 which empowers the Foreign Secretary to use the aid budget for 'promoting the development or maintaining the economy' of a country or improving the welfare of its population. The project did not meet these criteria.

ACTIVITY116

Read the extract from the case in *Cases and Materials* (15.1.3.1). Whom did the WDM purport to represent?

You should have concluded that one significance of this case was the fact that the WDM was held to have standing even though it was not representing the personal interests of people directly affected by the project. Its claim was to represent broader public interests in Third World issues.

The following factors were considered:

(a)   the importance of vindicating the rule of law;

(b)   the fact that the issues raised were important;

(c)   absence of any other challenger.

The latest case on *locus standi* is *R v Somerset County Council and ARC Southern Ltd, ex parte Dixon* [1997] COD 323. Sedley J held that public law is about 'wrongs' rather than 'rights' and that a person or a group may be in a very good position to bring the attention of the court to a 'wrong' notwithstanding the fact that they are not themselves sufficiently affected.

As you can see, there is no easy blueprint for establishing whether someone or a group has *locus standi*. There is, however, evidence of a liberalising trend. The Law Commissioner's proposed reforms to judicial review (*Administrative Law: Judicial Review and Statutory Appeals*, Law Com. No. 226, (1994)) reflects this trend by suggesting a two-tier test for standing. One tier for the applicant directly affected by a decision, the other for pressure groups and/or individuals applying for review in the public interest.

Do you agree that the expansionist view towards *locus standi* is to be welcomed? What advantages do you see?

The expansionist attitude adopted by the courts in relation to *locus standi* is arguably advantageous in that it widens the possibility of more effective checks and controls of the activities of public bodies, including, of course, the activities of government Ministers whose actions may remain unchecked for want of an application by someone directly affected by the decision, by bodies with more expertise than the average lay person.

15.3.6   DO GROUNDS FOR REVIEW EXIST?

Lord Diplock in *Council of Civil Service Unions v Minister for the Civil Service* [1985] AC 374 (commonly referred to as the *GCHQ* case) provided a useful three-fold classification of the grounds, any one of which will render a decision *ultra vires*:

(a)   illegality;

(b)   irrationality;

(c)   procedural impropriety.

You should, of course, bear in mind, however, that the grounds for judicial review are neither mutually exclusive nor exhaustive. You will find when you become more familiar with the grounds that they often overlap.

Remember that all we are basically doing is looking to see whether a decision-maker is acting *ultra vires* – if the decision is not *ultra vires* there are no grounds for review.

15.4 Grounds for Review

15.4.1 ILLEGALITY

A decision-maker cannot exercise any power that has not been conferred on him or her by law. Anything in excess or any abuse of powers conferred will be *ultra vires*.

Powers are often conferred by statute. By interpreting the original statute the court will decide whether the decision in question is *ultra vires*. It may be *ultra vires* for one of the following reasons:

15.4.1.1 The decision or activity is in excess of the powers conferred

In *Attorney-General v Fulham Corporation* [1921] 1 Ch 440 the Corporation was empowered under statute to maintain wash-houses but this power did not extend to the operation of a laundry.

Similarly in *Mixnam's Properties Ltd v Chertsey Urban District Council* [1965] AC 735 the Council had power to run a caravan site but this power did not extend to the imposition of regulations regarding contractual lettings between caravan tenants.

In *Bromley London Borough Council v Greater London Council* [1983] 1 AC 768 the House of Lords decided that the GLC was *ultra vires* in imposing higher rates on taxpayers in order to subsidise London Transport fares. Statute required that the services be run 'economically' but this did not extend to the subsidising of fares through higher rates.

R v Secretary of State for the Home Department, ex parte Leech [1994] QB 198 concerned a prisoner's rights of confidentiality of mail from his or her solicitor. Rule 33 of the Prison Rules 1964 gives prison authorities power to read and circumvent (if necessary) letters to and from prisoners to check they were bona fide. This did not extend to checking communications that did not breach security, and hence did not extend to letters to and from solicitors.

We have already considered *R v Secretary of State for Foreign and Commonwealth Affairs, ex parte World Development Movement Ltd* (see **15.3.5.2** above).

15.4.1.2 Abuse of power

In *Municipal Council of Sydney v Campbell* [1925] AC 338 the Council had power to compulsorily purchase land required for 'carrying out improvements in or remodelling any portion of the city'. It was held to be an abuse of that power to acquire land to obtain for itself an expected increase in the value of that land as the result of development of adjoining land.

Padfield v Minister of Agriculture, Fisheries and Food [1968] AC 997 holds that Ministers are under a duty to use discretionary powers to promote Parliament's intention, and will be acting *ultra vires* if they act counter to the policy and objects of the Act in question.

R v Secretary of State for the Home Department, ex parte Fire Brigades Union [1995] 2 AC 513 concerned a power conferred on the Home Secretary under s. 171(1) of the Criminal Justice Act 1988 to place the existing criminal injuries compensation scheme on a statutory basis. The House of Lords upheld the Court of Appeal decision, holding that it was an abuse of his prerogative power to introduce a radically different scheme unless empowered to do so by statute.

15.4.1.3   Errors of law and/or fact

Courts are more willing to review errors of law than errors of fact. Judicial review is not seen to be a suitable forum for factual disputes which involve cross-examination of witnesses etc.

Anisminic Ltd v *Foreign Compensation Commission* [1969] 2 AC 147 is the leading case on error of law.

Read *Anisminic* in *Cases and Materials* (15.2.1.1) in order that you fully understand the facts of this case.

Prior to this case there was an important distinction between errors of law 'going to jurisdiction' (jurisdictional errors of law) and errors of law 'within jurisdiction'.

A decision-maker who erroneously interpreted the law as providing a power which it did not was said to make a 'jurisdictional error of law'. Any decision taken under that power would therefore automatically be *ultra vires* because the decision-maker did not have power to decide in the first place.

An error of law within jurisdiction is the type of error made by a decision-maker who errs in law whilst exercising powers conferred. This type of error will not automatically render the decision *ultra vires*. The courts have discretion to intervene if the error of law appeared on the record of the decision. We shall cover this in **15.4.1.4**.

The House of Lords decision in *Anisminic Ltd* v *Foreign Compensation Commission* makes it (in most cases) unnecessary to make the above distinction. Their lordships decided that errors of law could be treated as going to jurisdiction even when it was an error made in the **process** of exercising power conferred rather than an error in deciding whether the power existed.

By considering issues and asking themselves questions that they were not empowered to ask (i.e., the nationality of the successor in title) the Foreign Compensation Commission had made an error in law which their lordships decided took them outside their jurisdiction.

Read *R* v *Lord President of the Privy Council, ex parte Page* [1993] 1 All ER 97 in *Cases and Materials* (15.2.1.1). Does every error of law affect a decision-maker's jurisdiction?

It would appear that all errors of law are jurisdictional errors, with just a few exceptions, notably the decisions of High Court judges and above (*Re Racal Communications* [1981] AC 374) and university visitors (*ex parte Page*). Bear in mind, however, that even if there has been a jurisdictional error of law the court may be precluded from reviewing if there is a successful exclusion clause as in *R v Registrar of Companies, ex parte Central Bank of India* [1986] QB 1114.

15.4.1.4   Error of law on the face of the record

Following the decision in *Anisminic Ltd v Foreign Compensation Commission* [1969] 2 AC 147 the distinction between errors of law on the face of the record and jurisdictional errors of law is probably rendered obsolete. However, their lordships in *Anisminic* did leave open the possibility of a decision-maker making an error of law within jurisdiction. As mentioned above, judicial review may be available where a body is acting within its powers but has erred in law whilst doing so and that error appears on the record relating to the decision.

In *R v Northumberland Compensation Appeal Tribunal, ex parte Shaw* [1952] 1 KB 388 a statute provided that all hospital employees who were made redundant should be paid compensation. The amount of compensation was to be calculated on the basis of not only the length of service in the particular hospital, but also to include periods of employment in any other local government service. The amount of compensation awarded by the tribunal reflected only the period of employment in the hospital and ignored previous service in other local government departments. The basis of the calculation was stated on the record of the tribunal's decision. The decision was therefore quashed.

This ground for judicial review is potentially very significant (if the distinction between jurisdictional and non-jurisdictional errors of law does still exist). because of the provisions of the Tribunals and Inquiries Act 1992 which compels tribunals to give reasons for their decisions, such reasons forming part of the record. It is therefore clear when an error of law has been made by referring to the record of the proceedings.

15.4.1.5   Errors of fact

An error of fact can also be challenged if the error is jurisdictional. A jurisdictional error of fact is where the existence of a particular state of affairs is a condition precedent to a decision-maker having jurisdiction in the first place. In *White and Collins v Minister of Health* [1939] 2 KB 838 the Minister had jurisdiction to order compulsory purchase only if the land in question did not form part of a park. On the facts, the land did not form part of a park and therefore his decision was *ultra vires*.

Cases involving non-jurisdictional questions of fact are subject to review on the unreasonableness standard and on the ground that the decision-maker has failed to give proper weight to the available evidence, or has refused to take account of evidence.

In *R v Secretary of State for the Home Department, ex parte Khawaja* [1984] AC 74 (see **Cases and Materials (15.2.1.2)**) it was held that there are three categories of 'factual' issues that are reviewable:

(a)   Jurisdictional questions of fact, as in *White and Collins v Minister of Health* and discussed above.

(b)   Non-jurisdictional questions of fact — where there is no condition precedent, judicial review may be available on the facts if it appears that a decision-maker has considered the facts and then decided unreasonably.

(c)   Non-jurisdictional question of fact — there may also be grounds for judicial review on the facts if the decision-maker has failed to give proper weight to all relevant facts when coming to his or her decision.

15.4.1.6   Unauthorised delegation

There is a presumption known as *delegatus non potest delegare* – a delegate cannot delegate his or her authority. Where power is delegated to someone, e.g., by statute, that person cannot then sub-delegate that power to someone else.

In *Vine* v *National Dock Labour Board* [1957] AC 488 the Board had power to dismiss dockers, but a sub-delegation of that power to a disciplinary committee which then dismissed Vine was *ultra vires* and the dismissal was held to be unlawful.

A more lenient attitude is taken towards administrative functions.

Read *Carltona Ltd* v *Commissioners of Works* [1943] 2 All ER 560 in *Cases and Materials* (15.2.1.3).

Make a note of the position with regard to sub-delegation within central government departments.

The *Carltona* **principle** acknowledges that there will be widespread sub-delegation in central government departments — this is unavoidable, it would be practically impossible for a governmental Minister to exercise all powers personally.

Statutes have expressly authorised extensive delegation in local government administration, e.g., the Local Government Act 1972.

15.4.2   IRRATIONALITY

Statutes conferring power on, for example, a Minister, often allow the decision-maker a certain amount of discretion. Grounds for judicial review can arise when that decision-maker does not exercise discretion properly or abuses the discretion conferred.

15.4.2.1   Failure to exercise discretion properly

A decision can be challenged when a decision-maker either:

    (a)   did not exercise discretion sufficiently free from outside influences, or

    (b)   abused the discretion conferred.

Let's have a look at grounds of review afforded as a result of the decision-maker failing to exercise discretion and/or allowing outside influences to decide for them. There are a number of situations when this will be the case, i.e., when:

    (i)   the decision has been made on the basis that the decision-maker is limited by some outside rule;

(ii)   the decision-maker does not make the decision personally but allows someone else to decide for him or her, i.e., there is unauthorised delegation of power (this of course also gives grounds for review in the illegality heading);

(iii) the decision-maker has developed a policy to aid decision-making, but has then refused to make exceptions.

Let us examine each of these separately.

15.4.2.2   Acting as though limited by external rules

Here, the decision-maker fails to exercise any discretion at all believing himself or herself to be bound by some external rule.

For example, a decision-maker who is required to take certain factors into consideration should have regard to the factors and take them into consideration rather than being dictated by those factors (*R v Stepney Corporation* [1902] 1 KB 317).

15.4.2.3   Unauthorised delegation

See **15.4.1.6**.

Compose your own definition of 'discretion'

A good working definition of 'discretion' in the context of administrative law is as follows:

> Where a person is given discretion to decide, that person is expected to exercise sound judgment after considering all relevant factors whilst keeping an open mind sufficiently free from external influence.

Any definition that includes elements of the above is therefore on the right track!

15.4.2.4   Decision-maker applies policy without flexibility

A decision-maker who is conferred with discretionary powers is expected to consider each case on its own particular set of facts and merits. Where decision-makers have developed their own policies and applied them rigidly, without considering whether the particular case has extenuating factors which would necessitate them making an exception, this will give grounds for review.

In *R v London County Council, ex parte Corrie* [1918] 1 KB 68 the council altered its policy with regard to sales of literature in parks. Existing permits were revoked and the council issued a statement to the effect that no further consents would be granted. The applicant was refused permission to sell a pamphlet, the council stating that no exceptions would ever be made, even in the most deserving cases. The reviewing court held that the council should have given consideration to the merits of the applicant's case.

Read *British Oxygen Co. Ltd* v *Minister of Technology* [1971] AC 610 in *Cases and Materials* (15.2.2.1). Make a note of the grounds for review and whether the application was successful.

You should have found the following:

British Oxygen Co. Ltd v *Minister of Technology* to be a case where a decision-making body had adopted a policy that was held by the House of Lords to be within the purpose of the Act of Parliament conferring the discretion. Their lordships could not find inflexibility because the decision-maker in question had indicated that they would be prepared to make exceptions to their policy on application involving 'novel' features.

15.4.2.5   Abuse of discretion

Courts will intervene if a decision-maker:

(a)   uses power for an improper purpose or to frustrate the legislative purpose;

(b)   makes a decision on the basis of irrelevant factors or fails to take account of relevant factors;

(c)   reaches a decision that is unreasonable in itself.

Let us examine each of these separately.

15.4.2.6   Use of power for an improper purpose or to frustrate the legislative purpose

There is much crossover with illegality.

Please read *Municipal Council of Sydney* v *Campbell* [1925] AC 399 and *Padfield* v *Minister of Agriculture, Fisheries and Food* [1968] AC 997 in *Cases and Materials* (15.2.2.2).

Ensure you understand why these cases fall into both categories, i.e., illegality and irrationality.

Municipal Council of Sydney v *Campbell* is an example of **illegality** in that the Council were abusing the powers conferred and **irrationality** in that they were failing to exercise discretion conferred in the way intended as they were guided by irrelevant factors.

Similarly, *Padfield* v *Minister of Agriculture, Fisheries and Food* is an example of **illegality** in that the Minister was abusing the powers conferred and thwarting legislative purpose and **irrationality** in that he was taking irrelevant factors into consideration.

15.4.2.7   The giving of reasons and irrationality

One element in the *Padfield* case was that the Minister had failed to provide reasons for his decision. His decision was, of course, held to thwart legislative purpose, but it was also held that if a decision-maker fails to give reasons for his or her decision the court may decide that there was no rational basis for that decision.

Padfield should be read in conjunction with *R* v *Secretary of State for Trade and Industry, ex parte Lonhro plc* [1989] 1 WLR 525 which modifies *Padfield* by stating that failure to give reasons will render a decision irrational only if all the available evidence points overwhelmingly to the decision-maker in question reaching a particular decision and the decision-maker then reaches a completely, unexpectedly, different decision.

Further, where a decision-maker fails to give good reasons for a decision, that decision can be challenged.

15.4.2.8   Forming decision on basis of irrelevancies or ignoring relevant factors

In *Roberts* v *Hopwood* [1925] AC 578 the House of Lords held that the socialist Poplar Borough Council had not taken into account the interests of ratepayers whilst exercising its discretion with regard to the level of employees' wages. *Bromley London Borough Council* v *Greater London Council* [1983] 1 AC 768 is also relevant.

In *R* v *Somerset County Council, ex parte Fewings* [1995] 1 WLR 1037, the local authority had imposed a ban on hunting on ethical grounds. The Court of Appeal said that the ban was unlawful if not imposed for the 'benefit, improvement or development' of the land pursuant to s. 122(1) of the Local Government Act 1972. By considering moral and ethical issues, the Council had taken irrelevant factors into consideration. The ban was therefore *ultra vires*. Can you see how this case also fits into the 'illegality' category?

Read *R* v *Secretary of State for Foreign and Commonwealth Affairs, ex parte World Development Movement Ltd* in *Cases and Materials* (15.1.3.1) making a note of the grounds for review.

The grounds for judicial review in *R* v *Secretary of State for Foreign and Commonwealth Affairs, ex parte World Development Movement Ltd* were as follows:

(a) Acting in excess of powers conferred and thwarting legislative purpose — the Foreign Secretary only had power to give financial assistance for 'sound development projects' — the Pergau Dam was not a sound development project — 'sound' was interpreted to mean 'economically sound', the project was anything but, an alternative scheme would have been £100 million cheaper.

(b) Taking irrelevant factors into consideration — the Foreign Secretary was guided by political factors, wishing to promote the UK's relationship with Malaysia.

15.4.2.9 Unreasonableness

Grounds for review also arise when a decision-maker reaches a decision that no reasonable person would have made. The leading authority is *Associated Provincial Picture Houses Ltd* v *Wednesbury Corporation* [1948] 1 KB 223. The Corporation granted a licence to the plaintiffs allowing them to operate on Sundays, conditional on them not allowing admission to children under 15. The plaintiffs argued that the condition was *ultra vires* on the grounds of unreasonableness. The Court of Appeal held that it was not unreasonable and stated that the test is not whether the court believes the decision to be so. The test is whether it is the sort of decision that a reasonable decision-maker would come to.

R v *Greenwich London Borough Council, ex parte Cedar Holdings* [1983] RA 17 holds that a decision is unreasonable if it is the kind of decision that is so outrageous that no right thinking person would support it.

See *R* v *Ministry of Defence, ex parte Smith* [1996] 1 All ER 260 (see *Cases and Materials* (**15.2.2.3**)) in which the Court of Appeal held that it was not unreasonable for homosexuals to be banned from the Armed Forces.

Unreasonableness, per se, is therefore a very high threshold test. Two standards of *Wednesbury* unreasonableness have emerged from the *ex parte Smith* case:

(a) Super-*Wednesbury* — involving 'soft-edged' questions, such as administrative only decisions. The courts are unwilling to intervene and take a very low-intensity approach.

(b) Cases involving more important issues, such as human rights or 'hard-edged' issues. The courts are more willing to intervene and exercise supervisory powers.

(See also Ivan Hare's article, 'Military Bases and Military Biases' (1996) 55 Cambridge Law Journal 179, in **Cases and Materials** (**15.2.2.3**), for discussion of the *ex parte Smith* case.)

However, in the case of *R* v *Cambridge Health Authority, ex parte B* [1995] 1 WLR 898 which involved a 10 year old girl dying from leukaemia, the Court of Appeal were still unwilling to intervene, even though the issues concerned what could arguably be the most important human right of all — the right to 'life' itself. The girl concerned had a 10–20 per cent chance of survival if she received a second bone marrow transplant and chemotherapy. Hospital doctors thought that the cost of the treatment far outweighed her chance of survival (£15,000 for chemotherapy and £60,000 for the bone marrow transplant). Her father sought judicial review. At first instance, Laws J held that the cost/benefit analysis used by the authority was not a sufficient reason to deprive the child of her right to life. The Court of Appeal, allowing the health authority's appeal, held that the matter was not justiciable. This indicates that the courts will not become involved in issues concerning allocation of scarce economic/financial resources even when human life is at stake.

Do you think it is possible for the courts to examine a decision for unreasonableness so objectively? Some people argue that judges inevitably bring their own personal views into their judgment and that it is impossible to operate in a 'vacuum'. If this is correct is the distinction between review and appeal blurred?

15.4.3 PROCEDURAL IMPROPRIETY

There are two heads to this category:

(a) The decision-maker has failed to observe procedural rules as stipulated in a statute or secondary legislation.

(b) The decision-maker has failed to observe the rules of natural justice or failed to act fairly.

Let us examine each of these separately.

15.4.3.1 Failure to observe express procedural rules

The consequence of such a breach depends on whether the rules themselves are classed as **mandatory** or **directory** in nature. This distinction is important. If the rules are held to be mandatory then breach of the rules will lead to the decision being quashed on an application for judicial review. If the rules are directory then the decision is not automatically *ultra vires*.

Unfortunately, Acts of Parliament do not always stipulate whether the rules are mandatory or directory.

Here are some examples of rules which have been held to be mandatory:

(a) where the rule involves giving affected persons prior notice of a decision in order that they have sufficient time to make representations and objections;

(b) where the rule involves the giving of notice of the right to appeal against a decision;

(c) where the rule involves publication of a decision within a stipulated time;

(d) where the breach involves any failure to observe rules relating to granting of planning permission as set out in the Town and Country Planning General Regulations 1992.

Here are some examples of rules held to be directory:

(a)   where the breach is of a trivial nature;

(b)   where those affected have not suffered substantial prejudice;

(c)   where substantial public inconvenience would be caused if the rule was held to be mandatory.

Why is it important to recognise the distinction between mandatory and directory procedural rules?

Breach of mandatory rules would render any decision *ultra vires* and the reviewing court could quash any decision made in breach of the mandatory rules.

This is not the case if the procedural rules are directory in nature. Where stipulated procedure is only directory by nature it is only there for purpose of guidance and does not have to be followed to the letter. Breach of directory rules will, therefore, rarely render a decision *ultra vires*.

15.4.3.2   Failure to observe the rules of natural justice and failure to act fairly

The rules of procedure and laws of evidence governing court proceedings do not apply to other proceedings, i.e., tribunals. The courts have therefore introduced standards to ensure that such proceedings are conducted fairly. These standards are known as the rules of natural justice. The rules embody two concepts. First, *audi alteram partem* – which means that a person should not be condemned without a fair hearing. Second, *nemo judex in causa sua* – which means that no one should act as judge in any matter if he or she has some kind of vested interest in the decision as all decisions should be free from bias.

15.4.3.3   The right to a fair hearing – audi alteram partem

When will this apply? Prior to the House of Lords decision in *Ridge* v *Baldwin* [1964] AC 40 it was accepted that the rules of natural justice applied to decisions of a judicial nature, but confusion reigned over whether these rules also applied to administrative or executive decisions. *Ridge* v *Baldwin* (see **Cases and Materials (15.2.3.1)**) was particularly significant in the history of the development of natural justice. Lord Reid said that the rules of natural justice can apply to administrative or executive decisions and should always be adhered to in the following types of situations:

(a)   where someone is dismissed from office; or

(b)   where someone is of deprived membership of a professional or social body; or

(c)   where someone is deprived of property rights or privileges.

This was taken a stage further in *Schmidt* v *Secretary of State for Home Affairs* [1969] 2 Ch 149. Lord Denning MR stated that there was now no distinction between 'judicial' and 'administrative' decisions and that the rules of natural justice applied wherever an individual has some 'right, interest or legitimate expectation'.

Cases subsequent to *Ridge* v *Baldwin* have introduced the concept of 'the duty to act fairly'. This was first introduced by Lord Parker CJ in *Re HK (An Infant)* [1967] 2 QB 617. The concept is sometimes used synonymously with 'natural justice', but it has also been used to describe a less onerous burden on the makers of decisions when the full rules of natural justice do not apply.

In *McInnes* v *Onslow-Fane* [1978] 1 WLR 1520, Megarry V-C said that natural justice was a flexible term which imposed different requirements according to the nature of the case. The closer a decision came to being termed 'judicial' the more applicable the full elements of the rules of natural justice. However, the closer a decision came to being 'administrative' in nature it was more appropriate to talk about the requirement of 'fairness'.

Let us take an example. Consideration of an application for a licence is an administrative task – the full rules of natural justice do not apply – the requirement is that of fair consideration of the application. In contrast, revocation of a licence is more of a judicial decision – it is taking away someone's rights – the requirement is therefore for the full elements of the rules of natural justice.

15.4.3.4   What constitutes a fair hearing?

As indicated above, the criteria for 'fairness' will differ according to each particular type of case. Where the full rules of natural justice apply a fair hearing will be expected to consist of the following elements:

(a)   adequate notice **must** be given to the person affected;

(b)   the person affected **must** be informed of the full case against him or her;

(c)   adequate time **must** be allowed for that person to prepare his or her own case;

(d)   the affected person **must** be allowed the opportunity to put forward his or her own case;

(e)   the decision-maker **may** be required to give reasons for his or her decision;

(f)   the affected person **may** be able to cross-examine witnesses;

(g)   the affected person **may** be entitled to legal representation.

Did you note the distinction between 'must be' and 'may be'?

In *Ridge* v *Baldwin*, the Chief Constable of Brighton was successful in his claim that the rules of natural justice had been breached as a result of his dismissal without being allowed a hearing and the opportunity to represent himself and answer the case against him. Lord Reid said that the right to a hearing existed whenever someone was going to be deprived of an office of employment or whose reputation was to be damaged in some way.

15.4.3.5   Does a 'fair hearing' always necessitate an oral hearing?

It is not always necessary for the hearing to be oral — sometimes written representations will satisfy the rules of natural justice or the duty to act fairly. In *R* v *Race Relations Board, ex parte Selvarajan* [1975] 1 WLR 1686 it was held that the Race Relations Board was acting fairly in considering written witness statements as opposed to allowing an oral hearing as the facts in the case were not in dispute.

Do you think the right to an oral hearing would exist in a case where the evidence consists of verbal evidence and/or where the facts themselves are in dispute? Or would the rules of natural justice be satisfied by the decision-maker considering written representations?

Case law suggests that written representations will suffice when the facts are not in dispute. Where this is not the case then the requirements of natural justice would seem to stipulate an oral hearing.

15.4.3.6 When will a decision-maker be required to give reasons for a decision?

Obviously it will assist a person affected by a decision to know the reasons behind the decision. The reasons themselves may provide grounds for review if, for example, the decision-maker has taken account of irrelevant factors or failed to take account of relevant factors. The giving of reasons may also assist a person to prepare his/her own case.

There is, however, no common law duty (as yet!) imposed on decision-makers to give reasons. But a series of recent cases have seen courts imposing this duty in the very interests of fairness. In *R v Civil Service Appeal Board, ex parte Cunningham* [1991] 4 All ER 310 the Master of the Rolls imposed a duty to give reasons on the CSAB.

In *R v Secretary of State for the Home Department, ex parte Doody* [1993] 3 WLR 154, Lord Mustill said that the Secretary of State had a duty to provide reasons as to the term of a life sentence. The prisoner concerned could challenge the sentence imposed only if it could be shown to be based on flawed reasoning.

In *R v Higher Education Funding Council, ex parte Institute of Dental Surgery* [1994] 1 WLR 242 Sedley J stated that there would be a 'breach of independent legal obligation' where reasons were not given in matters of importance. However, this duty to give reasons would only arise if fairness demanded that reasons be given or if the decision appears aberrant.

This was confirmed in *R v Mayor & Burgesses of the Royal Borough of Kensington, ex parte Grillo* (1996) April (1) Admin LR 165. Neill LJ in the Court of Appeal said:

> There may come a time when English law does impose a general obligation on administrative authorities to give reasons for their decisions but there is no such requirement at present.

SAQ 150

Can you think of how failure to give reasons might overlap with an area we have already discussed?

A failure to give reasons can give grounds under the catergory of irrationality. Do you recall *Padfield v Minister of Agriculture, Fisheries and Food* [1968] AC 997 and *R v Secretary of State for Trade and Industry, ex parte Lonrho plc* [1989] 1 WLR 525 discussed above? If not then take another look at them now.

A failure to give reasons also comes under the category of procedural impropriety in that the rules of natural justice may be breached if an affected person does not know the reasons behind a decision. Knowledge of the reasons upon which a decision is based may give grounds for review if it can be shown that there is some flaw in the reasoning. Cases like *R v Secretary of State for the Home Department, ex parte Doody* therefore have seen courts ordering reasons to be given in the interests of fairness.

(See also *R v Parole Board, ex parte Wilson* [1992] QB 740 in *Cases and Materials* (15.2.3.2).)

15.4.3.7 Cross-examination of witnesses

If the rules of natural justice or the duty to act fairly demand an oral hearing, is there the right to cross-examine witnesses? In *R v Board of Visitors of Hull Prison, ex parte St Germain (No. 2)* [1979] 1 WLR 1401 it was held that where witnesses were giving hearsay evidence (which is normally inadmissible in criminal proceedings in court), fairness may dictate allowing the person affected the opportunity to cross-examine, but in cases involving prisoners the Board of Visitors has discretion to refuse cross-examination if it would cause disruption.

In the House of Lords case *Bushell v Secretary of State for the Environment* [1981] AC 75, Lord Diplock said that whether fairness demands the opportunity to cross-examine witnesses depends on all the circumstances of each individual case, for example, the type and purpose of, and the issues involved in, the particular hearing and the type of evidence involved.

15.4.3.8 The right to legal representation

There is no **right** to legal representation and the courts have upheld statutory rules denying legal representation (*Maynard v Osmond* [1977] QB 240).

In cases where there are no statutory rules covering legal representation, case law again shows that the courts will uphold rules denying legal representation.

In *Pett v Greyhound Racing Association Ltd* [1969] 1 QB 125, it was held that legal representation should be a **right** in cases involving livelihood and reputation, but this was overturned in *Pett v Greyhound Racing Association Ltd (No. 2)* [1970] 1 QB 46.

In cases involving prisoners, boards of visitors have discretion to allow representation. The decision has to be based on the seriousness of the allegation, the ability of the prisoner to represent themselves and practical constraints.

15.4.3.9 Legitimate expectation and procedural impropriety

The courts have held that it is in the interests of fairness for decision-makers to honour promises, representations and established practice. But if the decision-maker proposes to change policy on which someone is relying, the affected person should be allowed the opportunity to make representations as to why the policy should not be altered.

The case of *R v Secretary of State for the Home Department, ex parte Asif Mahmood Khan* [1984] 1 WLR 1337 is a good example of how legitimate expectation fits into the category of procedural impropriety. The Home Office had issued a circular setting out the criteria for adopting a child from outside the UK. The applicant, who wished to adopt his nephew in Pakistan, went to great lengths to satisfy all the criteria only to find that his application was refused on the grounds that he had not satisfied further criteria which had not been mentioned in the Home Office circular. He argued successfully that he had a legitimate expectation that his application for adoption should be considered on the basis of the criteria he had relied upon unless he was offered a fair hearing and thus be given the opportunity to argue his own case for adoption.

You can also read *R v Liverpool Corporation, ex parte Liverpool Taxi Fleet Operators' Association* [1972] 2 QB 299 in **Cases and Materials** (**15.2.3.3**).

Legitimate expectations will be overridden in any cases where the issues involve questions of national security.

Does the doctrine of legitimate expectation fit into both categories of *irrationality* and *procedural impropriety*?

There is actually academic and judicial disagreement on this point and it is a developing area of law. In *R v Secretary of State for Transport, ex parte Richmond-upon-Thames Borough Council* [1994] 1 WLR 74, Laws J was of the opinion that legitimate expectation only gave grounds under procedural impropriety. The right to a hearing/to be consulted, etc., whereas in *R v Ministry of Agriculture Fisheries and Foods, ex parte Hamble Fisheries (Offshore) Ltd* [1995] 2 All ER 714, Sedley J said that the doctrine could also give substantive grounds i.e., under 'irrationality'.

Laws J was of the opinion that if the doctrine allowed substantive grounds for judicial review, public bodies would be effectively fettered from ever altering policy; Sedley J disagreed with this, arguing that it would not be restrictive to public bodies because it was not legitimate for people to expect that policies would never change!

The latest instalment can be seen in *R v Secretary of State for the Home Department, ex parte Hargreaves* [1997] 1 WLR 906. The Court of Appeal disapproved very strongly of moves towards recognising substantive legitimate expectation. Although the court was prepared to consider whether the Home Secretary's policy was *Wednesbury* unreasonable, they found the approach of Sedley J in *Hamble Fisheries* to be 'heresy'! It would appear that we are a long way off seeing 'legitimate expectation' established as a substantive ground for judicial review.

The doctrine of legitimate expectation fits into the category of irrationality in that if it can be shown that a person affected by a decision had a legitimate expectation that the decision-maker would exercise discretion according to certain principles then the decision may be irrational if those principles are ignored.

It fits into the category of procedural impropriety in that natural justice or the duty to act fairly could be breached if (see *R* v *Secretary of State for the Home Department, ex parte Asif Mahmood Khan* above) the affected person relies on representations and legitimately expects the decision-maker to reach a decision based on the same representations and the decision-maker then bases the decision on other factors of which the affected person had no knowledge without offering the opportunity to make representations, etc.

Read *Council of Civil Service Unions* v *Minister for the Civil Service* [1985] AC 374 in *Cases and Materials* (15.2.3.3). Make a note of the 'legitimate expectation' in this case. Why did it not assist the union members in their case?

The Council of Civil Service Unions' legitimate expectation was that they would be consulted before any changes were made to conditions of service. The Prime Minister had issued a directive (under prerogative power) to ban membership of trade unions at GCHQ without consulting the employees. The House of Lords recognised the legitimate expectation of consultation but held that this was overridden by the issues of national security involved.

15.4.3.10 *Nemo judex in causa sua*

Everyone is entitled to a hearing free from bias. Bias might arise in the following ways:

(a) The decision-maker has a pecuniary interest. In *Dimes* v *Proprietors of Grand Junction Canal* (1852) 3 HL Cas 759 a decision of the Court of Chancery was set aside because the Lord Chancellor who gave judgment was a shareholder in the company which benefited from the decision.

If a decision-maker does have a financial interest in the outcome of the decision (providing the interest is not too remote), the decision will be quashed on review.

(b) Actual bias — where a decision-maker has actually been biased in his or her decision the decision will be quashed on review.

(c)   Apparent bias — even if the decision-maker has not actually been biased at all, a decision may still be quashed if they have any professional or personal interest in the issues — **justice must be seen to be done**.

15.4.3.11   Professional or personal interest in the decision

In *R v Sussex Justices, ex parte McCarthy* [1924] 1 KB 256 a conviction for dangerous driving (i.e., criminal proceedings) was quashed when it came to light that the justices' clerk was a partner in the firm of solicitors acting for the plaintiff in related civil proceedings, even though it was shown that there was no actual bias.

In *Metropolitan Properties Co. (FGC) Ltd* v *Lannon* [1969] 1 QB 577 Lannon was the chairman of the Rent Assessment Committee hearing appeals from rent officers' decisions on fair rent applications from dissatisfied tenants. A landlord appealed against the level of rent deemed fair by the Committee. Lannon was also a solicitor and his firm had in the past handled applications for tenants of the landlord company. He therefore had a professional interest in the matter. Further, he lived with his father who was a tenant of the landlord company. He therefore also had some personal interest in the matter.

There was no proof of actual bias, but his personal and professional interests were sufficient for the Court of Appeal to quash the decision. Justice must be **seen** to be done.

15.4.3.12   What is the test for apparent bias?

Prior to the decision in the House of Lords case of *R v Gough* [1993] AC 646 two tests existed:

(a)   Is there a real likelihood of bias? This was the test used in *Metropolitan Properties Co. (FGC) Ltd* v *Lannon*.

(b)   Is there a reasonable suspicion of bias? This was the test used in *R v Sussex Justices, ex parte McCarthy*.

Which test would you prefer to use if you were trying to establish bias?

It is more difficult to establish bias using the 'real likelihood of bias' test – it is easier to establish bias using the 'reasonable suspicion' test. It is much easier to argue that people could reasonably suspect bias to have been present, than having to prove a real likelihood of bias.

Much confusion arose over which test to use. *R v Gough* provided some very welcome clarification in cases of alleged bias in decisions of justices, inferior tribunals, jurors or arbitrators. Their lordships held that the same test should be used when reviewing the decisions of any of these bodies. The test for bias is whether or not there was **real danger of bias**.

Read *R* v *Gough* [1993] AC 646 in *Cases and Materials* (15.2.3.4). Why did their lordships believe that there was no real danger of bias in this particular case?

Their lordships believed the juror's sworn statement that she had not been aware before sentence had been passed that Gough was her next-door-neighbour's brother (he being at one time Gough's co-accused). There was therefore no real danger of bias. The situation would have been completely different had the juror realised the relationship before the jury gave their verdict.

The *Gough* test was used in the Court of Appeal case of *R* v *K* (*Jury: Appearance of Bias*), *The Times*, 14 April 1995 which is in *Cases and Materials* (15.2.3.4).

If the reviewing court had used the 'real danger' test in *R* v *Sussex Justices, ex parte McCarthy* do you think the conviction would have been quashed? Does this test require the establishing of a *possibility* or a *probability* of bias?

In *R* v *Sussex Justices, ex parte McCarthy*, the magistrates' clerk (who you will recall was also the solicitor acting for the other driver in the civil proceedings) retired with the magistrates after all the evidence had been heard. The magistrates did not in fact consult the clerk, reaching their decision without any reference to him on points of law. The 'reasonable suspicion' test was used. As discussed above, this is relatively easy to satisfy. It would be reasonable to suspect bias to have taken place even though it had not actually taken place.

Had the 'real danger of bias' test been used, however, the question to be asked would have been whether there was a possibility of bias? It would seem that there was no possibility of bias affecting the magistrates' decision in *Ex parte McCarthy* as the clerk was never consulted. Had *Ex parte McCarthy* arisen today, therefore, it is quite likely that the conviction would not have been quashed!

R v *Secretary of State for the Environment and another, ex parte Kirkstall Valley Campaign Ltd* [1996] 3 All ER 304 confirms that the test in *Gough* applies to all public law cases, whether administrative, quasi-judicial or judicial in nature.

15.5   Remedies

An applicant may apply for one or more of the following remedies:

(a) **Certiorari**

An application for certiorari results in the decision being taken to the High Court in order to be investigated. If found to be *ultra vires* it will be quashed, i.e., declared invalid, so that it can be ignored. The parties will then be returned to their original pre-decision position.

Certiorari will not be granted against the Crown.

(b) **Mandamus**

This remedy deals with inaction. It enforces performance of public duties and can also be used to compel a decision-maker to exercise discretion properly, i.e., to take relevant considerations into account (*R* v *Birmingham Licensing Planning Committee, ex parte Kennedy* [1972] 2 QB 140) and to order a decision-maker not to abuse power conferred (*Padfield* v *Minister of Agriculture, Fisheries and Food* [1968] AC 997).

Mandamus is often applied for in conjunction with certiorari, e.g., in cases of breach of natural justice, certiorari will quash the decision and mandamus will compel a rehearing.

(c) **Prohibition**

Prohibition is very similar to certiorari but is used much less frequently. It acts to prohibit a decision-maker from engaging in *ultra vires* activities. Certiorari has retrospective effect on decisions already taken. Prohibition acts to prevent a decision-maker engaging in future *ultra vires* acts.

It is often sought in conjunction with certiorari. Certiorari will be sought in order to quash the decision in question; prohibition will be sought at the same time to prevent decision-makers putting the decision into effect.

It can be sought on its own in order to prevent a decision-maker considering an *ultra vires* exercise.

Prohibition will not be granted against the Crown.

The above orders are called 'prerogative orders' and can be applied for only in judicial review proceedings. The following orders can be applied for both in public and private law cases.

(d) **Injunctions**

Injunctions can be negative – i.e., forbidding a decision-maker doing something, or mandatory, i.e., to order a decision-maker to do something. In public law, injunctions sought tend to be negative in nature, because madamus will normally be sought in order to compel a decision-maker to carry out a duty.

Injunctions will be granted against Ministers acting in their official capacity (*M v Home Office* [1994] 1 AC 377) but will not be granted against the Crown.

(e) **Declarations**

Declarations do nothing more than declare the rights and obligations of the parties concerned. They are nonetheless very effective (see *Ridge v Baldwin* [1964] AC 40).

Declarations will be granted against the Crown.

(f) **Damages**

These may also be awarded in judicial review but only if the applicant also has private law rights — as in *Cooper v Board of Works for the Wandsworth District* (1836).

The Law Commission proposes 'de-latinising' the names of the prerogative remedies. It proposes the following changes:

Certiorari would become a 'quashing order'.

Prohibition would become a 'prohibiting order'.

Mandamus would become a 'mandatory order'.

15.6 Procedure for Applying for Judicial Review

(a) Write a 'letter before action'. The applicant or a lawyer should first write to the decision-maker in order to allow him or her the opportunity of remedying the situation. Failure to do this can result in application being rejected.

(b) The applicant has to apply for leave for judicial review as promptly as possible and in any event within three months of the occurrence of the alleged 'wrong'. The court does have discretion to allow late applications, but there would have to be very good reasons for the delay.

(c) Present position. The applicant seeks leave for judicial review. The application is made *ex parte* (without giving notice to the decision-maker in question) to a High Court judge by filing a notice (form 86A) in the Crown Office, together with a supporting affidavit verifying the facts relied upon. The judge can determine the application for leave without the necessity of a hearing, unless the applicant requests an oral hearing in the notice.

15.7   The Significance of Judicial Review within the UK Constitution

Do you support judicial intervention via judicial review or do you think it is wrong in principle for a non-elected body (i.e., judges) to have the power to interfere with the decisions and activities of elected bodies?

The above question necessitates a subjective answer, depending on your own particular viewpoint. There is no right or wrong answer.

The UK does not, of course, have a written constitution. As you will have learned fom earlier Chapters, our constitution is to be found in statutes, case law, customs and conventions. We do not have a constitutional court as in the USA where the Supreme Court has the power to rule legislation to be illegal if the provisions violate the Constitution.

We have witnessed the breakdown of the convention of individual Ministerial responsibility. Judicial review is, therefore, the only possible independent check on the activities of the executive. We have seen the House of Lords in *R v Secretary of State for Employment, ex parte Equal Opportunities Commission* [1995] 1 AC 1 hold that parts of the Employment Protection (Consolidation) Act 1978 were illegal as a result of contravening European law. In 1994, the Court of Appeal and the House of Lords ruled that the activities of the Foreign Secretary and Home Secretary were illegal and there are countless other examples of the courts vindicating the rule of law in judicial review decisions.

In the absence of a Bill of Rights or written constitution, judicial review presents a very powerful and crucial tool for aggrieved citizens and pressure groups.

The number of applications for leave to apply for judicial review has increased enormously over the last decade. More and more people are challenging the activities of public bodies as figures from the Law Commission's 1994 report clearly demonstrate:

1980   525 applications for leave

1992   2,439 applications for leave

1993   2,886 applications for leave

1994   1,851 applications for leave in the first seven months,
       compared with 1,728 for the same period in 1993

1996   over 3,900 applications for leave (58 per cent of which passed the leave stage).

Judicial review is one of the most exciting and fastest expanding areas of law.

15.8 End of Chapter Assessment Question

Geoffrey Wier, a member of Friends of the Countryside, an organisation with approximately 300,000 members nation-wide comes to you for advice.

He tells you that the Minister of Agriculture, Ben Hurr, has just authorised payment of £3 million to provide farmers with Swiftkill, a pesticide, in order to destroy a species of 'cannibal' worm, the *mulluscrophus* (fictitious), that is threatening to extinguish the normal domestic worm.

Ben, the Minister, has recently appeared on a TV chat show expressing his phobia of big worms and tells of a recurring nightmare in which he dreams he is being eaten alive by a giant worm. The *mulluscrophus* is approximately 2 foot long.

Geoffrey tells you that Friends of the Countryside have obtained expert reports which show that Swiftkill is not only extremely expensive, it is particularly dangerous to all wildlife and could wipe out at least a half of the country's wildlife. He tells you that the Minister could have authorised provision of an alternative pesticide, 'Mulluskull' which only has a lethal effect on the cannibal species of worms and has also been proven in clinical tests to kill in a humane way by anaesthetising and then destroying the nervous system. 'Swiftkill' on the other hand, acts by 'burning' through the insects/animal's respiratory system, but is a much quicker method of death.

The Minister is reported as saying that he would prefer the worms to have a painful, quick death as this might stop his nightmares.

Section 1 of the Dangerous Pest Act 1990 (fictitious) empowers the Minister to authorise payments for provision of pesticides to farmers for the purpose of 'destruction of environmentally dangerous insects or wildlife by means of efficient and humane methods'.

 (a) Advise Geoffrey whether Friends of the Countryside can challenge the Minister's decision.

 (b) On what ground(s) can the decision be challenged?

 (c) Can the Minister be compelled to give reasons for his decision?

 (d) What relief should be applied for?

See *Cases and Materials* (15.4) for an outline answer.

CHAPTER SIXTEEN

OMBUDSMEN

16.1 Objectives

This Chapter supplements **Chapter 15** on judicial review. At the end of this Chapter you should be:

■ familiar with the office of the Parliamentary Commissioner for Administration (PCA);

■ mindful of how the PCA receives and handles complaints;

■ able to appreciate the jurisdictional remit of the PCA;

■ aware of how both the Commissioner for Local Administration (complaints about local authorities) and the Health Service Commissioner (complaints about the National Health Service) operate.

16.2 Introduction

Consider the following scenarios:

■ You are a high-profile wealthy businessman. As a result of a miscalculation by the Inland Revenue, you suffer considerable financial loss. Their maladministration has damaged your creditworthiness, your business credentials and your good name in the community. What can you do?

■ Or what if you are at the other end of the income ladder? You are unemployed with a disability. You rely totally on State benefits to support yourself and your young family. The DSS lose your claim forms. They fail to apologise or provide any explanation for your temporary non-payment. As a result of their action, you and your young children suffer severe financial hardship. Have you any remedies?

■ Moving away from money. Let's say that you have an 80-year-old relative who is in hospital. She complains that, whilst receiving a bath, she was dropped by nurses. She says that this has happened before and you observe that she has severe bruising on those parts of the body where she landed. The nursing staff fail to provide any explanation, appearing indifferent to this and the fact that your elderly relative has also had personal possessions (books, flowers, fruit, cassettes) stolen from her bedside table. The hospital management fail to provide a proper remedy. To whom can you complain?

■ And finally, assume that your elderly relative is released from hospital. The local council, complying with a legal duty to house her, offer her accommodation in the top flat of a high-rise block. She accepts but immediately complains that the lifts are broken in the block. Unable to travel to the ground floor, she complains that she is virtually a prisoner in her own home. However, the council ignores all of her requests to be rehoused. How can she seek redress?

SAQ 155

Think of everything so far covered in the course. Which public law remedies are available here? How would you characterise these remedies in a diagram? A suggested diagram appears in *Cases and Materials* (16.1). And how useful is each remedy likely to be in responding to these scenarios?

You probably have identified two kinds of remedy: *political* remedies (Parliamentary questions, select committees, lobbying MPs), and *legal* remedies (judicial review). Each, however, has its limitations. Political redress is largely dependent on finding a sympathetic MP who is willing to argue your case in public. Even then he or she can only put political pressure on the relevant public body to respond positively to your grievance. On the other hand, legal remedies are potentially much more effective, offering the sanction of the law.

However, you should remember the strict procedural requirements which are necessary for a successful application for judicial review (see **Chapter 15**). These may rule it out as an option. Moreover, there may have been no illegality or procedural impropriety, providing no grounds for the complainant to apply for judicial review. Finally, the time and expense of judicial review may make it inappropriate for an individual who would just be satisfied with an apology or an explanation for a particular decision. Thus, to facilitate such contingencies and to offer a safety net to applicants who are unable to avail themselves fully of legal or political remedies, the services of Ombudsmen are provided.

In England and Wales there are three main Ombudsmen in the public sector. These are the Parliamentary Commissioner for Administration (PCA), the Commissioner for Local Administration (CLA) and the Health Service Commissioner (HSC). In this Chapter we will be focusing on these three Ombudsman although it is worth noting that there are a number of other, private sector, Ombudsmen in the UK, such as the Building Societies and the Legal Services Ombudsmen. The development of European Community law is reflected by the fact that there is even an EC Ombudsman, set up under the Maastricht Treaty (art. 138e), to consider allegations that the Community's institutions (with the exception of the European Court) have been guilty of maladministration.

16.3   Parliamentary Commissioner for Administration

16.3.1   THE OFFICE

The Parliamentary Commissioner for Administration (PCA) was created in 1967 by the Parliamentary Commissioner Act 1967. Each PCA is appointed by the Crown, so that despite the title, the Parliamentary Commissioner is not appointed by Parliament. So what does the PCA actually do?

Section 5(1) of the 1967 Act says that the PCA 'may investigate any action taken by or on behalf of a government department or other authority to which this Act applies'. Schedule 2 to the Act says that it applies to central government departments such as the Home Office, Treasury, Department of the Environment, the Foreign Office, the Ministry of Defence etc., In reality certain government departments provide the Parliamentary Commissioner with more business than others. For example, in 1996, 47 per cent of complaints related to the Department of Social Security (DSS), with dissatisfaction focused on the activities of the Child Support Agency accounting for more than half of these complaints. Similarly, in 1995, the DSS and its agencies received the highest number of complaints, five times more than the next highest target of complaints, the Inland Revenue which, in the 'complaints league', was followed by the Department of the Environment and the Department of Transport.

How significant is it, if at all, that in the last few years, the two Departments that have provided the majority of complaints which have been brought to the attention of the PCA, are the Department of Social Security and the Inland Revenue?

A good way of understanding the workings of the office of the PCA is to read through the Parliamentary Commissioner Act 1967 in *Cases and Materials* (16.2.1). How does it define 'maladministration' and 'injustice'?

The last decade has witnessed a dramatic increase in the work load of the PCA. A table charting the increase in the PCA's workload from 1987–96 is provided in *Cases and Materials* (**Table A, 16.2.1**). For example, in 1990, the PCA received 704 complaints, which were referred to him by 371 MPs. In 1993, the number had risen to 986 complaints from 429 MPs; in 1995, it was 1,706 complaints from 506 MPs; finally, in 1996, the PCA received a record 1,933 complaints from 566 MPs.

When the 1996 figures are broken down, two things are obvious. First, a high proportion of complaints which are referred to the PCA are rejected as they concern issues which do not fall within his remit — the PCA lacked jurisdiction in 1,419 (84 per cent) of the 1,679 cases which he examined in 1996 — see *Cases and Materials* (**Table B, 16.2.1**). Secondly, of those cases which are fully investigated by the PCA, a high proportion of complaints tend to be upheld. Thus, of the remaining 260 cases which were investigated in 1996, 189 (73 per cent) of these were upheld fully, 57 (22 per cent) upheld partly and, in only 14 cases (5 per cent), were the claims of maladministration totally rejected.

In answering **SAQ 156** earlier, you will have probably observed that the reason why a high number of the complaints which are referred to the PCA only relate to certain government departments (such as the Department of Social Security or the Inland Revenue) is that Departments such as these, on a day-to-day basis, tend to be in much more regular contact with members of the public than many other branches of government. Thus, since the office of PCA was set up specifically to protect individuals and groups of individuals, it was perhaps inevitable that successive PCAs would find themselves scrutinising the work of Departments which deal most directly with ordinary people.

Section 6(1) of the Parliamentary Commissioner Act 1967 states that a complaint to the PCA may be made by an individual or any body of persons. However, complaints may not be brought by 'a local authority or other statutory body', or by 'any other authority or body whose members are appointed by Her Majesty or by any Minister of the Crown or government department'. The Act also requires that the complaint must be made by 'the person aggrieved himself' (s. 6(2)). Thus, there is a 'victim' requirement so that, if an individual has suffered as a result of governmental maladministration, the victim alone can petition the PCA. Only where the complainant is unable to act for himself or herself, or has died, may the complaint be submitted by someone on the victim's behalf.

16.3.2   HOW IS A COMPLAINT MADE TO THE PCA?

Section 5 of the 1967 Act provides that complaints must be made within 12 months in writing to an MP, and referred to the PCA by the MP. Therefore, the complainant does not have direct access to the PCA: a complainant must approach the PCA through a member of the Commons. The White Paper, which preceded the then Parliamentary Commissioner Bill, made it clear that the reason for this was that Parliament should have the first opportunity to deal with the matter and that the PCA should not erode the authority of Parliament

But what happens when a complaint is sent directly to the PCA? In the past the PCA would simply tear it up and do nothing. In recent years, however, a custom has been established whereby the PCA will pass the complaint to the MP, with a note to explain that he will investigate the matter if the MP will refer it back to him.

In 1977, the legal pressure group, JUSTICE, criticised this 'MP filter system', and argued that UK citizens with grievances should have direct access to the PCA. Similar calls were made in the 1988 JUSTICE/All Souls Review of Administrative Law (see *Cases and Materials* (**16.2.2**). Even the Parliamentary Commissioner himself has advocated the removal of the MP filter, arguing in his 1993 report that 'the filter serves to deprive members of the public of possible redress'. However, successive governments have ignored these recommendations and the Select Committee on the Parliamentary

Commissioner for Administration (HC 33 of 1993–94) recommended that the MP filter system be retained 'but coupled with concerted attention to the means whereby access to the Ombudsman can be strengthened and enlarged'. This and other recommendations of the Select Committee are considered by Gregory, Giddings and Moore in *Cases and Materials* (**16.2.2**). According to the findings of Drewry and Harlow (*Cases and Materials* (**16.2.2**)), 'Labour's MPs are about five times as likely to favour direct access to their Conservative counterparts', but so far there is no evidence of any backbench pressure on Tony Blair's Government to give citizens the right of being able to go straight to the PCA. Thus, at least for the time being, the PCA is one of the few 'Ombudsmen' in the world who does not have direct access to the people the office was set up to protect.

ACTIVITY 126

It has been claimed that the office of the PCA 'is held in low esteem' (Drewry and Harlow). Construct the case for and against the individual's direct access to the PCA. The extracts in *Cases and Materials* (**16.2.2**) from the articles by Gregory, Giddings and Moore and by Drewry and Harlow will be of considerable assistance in undertaking this exercise.

Note the important wording of s. 5 of the Parliamentary Commissioner Act 1967 (see *Cases and Materials* (**16.2.1**)). The word 'may' gives the PCA a discretionary power in deciding whether or not to investigate a complaint. In *Re Fletcher's Application* [1970] 2 All ER 527, the court refused to issue an order of mandamus, which would have compelled the PCA to conduct an investigation. However, more recently it was established that there is nothing in either the role of the PCA or the statutory framework, which places the PCA beyond the bounds of judicial review (*R v Parliamentary Commissioner for Administration, ex parte Dyer* [1994] 1 WLR 621). Thus, a person unhappy with the PCA's decision not to investigate an allegation of maladministration can challenge it by way of judicial review. The courts are normally reluctant to interfere with the PCA's discretion and, in the *Dyer* case, the complainant (on the facts) failed in her attempt to challenge the PCA's refusal to pursue some of her complaints. Thus, even though Sedley J recently quashed the PCA's earlier decision that the Department of Transport had not been guilty of maladministration in *R v Parliamentary Commissioner for Administration, ex parte Ballchin* [1997] COD 146, such successful challenges tend to be rare.

ACTIVITY 127

How did Simon Brown LJ respond to the argument in *ex parte Dyer*, that the Parliamentary Commissioner should be answerable only to Parliament? Read the extract from his judgment and Marsh's criticisms of this decision in *Cases and Materials* (**16.2.2**).

16.3.3   MALADMINISTRATION

So far we have established that the office of PCA was established to investigate cases of injustice caused by central government maladministration. Thus you may be wondering what exactly is meant by 'injustice' or 'maladministration'? Congratulations if you noticed that the Parliamentary Commissioner Act 1967 (**Activity 125**) does not define these terms. When this legislation was proceeding through its Parliamentary stage, a Government Minister observed that the meaning of these words would be 'filled out by the practical processes of case work'. A preliminary definition of maladministration was offered by Richard Crossman who, as Leader of the House, had been responsible for the then Parliamentary Commissioner's Bill through the House of Commons. Known as the 'Crossman catalogue', he suggested that maladministration should cover 'bias, neglect, inattention, delay, incompetence, inaptitude, perversity, turpitude, arbitrariness and so on'. More recently, Sir William Reid, who was the PCA until 2 January 1997, gave some other examples of maladministration for the 1990s which include rudeness, failing to let people know what they are entitled to, giving poor or misleading advice, showing bias (i.e., on the grounds of sex, race etc.) and finally, showing an 'unwillingness to treat the complainant as a person with rights'.

Investigations completed by the PCA in the past indicate that maladministration and injustice will include:

- Financial loss.

- Being deprived of an opportunity to appeal against a decision.

- Deprivation of an amenity, e.g., the closing of a railway line.

- Loss of prison privileges, e.g., through being wrongly classified as a convicted prisoner while in prison on remand awaiting trial.

- Loss of access to a child, e.g., in one exceptional case, an error in a passport office led to a child being removed from the jurisdiction of the courts.

- An unjustifiable delay for a decision or, when it is given, the absence of any reasonable explanation.

- A departmental failure to handle similar cases consistently, e.g., no standardisation of departmental policy.

- Rudeness, offensive or inconsiderate behaviour by department officials, e.g., sometimes the complainant will be satisfied just with an apology.

- Finally, in his 1993 Annual Report, the PCA even noted that rigid adherence to the letter of the law which leads to injustice may be tantamount to maladministration. Think back to **Chapter 12** on the rule of law. Does this not add to the case against Dicey's strict interpretation of the rule of law? This seems to suggest that discretionary rule making in contemporary government is inevitable.

In relation to 'maladministration', the PCA has said that he looks on it 'as including any kind of administrative shortcomings'. But maladministration does not include the right to investigate the **merits** of a decision. Similarly, the PCA lacks jurisdiction to review statutory rules. The PCA has noted that, 'The contents of legislation and possible need for amendment to it are matters for Parliament itself to consider and not for me' (*The Guardian*, 5 June 1992). If you think back to **Chapter 7** on Parliamentary supremacy, you will not be surprised by the PCA's reluctance to usurp the functions of the legislature by questioning primary legislation.

SAQ 157

The influential pressure group JUSTICE recommended in 1977 that the PCA should be allowed to investigate any 'unreasonable, unjust or oppressive action'. What constitutional factors would preclude expanding the jurisdiction of the PCA? For assistance turn to the extract from the All Souls Review of Administrative Law in *Cases and Materials* (16.2.2) which considers some of JUSTICE'S recommendations.

16.3.4 INVESTIGATION

So how does the PCA carry out an investigation? The Commissioner must first notify the department concerned of the intention to investigate a complaint and then give it an opportunity to comment on the alleged facts. The investigation is held in private. The PCA may obtain information from any such persons and in such a manner as he thinks fit. The PCA has the same powers as a High Court judge to require any person to provide information or to produce documents. The PCA's duty to investigate complaints overrides any duty which may be imposed to maintain secrecy under the Official Secrets Act or any other rule of law. However, the PCA is not entitled to information concerning proceedings in the Cabinet.

Earlier in the book (**Chapter 2**) we looked at the Government's proposals to introduce a Freedom of Information Act but, at the time of writing, access to official material is regulated merely by an unenforceable Code of Practice on Access to Government Information (1993). The aim of the Code is to make public 'facts which the government considers relevant and important in framing major policy decisions' as well as giving the public 'reasons for administrative decisions to those affected'. A complaint may be referred to the PCA if a government Department fails to disclose information which should have been released under the Code. However, for the PCA (as well as citizens generally), the Code has a number of drawbacks. First, it only places a voluntary obligation on government to release information. The Code is not legally enforceable so that if the PCA considers that a government Department has failed to release information in accordance with the Code's guidelines, a legal remedy is not available. Instead, the relevant department may have to justify its actions before the Select Committee on the PCA but, as we saw earlier, the main drawback with this is that Select Committees lack any legal sanction and their work may be influenced by political factors. Secondly, a wide range of material is excluded from the Code — these exclusions include information which, if released, would harm national security and defence, international relations, the administration of justice, public safety, or might curtail frank internal discussion. Ultimately it is the government which will, almost always, have the power to decide whether something falls within one of these excluded categories. Thirdly, large sections of the public would seem to be unaware of the very existence of the Code. For example, in 1996, the PCA only investigated 12 cases (from a total of 44 complaints) relating to claims that there had been a denial of access to official information while, in his 1995

Report, the PCA lamented the fact that it was 'surprising' how 'nearly two years after the Code came into force, the public's use of it remains minimal'. Government in Britain is often said to be excessively secretive and perhaps this secrecy is illustrated by the fact that, until the Government's White Paper proposals in 1997, there was no statutory public right of a general right of assess to information held by public authorities.

The high degree of co-operation which successive PCAs have tried to foster with Government Departments means that information tends to be provided when requested. The PCA will use this information in conducting an investigation and at the end of the investigation that PCA will report to the relevant Department and to the MP who referred the complaint. If the PCA discovers maladministration, his report will include recommendations for dealing with the problem. The PCA also reports annually to Parliament which may examine all of his case reports.

The Parliamentary Commissioner's method of inquiry is inquisitorial rather than adversarial (see extract from former Commissioner Sir Idwal Pugh in *Cases and Materials* (**16.2.3**)). The fact-finding process means that the complainant will usually be interviewed by a member of the PCA's staff to determine whether the allegation of maladministration has any substance. Accordingly a backlog of cases is inevitable and on average it takes 13 months to complete an investigation. Yet delay is not the main weakness of the PCA's office. It is arguable that the main weakness is the broad range of activities from which the PCA is excluded.

16.3.5   EXCLUSIONS

The following areas are excluded from the jurisdiction of the Parliamentary Commissioner:

■ any matter where the ordinary courts of law provide a remedy or where there is a right of appeal to a tribunal;

■ foreign affairs;

■ extradition;

■ action taken in relation to contractual or any other commercial matters relating to government departments;

■ conditions of service for civil servants;

■ the armed forces of the Crown and matters affecting national security;

■ the hospital service and local government authorities (as we shall shortly see, these are catered for separately);

■ the conferment of honours or awards by the Crown;

■ matters relating to civil or criminal proceedings before a court of law;

■ the exercise of the prerogative of mercy by the Home Secretary;

■ criminal investigations;

■ 'matters relating to contractual or other commercial transactions . . . being transactions of a government department . . . or other public authority'.

This last exception is the most controversial. In the past a Parliamentary Select Committee on the PCA (1977–78) suggested that the PCA should be permitted to investigate complaints that a Government department 'had been improperly influenced in deciding which firms to include among those entitled to tender for contracts, or had made such a decision in an arbitrary manner'. This exclusion has also been criticised by a Royal Commission (1976) and the pressure group JUSTICE (1977), but successive governments have rejected such criticism by maintaining that such commercial activities are quite properly outside the remit of the PCA. However, it would appear that the potential effectiveness of the PCA is curbed by these commercial, as well as the other exclusions.

Think back to Chapter 5 and Sir Richard Scott's inquiry into the Matrix Churchill affair. What are the differences between an inquiry such as the one chaired by Sir Richard and an inquiry undertaken by the PCA? For some ideas turn to the views of the former PCA, Sir Cecil Clothier in *Cases and Materials* (16.2.4).

16.3.6   THE PCA: AN APPRAISAL

When the office of the PCA was established, the Labour MP Richard Crossman said that it would be 'a new and powerful weapon with a sharp cutting edge'. Drewry and Harlow (see *Cases and Materials* (16.2.2)) dismiss this as 'empty political rhetoric' and suggest that the PCA is 'capable of better things'.

Certainly, by now, you should be aware of the main criticisms which are levelled at the PCA. These are, to summarise, that the office of the PCA is weakened by the fact that its holder:

■   does not have direct access to the citizens who are making complaints;

■   lacks the power to undertake an investigation unless a complaint has been made;

■   is excluded from a wide range of governmental activities;

■   is required, in cases where an individual's complaint has been rejected, to send a report to the MP who referred the case to him or her, that explains the reasons for the decision. However, there is no comparable requirement to do this for the individual concerned. (You should have observed this from Marsh's criticism of the decision in *ex parte Dyer* [1994] 1 WLR 621, and in *Cases and Materials* (16.2.2).)

■   Finally, the recommendations in the PCA's report are not legally binding.

In the absence of any legal powers of enforcement, the PCA relies heavily on the co-operation of government Departments, which themselves are sensitive to charges of maladministration. Thus, it would seem that the PCA's most effective weapon is the sanction of bad publicity, and this is illustrated by two recent major investigations: the

PCA's reports into the Barlow Clowes affair and the Channel Tunnel rail link. We will now consider each of these in turn.

Barlow Clowes were investment brokers. In other words, they were financial 'middle-men', investing customers' money for profit. They were ostensibly a low-risk investment company, and had been given a licence to trade by the Department of Trade and Industry (DTI). Thus Barlow Clowes literature was stamped with the words, 'licensed by the DTI'.

In June 1988 it was discovered that there had been gross mismanagement in the running of Barlow Clowes. It had gambled unsuccessfully in high-risk markets and owed £190 million to nearly 19,000 investors and clients. Of particular significance was the transfer of assets to Jersey, where financial regulations were less stringent. The DTI neglected to spot this and had also failed to heed warnings from accountants Touche Ross. The PCA received 159 complaints from MPs. It was claimed that the DTI's negligence and failure to act had caused the investors to suffer severe financial loss.

The PCA, following what he described as 'the most complex, wide-ranging and onerous investigation ever undertaken by the holder of this office', found that there had been maladministration by the DTI. Initially the government responded negatively. It rejected many of the PCA's findings and refused to compensate investors. However, as a result of harsh criticism in the press, and 'out of respect for the office of Parliamentary Commissioner', the then Secretary of State for Trade and Industry, Nicholas Ridley, agreed that £150 million would be paid out in compensation, so that the investors received up to 90 per cent of what they had lost.

ACTIVITY 128

Read the extracts from the article by Gregory and Drewry, 'Barlow Clowes and the Ombudsman' in *Cases and Materials* (16.2.5). What do they claim are the 'special qualities' which the Parliamentary Commissioner brought to bear on the *Barlow Clowes* case?

The Barlow Clowes affair was arguably not a complete 'victory' for the PCA. Although compensation was paid out of 'respect' for his office, the government refused to accept responsibility for the inattention and mistakes of the DTI. Nevertheless the investors got redress, and this £150 million was of much greater practical significance than, say, a departmental apology!

As we have already established, the PCA lacks the power to force a government to comply with his or her findings but, in exceptional circumstances, the PCA can lay a special report before Parliament on a particular case (s. 10(3) of the Parliamentary Commissioner Act 1967). This has only, so far, happened twice before: the first time was in 1978 and led to s. 113 of the Local Government Planning and Land Act 1980; and the second was in 1995, following the PCA's report which had been critical of the Department of Transport's failure to accept the detrimental effect which the Channel tunnel rail link (CTRL) was having on property prices in the area affected by the proposed link. In 1997 an agreement was reached with the approval of the PCA, whereby those affected by the CTRL received compensation. You will find an explanation of the CTRL affair in the extract from James and Longley in *Cases and Materials* (**16.2.5**).

16.4   Local Government

16.4.1   THE COMMISSIONER FOR LOCAL ADMINISTRATION (CLA)

The Local Government Act 1974 extended the 'Ombudsman' principle to local government. Currently there are Local Government Commisssioners for England, Wales, and Scotland.

These Commissioners have the power to investigate complaints of injustice suffered as a consequence of maladministration in connection with the execution of administrative functions in local government. This includes allegations of unfair treatment made against district, borough, city or county councils; police authorities; fire authorities, urban development corporations; some functions of the National Rivers Authority; and appeal committees of grant-maintained schools.

In *R v Local Commissioner for Administration for the North and East Area of England, ex parte Bradford Metropolitan City Council* [1979] QB 287 (see *Cases and Materials* (**16.3.1**)), Lord Denning MR said that the Local Commissioner is concerned with the **manner** of the decision which led to the maladministration, rather than the nature, reasonableness of or policy behind that decision. Thus, maladministration is defined in a similar way for both the PCA and the CLA while, as with the PCA, the CLA's findings are subject to judicial review (*R v Commissioner of Local Administration, ex parte Croydon LBC* [1989] 1 All ER 1033). Another similarity for both the local and national Ombudsman is that complaints must be in writing and brought within 12 months from the day of the grievance. Complaints to the CLA usually relate to housing and town planning. For example, from 1995–96, the CLA received more than 15,000 complaints and of these 37.5 per cent were related to housing and 22.1 per cent to planning, with investigations taking, on average, just under a year and a half.

Unlike the PCA, the CLA (and also the Health Service Commissioner) can receive complaints directly from individuals. Originally there had been a 'councillor filter' to the CLA (a local government equivalent of the MP filter system), but the Local Government Act 1988 introduced the alternative of direct access to the CLA.

ACTIVITY 129

According to Geoffrey Marshall in *Cases and Materials* (**16.3.1**) what are the consequences of the 1988 Local Government Act's reform that complainants may choose whether to make complaints directly to the CLA rather than through a local councillor?

Notwithstanding this direct access, it should not be forgotten that there are considerable limits on the jurisdiction of the Commissioners for Local Administration.

The following matters are excluded from investigation by the Local Commissioner:

- any matter where there is a remedy before a court of law or tribunal or an appeal to a Minister;

- personnel matters in local government;

- contractual or commercial transactions within local bodies;

- matters which relate to how and what pupils are taught as well as to the management and organisation of local authority schools;

- public transport;

- action which affects all or most of the inhabitants in a particular area of a local authority.

The source of this last exclusion is s. 26(7) of the Local Government Act 1974. It provides that 'A Local Commissioner shall not conduct an investigation in respect of any action which in his opinion affects all or most of the inhabitants of the . . . area of the authority concerned.' What kind of scenario may this cover and what is the rationale behind this exclusion?

A good example of such a scenario is where city councils in the past increased community charge (poll tax) bills to take account of a loss of revenue from non-payers. The rationale governing this exclusion is that the services of the Local Government Ombudsman should only benefit individual complainants.

16.4.2 REMEDIES

The Commisioners for Local Administration are assisted by a reporting system. Having received a complaint, the CLA will notify the relevant authority and conduct an investigation. A report will be drafted and the local authority is under a duty to consider and respond to it within three months (s. 26 of the Local Government and Housing Act 1989). Should an appropriate response from a local authority not be forthcoming, a further report may be issued.

A local authority which fails to comply with a CLA ruling of maladministration may even be required to publish the report (at its own expense) in a local newspaper. This, however, is the ultimate sanction. Although a local authority must appoint a monitoring officer to examine findings of maladministration (s. 5 of the Local Government and Housing Act 1989), Local Government Ombudsmen lack strong enforcement powers. In approximately 6 per cent of cases where CLAs find maladministration, local councils fail to act. So what can be done? The 1986 Widdicombe Report (Cmnd 9797) recommended that complainants should be empowered to use adverse CLA reports to seek a remedy in the county court. While not accepting this proposal, the government clearly is aware of the failings of the Local Ombudsman system. In *The Citizen's Charter* (1991), the government warned that: ' . . . if difficulties continue we will take the further step of introducing legislation to make the Local Ombudsman's recommendations legally enforceable'. This is the position in Northern Ireland, and was the recommendation of Lord Woolf in the Tom Sargant Lecture (November 1996), but a government review of the CLA in 1996 decided against reforming the present system.

What are the advantages and disadvantages of making the CLA's powers legally enforceable?

Adopting such a proposal would certainly give Local Commissioners a more effective sanction. In Northern Ireland the recommendations of the equivalent office, the Commissioner for Complaints, are legally binding. However, the danger of introducing such legislation is that it could jeopardise the element of cooperation which often exists between local Ombudsmen and local authorities. Perhaps Local Government Ombudsmen operate most effectively alone and should not seek assistance from other sources.

As Himsworth observes:

> Ombudsmen . . . may have to accept that their influence will depend upon the prestige generated by their own offices in their own political systems. To look for external buttresses from Ministers, courts or select committees may do more to undermine than to support their authority. ([1986] PL 546 at p. 550.)

On the other hand, the public profile of the Local Ombudsmen is low. In 1987 a survey indicated that only 38 per cent of people knew of the existence of the Commissioners for Local Administration. Perhaps radical reform is necessary. C. Crawford [1988] PL 246 argues for the establishment of a new institution 'the Commission for Local Administration'. This Commission would enforce Ombudsmen's reports, issue administrative codes of guidance and review the work of the Local Ombudsmen.

In his 1994 Hamlyn Lecture, the former Lord Chancellor, Lord Mackay of Clashfern LC made the point that a strength of all systems of Ombudsmen is their ability to 'adjudicate between disputing parties without the trappings of going to court'.

What are the advantages of utilising the services of an Ombudsman and avoiding the courtroom? Make a list – some possible advantages are provided at the end of this Chapter.

16.5   Health Service Commissioners

The National Health Service Reorganisation Act 1973 established two Health Service Commissioners (one for England and one for Wales). Since their creation both offices have been held by the Parliamentary Commissioner for Administration although the government has recognised that as the work loads of each increase, it will become more difficult for the office to be shared by the same person. The Commissioners may investigate any alleged failure to provide a service which was the function of a health authority or any other action taken by or on behalf of such an authority.

A complaint may be made directly to the Commissioner or to the authority concerned and that authority may refer it to the Commissioner. A report of any investigation is sent to the authority concerned. However, if the Commissioner considers that injustice or hardship has been caused which has not and will not be remedied, he may make a special report to the Secretary of State, who must lay a copy of the report before Parliament. Examples of complaints which have been investigated include: the closure of a branch surgery; absence of pharmaceutical services; inadequate hospital records; delay in admission to hospital; charges for contact lenses; neglect of a woman in labour; failure to treat immediately a pregnant woman who had been involved in a car accident; and a failure to inform relatives that a patient had a terminal illness. Examples of medical maladministration in the Health Service Commissioners' 1994 Report include a suicide which might have been prevented, a patient who was forced to wait on a hospital trolley for 18 hours and a hospital which incorrectly issued three death certificates for the same recently deceased patient!

As with all other Ombudsmen, certain matters are excluded from the investigation of the Health Service Commissioners. These include areas:

■   where a remedy exists through a court or tribunal;

■   personnel matters;

■   contractual or commercial transactions;

- action taken by a family practitioner committee in the exercise of its disciplinary functions;

- action taken by persons providing general medical and dental services under contract with a family practitioner committee;

- action taken in connection with diagnosis of illness or care or treatment of patients where the action was taken solely in consequence of the exercise of clinical judgment.

The Health Service Commissioners received 2,219 complaints between 1996–97 (see *Cases and Materials* (16.4)) and in common with other ombudsmen, the Health Service Commissioners have no sanctions. However, adverse publicity resulting from publication of the Commissioners' findings may result in individuals obtaining redress. Once again the sanction of bad publicity is often the catalyst for change. (On the Health Service Ombudsman, see the extract by Gregory, Giddings, and Moore (1994) in *Cases and Materials* (16.2.2).)

16.6   Conclusion

In the UK there are three main public-sector Ombudsmen:

- the Parliamentary Commissioner for Administration (PCA);

- the Commission for Local Administration (CLA);

- the Health Service Commissioners (HSC);

As noted in **Activity 130**, each Ombudsman offers individuals an opportunity to obtain redress, without having to attend court. The advantages of this are:

- Complaining to an Ombudsman may be cheaper and speedier for an individual than engaging in time-consuming, costly litigation;

- Ombudsmen may also be less expensive on the 'public' purse than formal legal proceedings.

- Ombudsmen's techniques tend to be inquisitorial rather than confrontational or adversarial.

- Individuals who are frightened of the formal, traditional procedures in court are less likely to be intimidated into inertia by the less formal Ombudsmen.

The public-sector Ombudsmen are far from perfect. However, notwithstanding the weaknesses of the three Ombudsmen we have concentrated on, they perform an important role in acting as a safety net for individuals with grievances in their respective areas. After all, as Sir Cecil Clothier, a former Parliamentary Commissioner for Administration and Health Service Commissioner, has noted (*Public Law* 1986, p. 204): there is 'a curious paradox' that 'the more civilised a country is, the more likely is administrative injustice to be inadvertently done and the more need is there of an Ombudsman'.

INDEX